P9-CDK-402

# Scottish Cinema Now

# Scottish Cinema Now

Edited by

Jonathan Murray, Fidelma Farley
and Rod Stoneman

Scottish Cinema Now, Edited by Jonathan Murray, Fidelma Farley and Rod Stoneman

This book first published 2009

Cambridge Scholars Publishing

12 Back Chapman Street, Newcastle upon Tyne, NE6 2XX, UK

British Library Cataloguing in Publication Data
A catalogue record for this book is available from the British Library



ISBN (10): 1-4438-0331-6, ISBN (13): 978-1-4438-0331-1

# TABLE OF CONTENTS

# EDITORS' INTRODUCTION

## JONATHAN MURRAY

The past decade and a half was a period of unprecedented industrial expansion and creative achievement within Scottish film culture. Put in the simplest of terms, more films were made about and/or in Scotland, with more local and international production finance, involving and developing a wider range of indigenous creative talent, than at any previous point in cinema history. The essays in this volume, developed from the *New Scottish Cinema* symposium that took place in early November 2005 at the Huston School of Film & Digital Media, National University of Ireland, Galway, testify to and celebrate that fact. Yet as this introduction is written in early December 2008 the most recent public pronouncements on contemporary Scottish film culture's health are less than optimistic. See, for instance, various comments made by the actor Robert Carlyle around the time of the 2008 British Academy of Film and Television Arts (BAFTA) Scotland awards. Despite winning the Best Actor prize for his role in *Summer* (Glenaan, GB, 2008) Carlyle complained of Scotland that,

> We don't have a film industry here. I would argue that vehemently. An industry is something that feeds itself and grows. We make one film every 10 years that gets any kind of notice. You can't call that an industry. Over the past 12 to 15 years I have probably had about five or six scripts that have been Scots films shooting here. Not one of them has fucking happened. I don't know the answer to that. It's got to the stage now with my agent, if something Scottish comes in it has to be financed, otherwise I'm not going to read it because it depresses me. (Scott 2008)

Carlyle's comments go some way to indicating the true complexity of Scottish cinema's recent evolution. The decade or so since *Shallow Grave* (Boyle, GB, 1995) and *Trainspotting* (Boyle, GB, 1996) has delivered certain material and cultural advances while denying others, raising but also disappointing local expectations and aspirations at one and the same time. Carlyle's words of caution indicate the necessity of a critical approach that interrogates the aesthetic, industrial and ideological aspects of filmmaking in contemporary Scotland, rather than one content merely to celebrate the bald fact that such activity takes place more frequently and visibly than ever before, in however precarious a form.

Although this volume is titled *Scottish Cinema Now*, many of its essays propose that new historical scholarship, or reconsideration of well- and lesser-known figures and films from the past, form a necessary precondition for understanding fully the challenges of the present. Consider again, for instance, Robert Carlyle's above-quoted comments. Without wishing to dismiss or downplay the anxieties and reservations he voices, one can construct a historical "daisy chain" of such utterances in the Scottish context. As early as 1938, the documentary film producer and critic John Grierson could be found complaining that, "there is hardly a picture of Scotland but comes by grace of the alien and is false" (Hardy 1945, 145). In 1946, the BBC broadcaster Joseph Macleod was appointed Managing Director of a semi-voluntary organisation styling itself as the Scottish National Film Studios. This initiative aimed to finance and build a film studio in the Highlands, so that, in the words of promotional literature associated with the scheme, "young talent will be trained in the technical aspects of filmmaking and equipped to take their place later as creative artists and good Scots" (Bruce 1990, 77). The failure of such ambitions beyond the production of a single instructional short on road safety etiquette meant that in 1958, D. M. Elliot could still bemoan the fact that, "among the smaller nations of the world Scotland is almost alone in having no domestic film industry" (Elliot 1958, 41). Another decade on, John Grierson's celebrity lecture at the 1968 Edinburgh International Film Festival argued that Scottish filmmakers' shared predicament was one of endless wandering in a film industrial desert, forever "denied access to the means of production" (Grierson 1968). In 1976, Steve Clark-Hall, one of the first wave of aspirant Scottish independent producers to emerge in the late 1960s and early '70s, observed that, "the Scottish film industry, in any meaningful sense has yet to swing into being" (Clark-Hall 1976, 11). In 1982, director Charlie Gormley's debut feature *Living Apart Together* (GB, 1983) formed part of a then unprecedented wave of five Scottish features funded largely by the recently established Channel 4. Despite the euphoria surrounding this brief efflorescence, Gormley nonetheless cautioned that, "you can't really call it an industry here… there are around half-a-dozen blokes who have been around for ten to fifteen years and who want to make features" (Vaines 1982, 11). In 1995, the *annus mirabilis* of the "New" Scottish cinema which forms this volume's primary object of study, Eddie Dick, Chief Officer of the Scottish Film Production Fund, argued for the need to "normalise filmmaking," still "an abnormal activity" (Macnab 1995, 24) in Scotland. In 2000, Paddy Higson, by then the country's longest-standing and most experienced feature producer, grudgingly conceded that, "we've now got something which is almost a cottage industry… still not what you would call an industry" (Hamilton 2000, 15).

Thus, if the received critical view of the history of the British film industry is one of perpetual rebirth—artistic renaissance and economic crisis succeeding each other with metronomic regularity—Scotland's equivalent has always been understood by its constituents as stillborn or, at very best, in indefinite gestation: the late-'00s predicament bemoaned by Robert Carlyle is anything but new. What is also striking, however, about each of the comments quoted above—or at least those dating from the late '60s onwards—is that the contemporary circumstances each observer finds similarly unpropitious would have seemed unlikely and promising to their historical forebears. Revisiting the past offers a way of recontextualising and better understanding the nuances of the present.

A number of the essays in this volume demonstrate in different ways the extent to which this is so. Sarah Neely and Alan Riach's work on the mid-twentieth-century careers of pioneering amateur filmmakers Margaret Tait and Enrico Cocozza uncovers instructive precedents for the contemporary artists' film and video discussed by Neil Mulholland. Similarly, Marilyn Reizbaum forges new parallels between the creative and ideological uses to which Highland landscapes were put in certain seminal works of 1930s and '40s British cinema and the late-'90s/early-'00s Scottish films of Ken Loach. Colin McArthur revisits the early 1980s and Murray Grigor's hitherto underappreciated *Scotch Myths* (GB, 1983) not simply to reclaim a "lost classic," but also to highlight what he sees as the persistent marginalisation of non-classical feature filmmaking practices within more recent Scottish cinema. Conversely, Cairns Craig offers a provocative re-reading of a work widely acknowledged as seminal, Bill Douglas' *Childhood Trilogy* (GB, 1972-1978). Craig argues that what is typically seen as an aesthetic and ideological paradigm for new Scottish filmmakers is in fact a deeply problematic work, offering up an alienated representation of national culture and identity that, while formally accomplished, is culturally reductive and unproductive in equal measure. Christopher Meir compares and contrasts the early '80s and early '00s, discussing the international marketing campaigns for *Local Hero* (Forsyth, GB, 1983) and *Young Adam* (Mackenzie, GB/Fr, 2003). His juxtaposition of two apparently very different films aims to uncover a range of persistent external pressures and demands which Scottish filmmakers and financiers have had to negotiate over the last three decades, in their attempt to secure some kind of international critical and commercial visibility and viability for new Scottish cinema. Jane Sillars reclaims one of the most reviled representational traditions in Scottish culture, filmic or otherwise: the Kailyard image of small-town, domestic life. She argues that a wide range of contemporary Scottish film work demonstrates the ongoing creative and national cultural potential of a tradition routinely and rabidly dismissed in most twentieth-century academic commentary on Scottish culture. Alastair Scott examines a vital but hitherto overlooked institutional history within the development of Scottish film culture: that of the ongoing relationship between the British National Film and Television School, established in 1971, and successive generations of new Scottish filmmakers.

Elsewhere in this volume, Robert Carlyle's contemporary identification of the daunting financial, institutional and industrial pressures facing new Scottish cinema finds numerous echoes. In addition to already-noted contributions from McArthur, Meir and Scott, Duncan Petrie reconsiders the extended, optimistic analysis of the late-'90s situation offered in his seminal *Screening Scotland* (Petrie 2000). He concludes that many of the hopes raised by Scottish cinema's rapid expansion in the last few years of the twentieth century have remained unrealised in the early ones of the twenty-first, and that the present moment is one in which filmmakers, policy makers and critics need urgently to work together to (re)define the value and importance of a small national cinema such as Scotland's. This chimes closely with the analysis offered by Robin MacPherson. He traces the evolution of "Creative Industries" rhetoric within the Scottish film and television production sectors since the mid 1980s, concluding that cultural and political justifications for a publicly-subsidised national cinema have been woefully neglected and increasingly marginalised over the last two decades. MacPherson sees this situation as one in need of urgent rectification.

Finally, the contemporary example this introduction began with, that of Robert Carlyle and the actor's latest film, *Summer*, indicates another major theme of this collection. *Summer*'s very inclusion in, let alone its success at, the 2008 Scottish BAFTAs might cause some to look askance. Yes, the film's director, Kenny Glenaan, is a Scot, as is Carlyle, and the project's production financing package included a substantial contribution from Scottish Screen, the publicly-funded agency for film and television in Scotland. In other important regards, however, *Summer* cannot be said to be "Scottish" in any obvious way. The majority of the film's funding is non-Scottish; it is set in the English Midlands; perhaps the closest contemporary reference point for its story of fraught teenage relationships unfolding over a single season is not another Scottish film, but a British one (co-written and directed by a Pole), *My Summer of Love* (Pawlikowski, GB, 2004). Moreover, Kenny Glenaan's directorial career to date is not predominantly, let alone exclusively, Scottish by any stretch of the imagination. *Gas Attac*k (GB, 2001) is set in Glasgow, but the collective experience the film foregrounds is that of immigrant Kurdish refugees. *Yasmin* (Ger/GB, 2004) was made with a significant element of continental European finance, is set in the North of England, and focuses on British Muslim protagonists. The combined example of *Summer* and Glenaan indicates the extent to which, towards the end of the '00s, contemporary films and filmmakers can (indeed, *must*) be labelled "Scottish" without an automatic presumption that an extended or exclusive analysis of national history, society, culture and identity is what they will offer. Since the turn of the century, "Scottish" films have increasingly been financed on a pan-European basis, and the stories such movies narrate are, as in the case of *Summer*, often un- or only tangentially related to questions of national identity or specificity.

Recent or forthcoming work on Scottish cinema takes increasing notice of this fact. David Martin-Jones' *Scotland: Global Cinema* (Martin-Jones, forthcoming) posits an internationally inclusive rather than nationally exclusive remit, both in the films and filmmakers it singles out for discussion and in the critical conclusions it draws about these. My own *Discomfort and Joy: the Cinema of Bill Forsyth* (Murray, forthcoming) re-examines that filmmaker's early-'80s Scottish films in a manner foregrounding their non-nationally specific aesthetic and ideological characteristics, and examines at length Forsyth's late-'80s and early-'90s North American features, films almost totally ignored within the academic study of Scottish and British cinemas, largely, one suspects, because of their perceived deracination. Sarah Neely discerns "a recent trend in Scottish cinema, where issues of national identity are dealt with more tentatively" (Neely 2008, 161) than was the case as recently as ten years ago. She concludes that "the opening-up of modes of discourse within Scottish filmmaking should also be reflected in [Scottish] film criticism" (ibid., 162).

The "opening-up" Neely calls for is abundantly evident in this volume. Neil Mulholland reminds us of Scotland's established international reputation in the field of artist's film and video, a fact hitherto overlooked in the academic study of Scottish moving image cultures. Duncan Petrie's reconsideration of his arguments in *Screening Scotland* is explicitly informed by his subsequent time teaching in New Zealand and researching that country's cinema. Jane Sillars argues for Kailyard as an internationally legible and applicable, rather than nationally specific and reprehensible, representational discourse. Colin McArthur draws lessons from Eastern European film critical discourse in setting out the broad brushstrokes of the approach to the international promotion of Scottish cinema he would like to see taking place in the present. David Stenhouse argues that representations of Scottish culture and identity constructed by diasporic Scots have yet to be engaged with substantively within Scottish film and cultural criticism. John Hill analyses Ken Loach's late-'90s and early-'00s Scottish films, indicating the extent to which their nationally specific setting is only one constituent part of the socio-political analysis Loach sets out. Sarah Street argues that significant '00s films such as *Morvern Callar* (Ramsay, GB, 2002) and *Young Adam* should be seen as paradigmatic examples of contemporary "trans-national" rather than specifically "Scottish" cinematic practice. David Martin-Jones explores the extent which the discourses of identity put into play in much new Scottish cinema are sub- rather than (or as well as) supra-national in scope.

The expansion of Scottish cinema over the last decade-and-a-half has resulted not just in many more films from and/or about Scotland, but in the emergence of an ever wider range of questions to be posed about the country's relationship to the moving image. The editors of this book hope that readers find some of those questions (and better still, some productive responses to them) present in the following pages.

## Works Cited

Bruce, David. 1990. Hollywood comes to the Highlands. In *From Limelight to Satellite: a Scottish Film Book*, ed. Eddie Dick, 71-82. London/Glasgow: British Film Institute/Scottish Film Council.

Clark-Hall, Steve. 1976. Scottish Film Industry. *New Edinburgh Review* 34.2: 11-13.

Elliot, D. M. 1958. Film-Making in Scotland. *The Saltire Review* 5.15: 41-47.

Grierson, John. 1945. A Scottish Experiment. In *Grierson on Documentary*, ed. Forsyth Hardy, 144-148. London: Faber & Faber.

—. 1968. Edinburgh International Film Festival Celebrity Lecture. The John Grierson Archive, University of Stirling, ref. no. G7:14:1.

Hamilton, James. 2000. Northern Star. *Creation* May: 14-17.

Macnab, Geoffrey. 1995. Highland Reels. *Moving Pictures International* 8: 24-25.

Martin-Jones, David. Forthcoming. *Scotland: Global Cinema*. Edinburgh: Edinburgh University Press.

Murray, Jonathan. Forthcoming. *Discomfort and Joy: the Cinema of Bill Forsyth*. Oxford: Peter Lang.

Neely, Sarah. 2008. Contemporary Scottish Cinema. In *The Media in Scotland*, eds. Neil Blain and David Hutchison, 151-165. Edinburgh: Edinburgh University Press.

Petrie, Duncan. 2000. *Screening Scotland.* London: British Film Institute.

Scott, Kirsty. 2008. This is as good as it gets. *The Guardian*, November 21.

Vaines, Colin. 1982. Directing debut on own doorstep. *Screen International* 371: 11.

# ACKNOWLEDGEMENTS

This volume of essays emerges from *New Scottish Cinema*, a November 2005 symposium held at the Huston School of Film & Digital Media, National University of Ireland, Galway. Thanks are due to a number of individuals and institutions that helped make both that event and this book possible. Catriona Black, Steve McIntyre, David McKay and Martin McLoone all made important critical contributions to the proceedings in Galway. Fran Keaveney at the Huston School provided invaluable organisational support in setting up and running the event. A generous financial contribution from Scottish Screen made possible both the symposium and, by extension, this book. In the time between the original Galway event and this publication, both the Centre for Visual & Cultural Studies and the Research Board at Edinburgh College of Art provided financial support for editorial meetings on both sides of the Irish Sea. The editors would like to extend sincere thanks and gratitude to all of the above.

Jonathan Murray, Fidelma Farley & Rod Stoneman, December 17th 2008.

# DEMONS IN THE MACHINE: EXPERIMENTAL FILM, POETRY AND MODERNISM IN TWENTIETH-CENTURY SCOTLAND[1]

SARAH NEELY AND ALAN RIACH

Avant-garde film practices in Scotland have often been overshadowed by the dominance of a strong documentary tradition, and discussions of Scottish filmmaking are generally concerned with debates around national identity. These tendencies work to obscure the achievements of a number of important local filmmakers linked to the international avant-garde. This chapter will explore the work of two such figures: Orcadian poet, painter and filmmaker Margaret Tait (1918-1999) and Scots-Italian writer, academic and amateur filmmaker Enrico Cocozza (1921-1997). Both attended Centro Sperimentale di Cinematographia in Rome in the early 1950s, Tait after serving in the Royal Army Medical Corps, Cocozza after working as an Army interpreter for Italian POWs. Tait and Cocozza's poetic approach to filmmaking was admired by artists, other filmmakers, writers and, unsurprisingly, poets. Hugh MacDiarmid, who served as a subject for one of Tait's film portraits, published some of her written poetry and wrote about her in his 1960 *Scottish Field* article, 'Intimate Filmmaking in Scotland' (MacDiarmid 1998a, 415-7). Edwin Morgan favourably reviewed Tait's poems and later wrote a poem in tribute to Cocozza. Both Tait and Cocozza, to varying extents, were influenced by poetry, occasionally adapting and referencing the work of well-known poets in their own films.

Such links between poetry and filmmaking are well-established throughout the history of avant-garde cinema beyond Scotland.

[1] This chapter developed from a day seminar on the relationships between film and poetry in Scotland organised by Rae Riach at the University of Paisley. The research on Margaret Tait was supported by a small research grant from the Carnegie Trust for the Universities of Scotland.

Filmmakers such as Maya Deren and Jonas Mekas looked to poetry as source material for their films and as a way to explore and describe cinematic form and practice. More generally, William Wees establishes key distinctions between two different types of practice-based approach to the relationship between film and poetry. The term "poetry-film" describes films based on or directly inspired by poetry, while "film poem" refers to works characterised by "impressionistic or semi-abstract imagery carefully edited for rhythmic effects, complex formal relationships, and metaphorical or symbolic significance" (Wees 1999). Examples of such creative interrelations generally have been overlooked in historical accounts of modern Scottish culture, however. The importance of the poet laureate or the makar has long been established, but the achievements of film-makar peers such as Cocozza and Tait has gone largely unnoticed. If Edwin Morgan is the presiding, encouraging and enabling spirit for a generation of writers emergent in the 1980s and 1990s, should we not also bring Margaret Tait and Enrico Cocozza more firmly into the light of visible currency? Might they not be more enabling than they have hitherto been allowed to be? Cocozza's inventiveness was recognised within amateur filmmaking circles and Tait was celebrated by critics and savants of the avant-garde, but neither was satisfied by the limited opportunities available in mid-to-late twentieth-century Scotland to develop feature-length work. Although Tait succeeded latterly with *Blue Black Permanent* (GB, 1992), several other attempts made by the two never came to fruition. For instance, Tait sought development finance in the mid '80s for *Scars of Battle*, a never-made spy thriller about an ex-agent mourning the tragic death of his wife in Sri Lanka. Likewise, Cocozza's archival papers include a lengthy script for an unrealised feature project, *The Young Ned*.

Tellingly, the Scottish experimental filmmakers who received most significant institutional support and critical acclaim in the mid-to-late twentieth century most often did so by working outwith Scotland. Accordingly, their work is usually discussed outside a specifically national context. Most famously, Norman McLaren developed his approach to filmmaking at Glasgow School of Art, where he was a student, and set up the School's Kinecraft Society in 1933. Work produced by members of the Society was characterised by an avant-garde approach, but a few films are also notable for their social and political commitment. In 1936, McLaren and Helen Biggar, a fellow student and Kinecraft member, produced *Hell Unltd*, an anti-war film employing an innovative mix of animation and found footage. Many of the films produced by the Society's members were also submitted to the Scottish Amateur Film Festival, an annual event held at the Cosmo cinema (now the Glasgow Film Theatre). In 1935,

McLaren's film *Colour Cocktail* (GB, 1934) caught the attention of John Grierson. Grierson's interest in McLaren would inform the rest of the latter's career. Grierson invited McLaren first to join the GPO Film Unit, and later, the National Film Board of Canada. Cocozza and Tait's work was also seen by Grierson in later runs of the Scottish Amateur Film Festival. In 1951, Cocozza won the Victor Saville Trophy for most outstanding film for *Chick's Day* (GB, 1950). However, neither Cocozza nor Tait received the kind of offer Grierson made to McLaren. Both worked in Scotland for most of their intermittent careers as a result. Vitally, therefore, Cocozza and Tait were consistently influenced by and engaged with other streams of Scottish culture, even as they were compelled to assimilate and participate within the European and international filmmaking avant-gardes from a distance. McLaren has been lauded as internationalist "because he eliminated national and regional markers" (Dobson 1999) in nearly all of his work; in sharp contrast, Cocozza and Tait developed, through a combination of ingenuity and necessity, an obviously localised form of modernist practice. It is precisely in such terms that this essay documents and celebrates their achievements.

Neither Cocozza nor Tait chose to work outside international mainstreams, whether commercial or avant-garde, through active preference. Yet to a significant degree both turned necessity into virtue. They capitalised on freedom from the restrictions of working within an industrial framework and embraced an eclectic range of media, genres, forms and practices, both mainstream and avant-garde. Each displayed a serious commitment to experimentation with the material possibilities of film form. Like the modernist film which Jill Forbes and Sarah Street distinguish for its use of the camera more like a diary than a machine (Forbes and Street 2000, 20), Tait and Cocozza's work presents a fluid treatment of space and place. Although the oversight of their work and the general lack of support given to developing their skills is lamentable, their shared fate as truly independent filmmakers meant that their work was influenced uniquely by contemporaneous experimentations within other areas of Scottish culture, specifically, developments in modernist literature. Their respective oeuvres represent a remarkably vivid, intensely detailed local portrait of Scottish society and creativity in the middle of the twentieth century and beyond.

## Margaret Tait

Soon after returning to Scotland from her studies in Rome, Margaret Tait established Ancona Films with fellow student Peter Hollander.

Offices were listed in New York, Rome and Edinburgh, where Tait relocated in 1954, setting up her studio above a shop on Rose Street. There she held an annual 'Rose Street Film Festival', running parallel to the Edinburgh International Film Festival and intended to showcase the work of students from Centro Sperimentale. Later, after she returned to her native Orkney, she established her studio in an old Kirk and would screen films in local theatres, village halls, or occasionally her own home. For most of her career she used a Bolex camera that she had purchased on a side street when she was a student in Rome.

Given the fecund relationship between cinema and poetry that developed through her experimental film work, it is significant that Tait was committed to writing poetry as well as producing moving image work, and that key Scottish literary figures took an interest in both areas of her creative output. Of especial importance for this essay is the close relationship that developed between Tait and perhaps the most important of all twentieth-century Scottish poets, Hugh MacDiarmid. Tait published three books of poetry: *origins and elements* (1959), *The Hen and the Bees: Legends and Lyrics* (1960) and *Subjects and Sequences* (1960). She also wrote short stories and children's fiction. MacDiarmid published a number of Tait's poems in the magazine he was editing in the 1950s, *The Voice of Scotland*. From the 1930s on, MacDiarmid's poetry turned towards extended experimental forms of writing, predominantly in English but drawing in phrases and quotations from other languages and cultures. In this period the linguistic diversity of his work was matched by its wide-ranging reference to different disciplines such as science, biology, genetics, music and film. But throughout his writing career, MacDiarmid produced any number of poems dealing specifically with Scotland and Scottish subject-matter, and he repeatedly returned to composition in the language we call Scots. Intellectual enquiry, national disposition and formal experimentalism characterised MacDiarmid's writing at the time he encountered comparable qualities in Tait's literary work. Her 1959 collection *origins and elements* is characterised by free verse forms, openness of structure, line-breaks depending on syntax and conversational emphasis rather than repetitive rhythmic pattern, scientific subject-matter, love of paradox, wide-ranging literary reference (poems about Rimbaud, Emily Dickinson, allusions to D.H. Lawrence), analytic austerity rubbing shoulders with wry humour.

Edwin Morgan reviewed *origins and elements* in the autumn 1961 issue of *New Saltire*, in an essay entitled 'Who Will Publish Scottish Poetry?' Morgan was concerned to point out that Scottish publishers should take closer interest in what was happening with work produced in ephemeral, small-press or pamphlet editions. The poets he reviewed—Alan Jackson, Tom Scott, Alan Riddell, Ian Hamilton Finlay—achieved varying degrees of recognition, most notably Finlay, not only as a poet but as an internationally recognised artist. Alan Riddell, along with Finlay and Morgan, produced concrete poetry in an international movement that overlapped literary and visual forms. Morgan draws attention to Tait's "curious and interesting, though sometimes prosaic and wilful, poems on a great variety of subjects" (Morgan 1961, 51). He notes MacDiarmid's influence in scientific poems like 'Water' and 'Carbon' and in Tait's attack on the Calvinist disposition. Morgan concludes that Tait "gives the reader's mind something to work on" (ibid.) and praises her engagement with mental activity as opposed to rhapsodic entrancement. There is certainly an affinity between Morgan's own work and what he praises in Tait's.

Poems in Tait's 1960 collection *The Hen and the Bees* are more playful with sound patterns and vocabulary, focusing on animals ('Hen', 'Dog'), archetypal figures (Queen, King, Princess) and mythical gods (Thor, Loki and Baldar). The poems in her third collection, *Subjects and Sequences* (1960), are more varied and ambitious, collected under different section headings. 'Book I' is entitled 'Places, People and Events', and 'Book II', 'Sequences', includes poems on elemental sensations of sunlight, the role of the poet, Mary Queen of Scots, and children. The book has a larger physical format and the poems take advantage of this, with longer lines extending across the page then being brought back abruptly in one-, two-, or three-word lines, so that the conversational diction is formally arranged in a self-evidently self-conscious way. The poems show clearly the extent of their own artifice, while they are normally straightforward in their syntax, grammar and conversational tone. The range of poems and the consistency of their achievement are impressive. It is regrettable that Tait has been overlooked in modern anthologies, both of Scottish poetry and of poetry by women. She is more formally daring and in subject-matter much more radical than most of her contemporaries, "a remarkable critical forerunner in her poetry of what's now a recognisable Scottish literary voice" (Smith 2004, 9). No wonder MacDiarmid published her.

There were affinities between MacDiarmid and Tait, qualities of language and visualisation both artists share, representations of visual depiction (external scenes) and internal, abstract ideas, best summarised by the lines from MacDiarmid's 'On a Raised Beach':

> What the scene shows is never anything to what it's designed to hide.
> The red blood that makes the beauty of a maiden's cheek

> Is as red under a gorilla's pigmented and hairy face.
> (MacDiarmid 2004, 148)

Such an emphasis on immediacy and appreciation perhaps lay behind Tait making an intimate and expressive film-portrait of MacDiarmid. Tait's *MacDiarmid* (GB, 1964) combines poetry, film, music and song. The musical setting of MacDiarmid's 'The Eemis Stane' by the composer F. G. Scott provides the soundtrack while the words of MacDiarmid's 'Somersault' and 'Krang' are playfully interpreted through image, resulting in a memorable depiction of MacDiarmid teetering along an Edinburgh kerb. The film's subject is often decentred or out of focus and occasionally the camera shifts its attention to what might ordinarily seem subordinate objects of study: images of radios, clocks, books and newspapers, traffic and the sea, city and country. This amounts to a self-conscious occupation of time implicitly opposed to the exploitation of the viewer's time which is a commonplace of commercial cinema. In that cinema, time is consumable, waste-filled. In Tait's cinema, as in MacDiarmid's poetry, time is valuably lived, edged with movement and perception, unpredicted and unpredictable.

MacDiarmid's experimentation might be read as a strategy to move beyond established poetic expressions of Scottish life. Analogously, Tait's grappling with realism and representation can also be seen as a response to the dominance of documentary modes in mid-twentieth-century Scottish moving image culture. Although Tait subscribed to Grierson's idea of the "creative treatment of actuality," filming what was around her, she was wary of traditional documentary modes. She wrote:

> The contradictory or paradoxical thing is that in a documentary the real things depicted are liable to lose their reality by being photographed and presented in that 'documentary' way, and there's no poetry in that. In poetry, something else happens. Hard to say what it is. Presence, let's say, soul or spirit, an empathy with whatever it is that's dwelt upon, feeling for it—to the point of identification. (Tait 2004, 132)

Attention paid in *MacDiarmid* to the class- and culturally-coded linguistic registers so often associated with traditional documentary modes shows Tait's alternative approach to documentary in action. In 1964, BBC radio and television was generally sustained by voices whose received-pronunciation English was at the far end of the spectrum from the sounds of vernacular Scots voices. The musical settings of MacDiarmid's poems by F. G. Scott used by Tait bring the Scots tones and their velar fricatives into a high art medium, a fact which must have affronted certain contemporary arbiters of taste. By quoting such material, Tait's *MacDiarmid* evokes large questions about authority, the dissemination of information, how it is sanctioned or disapproved, and therefore how people are empowered or disenfranchised—all questions equally central to the poetic work of her film's human subject.

This question of language is crucial. The first MacDiarmid poem Tait uses in her film is 'You know not who I am'—a Scots version of a poem by the German Stefan George. It's worth pausing on this and looking at it in MacDiarmid's Scots and in an English translation (MacDiarmid 1993, 22). The poem catches the sense of the relation between spirit and form, an inherent quality in language itself, brilliantly. It seems to be about something you can't grasp or understand or comprehend, yet at the end, MacDiarmid identifies this quality as the thing that gives you courage, the wild and eager kiss that is always burning into your soul, something painful yet inspiring and vital:

***'You Know Not Who I Am'***

*After the German of Stefan George*

Ye kenna wha I am – but this is fac'.
I ha'ena yet by ony word or ac'
Made mysel' human…an' sune I maun tak'
Anither guise to ony I've yet ta'en.
I'll cheenge: an' yet my ain true sel' I'll hain,
Tine only what ye ken as me. I' vain,
Ye'll seek to haud me, an' ye needna murn,
For to a form ye canna ken I'll turn
'Twixt ae braith an' the neist: an whan I'm gane
Ye'll ha'e o' me what ye ha'e haen o' a'
My kindred since licht on earth 'good da'–
*The braith that gi'es ye courage, an' the fain*
*Wild kiss that aye into yer saul maun burn.*

***'You Know Not Who I Am'***

*After the German of Stefan George*

You know not who I am – but this is fact
I have not yet by any word or act
Made myself human…and soon I must take
Another guise to any I've yet taken.
I'll change: and yet my own true self I'll keep,
Losing only what you know as me. In vain
You'll try to hold me, and you need not mourn,
For to a form you cannot know I'll turn
Between one breath and the next: and when I'm gone
You'll have of me what you have had of all
My kindred since light on earth began to dawn –
*The breath that gives you courage, and the eager*
*Wild kiss that always into your soul must burn.*

The poem works in the Scots version in a different way, with a different kind of authenticity. The English is more like a black-and-white photograph where everything is in place and in focus. There's nothing ungraspable. But the Scots is both present and somehow elusive, hard and real but also fast-moving and emotionally quick.

Using the poem to bookend *MacDiarmid* was something Tait felt provided "a comment on the film and what it's about and on the partiality fully to be expected of a portrait" (Tait 2004, 133). Likewise, the images and audio fragments of MacDiarmid which Tait presents focus on the detail without trying to make any overarching generalisations. As with her other portraits, what she presents is a familiarity, something instantly recognisable but otherwise ineffable, unsayable, and utterly resistant to commercial imperatives. Tait's film brings out these elemental questions about energy, restlessness, time, growth and the creation of valuable things, both in nature and by human intervention.

Tait did experiment with the possibility of funding her filmmaking activities through established documentary routes. Her films briefly attracted the attention of Grierson, who commented on them admiringly after one of her 'Rose Street Festival' screenings. Yet nothing ever came of it. Her film *The Drift Back* (GB, 1956), about repopulation and the return of people from the Scottish mainland to Orkney, and from the Orkney mainland to its surrounding islands, follows traditional Griersonian lines most closely. One of her only fully-funded films, it was made with the support of the Orkney Education Committee and was intended to be the first of a series of films focusing on Orcadian subjects (Neely 2008b; Neely, forthcoming).

In many ways the budgetary and technological constraints Tait confronted often served a positive function in the development of her distinctive poetic style, in a way comparable to written poetry enlivened by its need for verbal economy. One of Tait's earlier experiments, *Calypso* (GB, 1955), was made with 35 mm film stock that she found while in Rome. Taking the stock's existing Calypso music soundtrack as her film's starting point, Tait handpainted a series of colourful figures to accompany the former. The quick succession of images and the inevitable slight variations in the painted figure reproduced over and over again cause the latter to tremble into life and reverberate with the energetic soundtrack. With many films, Tait would draw up an ideal plan, detailing what stock was necessary, what stock she had already and what she would be likely to obtain. This sometimes meant films were made over a number of years, as Tait accumulated the necessary footage. She would also consider the possibility of incorporating previously shot material into new films. These limitations demanded a degree of resourcefulness which often led to experimentation and innovation. Although Tait never had any involvement with the Free Cinema movement, its rhetoric expressing feelings of liberation from commercial restrictions have some resonance in her working methods. Many of Tait's films, her portraits in particular, make no effort to conceal the interaction between filmmaker and subject.

When Tait established the uncertain nature of garnering external funding and the difficulty of selling her short films to television, she decided to abandon hope of commercial prospects and allow herself to experiment fully with the poetic. Sometimes her films take the text of poems as a starting point of exploration. Tait's 1955 filmic interpretation of Gerard Manley Hopkins' 'The Leaden Echo and the Golden Echo' is one clear example. On other occasions Tait's development process reflects her own background as a poet. Films often began life in the pages of her notebooks. Lists of places, images or scenes carve out the rough, sculptural forms. Her film *Where I Am is Here* (GB, 1964) Tait describes as:

> Starting with a six-line script which just noted down a *kind* of event to occur, and recur, my aim was to construct a film with its own logic, its own correspondences within itself, its own echoes and rhymes and comparisons, all through close exploration of the everyday, the commonplace, in the city, Edinburgh, where I stayed at the time. (Tait 2004, 161)

The repetition and variation of images develop into a visual form of rhyming. A shot of birds sliding across the ice is juxtaposed against one of children doing the same. The impersonal and the personal, the general and the specific, the celebrated and the discarded, are each addressed with a shared observational intensity. The approach breaks with the authoritative and summative tendencies of documentary, but also challenges conventional articulations of Scottish culture. For Tait, there was an important distinction to be made between filming the "landscape" and filming the "scenery," particularly in Scotland where Tait felt scenery was too often shot out of convenience. Her landscapes aren't empty but are peopled. Her films often eschew grand scenic establishing shots and instead focus on the detail. Tait explains *Where I Am is Here* as a film "minutely examining the landscape of Edinburgh, or the townscape" (Tait 2004, 81). Tait's film poetry shares much in common with other avant-garde filmmakers, such as Maya Deren. For Deren, the poetic film inscribed a certain 'attitude'. She wrote: "If philosophy is concerned with understanding the meaning of reality, then poetry—and art in general—is a celebration, a singing of values and meanings" (Deren 1979, 123). Tait, in her short piece 'Film-poem or poem-film', points to the challenge for filmmakers in attaining the ideal Deren describes. Tait's fondness for Lorca's poetic notion of "stalking the image" (Tait 2004, 89) reflects her belief in the innate, lyrical qualities of everyday life. Her commitment to filming what was around her engaged with Lorca's idea that all things, regardless of their emotional or physical scale, must be given equal attention. In 'Now', a poem from *origins and elements,* the description of Tait's laboured attempts to register satisfactorily the movement of a flower opening its petals, and the disappointment felt when she concludes it is impossible to do so, illustrates her devotion to understanding a reality eluding cursory glances. It is the concern with empathy and identification, a decelerated manner of looking, which distinguishes Tait's films from more objective, documentary modes, but also from a tradition of subjective diary films (Neely 2008a).

## Enrico Cocozza

Like Tait, Enrico Cocozza harboured professional aspirations for much of his filmmaking career. The Scottish amateur filmmaking network provided a supportive structure for his activities. Although Cocozza was already actively involved in this network before studying in Italy, the years following his return to Scotland were particularly prolific. He established a film unit and built a small studio in Wishaw, producing 63 films between 1952 and 1960, including some for The Italian Consulate in Glasgow, The Scottish Film Council, and Star Informational films of New Jersey (Scottish Screen Archive ref. no. 3/7/3:2). He was also an active member of the Wishaw Film Society and served as honorary Treasurer and Secretary of The Connoisseur Film Circle, a club that eventually turned an old auction house behind Cocozza's mother's café into a cinema. Jean Cocteau, on whom Cocozza would later complete a PhD thesis, was listed as one of the society's patrons. Screenings were held three nights a week and members could borrow from a library of film books. Lectures also formed part of the Circle's activities: the brochure for its inaugural season of 1950-51 highlights the possibility of Forsyth Hardy delivering a lecture on Swedish cinema (Scottish Screen Archive ref. no. 3/7/20). Although the cinema's initial screenings largely consisted of European avant-garde films, eventually Cocozza would show his own work there. That Cocozza was equipped to both produce and distribute his own work meant he was able to operate relatively independently, restricted only by his ability to fund his productions.

Like Tait, Cocozza's creativity also took literary form. He was a writer of short stories, and his novel *Assunta: The Story of Mrs. Joe's Café*, named after his mother who owned the Belhaven Café in Wishaw, was published in 1987. That said, however, Cocozza's links with the 'film poem' are not as strong as Tait's. *Porphyria* (1836), Robert Browning's poem about a jealous man who murders his lover, was the basis for his 1960 film of the same name. Other projects, such as *Invocation* (GB, 1951), which Cocozza described as "a visual interpretation of a poem," (Scottish Screen Archive ref. no. 3/7/4) evoke Tait's slow, meditative pacing. A poetic montage gives up-close attention to a wide variety of trees and wildlife in the changing seasons. Shots are long in duration, pausing on the texture of the bark of a silver birch, the movement of a stream, the sky, budding flowers, building intrigue and suspense through the repetition and variation of images and visual rhyming. The ending is delivered with a comic edge, a hand popping out from the earth, wriggling out into the free air. It breaks the serious tone and departs in similarity from Tait's work, but is indicative of Cocozza's general playfulness and irreverence towards avant-garde conventions. While Tait occasionally expressed uneasiness with the term 'avant-garde' used to describe her work, Cocozza humorously interrogates avant-garde forms, presumably to challenge some of the established traditions in the amateur filmmaking circuit. Cocozza explains *Invocation* in his catalogue of work as "quite beyond the Cosmo audience at the Scottish Film Festival" (Scottish Screen Archive ref. no. 3/7/4). Similarly, he refers to his film *The Living Ghost* (GB, 1959-60), which like *Chick's Day* won the major award at the amateur festival, as his "last serious film—as pretentious as the rest" (Scottish Screen Archive ref. no. 3/7/4). Another film, *In the Shadow* (GB, 1957), he describes as "another of these heavy symbolic efforts that are merely an excuse for some good low-key photography that does not cover the dreadful acting" (Scottish Screen Archive ref. no. 3/7/4).

This sense of a challenge to canonical filmmaking conventions as strong as Tait's but more ludic in tone is captured in Edwin Morgan's poem 'Enricco Cocozza', in his 2002 collection *Cathures*. That poem marries Cocozza's sense of playfulness with Morgan's own. Morgan evokes and writes in the voice of Cocozza as persona, poking fun at Griersonian documentary: "*Drifters* was shown to the Herring Board: Even the herring were bored. Sorry John!" (Morgan 2002, 27) and later in the same piece declaims, "See worthiness? That is Scotland's shame" (ibid.). For Morgan, as for his Cocozza, Glasgow "is not worthy"—Glasgow "is Gotham City" (ibid.) and problems have to be lived, if you want to shoot them. Cocozza and Morgan shared the experience of growing up homosexual in the west of Scotland during the early twentieth century, and if Morgan's Cocozza recognises and realises his own sexual disposition alongside Eisenstein's—"He cruised the Berlin clubs..." (ibid.)—Morgan recognises how both these filmmakers used their own imagination to break through the restrictions of social contexts by means of their art. Morgan evokes Cocozza's film *Bongo Erotico* (GB, 1959) as "quite gallus, banging it out" (ibid.) and,

> Staring sultry at my favourite dancer
> As he sways in his sloppy satin knickers.
> Well it's not *Braveheart*… (ibid.)

It is rather, "flesh and heat / Fleshed out of Fifties forbiddenness" (ibid.). Morgan conjures up the cinemas he knew in Glasgow:

> The picture-palaces were glittering –
> Green's Playho se ('We want "u" in'),
> Grand Central, Classic, Curzon—
> Glittering but filled with shadows,
> Community of shadows on the screen,
> Community of shadows in the stalls,
> Great coming and going—
> (Morgan 2002, 29)

Morgan's poem is a celebration of creativity in a specific time and place, working against social oppression and difficult personal circumstance, but it connects the specific character of Cocozza to a wider Scottish cultural history in which both social oppressiveness and personal creative resistance is seen in a context of paradoxically shared isolation, recognition of which is consolation and social and creative empowerment. The poem ends:

> Whatever the shame, whatever the stain,
> Dante would sigh to see
> Those lost ones sitting in the smoky dark
> With their *mal protesi nervi*, and above them
> The pitiless projector's beam, behind them
> The pitiless projector's whirr, before them,
> The film, the film,
> The one they watched, the one I watch them in.
> To be free, you must show it, oh you must let it run!
> (Morgan 2002, 30)

Morgan's insistence on the value of Cocozza's film-making is taken to a further level of abstraction and affirmation in the poem-sequence entitled 'Demon' published at the end of *Cathures*. For Morgan, the Demon is a figure who intervenes in individual lives to remind us of the mischievous or perverse, the necessary energies in the dynamics of life. Whenever serenity threatens to turn into complacency, the Demon appears to upset what seems like stability. In 'A Little Catechism from the Demon' there is a reference to film which seems to fix an idea of what the medium can do:

What is the film? It rolls, it tells.
What is the film? *Under the Falls.*
Where is the theatre? Under the hill.
Where is the demon? Walking the hills.
Where is the victory? On the high tops.
Where is the fire? Far in the deep.
Where is the deep? Study the demon.
Where is the mountain? Set out now.
(Morgan 2002, 113)

This configuration of images suggests specific relations between aspiration and research, the work of watching, reading, studying, learning from film, rolling and telling in the theatre under the hill.

Biographically, Morgan's interest in cinema is suggestive. Born in 1920, his middle-class childhood and young manhood in Glasgow before and after his service with the Royal Army Medical Corps in the Middle East in the 1940s, saw increasing self-awareness of his homosexuality. In a city where public behaviour was closely observed and decorum insistently required, especially in certain professions, particular cinemas were well-established locations where such sexuality might be tacitly acknowledged. So Morgan's interest in cinema auditoria as well as films has an unconventional aspect that cuts across the accepted conventions of cinema's commercial or normative social priorities. When he writes at the end of 'The Second Life,' the title poem of his breakthrough volume of 1968, "Slip out of darkness, it is time" (Morgan 1968, 54), he is talking not only of Glasgow rebuilding itself, the snake shedding its old skin (as a boy Morgan's nickname was Kaa, the rock-python from Kipling's *Jungle Book*), or himself gaining a new confidence at the age of forty, but also implicitly of the moment when you emerge from a darkened cinema into the lighted city streets.

Similarly, perhaps Cocozza's reluctance to conform within a culturally and socially conservative climate informed his ability to experiment in other areas of his life, filming in the busy streets and parks of Wishaw and producing films that broke the established boundaries of the amateur circuit. At the Scottish Amateur Film Festival in 1949, his film *Fantasmagoria* was declared "the problem picture of the festival" (Scottish Screen Archive ref. no. 3/7/26:2). Filmed on Coltness Estate in Wishaw, the film is difficult to categorise. Essentially a horror movie, Cocozza himself plays 'the evil one' upsetting the estate. The film begins with a big orchestral score accompanied by an eerie but poetic voice-over, one part stylised montage and one part presentiment of *Plan 9 from Outer Space* (Wood Jr., USA, 1959). The festival adjudicator, Stephen Watts, a London film critic, described *Fantasmagoria* as "an experiment which quite clearly required courage", but noted the uneasy coexistence of "moments of drama and imagination" with "moments of profound obscurity" where one character could either be read as "Olivier playing Lear, or Santa Claus in a Glasgow store" (Scottish Screen Archive ref. no. 3/7/26:2). Watts surmised, "If the film were shown in London in a specialised cinema the reactions of the film critics would range from people walking out in the middle of it to people who would say it was a new art" (ibid.). Whether intentional or just a consequence of a limited budget and amateur actors, this conflict of meaning and intention is what makes Cocozza's work reverberate so powerfully. Even a decade later, when the Scottish Amateur Film Festival's adjudicator encouraged amateurs to "be bold—experiment with new ideas—avoid the conventional—don't ape the professionals," Cocozza's *Porphyria* was offered the suggestion that "the accent should not have been so localised" (Scottish Screen Archive ref. no. 3/7/26:4).

Cocozza's parodic engagement with a range of cultural texts informed his most innovative work, but also marked him out for some as 'unprofessional'. The demon in the fringes of Scottish filmmaking, he satirised the avant-garde, calling into question the strengths and weaknesses of amateur practices, but also the limitations of the preconceptions around Scottish filmmaking methods. His passionate engagement with, and inspired reinterpretations of, a wide range of film styles and genres share Morgan's sense of humour, but also his ability to re-imagine familiar settings in new contexts. In *Ad Infernum Buddy?* (GB, 1952) he parodies *Quo Vadis* (LeRoy, USA, 1951); *Robot Three* (GB, 1951) is a film about a mad scientist, reminiscent of Stevenson's *Dr Jekyll and Mr Hyde; Bongo Erotico* explores the genre of erotic film, shooting in negative and capturing the movements of sparsely clad dancers in his bedroom. *Chick's Day*, about a teen from Wishaw who commits a robbery, takes the gangster genre as its starting point. As with many of Cocozza's films, genre is not a sentence to creative confinement, but rather a site for artistic invention. The local dialect of the central character Chick forms the soundtrack's prominent voiceover. Rather than conform to generic conventions Cocozza retains local specificity, confidently appropriating various elements from a variety of genres. There are odd shifts in tone and Cocozza's approach is a playful one. In one scene involving the protagonist and his mother, the voiceover takes complete control of the soundtrack when her words are replaced by the protagonist's mocking, mimicked version. Sometimes the effect is a comic one, at others it is deeply moving. As Mitch Miller writes:

> This transference, from cool parody of documentary style analysis, to Cagney confronting the electric chair, his luck entirely spent, is effected without any perceptible incongruity. This is because, despite the affectation of gritty realism, the film is structured around Chick's own thoughts. (Miller 2002, 12)

In this sense, it is the employment of local dialect that enables the reinvention and reinterpretation of established genres, the incongruity that allows for the interrogation of entrenched modes. As Kenneth Broar writes, for Cocozza "his Wishaw locality, far from being a parochial or limiting factor, quite to the contrary *fed* his internationalism, and in turn this outward-looking spirit fed into his life in Wishaw" (Broar, 1999). *Chick's Day* was clearly successful in its ability to register with international audiences. The film had screenings in Moscow, Hong Kong, Australia and New Zealand and was distributed commercially by Contemporary Films of London. It also won awards in Spain and Portugal.

## Conclusion

While some see the work of filmmakers such as Cocozza, or even Tait for that matter, as failing to achieve the standards of professional mainstream film production, others praise the two for their experimentation. Whether looking at a particular time and place through avant-garde or other generic frameworks, where Tait and Cocozza's films best succeed is in their commitment to the present of the national society and culture from which both filmmakers worked. In this sense, Jonas Mekas' description of the film poem resonates in both Tait and Cocozza's work:

> These films, their subjects, their themes, are very small. Just maybe a feeling, a mood. When we go to a commercial film, a theatrical narrative or art film, and when we ask what is the subject of that film, we usually have many obvious, 'important' themes we can point out. But these other films are very unpretentious. They don't want to change you by force. They don't work, they do not plot, to undermine you so you will be this or that. (Mekas 1999, 192)

Yet it is also important to remember that neither Tait nor Cocozza were opposed to mainstream filmmaking. Cocozza regularly appropriated popular genres and the films most greatly praised by Tait were mainstream: she was, for instance, an admirer of Jerry Lewis' work. For her, meaningful films could be made across the wide range of industrial practices. Tait's *Blue Black Permanent* may be about poetry, but it is not by any stretch of definition a film poem. It is a feature film made with large cast and crew and informed by its (albeit low-level) industrial production context. But *Blue Black Permanent* does bear similarities to Mekas' description of the film poem, articulating a complex form of storytelling, complicating rather than consolidating the various points of view associated with the three generations of women depicted in the film.

In his essay 'Intimate Film Making in Scotland' MacDiarmid praises Tait's films as a singular achievement in the contemporary national context, "ploughing a lonely furrow, but she has set a process in motion which is bound to develop" (MacDiarmid 1998, 417). Relying largely on her own desire to make films, Tait was, as Mitch Miller describes,

> A square peg in the Tartan-cinema pigeonhole… worlds away from the Griersonian custodians of fact that dominated the Films of Scotland Committee, or the Scotch-misty London-manufactured stereotypes of the mainstream industry. (Miller 2006/07, 15)

A similar claim can be made for Cocozza. Many of his films are modernist in their playful approaches, intertextual referencing, fragmentation and subsequent shifts in subjectivity. Both Tait and Cocozza's work was mostly self-funded. The comparative lack of local support or recognition for their experimental films can be blamed on an inability to recognise work that broke with established forms of representation, a problem which still confronts many Scottish filmmakers today.

Tait and Cocozza both engaged with the local and the specific, but it was their dialogue with international traditions that pulled them outside the boundaries of popular debate within Scotland. While Tait's films were screened internationally, the majority of showings in Britain took place in England. Particularly within an avant-garde context, her work gained a significant degree of visibility after screenings at a number of festivals in the late 1970s and 1980s. This was a dilemma that Tait was acutely aware of. Writing for a dossier to accompany the *Desperately Seeking Cinema* event held at the Glasgow Film Theatre in 1988, she reflected back on the earlier stages of her career and "the dreadful days of the Films of Scotland Committee," describing how "everybody was expected to turn out the same sort of stuff; and it was all awful" (Orkney Archive ref. no. D97/27).

It seems natural, considering this restrictive local filmmaking environment, that Tait drew inspiration from as many sources as possible. MacDiarmid was of interest to Tait because of shared poetic pursuits, but for other reasons, too. Amongst the principal archive of Tait's papers in Orkney is a clipping of a letter that MacDiarmid wrote to *The Scotsman* in 1960, four years after the Films of Scotland Committee had been re-established. He writes:

> The hang-over of our past rural life has had most deplorable effects in the vast body of post-Burnsian doggerel, and, in my experience, the present folk-song cult plays into the hands of the great number of people who are hostile to all intellectual distinction and to experimental and "avant garde" work generally, and I regard their attitude as a menace to the arts not less serious than, and closely connected with, the pressure to reduce all arts to the level of mere entertainment. (MacDiarmid 1996, 100)

Tait, no doubt, would have agreed, as her impressive body of film and literary work testifies.

Recent years have seen an increased interest in both Cocozza and Tait. The Scottish Screen Archive and Lux (formed from the London Filmmakers Co-op and London Electronic Arts/London Video Access) have played a key role in ensuring the restoration, preservation and circulation of their films. In 2001, Scottish Television produced *Surreally Scozzese*, a documentary on Cocozza's life and work. In 2004, following the restoration of Tait's films, the Edinburgh International Film Festival hosted a retrospective of her work, supplemented by an international touring exhibition of the same. Tait and Cocozza's formal originality and their adept engagement with a range of cultural sources—global and local, generic and specific—demonstrates a willingness to take risks and sometimes to fail, and also to trust to the authenticity of one's own experience. Their significance in Scottish culture goes far beyond that of historical artefact. There is still much to learn from their empowering approaches to experimentalism. Their visions still have much to teach.

## Works Cited

### Primary Sources

Anon. 1950-51. Brochure for 'The Connoisseur Circle'. The Scottish Screen Archive, ref. no. 3/7/20.

Cocozza, Enrico. *The Young Ned,* unpublished film script. The Scottish Screen Archive, ref. no. 3/7/5.

—. Miscellaneous notebooks. The Scottish Screen Archive, ref. no. 3/7/3-4.

Tait, Margaret. Miscellaneous correspondence and notebooks. The Margaret Tait Papers, Orkney Archive, Kirkwall, ref. no. D97/27.

Watts, Stephen. 1949. Adjudicator's Statement at Cosmo Cinema, Scottish Amateur Film Festival, March 26. The Scottish Screen Archive, ref. no. 3/7/26.

## Secondary Sources

Broar, Kenneth. 1999. 'DR Enrico Cocozza Nov 6 1921-Dec 27 1997: A short biography'. The Scottish Screen Archive, ref. no. 3/7.

Cocozza, Enrico. 1987. *Assunta: The Story of Mrs. Joe's Café.* London: Vantage.

Deren, Maya. 1979. 'A Statement of Principles'. In *Film as Film: formal experiment in film 1910-1975, Hayward Gallery, South Bank, London, 3 May-17 June 1979*, 123. London: Arts Council of Great Britain.

Dobson, Terence. 1999. McLaren and Grierson: Intersections. *Screening the Past: an international electronic journal of visual media and history.* http://www.latrobe.edu.au/screeningthepast/firstrelease/fr1199/tdfr8d.htm (accessed May 12, 2008).

Forbes, Jill and Sarah Street. 2000. *European Cinema: an Introduction.* London: Palgrave.

MacDiarmid, Hugh. 1993. You Know Not Who I Am. In *MacDiarmid: Complete Poems, Vol I*, ed. Michael Grieve and W. R. Aitken, 22. Manchester: Carcanet. Alan Riach, English trans.

—. 1996. Letter to the *Scotsman.* In *The Armstrong Nose: Selected Letters of Hamish Henderson*, ed. Alec Finlay, 100. Edinburgh: Polygon. Originally published in *The Scotsman* (January 25 1960).

—. 1998. Films and the Scottish Novelist. In *Hugh MacDiarmid: The Raucle Tongue, Hitherto uncollected prose, Vol III*, ed. Angus Calder, Glen Murray and Alan Riach, 107-109. Manchester: Carcanet. Originally published in *Arts Review* (1947).

—. 1998a. Intimate Film Making in Scotland. In *Hugh MacDiarmid: The Raucle Tongue, Hitherto uncollected prose, Vol III*, ed. Angus Calder, Glen Murray and Alan Riach, 415-417. Manchester: Carcanet. Originally published in *Scottish Field* (October 1960).

—. 2004. On a Raised Beach. In *Selected Poetry*, ed. Alan Riach and Michael Grieve, 146-156. Manchester: Carcanet.

Mekas, Jonas. 1999. The Other Direction. *Poem Film Film Poem* 5: 190-195.

Miller, Mitch. 2002. Heavenly Mandates. *The Drouth* Winter: 9-15.

—. 2006/07. Recycled, re-imagined and resurrected: The return of Margaret Tait. *roughcuts* Dec-Jan: 15.

Morgan, Edwin. 1961. Who will publish Scottish Poetry? *New Saltire* 2: 51-56.

—. 1968. *The Second Life: Selected Poems of Edwin Morgan*. Edinburgh: Edinburgh University Press.

—. 2002. *Cathures: New Poems 1997-2001*. Manchester: Carcanet.

Neely, Sarah. 2008a. Contemporary Scottish Cinema. In *The Media in Scotland*, ed. Neil Blain and David Hutchison, 151-165. Edinburgh: Edinburgh University Press.

—. 2008b. Stalking the image: Margaret Tait and Intimate Filmmaking Practices. *Screen* 49.2: 216-221.

—. Forthcoming. 'Ploughing a lonely furrow: Margaret Tait and 'professional' filmmaking practices in 1950s Scotland. In *Amateur* Cinema, ed. Ian Craven. Newcastle: Cambridge Scholars Press.

Smith, Ali. 2004. The Margaret Tait Years. In *Subjects and Sequences: Margaret Tait Reader*, ed. Peter Todd and Benjamin Cook, 7-27. London: Lux.

Tait, Margaret. 1959. *origins and elements*. Edinburgh: private publication.

—. 1960a. *Subjects and Sequences*. Edinburgh: private publication.

—. 1960b. *The Hen and the Bees: Legends and Lyrics*. Edinburgh: private publication.

—. 2004. Film-poem or poem-film: A Few Notes about Film and Poetry. In *Subjects and Sequences: Margaret Tait Reader*, eds. Peter Todd and Benjamin Cook, 132-133. London: Lux.

Todd, Peter and Benjamin Cook, eds. 2004. *Subjects and Sequences: Margaret Tait Reader*. London: Lux.

Wees, William. 1999. Poetry-Films and Film Poems. *Film Poems* April.

http://www.lux.org.uk/forms/filmpoems/weesarticle.pdf (accessed November 11, 2008).

# REEL 2 REAL CACOPHONY: UNITED ARTISTS' TWENTY-FIRST CENTURY PICTURES

NEIL MULHOLLAND

Museum-scale works by Smith/Stewart, Jonathan Monk and Turner Prize winner Douglas Gordon saw Scotland became internationally acknowledged for black-box video installation work at the end of the twentieth century. The more self-consciously radical audio-visual art promulgated by peers involved with artist-run cooperatives in the late 1980s and early 1990s remains to be canonised, but their legacy is proving to be equally, if not more important for the production of recent Scottish audio-visual art than the more widely exposed tradition of video installation. Film and video work produced around co-ops such as Glasgow's Transmission and by artists working independently with video in an interventionist and ambient fashion are only just now entering the process of being archived by Scottish Screen and the REWIND project led by the University of Dundee. Interventionist, performative and environmental approaches—wherein the roots of audio-visual practice could be said to lie in Scotland—are undergoing an unprecedented revival of fortune. Yet many artists involved with such ways of working are also engaged with black-box video installation, as well as more open-source means of distribution without walls, such as DVD compilations, streaming AV, mobile-application-friendly MP4 and, most recently, ambient intelligence technologies (AmI). Scottish audio-visual work during the '00s defies categorisation: examining its terms of production, distribution and consumption draws out some of the complexities at play.

Recent dominant tropes and genres in Scotland appear to be equally fluid. A highly self-conscious and self-reflective focus on mechanics remains a key concern for many artists who continue the lineage of video art work "concentrated on the conditions of video as a mode of perception and production" (Rees 1999, 89). This introspective approach is increasingly balanced by artists following the lead of peers such as Bruce Nauman (USA) and Rebecca Horn (Germany), using video less as a primary medium for exploration and more a means to reject traditional media (ibid.). In such work the Structuralist eye of the man with the movie camera is subordinated to the promise of social adventures played out in front of the lens—a shift, perhaps, from the reel to the real. This is in part continuous with a wider trend of art practice since the mid 1990s concerned with social functionalism, finding a wider audience and encouraging a better quality of audience access and participation.

In the 1970s, formalist video art and the more socially functionalist modes of practice tended to be polarised as approaches. The spectre of modernist formalism was still a major bone of contention in the small, factionalised art world of 1970s Britain (Mulholland 2003). Contemporary art is now a vast global economy, one in which Scottish artists have excelled independently of the metropolitan scene in London. Early-'90s video art in Scotland swept aside the preoccupations metropolitan video art pioneers and the entire art video distribution network had established in the '70s and '80s, emulating instead the video art work produced by key analytical conceptual artists in New York in the early '70s. Glasgow artists in particular were cutting out the middle man and going straight to the centre of the international art market.

There are now many more artists and countless more opportunities for their practice than could possibly have been conceived in the 1970s. To what extent are once polarised varieties of approach now fluid and interconnected? In what ways do artists now circumvent genre by making use of their own production and post-production equipment? Are artists logically inclined towards polymathic multitasking tendencies, or is the current neo-baroque a product of a forced change of status for artists, a need to construct and occupy alternative social, aesthetic and economic roles in order to maintain a *raison d'être*? One way to address these questions is to examine the practices of a selected number of practitioners, to tease out the strategies and concerns that emerge. To this end, I will observe a few recent practices that exemplify some of the prevailing tendencies evident more widely in Scottish art. What follows here, then, is not an overview or survey but rather a few notes on approaches to practice that are worthy of further analysis and development.

## On Air: Ambient Video

David Hall's 16mm films *7 TV Pieces* (GB, 1971) are now regarded as seminal moments in the history of Scottish audio-visual art. Their importance lies less with the films themselves than in the strategies they employed. The short broadcasts were made on STV, Scotland's then new (and only) commercial television station, during ad breaks. Hall's ten *TV Interruptions* (August and September 1971) were made into the commercial flow of television spectacle, in those days of three channels a truly monolithic medium. This strategy of *détourning* a commercial medium, a form of subversive complicity widely practiced in environmental and public art practice, less concerned with the television and film industries than with public space, creating a unique situation in an environment, manifests itself in the work of a number of contemporary artists based in Scotland.

Peter McCaughey's practice, for instance, draws attention towards the peculiar invisibility of cinemas, environments that are constantly mutating: as the movie reel is changed, as customers turnover, as light flickers from frame to frame. McCaughey is not so much practicing as a site-specific artist, but rather as a psychological archaeologist, uncovering the moments in a cinema's working life that are perpetually being lost in time, the chain of meanings, motivations and longings that vanish in the blink of an eye. Since film is international, there is dialectical play between the local and global parameters of his site. On the one hand there is the specific cinema in which McCaughey may make his intervention; on the other, the cinematic memories the intervention can evoke.

A cinematic intervention, McCaughey's short film *Below Ground* (GB, 1998) transforms spectacle into spectre. A teaser for a Hollywood movie that was never made, *Below Ground* was shown frequently in cinemas around Europe. Shot on film using the language of the horror movie, the trailer was given its very own British Board of Film Classification certificate, a prop that represents the intimated movie in absentia. A rostrum shot of what might be a grave being unearthed and a probing camera zoom that takes us underground disclose nothing. *Below Ground* is bookmarked by McCaughey's longstanding interest in cinemas as sites in which artists can practice, and in contemporary art's complicity in the relations that govern all of its contexts of production, distribution and consumption. As an industry, cinema acts as a metaphor that allows these institutional issues to be dramatised in an entertaining way.

An early work by McCaughey, titled, with self-mocking precocity, *Classic* (September 1989), also involved excavation, digging for evidence of past viewing in an abandoned porn cinema in Glasgow. Found strips of film were stuck back together to produce a site-specific movie, screened in the old Classic cinema on Renfield Street. McCaughey has gone on to explore a number of abandoned cinema sites, including Glasgow's former ABC on Sauchiehall Street— *Coming Soon/Arc* (GB, 1999-2000)—and *The Futurist* (GB, 2004), centred on a Lime Street cinema during the 4$^{th}$

Liverpool Biennial. In both instances he establishes a relationship with the buildings' architecture as a dramatised space, facilitating events and playing in the ruins. *Coming Soon* reanimated the billboard outside the ABC to produce mixed messages and announce fictitious films that will never see the light of day. *The Futurist* reversed the cinematic gaze, turning series of CCTV cameras onto the former stage and screen where a variety of acts from the North West of England performed, their efforts relayed to passers-by on Lime Street. If the closure of both cinemas signifies the death of twentieth-century cinematic spectacle, it equally intimates the birth of the twenty-first-century surveying eye, one which picks and chooses what it wants to see. This cultural shopping experience McCaughey associates with the Variety and Music Hall origins of cinema auditoria. The viewer is given a greater degree of choice but the director remains the master of ceremonies.

## The Girl with the Handycam: Non-fiction, Pilgrimage and Performance

The Portapak revolution of the 1960s promised to put a camera in the hand of everyman, so bringing about the democratisation of media and message. The cost of video production and postproduction equipment has enabled more people to call it as they see it and so many more artists are taking up the challenges of DIY non-fiction production. In the 1980s Duncan of Jordanstone College of Art and Design in Dundee (DJCAD) pioneered the advanced use of this expensive technology in Scottish art schools. It has remained a key European centre for the production and development of video and electronic imaging work for the film and television industries. However, with more sophisticated technology cheaply available for home computers today, the opportunities for *artists* to work with new media are now dispersed, breaking DJCAD's monopoly on art-related expertise.

The travelogue adventure, based on a fixation with the utopian and the Other, is a particularly popular non-fiction film and video genre in Scotland. Sarah Tripp's *Anti-Prophet* (GB, 1998) involved the artist undertaking a pilgrimage of sorts to discover what people believe in. Each group of interviewees would suggest who Tripp should visit next in order to get to the bottom of her question. Tripp starts each interview with the seemingly innocuous question 'what do you believe in?' The effect is disarming: *Anti-Prophet* is a documentation of a performance, albeit a deliberately understated one. Freedom to engage with the unpredictable, performative practice of making the film is what remains all-important to

Tripp. Her *Testatika* (GB, 2001) is somewhere between artists' film and independent short film, commissioned by Scottish Screen and Manchester's Cornerhouse Gallery and screened at an array of international art and cinema venues. This non-fiction film tells the tale of the 'free energy' machine invented by the Methernitha religious cult based near Bern, Switzerland, and documents Tripp's journey there and to New Hampshire and Newcastle in order to understand more about the strange mythical technology. Tripp's approach to the moving image is tempered by a tendency towards précis, parsing down a seeming infinitude of values and desires into a suggestive, distilled form. She builds up plots around the social life of things. In this sense, her work relates closely to object making and gift giving. Maybe this is why objects play such a pivotal role in the construction of her narratives.

Like Tripp's work, Keith MacIsaac's videos sit on the edge of documentary filmmaking. They appear to be neutral but are clearly biased, judgemental even. MacIsaac mixes the use of direct address to camera in the animated, authoritative tone of an anchorman with occasional snippets of non-diegetic music and voiceover. A Vancouverite in the Old World, MacIsaac is enticed by European heritage culture often brushed-off in the rush to live in the future. With their genial repartee and spirited historical nuggets, his filmed travelogues lie somewhere between earnest Scottish hillwalking television series *Weir's Way* (STV, 1976-79) and docusoap satire *The Office* (BBC, 2001-2003).

Objects, mostly in the form of artworks, play an equally pivotal role in the construction of MacIsaac's work. *Bridgeness* (GB, 2005) is a thwarted campaign to convince the National Museum of Scotland to re-hang a distance slab which once lay on the Roman Antonine Wall between the Clyde and Forth. This not being seen as a cultural priority MacIsaac goes to great lengths to prove its importance. None of this back-story is divulged in the video itself. The expanded field of the *Bridgeness* project exists in the form of preparatory scrapbooks, exhibited alongside the video, featuring collage, letters and research notes that led up to the moment of production. In this sense MacIsaac is concerned with making the full pre-production process transparent, to the point where it becomes more important than post-production and distribution. The pre-production process has to be pieced together by the audience examining the evidence he displays. A series of *Bridgeness* collage, for example, divulge his attempt to enlist Celtophile Jimmy Page, of Led Zeppelin, to walk the Antonine Wall in order to promote MacIsaac's campaign. The collages *were* used to entice Page by showing him how he might look on the Wall if he were to get involved. To further encourage Page's celebrity endorsement, MacIsaac decided to hire a film crew and a helicopter, from which he expounds the virtues of the slab while flying over the remains of the Wall as if surveying a traffic jam. As a promotional tool for his cause, this is next to useless. The chopper clatter makes it impossible to hear MacIsaac's oration, yet his animated body language indicates his excitement at the dubious prospect of raising public awareness. Page, nevertheless, doesn't return MacIsaac's calls. The film is not the culmination of this body of work as the project remains incomplete until the slab is moved. Bricolage is thus a metaphor as well as a method: an unfinished project, incorporating a film-promo, is one that remains alive with possibility.

MacIsaac's brushes with cultural history extend to canonical modernist and postmodernist works by Henri Matisse—*Régina Flat/Studio Practice* (GB, 2005)—and Robert Smithson—*Glue Pour* (GB, 2006-07). Here, MacIsaac traces artists' pre-production of their oeuvre by visiting prominent sites in which they lived or worked. In *Régina Flat/Studio Practice* we encounter Madame Malaussena's home in the south of France, once the Hotel Régina wherein Matisse prepared his sketches for the Vance Chapel mural scheme. On a pilgrimage, MacIsaac has a chance encounter with Malaussena and, after some comical translation trouble, gains access to the flat. The resulting film collages archival footage of Matisse's studio, sketches filmed at his birthplace in Le Cateau-Cambrésis, Normandy and footage of the contemporary des res. Scenes are interspersed by MacIsaac's interview in New York with American art historian Donald Kuspitt, who enthuses bombastically on the Vance murals. Again we are given some access to the production process when MacIsaac can be seen handing over several hundred dollars to Kuspit before he starts answering any questions. The film ends abruptly with Malaussena's contact details, leaving us thinking that we've been watching a real estate promo. Again, it's very unlikely that MacIsaac's benevolent perseverance will aid Malaussena, but this only intensifies the peculiar blend of humour and humility found in his adventures.

*Skulptur Projekte Münster* (GB, 2007) takes this over-identification with the aura of the site of art production to yet greater extremes. The project originated in MacIsaac's desire to unofficially 'relocate' Michael Asher's *Caravan* (1977, 1987, 1997, 2007), a 1960s mobile home that has appeared in Münster every ten years since the project began in 1977. Asher's signature work, *Caravan* is supposed to travel to a new preordained location each week, thereby drawing attention to the changing face of the town. In some cases the original 1977 sites have vanished and thus the caravan has to be placed in storage. The *Skulptur Projekte*

*Münster* video appears to show the caravan being stolen and dumped in an (allegorically loaded) German forest, where it is later discovered by the police. The heist is shown in real time, a project fraught with genuine drama as witnessed in the protagonists' tense arguments during their getaway. The video culminates in a quiet shot of the caravan happily surrounded by trees, a natural habitat for a holiday home. The project lives on in international press cuttings documenting *Caravan*'s theft and rediscovery and in urban myths regarding whether or not these events actually took place.

## Every Artist is a VJ: Adventures on the Wheels of Reel

If, as in the respective cases of Tripp and MacIsaac, we internalise the gaze by reflecting it back towards the creative process itself, we also have to ask different questions of audio-visual art. What is the function of the performative within the spaces of exhibition and consumption? Video installation still flourishes, despite the avenues opened up by interventionist, ambient, non-fiction and performance approaches. Perhaps it goes without saying that galleries are sites which create different parameters for viewing audio-visual work than can be found in the cinema and the front room. The white cube, or black box as it more often becomes for the purposes of video projection, is a *tabula rasa*, a non-space to transform and play around in, but one that nevertheless comes with an abundance of cultural baggage. A heightened awareness of the constructed status of the black box *as a site* has therefore dramatically altered the ways in which audio-visual works are edited and produced. Since such work is time-based, the process of production and display is inevitably choreographed, dramatised or *performed* in many works that result from this raising of consciousness.

Torsten Lauschman's practice involves the use of audio and video in conjunction with photography, sculpture and found objects. While his is an art of system and process in the lineage of minimalism and conceptualism, it is, nevertheless, inclined towards the social, poetic and lyrical idiosyncrasies of Fluxus. *Suburbia in 3D: Chasing Butterflies* (Transmission Gallery, Glasgow, 2004) is a case in point. Digitally manipulated video images are projected onto the gallery walls. Branches tied to the gallery piloti cast shadows across the images to create an ambient environment—an immersive space in which the audience can dwell. The video footage of a park is at once obscured and amplified by the branches, while a diegetic soundtrack recreates the sounds of this urban sanctuary. In some cases the images are digitally cropped to fit with painted patterns on the wall. In this sense the work is for a black box environment, but it *détournés* that environment by making it resemble a suburban park on the one hand and a salon-style picture gallery on the other. *Mother and Child* (Transmission Gallery, Glasgow, 2004), a video portrait of his partner and new-born son sleeping, is presented in the form of an Orthodox Christian icon, the figures surrounded in gold leaf masking.[1]

Lauschman here exploits a number of tactics that are more than familiar to regular viewers of video installation. The use of loops, large screen projections and a darkened environment all induce a form of attention that is specific to the gallery-based video experience. It makes little difference to the audience if they enter half-way through a DVD loop, were this possible: the work has no discernible beginning or end. Like much video installation, Lauschman's work here is designed to be consumed in cycles or over an infinitely extendable period of time. The narrative-based approaches associated with classical Film Studies can play no meaningful role; instead we have to consider the work's impact upon our mood.

The techniques used to create such work are quintessentially postmodernist in their use of and attitude towards fragmentation. Lauschmann is heavily indebted to scratch video and a key advocate of this performative technique. In utilising Scratch's torrential montage of digitally manipulated imagery, hybridising music video and subcultural documentary (see Bishop 2003) he is far from alone among his international peers. Lauschmann's mastery of such video-stylo techniques is widely respected in Scotland and beyond, thanks to the more overtly politicised debate around this cut-and-paste approach to video that he has helped to revive, as much through his teaching work in Scottish and European art colleges as via his exhibitions and related events. During his 2004 Transmission exhibition, a series of consciousness-raising screenings took place in the basement lounge on Fridays and Saturdays. Here Lauschmann presented a series of experimental audio-visual works by a variety of artists, musicians, filmmakers and media activists. Clearly, one of Lauschmann's aims is to promote postmodern techno-creativity to a wider audience. His work is educational and enabling in this sense, showing a commitment to the radical aspects of video art that have been conveniently forgotten with the successful incorporation of video installation into the mainstream art world. Lauschmann's Transmission exhibition was a timely reminder that, in the 1980s, the gallery was an

---

[1] This work was later sold by Transmission at the 2004 Frieze Art Fair in London. This reveals that artist's video—as an *objet d'art*—is now increasingly difficult to distinguish from video installation into which it is often submerged or is supposedly genetically inseparable from.

important venue for the development of radicalised video practice, particularly during the period that Malcolm Dickson served on the committee.[2] Multimedia, in this guise, is end-user orientated.

Lauschmann's work takes its place within a notable revival of the early-'80s Scratch video movement in recent years in Scotland. This revival does not emerge from the tradition of artists who use video to shun the glossy production values of film and television. Rather, it comes from being raised on a diet of fast cuts, jagged composition, lighting and editing—techniques that are now commonplace in commercial television and film, the mainstream having fully absorbed the lessons of Scratch artists by the mid 1980s. This demarcated many contemporary artists in Scotland from video installation work produced in the country during the early 1990s, work which was more heavily influenced by American video art.

Early 1990s Scottish artists' video developed in synch with American conceptualism and, as such, was heavily indebted to its anti-aesthetic concerns. This ascetic aspect of video art can be seen in the work of Scotia Nostra artists, which parallels a rebirth of interest in the art of the early 1970s among Scottish artists active in the early '90s. Douglas Gordon's interest in video's ability to alter our viewing habits via time-shifting was equally a key concern of 1980s Scratch and related guerilla media. A corollary of this fixation with non-narrative forms is that many video artists who do not abandon the pleasures of narrative video and film are devalued and suppressed (see Beech 1999). This effectively surrenders the use of narrative dramatic forms to the film and television industries.

A result of this has been for artists to restrict their use of film to an (allegedly) critical role, as a commentary on the film industry (in art world terms this makes it continuous with conceptualist institutional critique) and/or the industry's hegemonic modes of attention and perception (visual pleasure and narrative cinema). In effect, this reduces the video artist to the role of couch potato consumer, a geeky (male) video junkie, a post-producer (see Bourriaud 2004) who rewinds, revues, speeds up and slows down the on-screen action.[3] Devoid of psychoactive, stimulating social environments in which to consume such moving images, such video art is

---

[2] Dickson is now the Director of Street Level Photoworks, which is in the same building as Transmission in Glasgow.

[3] Obviously this aspect of video viewing has had a major impact on film directors and audiences alike who have been raised on a diet of video. This makes for a more fragmented type of subjectivity - one more attuned to the smorgasbord of scratch video and multimedia that is commonplace to art practice today. Certainly, such effects were felt long before the '90s.

very often a passive—or, at most, autoerotic—viewing experience distinctly at odds with the aspirations of the pioneers of socially engaged artist's video; something that was highly visible in agit-Scratch work produced in Britain in the 1980s.

Scratch took a more active stance in relation to the post-production thesis, an equivalent of turntablism (Souvignier 2003). During the beer breaks at Flourish Nights—an informal series of film and performance evenings organised by artist Lucy McKenzie in Glasgow's Flourish studios—Lauschmann performed as a VJ using Final Cut, a jog-shuttle, video-crossfaders and a couple of laptops to mix audio and video sources in a club/gallery/studio hybrid environment. A guerilla media technique pioneered by experimental artists in the 1980s, VJing quickly became popular in nightclubs as the techno scene entered into the mainstream in the early 1990s. VJing clearly parallels turntablism and sampling, performative techniques and technologies widely used in dance music (and now in music generally). Seen in this neo-baroque context, the anti-auteur minimalist proclivities of early 1990s Scottish video art appear nostalgic for a pre-Scratch era—a time of more strictly limited recording and playback options: the 1960s.[4] The appropriation of *film*, moreover of classic *black and white* auteur movies, as in many of Douglas Gordon's best known pieces, makes such video work deeply conservationist and canonical in its concerns.

While such work was entering into the fold of major international contemporary art venues, AV technologies were developing at breakneck pace. Agit-Scratch morphed into techno-Scratch and the kind of genre mashups now associated with Bastard Pop.[5] The energy of anti-Thatcherite political filibustering transmogrified into a hedonistic aestheticism—the vagaries of PLUR (Peace Love Unity Respect)—much to the disdain of many Scratch pioneers. Bigger rave audiences and more nightclubbers meant better AV and IT budgets and so greater opportunities for technical experimentation with new MIDI-compatible platforms. The kinds of Scratch produced and promoted by Lauschmann are indebted to, rather

---

[4] In comparison with digital video, VHS is 'blackboxed', more difficult to manipulate or crack as a technological form.

[5] Bastard Pop made headway on the airwaves in the early '00s, skilfully broken into the mainstream by XFM's Remix Show in London, which encouraged young listeners to become top of the fops by sending in CDs burnt on iMacs. Home mixers sporting identity-protecting pseudonyms such as Freelance Hellraiser, Girls on Top, French Bloke and Soulwax pulled off inspiring and often hilarious mixes, combining metal with hip hop, grunge with R&B. By 2002, the major players of the bootlegging blip were signed up as Kylie and Cher's superstar megamixers.

than at odds with, this fast-paced entertainment industry development and thus to an aesthetics of free-play, frisson and to pleasure as an end in itself. While such performative graphic manipulations might go relatively unnoticed by revelers at a nightclub, the art audience remains perceptive towards the combination. Scratch, in this sense, is returning to its origins in independently organised culture, finding new audiences for a synaesthetic genre of video that has been rejuvenated with subcultural and pop cult significance thanks to its longer association with stage and nightclub lighting. Significantly, Ronnie Heeps, one half of the most innovative concert, club and rave lighting effects teams in Scotland—The Scottish Luminaries—now exclusively produces digitally manipulated animation, paintings and video. Heeps provided his technical services to many interventionist video artists in the '80s and '90s in Scotland, notably NVA's Angus Farquhar and Peter McCaughey. At the same time he was producing special looped, cut-up and spinning projection effects at UFO (Unlimited Freak Out), an acid-techno club night held at Glasgow's Tin Pan Alley venue. The name of the club echoes London's UFO, John Hopkins' famous Tottenham Court Road night in which psychedelic art and music mixed in the mid '60s.

Lauschman's particular contribution to the Scratch revival involves the extensive and inventive use of 'everyware' (Greenfield 2006), means of information processing that have diffused into everyday life, and virtually disappeared from view. For *Autumn Rhythm Film* (2002), Lauschman's solo show at The Changing Room, Stirling, he developed a digital feedback loop that recycled and automatically edited footage grabbed from the internet, a sampled archive of historical film stock and his own footage. Lauschman is able to remove himself from the editing process, putting an automaton in his place.[6] *Autumn Rhythm Film* exhibits an ambient intelligence (AmI)—it can adapt to the changing information it processes. This is a novel interpretation of video-stylo, where light *writing* is aided by new interpretive technologies shaped by their users. The work is a cybernetic device, a hybrid of nature and artifice, a metaphor for our burgeoning cyborg consciousness. The autopoietic feedback loop attests that, just as humans and animals form a continuum, the "social" and "technological" spheres cannot be so easily separated, since both are symbiotic, complex systems. Lauschman's work seems to herald some of the new subject positions we can expect as AmI grows apace. This is not a

[6] The work has parallels with Brian Eno's *77 Million Paintings* (2007-) in terms of the autopoietic production process, though Lauschman's work is illusionistic where Eno's is resolutely abstract.

passive process: Lauschman creates new uses, networks and artefacts for such technologies. This exploration of the creative potential of the technologies represents a crack or interpretative flexibility that can't be predicted by their designers. In Lauschman's hands the results are often amusing. A technologically updated homage to Fluxus and Cornelius Cardew, *Cold Water Quartet* (2005, Performance at the ICA, London) allows a goldfish to interact with an AmI device that translates its movements into music. The process of interaction reconstitutes new technological developments that are turned to aesthetic rather than functional outcomes.

As a means of creating and thinking live, of exposing the methods of production and integrating them into a cybernetic system that traverses the man-machine, Lauschmann's video-stylo is overtly *social* in its orientation in a way that non-narrative video loops are perhaps not. And yet Lauschmann does not by any means restrict himself to non-narrative video, producing a number of short films which have a clear narrative trajectory. This can be seen in works such as *Misshapen Pearl* (GB, 2003), a psychogeographical reading of the streetlamp. On its website, Axisweb quotes Lauschmann's thoughts on this work:

> What is a Streetlamp? I only pay her my attention if she bugs me, or if her light is too intense, or defective, or missing, or like now, if I give her my attention by breaking through the accepted everyday. In every other situation the streetlamp is for me just part of that disrespected environment, which I take for granted and which was created to be disrespected.

Lauschmann's non-diegetic voiceover reads the city discursively yet romantically. While some of his Transmission exhibition featured discreet works conjoined in the form of video installation, more recent shows tend to allow the composite works to retain their independence. Video, in this sense, is one media among many, but it's a medium that, in its reliance on editing to produce the illusionistic *effect* of a seamless stream of consciousness, is an allegory of Lauschmann's working practice, enabling more multilayered artistic production.

Lauschmann's rough-and-ready use of digital editing equipment to mix shot footage with animation can be seen in the work of a range of other artists working in Scotland, including David Shrigley (Glasgow), Ganghut (Dundee), Craig Mulholland (Glasgow), Mullen & Lee (Edinburgh) and Katy Dove (Glasgow), to name but a few prominent figures. Among these artists, Shrigley's animated work is the most well known, thanks to its inclusion in a number of pop promos—Blur's *Good Song* (2003)—and movies—*Hallam Foe* (Mackenzie, GB, 2007)—as well as to the massive popularity of his drawings and photographs. It is also distributed in DVD format for general home viewing (e.g. David Shrigley and Chris Shepherd, *Who I Am and What I Want*, 2005). Since he mainly produces drawings, Shrigley's videos are exclusively animation-based and very widely distributed in hard-copy, online via legitimate websites and through unauthorised filesharing on Web 2.0. The faux-naïf DIY aesthetics that attract such a wide and loyal fan base[7] to his work are, nevertheless, still very much evident in all that he does. This deliberate clunkiness makes Shrigley's work an ideal counterpart to the whimsical lo-fi character that typifies much Scottish pop music (Orange Juice, The Pastels, Teenage Fanclub, Belle & Sebastian, Malcolm Middleton, etc.).

It's therefore not surprising that younger artists such as Katy Dove should share this lo-fi approach while putting it to different ends. Like many of her local peers, Dove works with unadorned playschool media. Colouring in shapes with felt-tip pens and watercolour, she produces the kind of delicate forms and biomorphic sketches last seen alive in the abstract Plexiglas and pinboard animation of the Weimar Republic. Seminal influences are examples of early avant-garde film by Hans Richter and Oskar Fischinger. Dove's diverse repertoire of forms seem random and unconnected until they are digitally animated and rendered, software ensuring that any hand-made 'flaws' appear as integrated patterns. Cutting and pasting her drawings in regular digital formations, Dove amplifies audience attentiveness by giving them rhythm. The limitations of the sound and animation technology at Dove's disposal are used to her advantage, producing an effect that mimics modernist abstraction's somewhat clunky and naïve pursuit of unity in diversity. Many of Dove's early collaged films are optical noise, largely non-narrative and non-naturalistic images set to musical accompaniments that generate a pulse. Infectious and affecting, the right combination of sound and images radically alters the psychological mood. A robotically rhythmic psychedelic procession, *Motorhead* (2002) forms the video for Glaswegian electro group Devotone. Energy lines, dots and cut-out shapes threaten to coalesce to form facial features, but Devotone's synth lines ensure that the animation continually mutates allegorically-rhythmically. While these videos are mostly distributed through the black box space, Dove has also used other methods of distribution, notably in her

---

[7] Shrigley is perhaps unique in this sense; despite the accessibility and pop-cult aspirations, it's impossible to think of any other of his artist peers in Scotland as having *fans*. Unlike his contemporaries Shrigley doesn't exhibit any great desire to appropriate or allude to popular cultural forms in his art—his work *is* popular culture.

screensaver *forever changes* (2002), which was available from the Transmission Gallery website and via featuring on *Evil Eye is Source* (see next section). Such work has marked a shift away from the nocturnal, monochromatic video art that Scotland is popularly known for, away from the fixed camera and the passive document of a performance towards a kaleidoscopic cornucopia of colour and an active, performative approach to the construction of the audio-visual. It signals a very different attitude towards the idea of the spectacle and the ever-expanding array of audio-video technologies available *en masse*.

## She got a MTV eye on me, or, How I Learned to Stop Worrying and Love LCD

Artists' video in the 1970s exhibited an attitude towards TV underpinned by a scepticism and fatalism that owed much to the Situationists and vulgar-Marxism. Such a view was challenged by the more fan-oriented reading of TV by academics such as John Fiske (Fiske 1987, 1994). The paradigm shift that Fiske encouraged was reiterated by John Wyver in the early 1990s, in an article that has proven prescient to the situation Scottish artists now find themselves in:

> Along with many others, I have argued elsewhere that television was never as monolithic, as homogenous or as impoverished as the video world has invariably believed or stated it to be. And that television did not and does not only force the viewer to take the sort of passive spectator's position to which video is mean to offer a challenging alternative. (Wyver 1996, 317)

This has certainly been borne out in the intervening years. The proliferation of distribution networks and platforms for television has, in part, led to more risk-taking narrowcasting and interactivity—although not necessarily better programmes—than was possible even in 1991. Artists have benefited equally from more channels of distribution becoming available for their work: they are no longer limited to the gallery infrastructure or the antiquated cottage industry economy it continues to practice in order to foster exclusivity and value via scarcity (see Abbing 2004).

Theories of end-user interaction and prosumerist fan culture are central to understanding recent video production in Scotland, as *Evil Eye is Source* (2002), a video compilation curated by Luke Fowler, attests. Art Video compilations are nothing new, but they are normally assembled by resource centres and archives for the purpose of allowing curators to sample regional delights. Seldom are they curated with any imagination or verve, and even less often are they commissioned with a curatorial framework in mind. In contrast, Fowler's video compilation interpolates a fan base of a very different sort, one that is as drawn to popular music as it is to the art world. The project takes the form of a music compilation wherein ten Glasgow artists are paired with bands in order to collaboratively produce what are, ostensibly, a series of short music promos. Many of the artists embrace cheaply montaged narrative sequences and/or abstract animation, forms and techniques most commonly associated with scratch-y MTV music video from the earlier 1980s. In one sense *Evil Eye is Source* is nostalgic, reminiscent of an independent new wave pop culture that some of the artists involved were too young to participate directly within. In another, it is perfectly in synch with its time of release, a decade in which the musicians and artists working in Scotland have been particularly united (and often one and the same).

*Evil Eye is Source* builds on Fowler's pledge to situate the avant-garde in the public sphere. This is, in part, borne out by the tendency of his peers to exhibit in non-profit making public venues in Scotland. Generally speaking, Scottish artists' videos aren't commercially available unless the artist concerned happens to be represented by a major international gallery, a form of distribution that didn't exist *in Scotland* until the close of the 1990s. The distribution of editioned artists' video via commercial galleries is strictly controlled by the use of legal contracts—a legacy of conceptualism (Alberro 2003). Practices that have no material form exist in a legal framework and are subject to copyright licences in much the same way as mainstream cinema and television. This is, understandably, policed vociferously by commercial gallerists, since control over the strictly limited stock is crucial in maintaining its value. To overcome the high unit costs of such video, there would have to be a larger market for it or a commitment on behalf of the artist to an open source distribution of their work. The former is unlikely due to the restrictive industry practices of the contemporary art market, the latter difficult to sustain since video artists need to pay the bills like everyone else.

Given this, it's significant that the logic of mass distribution followed by television and mainstream cinema is applied to the video works contained in Fowler's compilation. In one sense, the compilation is more flexible than a Hollywood film; *Evil Eye is Source* videos can be shown anywhere at any time. This does not end their viability as far as public galleries are concerned, where the emphasis on the unique (or highly limited edition multiple) object is waning. But while mainstream distribution tends towards wide availability, independent art labels, like independent music labels, remain limited by the small demand. In effect, this safeguards the art world infrastructure and allows a video work such as *Evil Eye is Source* to remain within its discourse while driving its agenda via an indie philosophy that favours quality and risk over growth.

The internet has provided another option for artists looking for a low-cost, high-visibility solution to the hosting and distribution of audio-visual works. Ever ready to exploit novel methods and channels of organisation, Scottish artists have been quick to take advantage of this open source. The result is an approach to video that is driven from the grass roots up rather than from the top down. Artists working in Scotland are making use of digital media in ways that relate to the flotsam and jetsam of online moving image culture. Ewan Sinclair's works make use of pixelated forms associated with 8 and 16-bit platforms. Sculptural installations produced from kitchen sponges create a backdrop to his short looped GIF animations, moving landscapes and narrative paintings composed from an array of Flash characters available free online. The resulting animated collages resemble very early animated cartoons and make as little sense as a *Betty Boop* narrative. Jaygo Bloom's work samples sound from early video games and overlays them with real footage. *Tabla Pong* (2006), for example, features the *Pong* (1972) sound from Atari's classic console game in place of the rhythmic beats of a tabla drummer. His videos jog back and forth in the juddery manner of early laser-disk games or *Max Headroom*, as if the analogue footage and the digital processor were fighting it out in a final battle over representation.

By its nature, such digital work allows direct distribution to take place. Sinclair and Bloom's work alike are made for their websites[8]; Sinclair's works can even be distributed via email and SMS. Online platforms are also emerging via which such works can be curated and distributed, including Lauschmann's *Egoburger* (2005) and Gregor Wright's *Gregor* (n.d.). Despite their technophilic approach to online culture, these are not exclusively 'web-artists'. Sinclair and Bloom also exhibit their online works in galleries, film festivals and at one-night-only screenings, such as The Embassy's time-based arts event held quarterly in the vast neo-classical Sculpture Court at Edinburgh College of Art. Bloom makes scratch videos for Glasgow's *Death Disco*, a club night held at The Arches featuring DJs Shit Disco. This impacts just as much on the form their work takes, in so far as it functions rather like short stand-up comedy skits, perfect for Web 2.0 social networking sites as well as for a live event at which the audience fully expects to be entertained.

---

[8] Bloom: http://www.gabba.tv; Sinclair: http://www.pedalpanoptikon.com

With a less developed commercial infrastructure for visual art and therefore fewer of the commercial pressures that are attendant upon art production, Edinburgh-based artists have turned a great deal of attention to time-based, ephemeral events established via co-ops, in the lineage of early avant-garde British filmmakers. This has resulted in an upsurge of open screening and open source distribution organisations to support new audio-video work. As well as being the base of New Media Scotland, Edinburgh has been home to Aurora Projects, a series of exhibitions and one-off events hosted by artist Ruth Beale. Beale has used this as a forum for mixing time-based and audio-visual works with live performances by bands and DJs.

Old media plays an important part in this process of discovery and transmutation. In particular, Beale has raised awareness of key examples of early avant-garde film. In collaboration with Jo Smithers, Ewan Sinclair formed the *Pedal Panoptikon*, a small Super-8 cinema powered by bicycles. The ability to crack technology and turn it to alternative uses, if rather makeshift, is pursued with aplomb as an end in itself. Rather like Lauschmann's *Slender Whiteman* mobile DJ project—a sound system powered by solar panels that toured Scandinavia—*Pedal Panoptikon* is designed to tour and take old cinema reels to remote locations in Scotland that have little or no access to the cinema experience.

Analogously, The Magic Lantern, based in Glasgow and run by Penny Bartlett and Rosie Crerar, has developed an archive and a monthly independent film night that underpins and supports the hybrid ambitions of Scottish art, offering a smorgasbord of media. Artist-led cinemas are an important emerging trend, both as social and 'installation' experiences and as a novel means of distribution. With such organisations growing, it's equally significant that some artists, such as Sarah Tripp, are turning their hand to making dramatic *films*. This forms part of a tendency towards the convergence of media and genres that can be seen in the practice of a mounting number of 'artists' featured in the 2008 Glasgow Film Festival.

## To the glittering prize?

Does the rapid pace of media convergence mean that it is no longer possible to view recent audio-visual works exclusively as "art"? If so, then is it feasible to think of such practices in terms of "film" or "video"? The issue that dogged many "video artists" in the 1970s and '80s—how to get museums, galleries and collectors to buy and take care of their work in the same fashion as *objet d'art*—doesn't seem quite so pressing now. This battle has been won, but in victory it seems that it wasn't really worth fighting. Artists—if this is what they choose to call themselves—based in Scotland are internationally renowned for their independent organisational practice. They regularly found their own public and commercial spaces, studios and organisations, establish their own distribution networks and build relationships with art and film funders alike. They do so on their own terms and pay no attention to the restricting bureaucracies of medium specificity that once divided and ruled. The dangers of a quasi-modernist fetishising of any media are immense: a bogus division of the visual arts community, a suppression of debates that cut *across* visual media, a misrepresentation of creative practice as medium-specific, and closure on the dialogues and concurrences that enable an ongoing process of improvisation to extend creative audio-visual practice. The present neo-baroque diversification and flux suggests that we are witnessing a spectacular corrective to the Calvinism of '90s video installation and its closed conditions of display and distribution. A real cacophonic transformation, this is impossible to reverse. All this scratching will keep Scottish artists itching for more.

## Works Cited

Abbing, Hans. 2004. *Why are artists poor?: the exceptional economy of the arts*. Amsterdam: Amsterdam University Press.

Alberro, Alexander. 2003. *Conceptual art and the politics of publicity*. Cambridge, MA: The MIT Press.

Beech, Dave. 1999. Video after Diderot. *Art Monthly* 225: 7-10.

Bishop, Claire. 2003. Video Killed the Radio Star. *Flash Art (International Edition)* 36: 70-73.

Bourriaud, Nicolas. 2004. *Postproduction: La culture comme scénario: comment l'art reprogramme le monde contemporain*. Dijon: Presses du réel.

Fiske, John. 1987. *Television culture*. London: Methuen.

—. 1994. *Media matters: everyday culture and political change*. Minneapolis: University of Minnesota Press.

Greenfield, Adam. 2006. *Everyware: the dawning age of ubiquitous computing*. Berkeley: New Riders.

Mulholland, Neil. 2003. *The cultural devolution: art in Britain in the late twentieth century*. Aldershot: Ashgate.

Rees, A. L. 1999. *A history of experimental film and video: from the canonical avant-garde to contemporary British practice*. London: BFI.

Souvignier, Todd. 2003. *The World of DJs and the Turntable Culture*. Milwaukee: Hal Leonard Corporation.

Wyver, John. 1996. The Necessity of Doing Away with "Video Art". In *Diverse practices: a critical reader on British video art*, ed. Julia Knight, 306-320. Luton: University of Luton Press/Arts Council of England.

# *Scotch Myths*, Scottish Film Culture and the Suppression of Ludic Modernism

Colin McArthur

Scottish moving image culture has produced three masterpieces of ludic modernism: John McGrath and John Mackenzie's *The Cheviot, the Stag and the Black, Black Oil* (GB, 1974), Ian Pattison and Colin Gilbert's television series *Rab C. Nesbitt* (BBC Scotland, 1989-99) and Murray Grigor's *Scotch Myths* (GB, 1983), funded by Channel 4. Having celebrated the two former (McArthur 1978, 1998), I now wish to remedy the scandalous lack of critical attention accorded the latter, a lack symptomatic of the effective suppression of *Scotch Myths* and of modernism (ludic or otherwise) by Scottish film culture. Indeed, to address *Scotch Myths* is to wade knee-deep into the debates which traversed Scottish film culture in the 1970s and 1980s. It is ludicrous that a film constituting one of the key reference points in these debates has had no adequate description, far less analysis, of its subject matter and style.

But first, what is meant by "ludic modernism"? The phrase recalls, perhaps lies silently within, the increasingly prevalent term "ludic postmodernism". The assertion underlying the latter is that once there was this monolithic phenomenon, modernism, which was austere, all-embracing, elitist, lacking the common touch and, above all, humourless. Ludic postmodernism, the argument runs, has swept all this away. Unable to say anything useful about the real world if, as postmodernism has it, it exists at all, such discourse has recourse only to the complex glissandos of its own operations. The only appropriate stance is one of ludic irony. We may be going to hell in a handcart, but let's have fun on the way! (Ludic) postmodernism, unaware of the structuralist binarism of its own position, sets itself in opposition to its grim-faced predecessor, modernism, and travesties it in the process. Justus Nieland, by contrast, argues a range of contrary points:

> First, that modernism is funny, and the moderns inveterate laughers, gigglers, joke-pullers and devastating wags. Second, that modernism's ubiquitous laughter is overlooked, under-theorized, and downright gagged

> by the aura of high seriousness that still infuses critical descriptions of modernism. (Neiland 2006, 80)

This could serve as a rubric for *Scotch Myths* (and for Murray Grigor's work more generally). This essay seeks to locate the film within the ludic modernist tradition of the Surrealists, James Joyce and Samuel Beckett, arguing that it is simultaneously playful and politically serious, and that its effective suppression by Scottish film culture is massively retrogressive.

## The Exhibition

Several strands went into the making of what was to become the film *Scotch Myths*. The central one was Grigor's exhibition of the same name. This ran in a small St Andrews gallery in 1981 before transferring to the Edinburgh Festival. On each occasion the press and public response was substantial and generally sympathetic. Both the exhibition's wit and its serious political purpose were recognised (McArthur 1981/2). Ludic modernism is, it would seem, acceptable in the gallery if not on the screen. The exhibition included postcards, labels from whisky bottles and orange crates, tea towels, popular songs and the detritus of Scottish souvenir shops, and was mounted with considerable imaginative flair and a very light touch: one of the key installations was a version of Fingal's Cave with a pianola pounding out Mendelssohn's overture and spouting water at the piece`s climax. Grigor had clearly been influenced by the writings of Tom Nairn, particularly his essay "Old and New Scottish Nationalism" (Nairn 1977). Here, Nairn offered a scathing account of certain aspects of Scottish (popular) culture. He characterised these as pathological precisely because, unlike other European (popular) cultures, they had never been mobilised within the drive to create the nation. The British polity (including Scotland) had been settled in 1707, almost a century before the rise of nationalism in Europe and its colonial outposts. The political import of Grigor's exhibition was its deconstruction of Scottish (popular) culture and its anatomising of the figures (James MacPherson, Sir Walter Scott, Harry Lauder, etc.) who had projected internationally a pathological view of Scotland. *Scotch Myths* the exhibition implied that Scotland needed a radically different culture, one more attuned to the modern world.

## The Film

In order for *Scotch Myths* to become a television film the stasis of the exhibition had to some extent to become animated. Grigor achieved this by conjoining the gallery show with a theatrical piece he had written, *Breeksadoon*. This play on *Brigadoon* (Minnelli, USA, 1954), the representation of Scotland most loathed by Scots intellectuals of the late '70s and early '80s, is characteristic of Grigor's ludic modernism. The pun (a montage within a word) is one of the most favoured verbal strategies of modernism, deployed most deliriously by James Joyce in *Ulysses* (1922) and *Finnegan's Wake* (1939). Channel 4's commissioning of *Scotch Myths*, and its transmission of the film on Hogmanay, were themselves political acts. They threw down the gauntlet to those characteristic New Year's Eve broadcasts from Scotland constructed within the very discourses *Scotch Myths* took apart. That it found a home on the newly-created Channel 4 was partly due to the Channel's first Chief Executive, Jeremy Isaacs, being a Glaswegian well able to understand (and, one suspects, highly sympathetic to) the argument *Scotch Myths* was making. Additionally, the film's aesthetic innovation was precisely in line with Channel 4`s original remit to cater for minorities, a remit increasingly abandoned by those who succeeded Isaacs.

Costing just over £100,000 (achieved by making it within the film union's then-existing documentary agreement), *Scotch Myths* is a perfect exemplar of Poor Cinema—poor in resources, rich in imagination (McArthur 1993, 1994), a major attraction in a small, resource-strapped country. A key element of *Scotch Myths*' frugality is its refusal of classic Hollywood narrative. It does, however, gesture towards such narrative in the plot devices of a lost tourist bus and its discovery by a Scots aristocrat. Both these gestures earn their place in the film by referring to what is perhaps the most resonant date in Scottish history, 1745/6, the period of the last Jacobite uprising which sought to wrest the British crown back to the Stuart dynasty. A source of lachrymose nostalgia for many indigenous Scots (McArthur 1994a), "the '45" is perhaps also the key shaping mechanism in the identity narratives of transatlantic and other diasporic Scots (Ray 2001). In Grigor's film a tourist bus festooned with Scottish Tourist Board brochures referencing national history is lost on a heath which turns out to be Culloden Moor, the site of the 1746 battle which saw the defeat of the Jacobite army led by Charles Edward Stuart. Stuart, as Bonnie Prince Charlie, is one of the key *dramatis personae* in romantic discourse about Scotland. The tourists are "rescued" by Sir Johnny Stalker (Walter Carr). Stalker greases the palm of the tour guide (Freddie

Boardley) with banknotes bearing the faces of Sir Walter Scott and Robert Burns (Grigor is acutely sensitive to the circulation of national icons in the quotidian Scottish world), thus inducing him to reroute the tourists to Castle Dundreich, so that they might partake of "the Dundreich Experience," a series of Scottish historical charades. This narrative strategy ties together what are perhaps the two key sites of regressive discourse about Scotland, whisky and tourism. Sir Johnny's name and apparel (short red hunting coat) evoke a prominent brand of Scotch whisky, while his surname carries the whiff of the grouse moor and the reactionary role of the Scots aristocracy in fashioning images of Scotland. Given that *Scotch Myths* is primarily about international perceptions of Scotland and the Scots, Grigor's invocation of whisky (it will be a continuing motif in the piece) is an inspired narrative device. Not only is whisky the phenomenon which foreigners immediately allude to when thinking about Scotland or meeting a Scot, it also has profound implications for Scots' self-identity, touching as it does on questions of health, aggressive sociability and masculine rites of passage (McArthur 1991). The other dimension, tourism, prefigures VisitScotland's recurrent propensity—here it is no different from tourist boards throughout the world—to render the history of the nation as diverse "experiences." Within this framework the area round Stirling will now forever be "*Braveheart* country".

Another gesture towards classical Hollywood narrative is the very brief scene showing the arrival at Castle Dundreich of the actors who will embody the historical figures in the charades. The minibus they arrive in bears the words "17:45 Theatre Company". At one level this is a simple joke, referencing the (then) most politically radical Scottish theatre group, 7:84, with which several of actors appearing in *Scotch Myths* were associated. At another level, however, the detail joins with the earlier evocation of the 1745 uprising. This reconfirms that *Scotch Myths* is going to be a film not just about Scottish culture but also its most internationally resonant historical moments and figures.

*Scotch Myths*' third gesture towards classical narrative is less clearly motivated, but it too earns its place in the film by creating different resonances. The gesture in question has the famous Hollywood director Sam Fuller "as himself", upbraiding his personal assistant for being unable to find Castle Dundreich on the map. This is firstly an act of homage by Grigor to a great director, an assertion of cinephilia. Fuller, however, was not just *any* film director: he was talismanic. Beloved of the *Cahiers du cinéma* generation of critics-turned-filmmakers—Fuller appeared "as himself" in Jean-Luc Godard's *Pierrot le fou* (Fr/It, 1966)—he was the touchstone of a certain anti-literary, pro-image kind of cinema. To love Fuller was to love film. Additionally, Fuller's presence asserts the continuity between filmmaking and film criticism. Grigor had been Director of the Edinburgh International Film Festival (EIFF) from 1967 to 1972. His first major retrospective in that role had been of Fuller's work and, crucially, this inaugurated the policy, continued until the early '80s, whereby retrospectives would be accompanied by books of critical essays on their central figure or topic (Will and Wollen 1969).

Yet culturally resonant as Fuller's presence is within this scene, the sequence's most important meaning lies in its dramatic situation and its *mise-en-scène*. Scots and cinephiles would immediately recognise two men lost in the Scottish Highlands, discussing a place which does not appear on the map, as a reference to the opening of *Brigadoon*, the Broadway musical and subsequent Hollywood film most often cited as the nadir of debased Romanticism as it relates to Scotland (McArthur 2003a). The fact that mist swirls round the characters reinforces the *Brigadoon* connection, asserting that Grigor's film will not only be about Scotland and its history, but about the construction of these things in discourse. Underlining Grigor's lack of interest in classical narrative, Fuller and his hapless assistant quickly disappear from the film, only to reappear in its final moments in Grigor's perfunctory gesture towards narrative resolution. The meaning of *Scotch Myths* lies altogether elsewhere.

One of the most stable features of classical narrative cinema is coherence between actor and role, the individual actor embodying a single character (clearly there are exceptions, such as *Dr Jekyll and Mr Hyde)* throughout the time of the film. Different theatrical and cinematic traditions have posed other relationships between actors and roles, some ancient and non-western such as Noh, Kabuki and Bunraku, others western and modern(ist) such as the practices of Bertolt Brecht, Antonin Artaud and Jerzy Grotowski. The use of actors, and their playing style, in *Scotch Myths* probably draws most from Brechtian practice, in that Grigor makes no attempt to provoke identification with or sympathy for any of the personages: they are there to further a historico-cultural argument. While the actors playing the tour guide, the bus driver and Fuller`s assistant, plus Fuller himself, could be said to be performing broadly within the conventions of Euro-American naturalism, those embodying the historical personages use a heightened, declamatory mode of address quite alien to that tradition. Additionally and crucially, as individuals the latter group of performers are not coterminous with single historical figures. Several actors migrate from one historical or mythical figure to another: Alex Norton (James Boswell, Robert Burns, Napoleon, Felix Mendelssohn,

Prince Albert, John Brown), John Bett (James MacPherson, Ossian, Sir Walter Scott, Lord Byron, William McGonagall), Juliet Cadzow (Malvina Farquarson-Smith, Miss Moffat 1770, Bonnie Jean), Sorel Johnson (Queen Victoria, Mary Rose) and Bill Paterson (Samuel Johnson, Harry Lauder). In one scene Sir Walter Scott and Lord Byron (both in the body of actor John Bett) argue the merits of the former's construction of Scotland. Another clearly Brechtian device (also much used in *The Cheviot…*) is the punctuation of the action by songs, most of them composed and performed by Ron Geesin, who, as the Bonnie Hieland Laddie (here represented as a gap-toothed, grotesquely ugly but convivial character), provides a musical commentary throughout the film. Geesin shape-shifts, appearing as a bizarre cross between Bonnie Prince Charlie and Liberace. Playing a white piano, he disappears beneath the foaming billows of Fingal's Cave, a kind of surrealist transposition of the foaming grotto of Grigor's earlier exhibition.

In *Scotch Myths* Murray Grigor is a postmodernist *avant la lettre*, particularly in his obliteration of the distinction between high and low art. So central has this come to be seen in the definition of postmodernism, it is often forgotten how recurrent it was in modernism, too. The endless jokes in *Scotch Myths* are often demotic, as in the bus driver's take on Culloden Moor, "MAMBA country: miles and miles of bugger all". And, if historical figures such as James MacPherson, Dr Johnson and Sir Walter Scott are often regarded today as fixtures of high art, they exist cheek-by-jowl in this film with buffoons of popular Scottish culture such as Harry Lauder and William McGonagall. At one moment Scott declaims *The Lady of the Lake* (1810); at another he cuts his arse on the wine glass which, inveterate royal sycophant that he was, he had pocketed at the ceremony welcoming George IV to Edinburgh in 1822. *Scotch Myths*' melding of high and low art particularly links it to *Rab C. Nesbitt,* as does its unremittingly comic tone. The tone apart, the visual look and use of actors in *Scotch Myths* also connects it to another great modernist film, Hans-Jürgen Syberberg's *Ludwig: Requiem for a Virgin King* (W Ger, 1972). But whereas *Scotch Myths* provides (almost literally) a laugh a minute, Syberberg's film is sombrely didactic. However, the two films' engagement with history, their interrogation of Romanticism and their indifference to classical narrative set them in opposition to mainstream cinema. Finally, *Scotch Myths* is modernist in being a multi-discourse film, ranging outside the unities of time, space and action. The bus trip and the Fuller episodes exist in present-day "real" time and, at a pinch, the historical charades could be said to do so too, motivated as part of the performance of the Dundreich Experience being witnessed by the tourists.

Yet from time to time the charades erupt into historical reconstruction (another connection with *The Cheviot…*), as when James MacPherson is seen riding through the Highlands, collecting his "fragments of ancient poetry." The charades also segue on occasion into animation sequences, one of which is perhaps the most deliriously notable moment in the film. Sir Walter Scott and his faithful manservant (played by the Buster Keaton-faced Scots comedian Chic Murray, who also plays the whisky blender, Sir Rhosis Hue McRose of Glen Liver) are discussing the arrangements for George IV's visit to Edinburgh, which Scott choreographed. Describing the tartans which will be worn at the event, Scott deploys what has come to be called "the invention of tradition" (Hobsbawm and Ranger 1983). Informed that the tartan chosen for the kilt George IV will wear is known in the pattern books simply as Number 137, Scott, with increasingly rhetorical gestures, renames it successively as Stuart, Royal Stuart, Ancient Royal Stuart, Ancient Royal Hunting Stuart and Ancient Royal Hunting Dress Stuart. As he then declaims "Bring furrit the tartan and we'll tartan the kingdom," the screen explodes into festoons of plaid of every hue and the Scottish landscape itself becomes tartanised.

## The Suppression

Given the quite extensive press coverage of the *Scotch Myths* exhibition, the meagre response to the *Scotch Myths* film is puzzling. Even making allowance for the Hogmanay transmission (no newspapers on New Year's Day) the coverage is scant, just one press piece in the British Film Institute (BFI) cuttings file by the *Glasgow Herald*'s Julie Davidson. Davidson appreciates both the film's political import and aesthetic innovation, "possibly the most creative and discreetly bitter piece of self-analysis to come out of Scotland in years" (Davidson 1982, 7). She also recognises its likely difficulty for a general television audience. This point may help explain the lack of press cuttings, but this is not an absolute guarantee that no such coverage exists. It is simply that *Scotch Myths*' transmission was not covered by the BFI's designated list, broadly speaking, the major English, Scottish and some American papers and journals. The only other materials in the BFI cuttings file on *Scotch Myths* (apart from a Channel 4 press announcement) are three letters to *The Scotsman*. One, by P. H. Scott (a prominent Scottish nationalist and sometime spokesperson on culture for the Scottish National Party), attacks the film and two others (one by the present writer) defend it. Scott is the author of a book (Scott 1981) on his famous namesake, Sir Walter. In this he celebrates unambiguously the extent to which Scott's writings brought

Scotland to the attention of the world, while being blind, as David Daiches points out (Daiches 1981), to the pernicious Romanticism relating to Scotland that Scott's work engendered. P. H. Scott's hostility to *Scotch Myths* may be partly explicable by Daiches' citing of Grigor's exhibition as making good the lack in Scott's book.

Given the workaday factors such as the absence of newspapers around New Year, to call the (lack of) press response "suppression" would be to overstate the case. However, the term begins to have some validity in relation to the response of the institutions of moving image culture one would have most expected to engage with Grigor's film. This had been true in the setting-up of the project: Films of Scotland (the main sponsor of film production in Scotland at the time), Scottish Television and Grampian Television all turned it down for production finance. BBC Scotland had funded an early version of the script in the mid-1970s but did not follow through into production. This left Channel 4 to bring *Scotch Myths* to the screen, for the reasons outlined above.

*Scotch Myths* was also screened at the Festival of Film and Television in the Celtic Countries in 1984. It is instructive, however, to compare its programming there with that of another of Channel 4's early Scottish projects, Bill Bryden's *Ill Fares the Land* (GB, 1983), an historical account of the abandonment of the island of St Kilda in the 1930s (McArthur 1983). Bryden's film, an orthodox, quasi-Hollywoodean exercise much influenced by the films of John Ford, was given three prime-time weekend screenings at the festival. By contrast, *Scotch Myths* gained one midweek lunchtime screening. Clearly this represented the festival organisers' judgment of the kinds of audiences likely to be attracted to both films, and perhaps also indicates their own mainstream tastes. It is the behaviour of the Scottish Film Council (SFC), however, which most fully validates the term "suppression." The SFC flatly refused to acquire *Scotch Myths* for its Central Film Library or, amazingly, for the Scottish Film Archive, on the grounds that it was not important enough. No documentary evidence exists to confirm this assertion, but the chilly response to the film by the SFC as a whole was evident to me in the conversations I had with the institution's personnel. *Scotch Myths* would have sunk without trace at this point had I not been in a position (as Head of the Distribution Division of the BFI at the time) to ensure that it was acquired for the BFI Distribution Library and later included in a Critic's Choice season at the National Film Theatre. I also used Grigor's film as an aesthetic/political counter-model for a putative Scottish cinema in a review of the film *Local Hero* (Forsyth, GB, 1983) for the Channel 4 film programme *Visions* (1982-85).

*Scotch Myths* would be publicly screened intermittently thereafter, on Channel 4 as a St Andrew's Night offering and at some of the publicly subsidised regional film theatres in the major Scottish cities. Some material relating to the film (hopefully enough to strike a print or DVD from) eventually found its way into the Scottish Film Archive. It arrived there, however, by bequest of Murray Grigor himself and not as a result of a policy decision by the SFC. The SFC's suppression of *Scotch Myths* in the spheres of distribution, exhibition, archiving and education was fully matched by its grudging and meagre support for Grigor's subsequent projects, through its production funding mechanisms the Scottish Film Production Fund, and latterly, Scottish Screen. The extent of these bodies' chasing of the chimeras of, first, a European-style art cinema, then a full-blown "Hollywood on the Clyde" orthodox narrative cinema (and the consequent suppression of the kind of (ludic) modernism represented by *Scotch Myths*) can be followed in outline by reference to the writings of the key personnel controlling production (John Brown, Ian Lockerbie, Allan Shiach, Eddie Dick and Steve McIntyre) surveyed in Jonathan Murray's *That Thinking Feeling: A Research Guide to Scottish Cinema 1938-2004* (Murray 2004).

However, Scottish film culture's putative suppression of (ludic) modernism predates the SFC's early-'80s entry into film production. It might be said that every film culture operating in a market economy suppresses or marginalises modernism, usually by implication in the (often unspoken) institutional policies adopted, specifically, the belief that cinema's true nature manifests itself in the two-hour narrative feature film, with protagonist(s) and antagonist(s), coherent characters and an arc of action leading to narrative closure (Ellis 1982; Bordwell *et al.* 1985). Cineastes in every market-driven culture gravitate towards the narrative norm, and Scottish cineastes are no exception. At collective gatherings such as the annual Film Bang event in the 1970s, the cry was invariably raised that Scotland must have its own feature films. This was particularly poignant, since virtually the only film-producing mechanism in the country at the time, Films of Scotland, had grown out of the Griersonian documentary movement, and was therefore predicated, for political, aesthetic and economic reasons, upon the making of sponsored documentaries. The more imaginative cineastes working under Films of Scotland's auspices, such as Murray Grigor, Laurence Henson, Eddie McConnell, Douglas Eadie and Brian Crumlish, stretched the documentary form to breaking point. When something approaching a feature film, *The Duna Bull* (Henson, GB) was prised out of Films of Scotland in 1972, it was entirely orthodox in narrative terms. Moreover, this film echoed the ideological stance of Ealing or Ealing-style films about Scotland: *Whisky Galore!* (Mackendrick, GB, 1949), *The Maggie* (Mackendrick, GB, 1954), and *Laxdale Hall* (Eldridge, GB, 1953). In *The Duna Bull* a range of couthy Highland characters outwit (yet again) imperious southerners, here, the civil servants of the Scottish Office in Edinburgh. The history of the development and proliferation of publicly-funded film production in Scotland is ably described by Duncan Petrie (Petrie 2000), and can be read not only as an accelerating suppression of (ludic) modernism, but eventually of any kind of art cinema. This, however, is a reading Petrie chooses not to foreground explicitly. From the '70s on, successive institutional configurations and key personnel made concordats with the market and with classical narrative cinema, some, like Steve McIntyre, more reluctantly than others (McIntyre 1994 and 1996).

Though Scottish film culture's long march to the industrial model was largely a question of institutional and individual choice and taste, that process was also heavily over-determined by external forces. Two such forces, one economic, the other aesthetic, but both ultimately interpenetrated, were particularly important. The first was the neo-liberal economic policy first espoused by the Thatcherite Tory government from 1979 on. Within this the market was king and every public body had to pay its way or, at the very least, "give value for money." The financial discourse came to the fore within Scottish film culture with the report commissioned by the then Tory Secretary of State for Scotland, Michael Forsyth, following the Republic of Ireland`s "stealing" of most of the location shooting for *Braveheart* (Gibson, USA, 1995) through use of such devices as tax incentives and the provision of the Irish Army as extras. The report (Hydra Associates 1996) led to the setting-up of Scottish Screen and unambiguously installed the industrial model, relegating culture to a decidedly secondary role. Subsequent changes in the Scottish polity arising from devolution have resulted in the industrial model being tinkered with to add social criteria. It remains to be seen whether the new SNP government's *Creative Scotland* initiative (inherited from the previous Labour administration) will herald further changes.

Virtually contemporaneous with the rise of economic neo-liberalism was the emergence of what might be called story-structure discourse. Its generative mechanisms were the DIY screenwriting manuals of Syd Field (Field 1979, 1984) and the three-day story structure seminars of Robert McKee, which themselves ultimately emerged in book form (McKee 1999). To simplify somewhat, Field and McKee argued that every 90-120 minute narrative feature film script conformed to the same basic structure involving set-up, development and resolution; characters who were goal-driven (in simpler scripts having an external drive such as finding a lost object or person, in more complex ones also having an additional internal drive, such as purging a past mistake); and antagonists seeking to thwart the protagonists' aims. Field and McKee were quickly cloned, the provision of DIY screenwriting manuals mushroomed and soon (aspiring) scriptwriters, directors, producers, agents and actors were all spouting the storystructurespeak of plots, sub-plots, action arcs, turning points, false endings, etc. As I write I can see no less than twenty-four such manuals on my bookshelf, a mere fraction of those available. The title of one boils down what story structure discourse delivers: *Conflict, Action and Suspense* (Noble 1994). This pernicious triptych has not only hegemonised almost all film but is increasingly visible in ostensibly factual television as well.

I am comforted, however, that alongside the tiresomely repetitive DIY screenwriting manuals on my shelf there sits the most trenchant critique of story structure discourse, Jean-Pierre Geuens' *Film Production Theory* (Geuens 2000). Geuens demolishes the ideas underpinning classical narrative cinema: that the self is coherent, seamless and autonomous, as opposed to fractured, fluctuating and prey to the unconscious; that it acts on the world rather than the world acting on it; that human actions have entirely predictable consequences; and that the individual life is a plot rather than a chronicle. The emergence in the early '90s of the Scottish production mechanism *Movie Makars* ("makar" is an old Scots word for "writer") designed explicitly to introduce story structure discourse to Scotland, can be mapped onto both the over-determining economic and aesthetic forces referred to above. Or, perhaps better, it can be read as a local distilling of the latter. *Movie Makars* saw the emergence into the Scottish film production limelight of Allan Shiach, first Chair of Scottish Screen. Shiach incarnated perfectly both the economic and aesthetic master currents of the time. As Allan Shiach he was co-Chair of the Macallan whisky firm; as Allan Scott he was a practicing Hollywood screenwriter, a Jekyll and Hyde for the late twentieth century, except that in this case the two personalities were not in contradiction but instead pulled in exactly the same direction: the further industrialising and narrativising of Scottish cinema. Lest there be any doubt where that cinema was headed, one guest of honour at *Movie Makars* was the eminent Hollywood screenwriter William Goldman. It would be tedious to relate the Gradgrindian detail with which Scottish Screen now implements its industrial model. Those with the stomach for it should consult the Scottish Screen website, in particular the policy guidelines and application forms for its innumerable schemes at every level of production and training.

Collectively they constitute a manual for how to crush the life out of a creative project. Fortunately some, albeit a minority, of cineastes are able to reanimate the corpse at the moment of production. It goes without saying that a ludic modernist work such as *Scotch Myths* would have little chance of being funded under present policies, a fact confirmed by the virtual absence of Murray Grigor's name from Scottish funding rosters. Like that other great British modernist, Peter Greenaway, he raises the money for his projects, nowadays mainly about modernist architects, from continental Europe and to some extent North America.

## What is to be done?

So entrenched is the industrial classical narrative model in Scottish film production—a model, incidentally, which evolving technologies may render obsolete—that it is now a waste of time and energy to continue railing against it and proposing alternatives, even though one has a cultural and moral duty to remind younger cinephiles of what they have lost, and to honour the best examples of suppressed traditions such as *Scotch Myths*. There is, however, one battle that is still worth fighting. Scottish Screen still has—however marginalised and attenuated—a cultural remit, still housing within itself most of the mechanisms of a complete film culture, including film education, although the recent separation of the Scottish Film Archive and its relocation in the National Library of Scotland could be a sombre indication of what is to come. Scottish Screen, unlike its sister organisation the BFI—another body in danger of imminent dismemberment—never aspired to produce a substantial critical journal on the model of *Sight & Sound*. Scottish Screen is primarily an enabling facility for the production of "Scottish" films, the term being in inverted commas since the definition internal to Scottish Screen is economic rather than historico-aesthetic. As an enabling house, it does not venture far into the marketing of the films it funds, perhaps with the exception of the entry of these into international festivals. More generally, Scottish Screen apparently sees marketing as the job of the individual production companies it funds. Although its ethos is that of a traditional production company, in its adoption of the industrial model it does not follow through into marketing the way a traditional production company would.

Aside from billboards, radio and television advertising and trailers, the central marketing mechanism in the film business has been the campaign book on each individual film which would be sent to every local cinema manager. Perfectly understandably, these books made little claim to cultural enlightenment but were primarily mechanisms to maximise ticket sales. To take a concrete example, the campaign book for *The Big Heat* (Lang, USA, 1953) issued by Columbia Pictures' British subsidiary in 1954 runs to four pages. The first page gives key information such as credits, synopsis, certification details and running time, the second page a more detailed account of the film and little anecdotes primarily about the stars, and a [kind of] summarised interview with lead player Glenn Ford. The little anecdotes continue on the third page which begins to make clear who, exactly, the campaign book is aimed at: individual cinema managers. A reference to the novel on which the film is based urges managers to ensure that local bookshops stock and display the novel prior to playdate. About half of page three is taken up with a section headed "Exploitation," which offers suggestions for drumming up business: local police giving pep talks on crime before the film begins, tying the film in with local gas and electricity showrooms because of its title, and so on. Page four details the diversity of posters, stills and trailers to be had from Columbia's branch offices in major British cities.

The unremittingly commercial discourse of these campaign books is quite understandable from companies which rarely claimed to be anything other than money-making machines. Needless to say, the books show no evidence of any attempts to induce audiences to reflect on the film in question, far less wider issues of film culture. But Scottish Screen is ostensibly not simply a money-making machine. Were it to up its profile in the marketing of the films it funds, Scottish film culture could reasonably demand that Scottish Screen's promotional discourse be *cultural* as well as commercial. Where then might it look for a cultural model of film promotion? Good examples to ponder are found in the magazines and brochures produced by the film-exporting arms of the former socialist republics of Central and Eastern Europe. Here, commercial promotion took second place to raising the profile of Communism in general and the individual states in question. For instance, in 1966 Sovexportfilm produced a bulky brochure on *Lenin in Poland* (Sergei Yutkevich and Jan Rutkiewicz, USSR/Pol), the USSR's entry to that year's Cannes Film Festival. This runs to twelve large-format pages, including a long, serious critical essay on the film and, somewhat incongruously (even Soviet publications are not free from contradictions), a double-page spread of photographs of Soviet actresses of the time.

More impressive—in intellectual if not presentational terms—is the bi-monthly *Hungarofilm Bulletin,* produced very cheaply in A4 format, almost like a *samizdat* production. Characteristically, it ran to forty pages in English and tended to be devoted primarily to one film. One issue was given over to *The Round-Up* (Hun, 1966), the celebrated film by Miklós

Janscó about the Kafkaesque methods of the Habsburg secret police in identifying the ringleaders of an abortive mid-nineteenth-century uprising by Hungarian patriots. The publication contains a Janscó filmography; three pages of stills; a twelve-page analysis of the film by a noted Hungarian film critic; a nine-page interview with Janscó; and bio-filmographies of Tamás Sembó, Director of Photography, and Janós Görbe, leading actor. Both the critical essay and the interview are serious and unfrivolous, substantially concerned with the philosophical, moral and formal aspects of cinema. The bulletin is exemplary in the seriousness with which it approaches cinema, even if its production is austere by Western standards.

In many respects the most attractive publication to come out of Communist Eastern Europe was *Film Polski*, the regular magazine in French and English, of the Polish film industry. It managed to adopt several of the features of Western film magazines while retaining a serious discourse about cinema. A characteristic issue of 1965 has photographs of Polish actors on the back and front covers; three pages of photographs of and statements from participants at the Krakow Film Festival; a double-page spread on a new Polish feature film, *Three Steps on Earth* (Jerzy Hoffman and Edward Skórzewski, Pol, 1965); a double-page spread on the films of Andrzej Wajda and three double-page spreads on his latest film, *Ashes* (Pol, 1965), an adaptation of a famous novel about the role of the Polish Legion in Napoleon's army. There are briefer sections on films in production, industry news and new Polish films being set up. *Film Polski* remains serious about cinema, although the lavish illustration and generally shortish articles may have achieved a good balance between criticism and promotion without becoming a vehicle for fragmented bits of information and gossip.

Yet what is perhaps the most aspirational model for contemporary Scotland comes not from the Communist East but from the non-Communist West: the quarterly *German Films*. Established in 1954 and with a current budget of 5.7 million Euros, it runs to over eighty pages in full colour. Issue 2 of 2005 contains a ten-page article on documentary film in Germany; four double-page features on German film personnel (directors, producers, an actor); five pages of industry news; ten pages on films in production; thirty pages, each one devoted to a new German film; and four pages which are part of an ongoing discussion of key German films of the past. *German Films* represents an exemplary mobilisation of shareholders, supporters and institutions around the common purpose of promoting German cinema in a non-hucksterish, intellectually serious manner.

Much of the hype emanating from Scottish Screen has been about the efflorescence and international success of recent Scottish cinema. Some of this has been justified, most of it empty tub-thumping. An equally significant development has been the growth of Film Studies at all levels of the Scottish educational system. It is unclear the extent to which the personnel making up this development see themselves as a collective. If and when they do, they will have every right to demand not only that Scottish Screen continue allocating a significant amount of its resources to Film Studies, but that its publications adhere to the highest intellectual standards. Part of the demand might be for a publication along the lines of the better models discussed above. As well as promoting Scottish cinema in the here and now it might, like *German Films*, retain the memory of Scottish cinema past. Who knows, it might even recall lost masterpieces like *Scotch Myths.*

## Works Cited

Bordwell, David, Janet Staiger and Kristin Thompson. 1985. *The Classical Hollywood Cinema: Film Style and Mode of Production to 1960.* London: Routledge.

Daiches, David. 1981. Scott's Double Vision. *The Scotsman.* September 19.

Davidson, Julie. 1982. A Kind of McSon and Lumiere. *Glasgow Herald.* December 28.

Ellis, John. 1982. *Visible Fictions: Cinema, Television, Video.* London: Routledge.

Field, Syd. 1979. *Screenplay: The Foundations of Screenwriting.* New York, Dell.

—. 1984. *The Screenwriter`s Workbook.* New York: Dell.

Geuens, Jean-Pierre. 2000. *Film Production Theory.* New York: State University of New York Press.

Hobsbawm, Eric and Terence Ranger, eds. 1983. *The Invention of Tradition.* Cambridge: Cambridge University Press.

Hydra Associates. 1996. *Scotland on Screen: the Development of the Film and Television Industry in Scotland.* Glasgow: Scott Stern Associates.

McArthur, Colin. 1978. *Television and History.* London: British Film Institute.

—. 1981/2. Breaking the Signs: 'Scotch Myths' as Cultural Struggle. *Cencrastus* 7: 21-25.

—. 1983. Tendencies in the New Scottish Cinema. *Cencrastus* 13: 33-35.

—. 1990. The Rises and Falls of the Edinburgh International Film Festival. In *From Limelight to Satellite: a Scottish Film Book*, ed. Eddie Dick, 91-102. Glasgow/London: Scottish Film Council/British Film Institute.

—. 1991. A Dram for All Seasons: the Diverse Identities of Scotch. In *Scots on Scotch*, ed. Phillip Hills, 87-102. Edinburgh: Mainstream.

—. 1993. In praise of a poor cinema. *Sight and Sound* 3.8: 30-32.

—. 1994. The Cultural Necessity of a Poor Celtic Cinema. In *Border Crossing: Film in Ireland, Britain and Europe*, eds. John Hill, Martin McLoone and Paul Hainsworth, 112-125. London/Belfast: British Film Institute/Institute of Irish Studies/University of Ulster.

—. 1994a. Culloden: a Pre-emptive Strike. *Scottish Affairs* 9: 97-126.

—. 1998. The Exquisite Corpse of Rab(elais) C(opernicus) Nesbitt. In *Dissident Voices: the Politics of Television and Cultural Change*, ed. Mike Wayne, 107-126. London: Pluto Press.

—. 2003a. *Brigadoon, Braveheart and the Scots: Distortions of Scotland in Hollywood Cinema*. London: I. B. Tauris.

—. 2003b. *Whisky Galore! and The Maggie*. London: I. B. Tauris.

McIntyre, Steve. 1994. Vanishing Point: Feature Film Production in a Small Country. In *Border Crossing: Film in Ireland, Britain and Europe,* eds. John Hill, Martin McLoone and Paul Hainsworth, 88-111. London/Belfast: British Film Institute/Institute of Irish Studies/ University of Ulster.

—. 1996. Art and Industry: Regional Film and Video Policy in the UK during the 1980s. In *Film Policy: International, National and Regional Perspectives*, ed. Albert Moran, 215-233. London: Routledge.

McKee, Robert. 1997. *Story: Substance, Structure, Style, and the Principles of Screenwriting*. London: Methuen.

Murray, Jonathan. 2004. *That Thinking Feeling: a Research Guide to Scottish Cinema 1938-2004*. Edinburgh/Glasgow: Edinburgh College of Art/Scottish Screen.

Nairn, Tom. 1977. *The Break-Up of Britain: Crisis and Neo-Nationalism*. London: New Left Books.

Nieland, Justus. 2006. Editorial Introduction: Modernism's Laughter. *Modernist Cultures* 2.2: 80-86.

Noble, William. 1994. *Conflict, Action & Suspense*. Cincinnati: F&W Publications.

Petrie, Duncan. 2000. *Screening Scotland*. London: British Film Institute.

Ray, Celeste. 2001. *Highland Heritage: Scottish Americans in the American South*. Chapel Hill, NC: University of North Carolina Press.

Scott, Paul H. 1981. *Sir Walter Scott and Scotland*. Edinburgh: William Blackwood.

Will, David and Peter Wollen, eds. 1969. *Samuel Fuller*. Edinburgh: Edinburgh International Film Festival.

# NOSTOPHOBIA

CAIRNS CRAIG

Jonathan Murray (Murray 2004, 2) dates the emergence of a distinctive Scottish film culture to Bill Forsyth's *That Sinking Feeling* (GB, 1979), a film whose title proved to be all too appropriate to the year of its release, that of the devolution referendum that sank the Labour government of Jim Callaghan and led directly to Margaret Thatcher's dominance of the 1980s. 1979 is, however, framed by two of the most powerful and acclaimed films in Scotland's problematic cinema history: Bill Douglas' *Childhood Trilogy—My Childhood* (GB, 1972), *My Ain Folk* (GB, 1973) and *My Way Home* (GB, 1978)—and Michael Radford's version of the Jessie Kesson novel, *Another Time, Another Place* (GB, 1983). *My Childhood*, which failed to find funding in Scotland because it did not project a sufficiently positive image of the country, turned into a trilogy funded by the British Film Institute; its critical reputation is in inverse proportion to the budget of less than £40,000 for which it was made. The *Trilogy* has taken on an almost legendary status as one of Britain's truly innovative cinema creations. The 2008 British Film Institute DVD release of the work is, for example, emblazoned with *The Observer* film critic Philip French's view that Douglas' films constitute "not just as a milestone, but… one of the heroic achievements of the British Cinema."

The *Trilogy* was also indicative of a contemporary turn by British directors towards a European arthouse tradition of filmmaking. Michael Radford's *Another Time, Another Place*, winner of a whole series of European prizes, was one of the major outcomes of this development. Radford, born in India to an English father and Austrian mother, had only a brief period of acclimatisation to Scottish culture as a teacher in an FE college in Edinburgh, but a television film of Jessie Kesson's *The White Bird Passes*, made for BBC Scotland in 1980, led to the plan for a larger-scale adaptation of one of Kesson's other works. *Another Time, Another Place* was to be the beginning of a very successful international directorial career that produced films such as *1984* (GB, 1984) and *Il Postino* (Fr/It/Bel, 1994). Douglas, by contrast, produced only one more full-length film, *Comrades* (GB, 1986), before his early death in 1991.

*My Childhood* and *Another Time, Another Place* are linked in narrative terms by the fact that both look back to the Second World War, and each film has as its main protagonist a character who develops a relationship with prisoners of war working on the land. In *My Childhood*, a German POW, Helmut (Karl Fieseler), befriends Jamie (Stephen Archibald), who is one of two brothers deserted by their respective fathers and living in abject poverty with their grandmother (Jean Taylor Smith) in a desolate, run-down Scottish coalmining town. For Jamie, Helmut—one of the 'enemy' as an air-raid shelter scene underlines—has become a surrogate for the father who has abandoned him. Together they read a children's book and begin to learn each other's languages. Helmut's inevitable departure leaves Jamie bereft: while the prisoner of war can return home, Jamie is already at home but has no home. In the film's final sequence, he leaps on to a coal wagon that gradually disappears beyond the boundaries of the village. In *Another Time, Another Place*, the central character, Janie (Phyllis Logan), is a "young woman" (as she is called throughout Kesson's novel), married to a dour farmer (Paul Young) some fifteen years her senior, and on whose farm are quartered Italian POWs. She is fascinated by their very different culture, full, as it seems to her, of a sensual responsiveness to life that is entirely absent from her own. When she becomes romantically and sexually involved with the Italians, it is at terrible cost to all parties.

The introduction of these POWs into two of the most striking Scottish films of their period may not, given the smallness of the sample, be statistically significant, but it is, I want to suggest, culturally so, especially in relation to the environment in which Scottish film culture itself developed. The besetting sin of Scottish cinema, according to its critics, has been its nostalgic concentration on a rural Scotland invested with a romantic sense of isolation from the modern world. Scotland becomes the setting for a sense of communal belonging which has a magical ability to transform the outsiders who encounter it, changing them from brutal, or simply insensitive, participants in a modern society into sympathetic discoverers of the values of a simpler but more humane way of life. *Whisky Galore!* (Mackendrick, GB, 1949) and *Local Hero* (Forsyth, GB, 1983), are often cited as characteristic Scottish versions of a trope whose archetypal embodiment is Vincente Minnelli's *Brigadoon* (USA, 1954), in which two American tourists discover a Scottish village that only comes to life for one day every hundred years. Industrial urban Scotland—and, after all, Scotland was by 1900 one of the most industrialised and urbanised countries in the world—has no part in this mythic structure. Instead,

Scotland exists as an idyllic antithesis to modernity, the lingering memory of a world only reachable through the illusions of art.

For the POWs in *My Childhood* and *Another Time, Another Place*, however, rural Scotland is a far-from-idyllic discovery. *My Childhood*, shot in black and white, reduces the landscape to a featureless flatness, like the suspended lives of the prisoners whose labour, under the eye of a soldier with a gun, is punishment. The colour of *Another Time, Another Place* is used to emphasise how colourless the landscape is—as bleak in its monotony as the work that has to be done on the farm. In both films, what the POWs ironically underline is how much more freedom they have than the people of the community among whom they temporarily live. The prisoners have a home to which, one day, they will return, whereas the Scots are trapped in an imprisonment that is apparently without end and which leaves them with a sense of homelessness even when they at home. As Jessie Kesson's novel puts it:

> Times like these, the young woman felt imprisoned within the circumference of the field. Trapped by the monotony of work that wearied the body and dulled the mind. Rome had been taken. Allies had landed in Normandy, she'd heard that on the wireless. 'News' that had caused great excitement in the bothy, crowded with friends, gesticulating in wild debate. Loud voices in dispute. Names falling casually from their tongues, out of books from her school-room days. The Alban Hills, The Tibrus… O Tibrus, Father Tibrus. To whom the Romans pray… Even in her schooldays those names had sounded unreal. Outdistanced by centuries, from another time. Another place. (Kesson 1983, 101)

The "young woman" is the real prisoner, the "servant of circumstances" (ibid., 115). Her brief relationship with one of the prisoners will confirm the sensual poverty of the world in which she lives, just as Jamie's relationship with Helmut will confirm the material and spiritual poverty of the 'family' in which he is growing up. The prisoners may be nostalgic for their homelands, but nostalgia for them is possible because they come from places rich in culture, rich in colour. No such nostalgia is possible for the Scots, whose memories are, like Janie's, only of a lost world they were once introduced to in school, or, like Jamie's, of a life of exclusion and rejection.

Both these films succeed in evading the nostalgia for a return to an idealised, rural Scotland by seeing the nation in the light of the real nostalgia of POWs who ache to return to their true homelands. In focusing on prisoners of war, these films are actually recovering the original meaning of the term nostalgia, which was coined by the Swiss physician

Johannes Hofer in the late seventeenth century to describe the condition of extreme homesickness among Swiss mercenaries fighting far from home on behalf of another people's culture. The "symptoms" of the "nostalgic" were said by Hofer to be despondency, melancholia, excessive emotion (including profound bouts of weeping), refusal of food and a wasting away which sometimes ended in attempts at suicide (Davis 1979, 1). These, however, are not the symptoms of the POWs in Douglas' *Trilogy* but rather those of Jamie's family members. His grandmothers both waste away in bouts of weeping and melancholia; his mother, incarcerated in an institution, hides under the sheets when Jamie goes to see her, refusing contact with the world as she, too, wastes away. In the children's 'home' to which he is sent, Jamie himself refuses food and his 'despondency' and 'melancholia' are such that he agrees to be taken back by his father, despite his awareness that there is no home for him to return to. Nostalgia, in its original context, was a disease of wartime and military service, related to distance from a physical home and the unlikelihood of ever being able to return to it. In the case of both Jamie's family and Janie's marriage, however, the context is reversed—nostalgia is a disease which, through dispossession and poverty, has come to afflict a civilian home front population, where 'home' has come to represent just as profound a separation from origins and community as being at war did for Hofer's Swiss soldiers. In Douglas and Radford's films, the Scottish characters' desire to escape from their 'imprisonment' may be just as powerful as that of the POWs, but the former have no place to return to. They are displaced persons for whom 'home' can mean only deprivation and loss and for whom nostalgia can have no object. In *Another Time, Another Place*, the Italians make themselves at home, creating their own Marian shrine in the bothy where they live; Janie, ostensibly at home, can in fact only find it indirectly—and briefly—in enemy aliens. Her desire is for that other place, nostalgia for a lost potentiality. Jamie in *My Way Home* reverses the nostalgia of seventeenth-century Swiss soldiers by finding his real home, an alternative to his childhood one, through the army and through his consequent displacement to serve in a distant country.

Whatever its roots in Bill Douglas' personal experience, *My Childhood* and its sequels have been read not simply as the account of the life of one extremely unfortunate family (and briefly, after all, we are given glimpses of the rest of the mining community as one full of happy children). Rather, the *Trilogy* has been viewed as an iconic overturning of the nostalgic representation of the Scottish nation. Andrew O'Hagan, for example, seeks to locate the significance of his own childhood through Douglas' work:

> I thought of how my own growing awareness of small-town life had been given a painstaking visual language in the films of Bill Douglas. It was an awareness of broken promises and crumbling illusions—both inside my home and outside, in the shambolic 'ideal corporate living space' that was the Scottish new town. Scotland, my own imagined community, had produced an artist who mocked the quixotic posturing of a bogus national identity—exploding the tired, iron platitudes of family loyalty, couthy neighbours and yer ain fireside. (O'Hagan 1993, 206)

The nostalgia of Scotland's filmic history and cinematic self-representation is overturned in the "flickering shadow-play of great cinematic art" (ibid.), an art capable not only of reshaping our sense of Scottish film but having also "the capacity to break with our traditional sense of nationhood" (ibid.). Scotland is not a nation about which to be nostalgic: "Scotland's search for a noble identity, as ever, means nothing more than the ceremonial waving of a blank banner and collective aversion of eyes from prevailing, indigenous social injustice" (ibid., 212). 'Home', for O'Hagan—and, he assumes, for Douglas—is a place one has to discover by travelling in "the opposite direction from the religious pieties and cultural prejudices" which represent "the traditional values and supposed certainties of [our] Scottish roots" (ibid., 213). "Will I never get out of this place?" Janie keens in *Another Time, Another Place*.

In framing the key date of a Scottish feature film culture's emergence, Douglas and Radford's films also frame the terms of the critical debate by which that culture was defined. On one side was the nostalgic indulgence of Scotch myths—what came to be known as Tartanry and Kailyard (McArthur 1982)—and on the other a realism which could force its audience to acknowledge Scotland as a place of exploitation, suffering and repression. As Joyce McMillan puts it, focusing on the first two parts of Douglas's *Trilogy*:

> The standard iconography of working-class community life, in Scotland as elsewhere in the industrialised world, is all to do with compensatory virtues of warmth and solidarity, with the innate decency and the family values that, in legend, kept the home fires burning and the doorsteps gleaming white even in the toughest times; with the sense that 'we', the workers, were more caring people, for all our poverty. It takes a brave man to drive a coach and horses of bitter memory through all that. (McMillan 1993, 220)

The power of Douglas' work lies in its ability to unravel the myths by which Scotland conceals itself from itself, or, as O'Hagan puts it, in the films' "critical assault on the cultural tradition that draws much of its force from the Kailyard" (O'Hagan 1993, 210). Andrew Nash has argued that the Kailyard myth has its roots in the identification of Scotland with Burns' depiction of rural life (Nash 2007, 22), and, in particular, in the religiously devoted farming family of 'The Cotter's Saturday Night' (1785):

> The chearfu' Supper done, wi' serious face,
> They, round the ingle, form a circle wide;
> The sire turn o'er, wi' patriarchal grace,
> The big *ha'-Bible*, aince his *Father's* pride.
> His bonnet rev'rently is laid aside,
> His *lyart haffets* wearing thin and bare;
> Thos strains that once did sweet in Zion glide,
> He wales a portion with judicious care,
> '*And let us worship GOD!*' he says, with solemn air.
> (Burns 2001, 90)

Douglas' films, with their absent, careless fathers, no less than *Another Time, Another Place*'s presentation of "the young woman" trapped in the power of an apparently infertile patriarchy, can thus be seen to "explode effectively the fanciful mythology which has long held sway in romantic tales of Scottish childhood, family and community" (O'Hagan 1993, 207). The abused child and the repressed wife, living in the constrictions of a poverty both material and spiritual, refute Burns's belief in a community where, "With joy unfeign'd, *brothers* and *sisters* meet,/And each for other's welfare kindly speirs," and treat with irony his plea that "Heaven" may "their simple lives prevent/From luxury's contagion" (Burns 2001, 92). Poverty in these films cannot be the basis for communality or for spirituality: such virtues can be encountered only through the people classified by the nation as the 'enemy', prisoners nostalgic for another place.

The debates from which Scottish film criticism emerged, therefore, were ones in which criticism saw its function as *resistance* to the falsehoods apparently endemic to traditional Scottish film—what Colin McArthur dubbed the "Scottish Discursive Unconscious" (McArthur, 1996)—and by the effort to identify and encourage films which, like Douglas and Radford's, could be read as negations of those traditions. This, however, was not an argument about Scottish film culture but about the influence of Scottish culture on film: the source of the problem was in the national culture as much if not more than in the specific conditions under which films were made in Scotland. As Colin McArthur puts it,

> The Scottish Discursive Unconscious has been constructed over several centuries, its key architects including James 'Ossian' MacPherson, Sir Walter Scott, Felix Mendelssohn, Queen Victoria, Sir Edwin Landseer and Sir Harry Lauder. Within it a dream Scotland emerges which is highland, wild, 'feminine,' close to nature and which has, above all, the capacity to enchant and transform the stranger. (McArthur 2003, 12)

It is not film which is the problem but film's inheritance of over two hundred years of Scottish misrepresentation, a misrepresentation which "has come to suffuse every sign system: literature, music, easel painting, photography, advertising, right down to film and television in our own day" (ibid.). It is not film-in-Scotland which is the problem but Scotland itself, the whole development of its history and its culture: "the dire outcome is that, when Scots set out to produce images of their own country, Tartanry and Kailyard exercise a magnetic pull on them, irrespective of what they may wish to do or what they think they are doing" (McArthur 1986, 8). Importantly, this is not simply the condition of any small country in the era of industrialisation and imperial expansion: it is, as Tom Nairn had argued in *The Break-up of Britain* (1977), a situation in which Scotland is unique because "there was to be only one example of a land which—so to speak—'made it' before the onset of the new age of nationalism" (Nairn 1977, 108); "a prodigy among nations, indeed," (ibid., 109) its "previous astonishing precocity led it, quite logically, to what appears as an equally singular 'retardation' or incompleteness in the period which followed" (ibid., 116). Scotland's problem is that it is not *normal*, and "this freak by-product of European history" produces a culture which suffers from 'a characteristic series of sub-national deformations or 'neuroses'" (ibid., 129). Scotland managed to become a "modern" nation without going through the stage of nationalist self-definition which, on the model of nationalism's relation to modernisation as laid out by Ernest Gellner, was to be "typical" of the route to modernity for European nations. As a consequence, its development was "one which naturally appears as 'neurosis' in relation to standard models of development" (ibid., 153). Nairn's ideas helped shape the agenda of the *Scotch Reels* event at the 1982 Edinburgh International Film Festival, and the volume of essays which emerged from it (McArthur 1982), but if Hofer's original account of the neurosis of nostalgia emphasises how it leads to "despondency, melancholia, excessive emotion" and to the decline of the body, then its opposite would be an abnormal fear or dislike of home, one which leads to the revitalisation and the flourishing of the self as soon as it is released from the degenerative condition of a despondent and melancholic homeland.

A word is needed for this profound revulsion from the representation of the nation in Scotland's cultural past, this profound refusal of the nostalgia of/for the homeland. We might designate it, following a suggestion of Fred Davis, as "nostophobia" (Davis 1979). Like Jamie or Janie, the nostophobe can flourish only by recognition of the fact that s/he is a prisoner in a homeland whose history will produce neurosis unless s/he can escape from that destructive environment into one which allows for Nairn's "standard models of development." Nostophobia of this kind was typical of much Scottish culture in the 1960s and 1970s: in an 'Open Letter to Archie Hind', for instance, published in *Scottish International* in October 1971, John Lloyd challenged the form of Hind's support for the workers of the Upper Clyde Shipbuilders:

> The cutting edge is the guilt Scots often appear to feel that they are writers/artists/intellectuals at all, and not part of the nitty gritty of boots and shovel, pick and piece-bag. It's as though they develop a mental castration fear. Having dared to develop the mental organ until it stands up above those of his fellows, the one thing the Scot wants to do is to disguise it, in case someone takes a chop at it. (Lloyd 1971, 17)

By contrast, Lloyd explained how,

> I like living in London much of the time. It was in London that I learned various pleasures like, for example, LSD (the drug), wearing my hair long, that I began to gain a measure of sexual freedom and feel a gradual loosening of the tightness of my own inhibitions. Now all these things could have happened in Govan, perhaps, but in London it was easier. (ibid.)

Scotland is the place where intellectuals are mentally castrated, London where they are sexually liberated. A conference, 'What Kind of Scotland?', sponsored by *Scottish International* in April 1973, was reported by John Herdman in that magazine. His opening paragraph recounts psychiatrist Aaron Eesterson's idea that "people are often driven mad directly by the behaviour towards them of members of their own families," and muses on how, for the audience, this must have raised the question of,

> How far the tensions of a small, cramped national society like that of Scotland, not dissimilar to a family in many ways, may help to induce various kinds of corporate madness in the Scottish people. (Herdman 1973, 11)

Nostophobia assumes that the homeland suffers, and suffers uniquely, from a distortion and repression of the self that can only be cured by flight. So Tom Nairn, in a letter to *Scottish International*, projected a future in which Scots could be the new wandering Jews of Europe, dislocated from their national homeland and so able to escape from the (inevitably) disabling effects of national identity:

> The cultural nationalist invariably sees a fruitful culture as rooted in an internal wealth and psychological development: in the inner depths of the national personality's *Id*, as it were. For him it's roots or nothing. Outside them there is nothing but (I quote again from your editorial of No. 1) 'a colourless or promiscuous internationalism… to nobody's advantage'. But this antithesis itself belongs to the universe of nationalism (as does its corollary, the primary commonplace of the past age, that an achieved nationalism is the necessary precondition of 'true' internationalism)… Europe's new 'Jews' are far more likely to be… delinquents from the outer edge: cultural nomads from the barrens, so to speak. (Nairn 1973, 7)

A new "chosen people" of the post-nationalist world, the Scots would be able to assert their European significance precisely to the extent that they escaped from, rather than commited to, "the national personality's *Id*." Recognising their national—or, at least, their *nationalist*—failure—"not having 'roots' of the requisite kind has been their chief advantage in life" (ibid., 8)—will liberate Scots to become to the true new Europeans. They would become inheritors of an Enlightenment which was built on "our critical ability to rise above a relatively weak national inheritance in a manner at once intellectual and universal in its aim" (ibid., 7). Scots would be allowed thus to fulfil the agenda set by the first issue of *Scottish International*, which insisted that the nation must escape "a self-conscious cultural nationalism… leading to bad habits of stereotyped thinking and unwillingness to look at the situation as it really is" (quoted in ibid., 7). "Look[ing] at the situation as it really is," and in negation of its previously nostalgic representations, is always the claim of the nostophobe: nostalgia conceals, nostophobia reveals.

What such accounts fail to recognise, however, is how ingrained nostophobia has been in modern Scottish culture. The nostophobe always presents his or her realisation of the bleak reality of that culture as a radical breakthrough, as the recovery of sanity in a world of pathological illusion. Nostophobes never acknowledge, however, that their own responses are the expression of a pattern just as powerful—and just as baleful—as the one they want to overthrow. If, as is claimed, nineteenth-century Scotland was the country of nostalgia, then twentieth-century

Scotland has been the country of nostophobia. Far from being the minority opposition in modern Scottish culture, nostophobia has been, in fact, the ideology of the cultural establishment. Ironically, since many nostophobes—like Andrew O'Hagan—are anti-nationalist, the roots of nostophobia are actually in the nationalism of the Scottish Renaissance movement in the years after the First World War. The agenda of "Hugh MacDiarmid," C.M. Grieve's alter ego, was a radical reversal of what he claimed to be nineteenth-century Scottish culture's entrapment in the influence of Robert Burns. "Not Burns, Dunbar" was the slogan, as though the rooting of Scotland in its late medieval creative achievements was not itself the product of Burns' establishment of the significance of Scots, and dependent on the editorial efforts of scholars like David Laing, who had, between the 1830s and 1860s, made the work of the medieval makers available to a modern audience. What the "Back to Dunbar" movement actually signified was a nostophobic rejection of all of Scotland's cultural achievement in the intervening period, as can be seen, for instance, in Neil Gunn's reply to an article that had mocked MacDiarmid's "Back to Dunbar" agenda in 1928:

> Artistically in the modern world Scotland doesn't exist. No music, no drama, no letters, of any international significance. Why is this all-round sterility so complete, so without parallel in the life of any modern nation? Should not an honest attempt be made to answer that question before attacking the very movement that is trying to do so? (Gunn 1987, 150)

Scotland is a country of "all-round sterility." If nostalgia is the outcome of the selective recollection of the nation's noble and harmonious past, then the outcome of nostophobia is an equally selective amnesia which rejects everything that does not fit the degraded and discordant structure of that past. MacDiarmid's nationalism was rooted in just such a rejection and set the pattern for the analysis of Scottish culture through the 1960s and '70s: the major critical assessments of Scottish culture, from Edwin Muir's *Scott and Scotland: the Predicament of the Scottish Writer* (1936) to David Craig's *Scottish Literature and the Scottish People 1680–1830* (1961) to John Speirs' *The Scots Literary Tradition: An Essay in Criticism* (1962) are all accounts of the inevitable decline of Scotland, of the failures and failings of Scottish culture. As David Craig summarised it in an essay in Hugh MacDiarmid's journal *The Voice of Scotland*:

> In a culture so thin and so badly placed as the Scottish there were few conflicts in society that did not lead to waste and confusion. Much of the national spirit, often in rabid form, went into the Low Kirk religion, but its

> spirit… was irreconcilable with the cultivated ethos… it led directly to the Disruption of 1843. This is another of the deep dis-unities which ran off the energies of the 18th century Scotland into dispute and partisan bitterness, anyway characteristic of the race, which made for a stultifying monotony of idiom, religious, political, poetic—an inhumane extreme of partiality, in which positions defined themselves more by violence of opposition than by their positive natures. (Craig 1956/57, 28)

Scotland is a place incapable of achieving "the cultivated ethos" because of the "partisan bitterness… characteristic of the race."

This nostophobic negation of Scotland as a place of value could only be satisfied by the presentation of the nation as a place from which, like a prisoner of war, one felt almost legally required to attempt to escape. Douglas' *Trilogy* did not arrive, in other words, simply as a filmic challenge to the nostalgic traditions of Scottish film-making but as a filmic fulfilment of the long-established nostophobia of much of the Scottish intelligentsia. Thus, Jamie's liberation in part three of the *Trilogy* comes in Egypt, when he is shut up in an army camp—when he has become the equivalent of those POWs with whom, as a boy, he had consorted. Of course, nostalgia for him is impossible—he has no home to mourn—and so he has to learn the value of "home" from someone else's nostalgia, that of his friend Robert for England. "Home" is written across Robert's calendar on the day their tour of duty is due to end and as they prepare to leave Robert invites Jamie to visit him. The film concludes with a long-held image of a rich orchard in bloom, the place to which Robert invites Jamie to "look us up; you can call it home." The orchard home is the absolute antithesis of the treeless landscapes of the Egyptian desert in which they have met, a desert which also metaphorically replicates the infertile desert in which Jamie has grown up. Through Jamie's soldiering, in his deployment far from home, Douglas effectively backtracks into the origins of the word "nostalgia" but allows Jamie—like generations of Scottish intellectuals—to acquire his nostalgia at second hand, nostalgia for a culture whose past has a real "cultivated ethos."

Through the influence of Douglas' work the well-established nostophobia of Scotland's mid-century culture has become inscribed into its contemporary film culture. It is both parodied and reinforced in *Trainspotting* (Boyle, GB, 1996) in Renton's rant (located in symbolically "Scottish" natural scenery) about Scotland as country so unfit that it has been colonised by "wankers", and in the narrative of Lynne Ramsay's much acclaimed *Ratcatcher* (GB/Fr, 1999), a film full of allusions to and echoes of Douglas' *Trilogy*. *Ratcatcher* is built around a family's desire for a new home, a desire that is continually undermined by the condition of a country which is, quite literally, because of the bin-men's strike, a midden. The family's utopian walk through a field of corn to a new home at the film's conclusion is an ironic version of Douglas' orchard—except that it is a scene which cannot ever occur in reality, being the unrealisable after-image of their son's utopian hopes as he commits suicide. *Ratcatcher* constructs an image of its culture and its society in which the only possible desire is not nostalgia for a lost past but nostalgia for a promised future that will never happen. Simply because it has switched its nostalgia from past to future, or, in Douglas' case, from Scotland to England, does not make it any the less nostalgic. Nostophobia is always the doorway to an alternative nostalgia.

Indeed, Douglas' *Trilogy*, despite all the plaudits about its "realism," runs on the most conventional of narrative lines about working-class life. A boy or a young man with a special talent—think of *This Sporting Life* (Anderson, GB, 1963), *Kes* (Loach, GB, 1969), *Billy Elliot* (Daldry, GB/Fr, 2000) or even *The Full Monty* (Cattaneo, GB, 1997)—allows Douglas both to explore a working-class environment while insisting on the individual's ability to transcend it. It is a transcendence, however, which is either temporary—the protagonist is drawn, inevitably and tragically, back into the limitations of the community from which he has sought escape—or, if permanent, simply emphasises how rare and arbitrary such escapes must be. Douglas plays a skilful game with this narrative: Jamie is allowed to tell his family and to tell Robert that he hopes to be an artist or a film director, and the head of the "home" to which he is sent tells his father he ought to be sent to art school, but unlike the protagonists of the other British working-class films mentioned above we never see him actually engaged in activity which will lead to this conclusion. Jamie's life, therefore, is presented as being bleakly empty of creative activity, while Douglas' own was in fact the reverse: his obsession with film was not only sufficient to get him regularly into the local cinemas but to inspire him to send off drawings to Hollywood film studios in the hope of getting a job. No such efforts divert Jamie from his inner torment. The absence of such creative activity in what we see of Jamie's life allows him to seem trapped within the determining boundaries of his working-class experience: his assertion that he wants to be an artist or film director remains, at the level of plot, merely utopian—except, of course, that the film itself is its realisation.

In other words, the "realism" of Douglas' *Trilogy* is selectively *unrealistic*; it is through the suppression of the real events of Douglas' own life that it generates its iconic, nostophobic power. There is a moment, however, at the beginning of *My Ain Folk* when the black-and-white of the rest of the film is suddenly displaced by colour—the colour of a *Lassie* film with a backdrop of American pastoral by which the boy's upturned face is mesmerised. The film immediately cuts, of course, to the contrastingly bleak and colourless world of the coal mining town, but it points to what Douglas himself acknowledged in his essay "Palace of Dreams:"

> For as long as I can remember I always liked the pictures. As a boy I spent so much time in cinemas, a friend suggested I take my bed with me. I would have, had it been possible. That was my real home, my happiest place when I was lucky enough to be there. Outside, whether in the village or the city, whether I was seven or seventeen, it always seemed to be raining or grey and my heart would sink to despairing depths. I hated reality. (Douglas 1978)

"Home" is, in effect, the world of film: it is the world of film itself for which Jamie and Douglas are nostalgic, and which drives their nostophobia towards their actual home.

Because the theory of film has been driven largely from and in relation to the major producing centres, we take too little account of the extent to which cinema, in the first half of the twentieth century, quite literally displaced and made redundant the traditions of local popular culture. In the music halls which the cinemas replaced, even touring companies would incorporate material specifically tailored to their local audience, or would incorporate specifically local performers. The music hall's mode of address was interactive: film, as Adorno and Horkheimer disenchantedly pointed out, was not only consumed passively but was designed to encourage passivity:

> All the other films and products of the entertainment industry which they [the audience] have seen have taught them what to expect: they react automatically. The might of industrial society is lodged in men's minds. (Adorno and Horkheimer 1979, 126)

The effect, Adorno and Horkheimer believed, was one in which,

> The whole world is made to pass through the filter of the culture industry. The old experience of the movie-goer, who sees the world outside as an extension of the film he has just left (because the latter is intent upon reproducing the world of everyday perceptions), is now the producer's guideline… Real life is becoming indistinguishable from the movies. (ibid.)

This may have been the case in Frankfurt, Berlin, Paris or in the Los Angeles where Adorno and Horkheimer had taken refuge during the Second World War and where *The Dialectic of Enlightenment* (1944) was written, but movies had the absolutely opposite effect in places which had no access to the scale of audience and the scale of industrial production necessary for making them. Instead of "real life becoming indistinguishable from the movies," the movies represented a "real" life which rendered the actuality of local culture empty, insignificant, and unrealisable within the creative processes of modernity. Life had to imitate the elsewhere of the movies—as John Byrne's plays comedically insisted—if there was to be a continuity between film culture and local culture. Douglas, sitting down to create a film after he graduated from film school, could not attempt costume drama or adaptations of contemporary novels because of cost. The restrictions of the medium for which he was writing forced him to write about his childhood: "strangely enough, my trilogy is not about a dream world, but about the real landscape I had wanted so badly to escape from" (Douglas 1978). Except, of course, it is not "the real landscape" but the nostophobic recollection of that landscape as refracted through its absence from the world of film, through its estrangement from the filmic world, through its creator's and its protagonist's nostalgia to be at home in the world of film. The form of film, in its mid-twentieth-century technological development, insisted that local culture could only be represented as a nostalgic place lost in time or as its nostophobic antithesis, a place for which no nostalgia is possible. The latter, however, is still a world of *escape* to audiences in Venice or Cannes or New York.

That the narratives of Scottish films are driven by modes of escapism—whether the escapism of the fantasy narratives of *Whisky Galore!* or *Local Hero* or the escapism of the "realistic" films which show someone, like Jamie, fleeing his destructive environment—is not a commentary upon Scotland but a commentary on the nature of film itself in the first fifty years of its development. Film is an inherently nostalgic medium: even the most "realistic" of movies frames a time which, through time, becomes "another time, another place," and the possible location of a lost emotional homeland. Film made its audiences, like Jamie and Janie, homeless at home, nostalgic for that other time, that other place of the film itself—which those audiences could then be sold as a real place to visit in the form of Disneyland.

Walter Scott, despite the abuse heaped on him for creating a national nostalgia, never allowed his readers to forget that they were *readers* and that the purpose of their reading was founded on the pleasure of illusion, on what Sandy Stranger, in Muriel Spark's *The Prime of Miss Jean Brodie*

(1961), calls "The Transfiguration of the Commonplace" (Spark 1965, 35)—a feat achieved, incidentally, by the novel itself but not by the film based on it. It is such a transfiguration of the commonplace that Douglas' *Trilogy* achieves—a transfiguration just as magical, and just as distant from representational realism, as the films—like *Whisky Galore!* or *Gregory's Girl* (Forsyth, GB, 1981)—to which it has been so regularly opposed. Nostophobia is no escape from nostalgia: it is the product of that profound nostalgia for film itself which was produced by the first wave of globalised mass entertainment. As Andrew O'Hagan nostalgically recalls, a Scottish childhood was one in which "'I stretched out on the grass chewing my hands, reading about the lives of American movie stars in large-format colour books," one in which "I lost myself in "Garbo's laugh, Lombard's crash, or Marilyn's fatal affairs with the Kennedys" (O'Hagan 1993, 205). Nostophobia is not an escape from national nostalgia: it begins and ends in identification with someone else's nostalgia.

## Works Cited

Adorno, Theodor and Max Horkheimer. 1979. *Dialectic of Enlightenment*. London: Verso.

Burns, Robert. 2001. *The Canongate Burns*. Ed. Andrew Noble and Patrick Scott Hogg. Edinburgh: Canongate.

Craig, David. 1956/57. Burns and Scottish Culture. *The Voice of Scotland: A Quarterly Magazine of Scottish Arts and Affairs* VII 3-4: 24-32.

—. 1961. *Scottish Literature and the Scottish People 1680–1830*. London: Chatto & Windus.

Davis, Fred. 1979. *Yearning for Yesterday: a Sociology of Nostalgia*. London: Collier Macmillan.

Douglas, Bill. 1978. Palace of Dreams: The Making of a Film Maker. http://www.ex.ac.uk/bdc/palace.shtml (accessed November 15, 2008).

Gunn, Neil. 1987. *Landscape and Light: Essays by Neil Gunn*. Ed. Alastair McCleery. Aberdeen: Aberdeen University Press.

Herdman, John. 1973. What Kind of Scotland? *Scottish International* May/June/July: 11.

Kesson, Jessie. 1983. *Another Time, Another Place*. Edinburgh: B&W.

Lloyd, John. 1971. Open Letter to Archie Hind. *Scottish International*, October 17.

McArthur, Colin, ed. 1982. *Scotch Reels: Scotland in Cinema and Television*. London: British Film Institute.

—. 1986. *The Cinema Image of Scotland*. London: Tate Gallery.

—. 1996. The Scottish Discursive Unconscious. In *Scottish Popular Theatre and Entertainment: historical and critical approaches to theatre and film in Scotland*, ed. Alasdair Cameron & Adrienne Scullion, 81-89. Glasgow: Glasgow University Library Publications.

—. 2003. *Brigadoon, Braveheart and the Scots: Distortions of Scotland in Hollywood Cinema*. London: I. B. Tauris.

McMillan, Joyce. 1993. Women in the Bill Douglas Trilogy. In *Bill Douglas: A Lanternist's Account*, eds. Eddie Dick, Andrew Noble & Duncan Petrie, 219-226. London: British Film Institute.

Muir, Edwin. 1982. *Scott and Scotland: the Predicament of the Scottish Writer*. Edinburgh: Polygon.

Murray, Jonathan. 2004. *That Thinking Feeling: a Research Guide to Scottish Cinema 1938-2004*. Edinburgh/Glasgow: Edinburgh College of Art/Scottish Screen.

Nairn, Tom. 1973. Letter to the Editors. *Scottish International* April: 7-8.

—. 1977. *The Break-Up of Britain: Crisis and Neo-Nationalism.* London: New Left Books.

Nash, Andrew. 2007. *Kailyard and Scottish Literature*. New York: Rodopi.

O'Hagan, Andrew. 1993. Homing. In *Bill Douglas: A Lanternist's Account*, eds. Eddie Dick, Andrew Noble & Duncan Petrie, 205-218. London: British Film Institute.

Spark, Muriel. 1965. *The Prime of Miss Jean Brodie*. Harmondsworth: Penguin.

Speirs, John. 1962. *The Scots Literary Tradition: An Essay in Criticism.* London: Faber & Faber.

# THEY KNOW WHERE THEY'RE GOING: LANDSCAPE AND PLACE IN SCOTTISH CINEMA

MARILYN REIZBAUM

The Highland scene in Danny Boyle's *Trainspotting* (GB, 1996) has been much touted. Adapted and expanded upon from Irvine Welsh's 1993 novel by screenwriter John Hodge, the sequence deploys Scottish landscape as the *sine qua non* of the cinematic. The landscape becomes conscious prop, counterpoised with a countervailing, rivalling or superseding landscape that is the urban space, posited as real space—parodically, really "Scottish". Poised on the mini-platform of a rural train station as though it were a life raft, the boys are afraid to step off into the yonder, which, now displaced from its former glory as the real McCoy, promises no relief. "Well what are you waiting for... doesn't it make you proud to be Scottish?" Tommy (Kevin McKidd) asks as he moves into the frame, striding toward the hills. Renton (Ewan McGregor)'s rant brings the view into view as colonised space: "it's shite being Scottish." They conclude that a walk in the country is no shot in the arm.

It is not the aim of this essay to illustrate the misdirected legacy of the filmic production of the Scottish highland landscape as nationally authentic/nation location, evident in films like *Braveheart* (Gibson, USA, 1995) or even *Local Hero* (Forsyth, GB, 1983). It is my intention instead to elaborate on Colin MacArthur's idea about a "Scottish Discursive Unconscious" (McArthur 1996). Though labelled as such by McArthur only in the mid '90s, as Duncan Petrie notes, the idea has been used consistently by McArthur and others to argue that externally produced images of Scotland typically "naturalise[] essentially negative or regressive images of Scotland and Scots" (Petrie 2005, 214). Here, I question this contention by examining an "outside" view of Scottish discursive spaces by directors like Hitchcock, Michael Powell and Ken Loach.

Critics like Petrie argue that *The 39 Steps* (Hitchcock, GB, 1935) and *The Edge of the World* (Powell, GB, 1937) "in different ways characterise the dominant external cinematic construction of Scotland," (Petrie 2000, 32) but by this I think Petrie means that such films offer a non-authentic vision and it is this assumption I wish to interrogate. It would seem logical to implicate these early outside influences in the production of a certain notion of Scottish authenticity in film, but I will argue, perhaps counter-intuitively, that their interest in and employment of the Scottish backdrop for their own filmic purposes, at least in the cases of Powell and Hitchcock, *exposes* the naturalizing process that McArthur identifies (McArthur 1982, 68). Furthermore, the landscape itself, in all of its empty splendour, is such a regressive image of Scotland, being a product of a history of political erasure, thereby ironically becoming a major aspect of "dominant regimes of imagery" (McLoone 2001, 185). Though the producers of *Brigadoon* (Minnelli, USA, 1954), for example, are often reviled for the choice to set the film in a Hollywood studio in order to realise or match their idea of the Highland dreamscape, the terms of their move might serve to turn the plaint back on their detractors: it's not actually the authentic Scotland Minnelli and his colleagues were unable to find, but the imagined one (see Hardy 1990, 1; McArthur 2003, 70-71). One could argue that the filmmakers then did not understand that the landscape they encountered was as "mythical" or trumped up in some sense as the one they sought, but that is somehow beside the point. The famously reverberating remark attributed to *Brigadoon* producer Arthur J. Freed is that in Scotland, he could find nothing that looked like "Scotland." After all, in a film that is about the construction of American mythscapes in a Cold War era, Minnelli *et al.* seemed to know where they were going when choosing the Hollywood set as location.

One deeply ironic effect of the Clearances was to etch more finely into the Highland landscape the signature barrenness that would be and is still today equated with its majesty—the ruse of unoccupied space (because occupied politically), the roaming sheep, the engineered view. In being a kind of monitor of that history, film's employment of that landscape also provides a practical view of certain debates in the film industry, between the realism or documentarism of the '20s and '30s and the new film aesthetic, provided by the "pure cinema" of Alfred Hitchcock or the "composed film" (Christie 1994, 69) of Michael Powell (and Emeric Pressburger), for example. An unintended effect, perhaps, of this employment has been to deepen the irony in the re-mastering of these landscapes into backdrops even while producing a witting and uncanny sense of them as providing a backdrop to a (film) history the films are making. Furthermore, in becoming a fetish object—a result, in part, of the erasures that have produced it—the landscape is often suggestive of the gnomonic, delimited by what's missing, a political castration.

I want to consider this idea of the fetish or manufactured landscape by looking at three early films, two by Powell—*The Edge of the World*, *I Know Where I'm Going!* (Powell and Pressburger, GB, 1945)—and one by Hitchcock—*The 39 Steps*—along with two of Ken Loach's late-'90s/early-'00s Scottish trilogy—*My Name is Joe* (Sp/It/Fr/GB/Ger, 1998), *Sweet Sixteen* (GB/Ger/Sp, 2002)—that utilise the Scottish setting in this way. In using Loach here, I am not only drawing a line of non-native filmmakers' engagement with Scotland, but also working against the perception of his work as reductively documentarist, just as his precursors, in particular Powell, resisted that model of filmic authentication (both for the subject and the medium). Ken Loach's aims in this regard might be seen as more ideological and discursive and less filmic in nature, but I argue he uses the landscape in conjunction with his idea of disclosure—bringing his subjects into view by way of what the camera can see. Loach sees landscapes and politics as eminently intertwined. And it is my contention that the encounter between place and director was transformative for each. Many have discussed the set that the Scottish landscape provides for filmmakers, but few have addressed it as set, a filmic beneficiary of a historical byproduct.

Powell and Hitchcock notably used the Scottish landscape in their early films. In fact, both are said to have cut their cinematic teeth on the films that feature it prominently—*The 39 Steps, The Edge of the World, The Spy in Black* (Powell and Pressburger, GB, 1939), *I Know Where I'm Going*! Some effort has been made to explain their choice of remote sites (see Moor 2005, 118). Powell, Hitchcock and Loach are, of course, technically outsider directors, non-natives who identify the Scottish space as other in some way, and yet they are also at once British, technically working at home (see Petrie 2000, 32-33). Part of the relevant Scottish history requires an observance of the certain splits that delimit the landscape—north from south, Highland from Lowland, island from mainland, insider from outsider—in both geographical and psychic ways. When looking at these films together one finds a remarkable affinity in the use of location, actors, stories of disinheritance, right down to the music.

The idea of "erasure" or invisibility/emptiness when talking about landscapes is of course both paradoxical and here to the point. *The 39 Steps* is ostensibly about espionage but it is often observed that Hitchcock's film empties the source—John Buchan's 1914 novel—of its theme of wartime British patriotism. It becomes a heuristic move to do so, in that the narrative skeleton becomes a disguise or camouflage for the "real" intrigue of illicit encounters: those potentially amorous meetings between Hannay and Annabella, Hannay and Margaret, and Hannay and

Pamela, whose *amore* is clinched. Robert Donat plays the incidental spy, who is presented as, not so incidentally, Canadian, and therefore a colonial rather than an Englishman. This is one of the details Hitchcock changes from the novel, where Hannay is a Scot displaced to South Africa—about the same difference, except that this permits another kind of switch on the part of Hitchcock, where he himself, in a sense, is now the English intruder, producing a common feature of, especially, Kailyard Scottish film. Annabella, the Garbo-ish actual spy for hire, with Germanish accent in tow, is played by Lucie Mannheim, a German actress of Jewish background, expelled by the Nazis, adding yet another layer to the backdrop of erasures and intrigue. Margaret, the oppressed or abused wife in the austere Highland croft, is notably played by Peggy Ashcroft, in one of her first film appearances. Finally, Pamela is one of Hitchcock's first blondes, played by Madeleine Carroll. One might say further that the film's focus is on camouflage or concealment and in this way the setting becomes a symbol of its intent. While part of its focus is the perfectability of the machine—the human mind as machine (Mr. Memory), but most importantly the machine that is the camera—the film is chiefly concerned with the idea of undetectability and the way the camera mimics this idea, ostensibly concealing itself in the act (Hitchcock's cameos doubly mimic this double role of disguise, the passive bystander, no less). The novel's aims and even the novel itself, one might say, constitute the MacGuffin of the film, a term coined by Scottish screenwriter Angus MacPhail with a Highland motif that embodies the idea of camouflage that the setting represents (see Truffaut 1967, 138). In his adaptation, Hitchcock reveals his fetish subjects—femme fatales and invasive machines. What you see is hidden in plain sight, in that the empty space is the purloined landscape; the art of detection is nothing more and nothing less than another form of scopophilia, with a particular investment in the view.

Hitchcock adapts Buchan's novel in three important ways for our consideration here: he changes and displaces the book's central figure as marked in the title, thereby conflating the subject and the location—in the novel, the "thirty-nine steps" refer to a secret landing place for a spy airplane, actual steps, whereas in the film it is the code name for the spy ring (Blackstone in the novel); he changes the nature of the secret from plans to thwart a German invasion into Britain to plans for the development of silent (read, undetectable) aircraft; he imports the subplot of Mr. Memory in the London Palladium as a way of framing the story—he is a freak whose performance of remembering is the warped key that unlocks the secret. All of these changes, I would argue, pertain to the Hitchcockian method, bringing the novel to heel on its terms.

While unlocking is certainly a prominent motif in *The 39 Steps*, akin to the metaphor of detection, Hitchcock is purported to have said in this connection that "what interests him is the drama of being handcuffed" (Spoto 1999, 148-149). The famous handcuffs that bind Pamela and Hannay are strangely notational of romance. The image of the couple's joined hands in the very last shot of the film is marked by the dangling cuffs, still attached to Hannay, and retroactively to the illicit nature of their initial connection—the aggressively stolen kiss on the train and the famous bedroom scene in which Hannay initially cuffs them together. This image of the cuffs, of course, is suggestive in a number of ways, doing the double work of both policing and enabling transgressive acts. The handcuffs themselves, so prominent in the film, suggest, too, Hitchcock's takeover of Buchan's tale, where the "plan" may be in the wrong hands. This idea of "wrong hands," like that other common theme in Hitchcock films of the "wrong man," or mistaken identity, brings together the political and romantic plots in keeping with Hitchcock's persistent insinuation in his films of romance as male entrapment, a destabilization or opening up of what should read as the triumph over foreign threat (see Devas 2005, 45-54). Like the old chestnut the real master spy Jordan (Godfrey Tearle) offers Hannay in his Highland hideout, when referring to his own efforts at deception—"I guess I've been leading you down the garden path—or is that 'up' the path?"—the local(e) is all-encompassing and revealing. Jordan's worry about getting the idiom with its lewd insinuation wrong, expressed in his qualification, is what displays his non-nativism; either direction produces the same outcome here. The subterfuge, as the plot unfolds, is in the romance of the landscape doubling as the romantic entwinement of the couple.

Garden paths return us to the up and down or the north and south of the Scottish landscape and to the first and perhaps major of Hitchcock's alterations of the source, as mentioned above. In the same way that the ending of *The 39 Steps* brings together the frames of espionage and romance or the "real" *politik* and performance, so, too, the title's transcription of the film conflates the location with the subject, i.e. the meeting place becomes the whole operation. We see Hitchcock's adaptation configured in his adjustment of the title of the novel from the number written in letters to numerals. What this suggests, despite the popular assumption that the subject presented by that title is the film's MacGuffin, is that, in fact, the setting, or the set, the *mise-en-scène*, let's say, is the story. The numeral "39" becomes the visual notation of Hitchcock's pure cinema. This aim is beautifully realised in Jordan's decorous presentation to Hannay of the view from his window in the fabricated location of *Alt na Shellach*, a view of which he proclaims they (he and his spy family) are very proud. This becomes a pretense for menacing Hannay with the visual of the police combing the landscape, just as the invitation in the view belies a history of treachery. This mechanical intrusion, as it were, into the landscape is everywhere: from the Highland rail with its Flying Scotsman, the keystone cops swarming like sheep, to the motor cars (Hannay's so-called disguise is comically as a motor mechanic looking for work in the Highlands), to the remarkable hovering helicopter, doubling as a camera, perhaps, though it looks more like something out of *The War of the Worlds*. These intrusions along with the natural features of water—the sheep are not natural to the landscape, of course, having been imported—highlight the artificiality of the natural setting, which the stern crofter claims was made by God, unlike the city: Hitchcock's little joke. This mechanical onslaught upon the landscape, which seems to repopulate it, in a kind of perverse turnaround of history's denuding of it, is reminiscent of Hitchcock's use of other monumental intrusions into the landscape, such as Mt. Rushmore in *North by Northwest* (USA, 1959). This production of the ruined idyll, while bringing "Hitchcock" into view, perhaps not so coincidentally provides a corrective to the manipulation of the space by history.

Finally, to conclude at the beginning, when Annabella—the spy who invites herself out of the cold into Hannay's flat—staggers into his bedroom with a knife in her back, she clutches a map of the Highlands of Scotland. The location *Alt na Shellach*—which is fabricated—is circled. But the viewer can hardly make it out as the camera has focused on a site to the right of this, an actual place in the area of Rannoch Moor, called KILLIN, written on the map in capitals. In this view, the camera almost loses sight of the key location, the drop spot, revealing instead the symbolic coincidence of the sinister surroundings. This is classic Hitchcock "slapshtick," throwing us off in every sense, bringing us in for the kill, as it were. It is important to note that Hitchcock made another major change in the adaptation from Buchan's novel, by moving the Scottish location from the Borders to the Highlands, knowing, it seems, that the latter would provide more potential for such MacGuffinesque diversions and appreciating, as an Englishman can, majesty's potential for kitsch.

My interest in this general topic began with Michael Powell's *The Edge of the World*, filmed entirely on Foula, the westernmost of the Shetland Islands. This is the film that brought Powell the acclaim that made his career. As Powell tells it, he had become fascinated with an account he had read of the forced evacuation of St Kilda, in the Outer

Hebrides, but unable to film there, he found Foula instead (which he names Hirta in the film, meaning "death" in Gaelic). The abandonment of St Kilda was reflective of the changing economy, which made the sustenance of such remote life unviable, and though seemingly distant from the Clearances, it was, in fact, a reenactment of the earlier scene, since the islanders still served at the pleasure of the laird, as Powell's film shows. Sheep figure prominently; indeed, the evacuation could be seen as an inverted exodus and this play on a homecoming is suggestive of the inversion of intent that obtains in the landscape. A BBC documentary made some 50 years later (and contained as an extra on Image Entertainment's 2003 DVD re-release of *The Edge of the World*) returned Powell to Foula with several of the actors from the film. In a strange reminiscence, the interviewed inhabitants recount the benefits and drawbacks of Powell's choice of their island: paradoxically, the attention they received came hand-in-hand with an expectation of their departure from the island, documented so dramatically by *The Edge of the World.* Powell and his film seemed to forget that they were just acting. As becomes clear in Powell's work here, the act is necessary. Much of what has been said about Hitchcock's use of the landscape may be applied to Powell's cinematic aims. Additionally, in this and his other Scottish films (*The Spy in Black*, *I Know Where I'm Going!*), he taps into the hyper-real as well as the melodrama of the elements to produce a highly stylised effect. The power here is less sinister than in Hitchcock and more dangerous. Like *The 39 Steps*, the title (*The Edge of the World*) works to conflate the setting with the subject of such danger—the edges are everywhere, including the double edge of the island's allure. This early film (1937) is often lauded for being a paean to island life, or more accurately, to the death of the island; situated on the other side of his career from what has been claimed by many to be the making and unmaking of it—*Peeping Tom* (GB, 1960)—*The Edge of World*'s loving lens seems no less fixated on killing.

In the climactic scene of the epic race between the island scions, representing the split within the community between those who see evacuation as inevitable and are willing to go with it (not as simple as an embrace of the modern) and those who are intransigent (their attitude, again, not simply portrayed), the lighting behind the beckoningly majestic and deadly cliff works like a kind of curtain. As Robbie Manson (Eric Berry) falls to his death, the camera cuts to the stylised image, the montage of affect—the grandmother's profile, the silent tragic chorus that is the women standing on the cliff; and everywhere, such as in the water that moves through the scene coincident with the fall, as if a curtain on a stage, the scenery's foreclosure on the history. It is the stuff of optical illusion, throwing the viewer emotionally off-kilter since the images of the landscape are consistently double: it has an artificial—comic, melodramatic, almost kitsch—quality that is continuous with the framing mood of tragedy. Unlike the symbolism of Russian or surrealist film, where the naturalistic image may be cut or hyperbolised in some way, here the ostensible real is the special effect that produces the melodrama.

The plot as such seems quite predictable, even sentimental: the families are estranged; the sister of the boy who falls to his death is forbidden from marrying his rival who survives; he leaves and she has his baby, unbeknownst to him; the families are reunited through the baby, and despite the new life are forced to leave the island. But the audience cannot predict the landscape, which remains steadfastly moody and dramatic. Powell was lauded for his dramatic camera work and some, like the documentarist John Grierson, tried to cast the film as documentary. But Powell resisted for good reason. After all, the island was only acting. In what is a different kind of rehearsal of the history of erasures in Scotland from that of Hitchcock, Powell's meta-narrative fixates on the idea of a lost horizon—a cinematographically piquing proposition in its own right—on the landscape's quality of being an extension of the camera... peeping back at him.

Whereas the final image of *The 39 Steps* are the joined hands, cuffs dangling, the last of *The Edge of the World* is the small gravestone of Peter Manson (John Laurie), the father of the boy who dies in the race, who himself dies when climbing down one of the cliffs to retrieve a chimerical egg—what is meant to be a memento of his lost island. Instead, the island loses (or keeps?) him. Each concluding frame acts as a kind of insigne or motto whose subject is co-optation, disguised as co-operation. Manson's epitaph reads "GONE OVER." Indeed, *he* has become the *memento mori* of an irretrievable history and a marker of a shift in Powell's filmmaking to a concern with the medium, not at the expense of the setting, but in tune with it.

*I Know Where I'm Going!*, coming eight years after *Edge...* and being one of the first Archers' films with Powell's directorial partner Emeric Pressburger, does similar things. It is distinguished from the earlier film in a number of ways, but mostly by its humour. The film's subject is "fancy," with its double entendre of a play on magical space and articulated desire. Much has been made of this film as fairy story, a romantic homage to the mystical Scottish landscape, and many have compared it to *Brigadoon* in its seeming offer of a "timeless never-never land" refuge. Others point to the serious undertow of post-war anti-materialism in it, or the subplot of repressed desire (see, for instance, Petrie 2000, 39; Moor 2005, 118-125). *I Know Where I'm Going!* begins with and sustains throughout a pronounced mockery of pretentious wealth as represented by the (never-seen) industrialist Bellinger, whom Joan Webster (Wendy Hiller) is going to Killoran to marry—for his money, it is suggested. It ends with her turnabout toward Torquil (Roger Livesey), the somewhat disenfranchised laird of Killoran, and away from the island itself. In every case, the audience is "charmed," an apt and misleading term in assessments of the film.

In the commentary presented as part of the 2001 New Criterion DVD re-release package, both Kevin Macdonald and Ian Christie suggest that Highland history is a backdrop to the film, if not directly in evidence. Christie comments that the effect of the *mise-en-scène* is always of empty space, regardless of the number of people who may be in any scene. Even more interesting, Macdonald, Pressburger's grandson, makes the claim for the film as having a Continental sensibility, in the rhetorical and mystical dimensions of the place. He hears, for example, the inflection of Yiddish (Bashevis Singer folk wisdom) in Torquil's retort to Joan's initial, unseeing query about the impoverishment of her surroundings. The islanders are not poor—they just have no money: "that is something entirely different," he avers. It is true that several other members of the production team, along with Hungarian Pressburger, were Jewish continentals: musical composer and director Allan Gray, production and art designer Alfred Junge, cinematographer Erwin Hillier. Even Powell, Macdonald suggests, is foreign to Scotland, not only because he was English-born, but also because he had done most of his film study in France. This sense broadens the political implications in the analogue of a kind of Diasporic space of displacement, both for the Scots and the Jews, themselves historically aligned as out of place in the Kingdom, here connected through a kind of collusion of representation: the landscape is symbolic. The film is filled with thresholds framed in darkness, as when Joan steps into the somewhat dilapidated grand house on Mull (the island where the film is set), a seeming ruined idyll, before setting off on the treacherous journey to Killoran, here both a symbolic space and like Hitchcock's Killin, actual. Such symbolic thresholds are reminders of the composed or synthetic cinema that Powell sought to perfect (independent framing that permits technological ingenuity, such as the managing of Roger Livesey's absence from the location shoot): the Highland setting is counter-intuitively, it might seem, most suitable for the creation or manufacture of "authentic space."

Those who would object to such a reading, having been charmed by a seeming romantic view, should consider certain scenes: for instance, the tartan hills that figure in Joan's train nightmare as she moves up to Scotland from England on what she calls the "Scotch express." In her dream, she envisions her wedding and her transformation into the magnate dowager. As the train gets closer to her dream destination—she tells her father when she announces to him her imminent betrothal that she has been to Killoran in her dreams many times, sufficient, it seems, to feel familiar—we see her bizarre dreamscape and the voiceover announces the arrival at the Scotland/England border, yet another dark threshold. The musical accompaniment to this scene is "The Banks of Loch Lomond," fitting in how its sentiment of loss has been rehabilitated into the sentimental anthem of kitsch Scottishness, conveyed often in a jaunty tempo. The images of the overlaid hills in Joan's dream have a similar kitsch quality, as though an unconscious projection of the imposition of tartan, yet another example of constructed Scottishness arising out of the erasures and then re-appropriation of clan dress produced by the eighteenth-century Act of Proscription and its subsequent revocation by the British Parliament (Trevor-Roper 1983). The symbolic import of this vision beyond Joan's personal drama provides in yet another sense the return of the repressed.

Another telling counter-example comes in the climactic Corryvreckan scene (the Gaelic Charybdis), so much like the one in *Edge...* that also employs the squall curtain, making Powell's "composed cinema" palpably apparent. The curtain seems to come down on the direction Joan thought she was headed in; the storm closes in on the boat, pushing it toward the whirlpool, as Joan moves to secure her trousseau, which promptly "goes over." In this scene, Joan, too, goes over, to the legend of Corryvreckan, whose telling is only completed by Torquil at this precarious moment. The legend as used here is rife with modern tropes of consuming desire and tests of love that involve the breaking of bonds or bounds. In order to go over to Killoran, doubling as the disenfranchised laird, she has to break faith with Bellinger, and not arrive. *I Know Where I'm Going!* in fact ends very like *The 39 Steps*. Torquil, too, goes over to legend by breaking the curse of the Castle of Moy. By stepping over its dark threshold, he submits to the curse that will render him a prisoner, "chained to the woman he loves until the end of his days." The sinister implication is reminiscent of Hitchcock's ambivalent takes on love, though here the message is discursively rather than notationally rendered, in the inscription of the curse that appears outside the castle: the legend underwrites the image of the happy couple, standing in the ruins, seeming more ambivalent about the idealised setting than the romance. Moor has suggested the film displays the directors' typical scepticism towards the primacy of either the camera or the natural landscape and that the ancient myths that they bring into play, full of loss and bloodshed, "offer no rosy view of Old Scotland as utopia" (Moor 2005, 124). He concludes that "'Real Scotland' is just within the film's reach, but it is its re-creation which makes the viewer long for its distant reality (ibid, 120).

There are a number of remarkable correspondences between these early films by Hitchcock and Powell, the latter, younger man perhaps paying homage to the former, elder one. Powell worked for Hitchcock as a stills photographer on *Blackmail* (GB, 1928) and *Champagne* (GB, 1929). Both directors appear in their respective works (Powell taking a small acting role in *Edge...*), though such appearances did not become signature for Powell. Scottish actor John Laurie appears in *The 39 Steps*, *Edge...* and *I Know Where I'm Going!*. In one of the more uncanny connections, the same music is used in the climactic scenes of both *The 39 Steps* and *Edge...*, though they are not attributed to the same source in the films' respective credits. The well-known editor Derek Twist worked for both directors. While I cannot make a direct connection between Powell's early interest in the Scottish landscape and Hitchcock's uses of it in *The 39 Steps*, it seems unsurprising that this landscape and history would suit the early aims of directors who sought a departure from the mainstream British film industry in their own backyard—whose hiddenness in plain sight became their heuristic subjects.

Turning to Ken Loach's Scottish films, we encounter a director acutely aware of the politics of landscape and the politics of the British Isles. Loach is both lauded and dismissed for foregrounding politics in his film work, his brand of British realism sometimes seen as a throwback to the documentarism Hitchcock and Powell eschewed. But Loach is not interested in authenticity so much as in an aesthetics of real politics (not necessarily *realpolitik*). Pre-'90s British critical dismissals of Loach tended to focus on a critique of what was seen as his retrograde form or (Marxist) politics. In recent years, however, Loach has come slowly back into favour in the contemporary moment's return to or search for the "real," a return to what is now the art of documentary—the "unpremeditated documentary look" (English 2006, 262). My initial approach to Loach came through work on Scottish and Irish intersections, and Loach's continuing interest in both places has been salutary. In his Scottish films (as elsewhere in his career) Loach often throws an idealised rural setting into relief by contrasting it with the urban. Loach works counter to the recuperative tendency, visible in Scottish films such as

*Ratcatcher* (Ramsay, GB/Fr, 1999), which posits open, empty space as redemptive or therapeutic.

Several scenes in *My Name is Joe* and *Sweet Sixteen* seem particularly relevant to this discussion. *Joe* has been praised mostly for its would-be documentary realism: its urban grit, its use of local non-actors, the virtuoso performance of Peter Mullan as the recovering alcoholic central character. It seems that such praise has something to do with the locale. That is, Scottish subjects are "case studies," since in one important way the film is about alcoholism. This is reflected, as though anticipated critique, in a sequence where Joe, in an effort to help one of his charges—his efforts at his own rehabilitation are projected onto his community—undertakes to do a drug run for a local crime boss. Ironically, Joe needs to pick up the drop in a Highland town, where he, to use a phrase, is a fish out of water. The locale is presented as set, a façade exploited and even produced by some outside "criminal" element. Joe comically uses the public phone box for the call to receive directions, comical because of the kitsch filmic history associated with that image of technology submerged in a landscape that does not seem to and should not accommodate it. The phone produces the effect of isolation rather than communication and this is usually a signal of the romance of the landscape. In this case, the clichés of both the pastoral and urban/criminal serve to debunk Joe as misfit, which in turn applies to the misfit nature of the clichés themselves. Joe is mocked by the crime boss for his lack of recognition of the locale: he has trouble sighting the drop-off place, the Stella Maris Inn—"It's Latin," snaps the voice on the other end of the line. "What?" asks Joe uncomprehendingly; "I just thought you might want to know what it fucking means," comes the belittling response. Leaving aside the obvious religious reference that Joe cannot recognise, this exchange seems like a parody of the civilising impact of the colonising force, one that quickly drops its pretense and speaks a language they both "fucking" understand. The exchange is shot through with that qualifier, the lingo imitating the condition of being fucked over. Joe is also not familiar with the remote entry key for the car waiting for him and sets the alarm off when entering. When Joe nervously asks a local to help him, the man jokes that he might be observing a robbery. This slapstick worthy of the keystone cops is not an uncommon feature of even Loach's most serious films. The effect is to disarm the fetishised narrative and, in this case, Joe is literally disarmed momentarily: the seeming conflation of narratives of romance and crime, as we saw in Hitchcock, are suggestive of the historical narrative in the backdrop of this story, which has become the romance of the crime.

Another such disarming moment comes down the road from the drop-off town, when Joe stops for a break at a van selling roadside refreshments. A piper is exploiting the space and tourists are everywhere snapping photos. The scene is positively kitsch, along with the tunes the piper is playing. Drawing heavily on his cigarette in the idyllic setting, which the camera knowingly pans, Joe has an exchange with the caravan attendant, the other "native" in the scene besides him and the piper. The piper only knows three songs, the attendant says with a kind of weariness: Scotland the Brave, the Skye Boat Song and "Flower of Scotland." Joe muses that "he probably sells shortbread... Bonnie Scotland, eh?" The routine is familiar. The scene plays out as exploited prop, ironic not just in relation to "real" Scottish lives, but as a certain kind of myth of sublimity (as in *Trainspotting*).

*Sweet Sixteen* has been lauded similarly for its "authenticity" and performances and again its subject of drug rehabilitation is often read as a Scottish "case." It is a coming-of-age story whose story cannot unfold. The cliché of this narrative is treated like that of idyllic space—hackneyed and unproductive. Like *Trainspotting*, which needed re-dubbing for American audiences, *Sweet Sixteen*'s Greenock voices are interpolated by English subtitles. I think it is lost upon most reviewers that the cliché of the tragically thwarted life plays out as a caricature of itself in the same way that the kitsch symbology of Scottishness seen in *My Name is Joe* has both tragic and comical dimensions. One important difference between the films, which also produces a salient counterpoint, is that the story of Liam (Martin Compston), *Sweet Sixteen*'s central character, retains a heroic dimension whereas the heroism of Joe is undercut by a refusal to naturalise the tragic elements of the environment. Liam's heroism might also be tied to a recurrence of the ideal of the landscape as escape. His fantasy about moving with his mother to a caravan in West Kilbride, the village located down from Greenock on the Firth of the Clyde, becomes the motivating force behind his daring and ultimate self-destruction.

When we see Liam at the campsite, he is looking longingly into the window of a caravan for sale. The camera takes us inside the enclosed space. It is compact and tidy. Its basic set is idealised through his imagination of it—a room with a view from the other side of the Isle of Arran, which might momentarily seem to tap into the cultural imaginary of the landscape. But there is no majesty except in Liam's vision of it as removed from the tenement spaces of his Greenock neighbourhood. Greenock had grown up around the industrial docks, which now mark its ruin in a kind of parody of the emptying out of the thriving landscape that was the Highland crofts. The obsolescence of the inhabitants of the

Highland scape—the roaming sheep—is now reproduced in these urban denizens, arguably through a similar political impulse. Liam's criminal entrepreneurialism, which perversely mimics the Thatcherite prescription for urban renewal, a particular failure in the outlier parts of the United Kingdom she used as political guinea pigs and/or scapegoats, becomes the means of his downfall.

In Charles Barr's tribute to the relationship between Hitchcock and Powell within British cinema, he places Ken Loach in opposition to them, describing him as "bracingly scornful of any talk of the art of cinema; he would hardly claim to 'love films' or 'love cinema'" (Barr 2005, 8). Barr suggests that film is a medium of convenience for Loach, trumped by the social message. To make his point about film as art by contrast, Barr praises the signature feature of personal appearance employed by both Powell and Hitchcock—the modernist tick of authorial self-referentiality—a way of implicating themselves in the artifice. To illustrate, Barr points to Powell's cameo in *The Edge of the World*:

> It starts with a tourist couple arriving on a yacht, at a deserted island. The man identifies it on a map, and tells their guide that they will stop there and have a look… the yachtsman is Michael Powell himself, and the woman is Frankie Reidy, later to be his wife… The story itself, framed in long flashback, is unashamedly melodramatic. It is narrated not by the traditional neutral 'voice of God' commentary of documentary but by one of the main participants. And it is introduced by the visiting yachtsman and his wife, who act as a kind of surrogate for the audience, being introduced to this exotic place and then settling down to be told about it. It is not an objective piece of documentary, but a story into which the audience and the primary narrator, Powell himself, are inscribed at the start. (ibid, 8-9)

The meaning of Powell's self-inscription here is more assumed than articulated. Barr argues, and it seems we may take it for granted, that by placing himself inside the film, Powell exposes the conceit of documentary objectivity. But it seems to me that Barr misses some important points regarding the implications of Powell's particular role here. Powell plays the English tourist to this remote "exotic place," as Barr terms it. Given Powell's interest in Scottish history, he would have been aware of another signal his presence conveyed—the cliché of the English intruder, who is not only historically inscribed in the landscape, but who inscribes its "exoticism." We know that Hitchcock's appearances might be said to function in different symbolic terms. He offers himself up as his own MacGuffin: searching for him has become a fetish of his audience. As every one of his films begins, he is missing—something like the Scottish landscape he employs so early on. Its mystery is not in its majesty but in what is concealed. I don't refute Barr's claim that Powell and Hitchcock eschewed documentarism, though I would argue with his characterization of that form as necessarily unartistic and, more importantly for my argument here, with his assessment of Loach in these terms. All were aware of the setting or landscape as visual commodity. And as Powell and Hitchcock both insisted until the very end of their careers, and perhaps most emphatically in their later twin works—*Psycho* (USA, 1960) and *Peeping Tom*—it is the camera more than the director that surrogates the audience. Viewer, beware.

## Works Cited

Barr, Charles. 2005. Hitchcock and Powell: two directions for British Cinema. *Screen* 46.1: 5-13.

Christie, Ian. 1994. *Arrows of Desire: The Films of Michael Powell and Emeric Pressburger*. London: Faber and Faber.

Devas, Angela. 2005. How to be a Hero: Space, Place and Masculinity in *The 39 Steps*. *Journal of Gender Studies* 14.1: 45-54.

English, James F. 2006. Local Focus, Global Frame: Ken Loach and the Cinema of Dispossession. In *Fires Were Started: British Cinema and Thatcherism*, ed. Lester D. Friedman, 259-281. London: Wallflower Press.

Hardy, Forsyth. 1990. *Scotland in Film*. Edinburgh: Edinburgh University Press.

McArthur, Colin. 1982. Scotland and Cinema: The Iniquity of the Fathers. In *Scotch Reels*: *Scotland in Cinema and Television*, ed. Colin McArthur, 40-69. London: British Film Institute.

—. 1996. The Scottish Discursive Unconscious. In *Scottish Popular Theatre and Entertainment: historical and critical approaches to theatre and film in Scotland*, eds. Alasdair Cameron and Adrienne Scullion, 81-89. Glasgow: Glasgow University Library Publications.

—. 2003. *Brigadoon, Braveheart and the Scots: Distortions of Scotland in Hollywood Cinema*. London: I. B. Tauris.

McLoone, Martin. 2001. Internal Decolonisation? British Cinema in the Celtic Fringe. *The British Cinema Book 2nd Edition*, ed. Robert Murphy, 184-190. London: British Film Institute.

Moor, Andrew. 2005. *Powell & Pressburger: A Cinema of Magic Spaces*. London: I .B. Tauris.

Petrie, Duncan. 2000. *Screening Scotland.* London: British Film Institute.

—. 2005. Scottish Cinema dossier: introduction. *Screen* 46. 2: 213-216.

Spoto, Donald. 1999. *The Dark Side of Genius: The Life of Alfred Hitchcock*. New York: Da Capo Press.

Trevor-Roper, Hugh. 1983. The Highland Tradition of Scotland. In *The Invention of Tradition*, eds. Eric Hobsbawm and Terence Ranger, 15-41. Cambridge: Cambridge University Press.

Truffaut, François. 1967. *Hitchcock*. New York: Simon and Schuster.

# 'BONNIE SCOTLAND, EH?': SCOTTISH CINEMA, THE WORKING CLASS AND THE FILMS OF KEN LOACH

JOHN HILL

Duncan Petrie identifies the emergence of a "new Scottish cinema" (Petrie 2000, 172) in the mid 1990s. Somewhat unexpectedly, perhaps, Petrie's list of relevant films includes *My Name is Joe* (Loach, Sp/It/Fr/GB/Ger, 1998). While the film is, of course, set in Scotland, its director, Ken Loach, is a long-established English filmmaker with no record of interest in either Scotland or the Scots prior to the 1990s. Nevertheless, there can be little doubt that Loach's contribution to raising the profile of Scottish cinema during this period was substantial. *My Name is Joe* was followed by further collaborations with the Scottish writer Paul Laverty—*Sweet Sixteen* (GB/Ger/Sp, 2002) and *Ae Fond Kiss...* (GB/Bel/Ger/It/Sp, 2004)—which together acquired the status of an unofficial Scottish trilogy. Scottish sequences or characters also appeared in *Riff-Raff* (Loach, GB, 1991), *Carla's Song* (Loach, GB/Ger/Sp, 1996), *Tickets* (Kiarostami/Loach/Olmi, It/GB, 2005) and *The Wind that Shakes the Barley* (Loach, Ire/GB/Ger/It/Sp/Fr, 2006). Moreover, although these films show a great deal of continuity—in theme and style—with films that Loach made (with other writers) in England, they also cultivate a relatively distinctive view of contemporary Scotland. The discussion that follows, therefore, will begin by suggesting some of the reasons prompting the Scottish turn in Loach's work, before going on to consider the kind of representations of Scotland to which it led.

If Loach's association with a new movement in Scottish filmmaking was unexpected, it is also explained in part by the institutional and political changes that were occurring at the time. As Petrie and others have indicated, the arrival of a "new Scottish cinema" in the 1990s was not only the result of new talent and sources of creative energy but also depended upon the increased availability of financial support devoted to filmmaking in Scotland. Although the Scottish Film Production Fund was established in 1982, its levels of funding had been relatively modest. The decision of the UK government in 1995 to allocate a share of National Lottery revenues to film (initially administered in Scotland by the Scottish Arts Council and then by Scottish Screen) led almost immediately to the injection of new funds into Scottish film production and a growth in the number of films made. Thus, despite Loach's reservations that the Lottery constituted a "tax on the poor" (Anon 1998, 2), all parts of his Scottish trilogy benefited from the backing of Scottish Lottery funds. The Glasgow Film Fund also supported *Carla's Song* (set partly in Glasgow) and *My Name is Joe*, while the Glasgow Film Office (established in 1997) assisted both *Sweet Sixteen* and *Ae Fond Kiss*.... Although Scottish funding comprised only a proportion of the films' overall budgets, the sums involved were still sufficiently substantial to attract an established filmmaker to work in Scotland and make use of Scottish locations.

However, while the move to Scotland in Loach's work may be related to the increased availability of public funding for film there, this does not tell the whole story. What also appeared to make Scotland an attractive place for him to work was the difference in political climate from that existing in England. Although the Conservatives under Margaret Thatcher came to power in the UK in 1979, there was little support for their brand of economic neo-liberalism and socially divisive politics in Scotland. During the years that followed, electoral support for the Conservatives in Scotland carried on falling with the result that, in 1997, only seventeen per cent of Scots voted Conservative and not a single Tory MP was elected to Westminster. As David McCrone explains, the Conservatives' "attack on state institutions—the nationalised industries, the education system, local government, the public sector generally" came to be regarded, given the cultural significance of public institutions for Scottish identity, as "an attack on 'Scotland' itself" (McCrone 1992, 172).

Due to the strength of anti-Conservative sentiment in Scotland at this time, the country could be seen to provide a relatively congenial environment for a socialist filmmaker such as Loach. This was particularly so given the way in which the discourse of class continued to survive in Scotland despite the changing character of the nation's workforce. Resistance to post-'79 English Conservative rule involved a continuing attachment to collective values that often found expression in the language of class identity and politics. Paterson *et al* cite evidence that a majority in all socio-economic groups within Scotland perceive of themselves as "working class," indicating how "Scotland still thinks of itself as being a working class country" (Paterson *et al* 2004, 101) despite the changes in patterns of employment wrought by the move towards a post-industrial economy. Given Loach's own commitment to the politics of class struggle, it could be argued that Scotland's continued maintenance of a consciousness of the politics of class, as well as the virtues of collectivism, chimed with Loach's own political outlook.

However, the discourse of class in Scotland also possessed strong associations with national identity that did not sit entirely easily with Loach's own—internationalist—view of class politics. It has been a consistent premise of Loach's politics that class solidarity cuts across national identifications. Thus, despite the ostensive nationalism of his dramatised account of the Irish War of Independence and the ensuing Civil War in *The Wind that Shakes the Barley*, Loach has claimed in relation to the film that people "have much more in common with people in the same position in other countries than they do with those at the top of their own society" and that he'd therefore "encourage people to see their loyalties horizontally across national boundaries" (Loach 2006, 9). Indeed, it is precisely this sense of 'horizontal' identification that animates Loach's contribution to *Tickets*, in which three Celtic fans (and shopworkers) on board a train for Rome assist a family of Albanian immigrants before they themselves are helped to escape the police by Italian football supporters. Given this commitment to the primacy of class over other forms of cultural identification, there is therefore a sense in which Loach's Scottish films do not overtly seek to dramatise their "Scottishness". Thus, in an interview on the DVD release of *My Name is Joe*, scriptwriter Paul Laverty suggests that "no great premium" is placed upon the Glasgow location which he argues is no "less or more complex than any other city". Loach has also suggested how Glasgow—with its "strong working-class culture"—possesses much "the same quality as Liverpool," (Mottram 2004, 22) a city that had previously provided the location for a number of Loach productions ranging from *The Big Flame* (BBC, 1969) through to *Raining Stones* (GB, 1993). This might suggest how, as a result of the necessities of raising production finance, Glasgow came to function as a kind of surrogate location in Loach's films, a sort of Liverpool-in-disguise. A recurring ambition of Loach's work is to tell stories focused on individuals and their families which nonetheless demonstrate a degree of 'typicality' or social representativeness. It could be argued that the impulse to represent, and be representative of, the general experience of the urban working class in contemporary Britain, rather than the specificities of the Scottish experience, primarily animates the representational strategies of films such as *My Name is Joe* and *Sweet Sixteen*.

However, given the emphasis upon the actuality of place and accuracy of observation in Loach's films, there is inevitably a degree of movement between the local and the general in the way in which they portray character and place. This is clearly so of Loach's Scottish films. The "representativeness" of their stories may relate primarily to issues of class but their emphasis upon the "authenticity" of location and accent (the source of considerable comment in the English press) entails that the films retain strong "national" connotations as well. However, films set in Scotland (no matter how "authentic") are never discursively "innocent" but inevitably occupy a position in relation to pre-existing traditions of representation. The enduring influence of the edited collection *Scotch Reels* (McArthur 1982) means that many of the key arguments concerning Scotland's cinematic representation have by now become extremely familiar. McArthur identifies how, despite the transformation of Scotland by industrialisation and urbanisation during the nineteenth century, cinematic imagery of the nation remained indebted to the discourses of Tartanry—romantic evocations of the Highlands—and Kailyard—sentimental portraits of small-town life (McArthur 1982, 40-69). Indeed, one of the purposes of my own contribution to *Scotch Reels* was to identify and analyse one of the few films that sought to address contemporary Scottish urban life prior to the 1980s, *The Gorbals Story* (MacKane, GB, 1949) (Hill 1982, 100-111; see also Hill 1977, 61-70). While both Tartanry and Kailyard continue to survive in new, and often knowing, forms, Scotland's cinematic representation has, nevertheless, become considerably more varied in recent years. It is no longer possible to identify the representation of city life as the 'absent' cinematic discourse that it once appeared to be. Indeed, due to the role of local city-based agencies with a remit to attract films to Glasgow and Edinburgh, the majority of Scottish feature films are now set and shot in Scotland's two main cities (Turok 2003, 556).

Loach's realist aesthetic and socialist outlook has encouraged an emphasis upon the city, perceived as a product of industrial capitalism, the home of the industrial working class and the traditional base of organised labour. It is therefore unsurprising that his Scottish films should choose the Glasgow area, with its associations with heavy industry and labour militancy, as their main setting. In doing so, the films do not entirely ignore the country but, in line with the spirit of urban realism, largely define its significance in relation to city life. Thus, just as *The Gorbals Story* had sought to highlight the irrelevance of Tartanry to the inhabitants of Glasgow slums, so Loach's films exhibit a similar kind of demythologising impulse towards romantic and touristic views of the Scottish countryside. This is particularly clear in *My Name is Joe* when Joe (Peter Mullan) abandons the city for the only time in the film, in order to collect a car, containing drugs, from outside a seaside B&B. On his return drive to Glasgow he stops off at a "Highland" tourist location (identified as Glencoe in the script) where he observes a piper playing *Scotland the Brave* while a group of tourists (most of whom seem to be Japanese) gather round to take photographs. Observing the scene from a distance, Joe engages in sardonic banter with the woman serving him tea from a caravan kiosk ("Bonnie Scotland eh?," "Bonnie Scotland right enough"). Recalling the famous "It's shite being Scottish" sequence from *Trainspotting* (Boyle, GB, 1996), Loach's scene gently pokes fun at the commodification of Highlands mythology and puts into question the latter's relevance to contemporary urban life.

Joe's drive through the Scottish countryside is also reminiscent of a scene in another Scottish film, *A Sense of Freedom* (John Mackenzie, GB, 1981), concerned with the exploits of the Glasgow criminal and "hard man", Jimmy Boyle. Before his eventual transfer to the Barlinnie Special Unit, Boyle achieved notoriety for his extreme violence and refusal to submit to the discipline of prison life. At one point in the film, Boyle (David Hayman) is transferred to Nairn Prison. A short sequence shows a car containing Boyle racing through the Highlands. As the rest of the film has taken place within the confines of either the city or jail, these shots provide an unexpected sense of release (for viewer and Boyle alike) from the atmosphere of claustrophobia and confinement that has pervaded up until this point. In a similar fashion, Loach's Scottish films may also be seen to set up a contrast between the temporary "escape" provided by the country and the sense of "imprisonment" characteristic of the urban environment. In *Carla's Song*, George (Robert Carlyle) and Carla (Oyanka Cabezas) escape to Loch Lomond on George's double-decker bus and enjoy a bottle of champagne. However, not only is the romance (and "romanticism") of the sequence undercut by the bus sticking in mud, but Carla's fleeting moment of happiness is followed by a suicide attempt on their return to the city. In *Sweet Sixteen*, Liam's aspiration to escape from his drab housing estate is symbolised by a caravan located on a hill overlooking the Clyde estuary (which he enthusiastically describes as "paradise"). This too proves a forlorn dream and the caravan is subsequently discovered burnt to the ground, just as the telescope he had used to view Saturn is smashed. It has been a common feature of films associated with Tartanry and Kailyard to employ narratives involving an outsider's encounter with a fantasy Scotland. In Loach's films, however, the nightmare realities of poverty and deprivation ensure that characters' hopes are dashed and their desires remain unfulfilled.

In this respect, the films may be seen to counterpose an unrealistic, romantic view of the country (and vision of rural "escape") to the grim, down-to-earth "realities" (and confined spaces) associated with the city.

This does not mean, however, that the representation of the city succeeds in avoiding its own romanticising tendencies: the Scottish city, and especially Glasgow, has generated its own cultural mythologies. In the debates surrounding Scottish cinema, the analysis of these myths has tended to crystallise around the idea of "Clydesidism". In his original *Scotch Reels* argument, Colin McArthur did not actually employ the term but suggested how certain films, such as *Floodtide* (Wilson, GB, 1949) and *The Gorbals Story*, sought "to define the meaning of Scotland in relation to the Clyde" (McArthur 1982, 52). Subsequent discussion, however, invested the term with more precise associations. Douglas and Ouainé Bain, for example, identified Clydesidism with "the valorisation of the Scottish male industrial worker, especially in shipbuilding, steel, heavy engineering and mining" which they suggested could be found in "progressive and socialist" (Bain/Bain/Skirrow 1983, 4) films such as *Seawards the Great Ships* (Harris, GB, 1960) and *The Brave Don't Cry* (Leacock, GB, 1952), the latter's Ayrshire setting extending the meaning of Clydesideism beyond the banks of the River Clyde. While in this view, Clydesidism is identified as a celebratory (but, from the viewpoint of feminism, problematic) mode, it has also been held to possess much more negative connotations. David Bruce links Clydesidism with a "mini-genre" of "hard man" films (such as *A Sense of Freedom*) dealing with "working class violent crime" and possessing "overtones of poverty, sectarianism and stubborn refusal to be beaten by the system" (Bruce 1996, 124; see also Petrie 2004). Although these two groups of films invest the Clyde with apparently opposing meanings, they nonetheless share an emphasis upon the male working class and its association with toughness and virility, whether in the form of hard physical labour or hard fighting and drinking. Indeed, made not long after one of the last bursts of heroic Clydesidism—the Communist-led Upper Clyde Shipbuilders (UCS) work-in of 1971-2 aimed at keeping the shipyards open—late-'70s/early-'80s "hard men" films and television dramas may be seen to grapple, almost obsessively, with the status of working-class masculinity in an era of industrial decline. In one of the most discomfiting of these, John Mackenzie's television film *Just a Boy's Game* (BBC, 1979), the inevitable violent "showdown" occurs in the shadow of the shipyards, with one of the participants tripping and falling to his death in the Clyde. Here, the imminent demise of the shipyards appears to threaten redundancy not only for traditional forms of manual labour but also the culture of "hardness" associated with heavy industry as well.

The vicissitudes of the working class has, of course, also been the major preoccupation of Loach's films since *Riff-Raff*. Thus, while his

Scottish films maintain considerable similarities with those set in England (such as *Raining Stones*), their use of Scottish locations also means that they cannot avoid an engagement with the patterns of representation historically associated with Clydesidism. They were made, of course, at a time when Scottish heavy industry had experienced a sharp decline: by 2001, manufacturing accounted for only thirteen per cent of jobs in Scotland (Paterson *et al* 2004, 84-85). Given the collapse of heavy industry, and the failure of trade union action to halt the process, it is hardly surprising that Loach's Scottish films should avoid any heroic portrayal of manual labour or celebration of the spirit of "Red Clydeside". The beginning of *Carla's Song* introduces us to the character of George, a Glasgow bus-driver characterised by anti-authoritarianism and sympathy for the underdog. However, his rebelliousness is confined to provoking the irritation of low-level officials and it is Nicaragua, rather than contemporary Scotland, that the film identifies with a genuine spirit of revolution (and George subsequently fails to participate fully in this). As a filmmaker, Loach has always been sceptical about the prospects of radical political change in Britain. Even in his most provocative television drama, *The Big Flame* (1969), the workers' take-over of the Liverpool docks is shown to fail due to a lack of trade union leadership and the state's resort to military force. In 1969, however, it was at least still possible to imagine how organised, collective action might mount a serious political challenge to capital and the state. By the 1990s, this moment has long since passed. Loach's portraits of the working class focus instead on the destructive effects of de-industrialisation, mass (male) unemployment and associated economic hardship.

*Sweet Sixteen*, for example, is, like *Just a Boy's Game*, set in Greenock on the Clyde estuary (a town, according to the earlier film, "built on yards" and that "exists because of them"). In *Just a Boy's Game* the men still have jobs, no matter how unsatisfying and under threat. In *Sweet Sixteen*, cranes continue to dominate the skyline but none of the film's characters are employed as shipyard workers. As a result, films such as *My Name is Joe* and *Sweet Sixteen* lay stress upon the limited scope for action now available to the main characters, bleakly charting the ways in which force of circumstance imposes upon them. In *My Name is Joe*, Joe is a recovering alcoholic who achieves a degree of self-respect through his management of the local football team, an unlikely group of no-hopers faced with expulsion from the league. He also embarks upon a tentative romance with a social worker, Sarah (Louise Goodall), who encourages him to deal with the shame he feels about his violent assault on a female drinking companion. By the end of the film, however, Joe has returned to drink, his relationship has collapsed and a member of the football team, Liam (David McKay), whom he has tried to help, has been driven to suicide. In *Sweet Sixteen*, teenager Liam (Martin Compston) aspires to make a home for his mother (Michelle Coulter) when she is released from prison. Although his money-making schemes initially prosper, his dreams are in shreds by the end of the film: his mother has rejected him and he is in flight from the police after stabbing her boyfriend.

The strategy of the films, in this regard, is not only to provide vivid reminders of those who have lost out in the transition from an industrial to a services-led economy, a process that encompassed the resurgence of a "new Glasgow", but also to insist upon the centrality of economic factors in accounting for the problems that the characters face (and, therefore, the considerable difficulties that are involved in "solving" them). In this respect, the films seek to avoid explaining the actions of characters simply in terms of psychological make-up or moral outlook but to demonstrate how they result from the social and economic pressures that weigh upon, and restricted opportunities open to, them. Thus, Joe's decision to help Liam by doing a job for the drug-dealer McGowan (David Hayman) has disastrous consequences but is shown to have been forced upon him by the lack of economic alternatives. As he subsequently explains to Sarah:

> I'm sorry but we don't live in this nice, tidy wee world of yours. Some of us cannae go to the polis. Some of us cannae go to the bank for a loan. Some of us cannae move house and fuck off out of here. Some of us don't have a choice.

Despite Joe's alcoholism, it is the use of hard drugs that is identified as a particular scourge within the deprived communities of the west of Scotland in the late '90s. Indeed, as early as *Riff-Raff* Loach had introduced a brief Glasgow-set scene in which Stevie (Robert Carlyle) returns to the city for the funeral of his mother and encounters his brother and his wife, both recovering junkies. Heroin use, of course, also formed a central feature of *Trainspotting*, set in the estates of Leith (near Edinburgh). Although that film could hardly be said to glamourise drug use, its employment of attractive young actors, pop soundtrack, witty voice-overs and general air of self-conscious knowingness did render it vulnerable to charges of "heroin chic". In Loach's universe, however, heroin use is divested of rock culture associations and much more firmly linked to class disadvantage and material hardship. Renton (Ewan McGregor)'s famous voice-over at the beginning of *Trainspotting* ("choose a job, choose a career, choose a family, choose a fucking big television, choose washing machines, cars, compact-disc players and electrical tin openers") invokes the rhetoric of bohemianism and its rejection of social conformity and materialism. Loach's films imply that the majority of these acquisitions do not lie within the grasp of their working-class characters in the first place.

However, while drug use features prominently in both *My Name is Joe* and *Sweet Sixteen*, the films' emphasis is less on "the needle and the damage done" and more on the role drugs play within the "local economy". It is, of course, a convention of gangster films to allegorise crime as a kind of extension, or mimicry, of "normal" business practices. Similarly, in *Sweet Sixteen*, the vacuum left by traditional manufacturing appears to have been filled by the new service industry of illegal drug supply. In an ironic commentary on the "enterprise culture" championed by successive UK Conservative and New Labour administrations, the film indicates how drug-dealing provides one of the few "career opportunities" still available to ambitious but socially disadvantaged youngsters. Liam seizes the "business opportunities" available to him by gravitating from selling stolen cigarettes in pubs to working for the local "Al Capone" figure, Douglas (Jon Morrison), who operates under the cover of a smart health club typical of the new middle-class Glasgow. There is, in this respect, a further parallel with *Trainspotting*. On moving to London, Renton relishes the amorality of the enterprise culture and betrays (the majority of) his friends by stealing the proceeds from a drug deal: the money offers the means of getting away from the environment and friends that have dogged him and of making a new start. In *My Name is Joe* and *Sweet Sixteen*, however, the resort to drug-dealing is destined to prove a false avenue of "escape". The main characters end up in worse circumstances than those in which they began. At the time of the release of *Shallow Grave* (GB, 1995), Danny Boyle, director of both that film and *Trainspotting*, expressed his admiration for Loach but worried that his recent work "hadn't moved on" (Bennett 1995, 36). In this respect, *Trainspotting* may be read as an attempt not only to "move on" from Loach's style of observational realism but also his class-based, or "environmentalist," account of character.

Given the male-centred nature of the films' narratives, the main characters' lack of success in achieving their goals also involves a commentary on the impact of unemployment and poverty upon traditional forms of working-class masculinity. During the 1990s, a number of successful British film comedies indicated how the erosion of manufacturing in the north of England had impacted upon traditional definitions of masculinity. This was also so of the Scottish comedy, *On a*

*Clear Day* (Dellal, GB, 2005), in which Frank (Peter Mullan) loses his job as a shipyard worker but regains his self-respect (and that of his group of male friends) through swimming the English Channel. *On a Clear Day* proposes a symbolic resolution of the "crisis of masculinity" through a recovery of homosocial community. In Loach's films, however, no such salvation is available. The bonds of male friendship, such as those between Liam and Pinball (William Ruane) in *Sweet Sixteen*, dissolve in the face of the pressures imposed upon them. Pinball sets fire to Liam's caravan, Liam is instructed to "take care" of Pinball by Douglas. The "relearning" of male roles also proves much more problematic than in working-class comedies such as *The Full Monty* (Cattaneo, GB, 1997). Despite Liam's insistence that he will make money through the use of his "heid" he is ineluctably drawn into a criminal underworld dependent upon the threat of physical violence. This continues to trap him in the very culture of "hardness" from which he aspires to escape. As in an earlier film such as *The Big Man* (Leland, GB, 1990), in which an unemployed miner (Liam Neeson) is forced to become a bare-knuckle fighter, Liam's repeated beatings (at the hands of both his own family and other dealers) may be seen to mock the aura of physical dignity and pride that once attached to the male working-class body and the performance of traditional forms of manual labour.

The bleakness of the men's situation is reinforced by the Loach films' treatment of female characters. Historically, women have played a symbolically important role in images of Scotland by giving embodiment to the nation's "spirit" or its supposedly "natural" state. According to John Caughie, the portrayal of women in Tartanry and Kailyard may be linked to a "specifically masculine yearning" for the redemptive or regenerative qualities that women may be taken to provide; in Clydesidism, Caughie suggests, women are called upon to sustain men through "the uncertainties of post-industrial manhood" (Caughie 1990, 16). While this is certainly the case in a film such as *On a Clear Day*, it is not generally so in Loach's films, in which men search in vain for the love and support that they crave. For all her professionalism and caring qualities, Sarah is unable to make the imaginative leap into Joe's world. Her rejection of him prompts his disastrous efforts to extract himself from McGowan's clutches. Although Liam's sister Chantelle (Annmarie Fulton) does her best to look after him in *Sweet Sixteen*, it is his desire for his mother's affection that prompts most of his actions. At the end of the film, however, the latter abandons him (and the flat that he has acquired for her) in order to return to her boyfriend Stan (Gary McCormack). This sets in motion the film's final chain of tragic events. In a remark that appears to possess more general applicability, Sabine (Anne Marie Kennedy) in *My Name is Joe,* says of her relationship with Liam (and their little boy) that "it's me that let him doon". Although the films seek to avoid the moralising discourses commonly directed at family dysfunction (and deficient mothering), pointing to the economic causes that underpin them, the difficulties confronting the male characters are generally exacerbated by the collapse of the certainties traditionally associated with the "feminine" role.

At the beginning of the essay, it was suggested how the social and political climate in Scotland—opposition to Thatcherism and, subsequently, to aspects of New Labour, growing self-confidence through devolution and a continuing attachment to "communitarian" values—made the country a congenial place for Loach to work. As the preceding analysis would suggest, however, these features have found relatively little expression in films such as *My Name is Joe* and *Sweet Sixteen*. Loach has, of course, stressed the comedy that he unearths from even the most desperate of situations, citing, for example, the antics of the football team in *My Name is Joe*, as well as the resilience his characters demonstrate in the face of economic and social disadvantage. Yet given the relentless downward spiral in which characters are caught, and the denial of any viable escape route to them, *My Name is Joe* and *Sweet Sixteen* remain overwhelmingly pessimistic in tone (possibly the most pessimistic that Loach has made). Even Peter Mullan, the lead actor of *My Name is Joe*, was moved to qualify his admiration for Loach's work with the observation that Liam's suicide at the close of the film was "absurd," achieving "nothing except moving an audience to tears" and offering "no insight into other options he might have taken" (Spencer 1999, 14). Significantly, Mullan's own directorial debut, *Orphans* (GB, 1997), completed shortly before the filming of *My Name is Joe*, covers much of the same ground as the Loach films—the trauma of deindustrialisation, the crises of masculinity—but attempts to extract a degree of optimism from its angst-ridden tale of a family coping with the death of their mother (conceived as a loose symbol for traditional forms of Scottish identity) (see Murray 2001; Martin-Jones 2004). As Mullan's remarks would indicate, the pessimism and discourse of failure to be found in Loach's films appears to acquire a particular significance in the Scottish context. An elegiac tone and sense of national loss has been a longstanding feature of cultural representations: Tartanry relies upon discourses related to the massacre of Glencoe, the Battle of Culloden and the Highland Clearances, while Clydesidism is preoccupied with the demise of shipbuilding and other heavy industries. While virtually all of Loach's films made in the UK since the 1990s have focused on the collapse of heavy industry and its impact upon the traditional (male) working class, this possesses a distinctive ideological resonance in the Scottish context, perhaps assuming a "national-allegorical" dimension.

However, while the films' narratives of victimisation and failure may draw upon a longstanding tradition of representation, there is, given their production context, an element of irony that this should be so. As previously noted, the funding available to support filmmaking in Scotland has been the product of public initiatives designed to promote Glasgow as a financially attractive place to work and to encourage the kind of local "creative economy" regarded as necessary for urban regeneration. The production of films such as *My Name is Joe* and *Sweet Sixteen* played an important role in raising the profile of Scotland as a centre for film production and helped circulate images of the nation around the world. However, the desire to reinvent Glasgow as a "vibrant contemporary creative hub" is, to some extent, subverted by the reliance of the films themselves on images of Glasgow as "a depressed and depressing post-industrial dystopia" (Murray 2007, 34). This irony has not gone unremarked. The local Labour MP, David Cairns, worried that *Sweet Sixteen*'s bleak portrait of the Greenock area would act as a deterrent to investment while others fretted about the impact of such images upon tourism (Garside 2002). Referring to Loach as "our Visiting Professor of Doom," Channel 4's Head of Nations and Regions, Stuart Cosgrove, also complained that screen representations like his have "tilted Scotland too far in the direction of perceived failure" and that, while "poverty and deprivation" remain a "challenge," they do not constitute the "defining characteristic" of contemporary Scottish experience (Cosgrove 2005).

By 2005, however, Loach and Laverty had in fact moved in a new direction and produced, possibly as a result of earlier criticisms of their work, a considerably more upbeat account of contemporary Scotland. Partly conceived as a response to the changing atmosphere towards Muslims in wake of the events of 11 September 2001, *Ae Fond Kiss...* deals with a romance between a second-generation Glaswegian Asian, Casim Khan (Atta Yaqub), and an Irish-Catholic teacher, Roisin Hanlon (Eva Birthistle). Increasing emphasis placed upon romantic encounters such as those between Stevie and Susan (Emer McCourt) in *Riff-Raff* and George and Carla in *Carla's Song* has been one of the more striking features of Loach's films since the 1990s. However, while romance is shown to provide redemptive possibilities, allowing characters to uncover new aspects of themselves, films such as *My Name is Joe* also lay stress on how romantic success or failure depend upon social and economic factors and not just personal attributes. In *Ae Fond Kiss...* it initially appears as though religious and ethnic differences will prise the couple apart. Although Casim and Roisin have embarked upon a relationship, Casim has omitted to tell Roisin that he is due to marry a cousin from Pakistan, an arrangement which, out of loyalty to his family and religion, he feels unable to renege upon. Roisin, in turn, is confronted by the prejudice of the local parish priest who refuses to sign the Certificate of Approval that would allow her to take up a permanent post at the Catholic school where she works on the grounds that she is living "in sin" with a non-Catholic ("we're stuck in the middle," she subsequently complains to Casim). The title of the film derives from a Robert Burns song about parting: "Ae fond kiss, and then we sever!/Ae farewell, and then forever". The song's gloomy sentiments appear to anticipate, as in other Loach films, the breakdown of Casim and Roisin's relationship. Thus, after Casim has told Roisin he is not her "match," the song is heard on the soundtrack over shots of Roisin crying and Casim driving away in his car.

To this extent, *Ae Fond Kiss…* makes use of the relatively well-worn narrative convention of love across the cultural divide to comment on the state of contemporary race relations. It does so, however, in a way that seeks to avoid mapping these in terms of a simple contrast between tradition and modernity. Although Casim's father, Tariq (Ahmad Riaz), is shown to be opposed to his children's exercise of the normal Western "freedoms" (choice of partner, choice of university course), the film is also at pains to emphasise how Tariq's outlook has been shaped by his experience of colonialism, migration and racism. Moreover, even though it may possess the air of a somewhat contrived "balance," the film's emphasis upon the narrow-mindedness of the Catholic Church also acts as reminder that the "West" itself is hardly to be regarded as a repository of secular rationalism. By making Roisin Irish rather than Scottish, the film also hints at how both Ireland and Pakistan have both been shaped by a colonial legacy of partition and historic patterns of emigration. However, somewhat remarkably for a Loach film, *Ae Fond Kiss...* also strives to overcome the in-built pessimism of its narrative set-up and demonstrate that the couple possess the capacity to overcome the divisions that separate them. This is not only an unusual characteristic of a Loach film but a significant one given the period in which the film was made. The events of 2001 and its impact upon British Muslims had prompted the production of a number of films and television dramas, such as *Yasmin* (Glenaan, Ger/GB, 2004) and *Bradford Riots* (Biswas, GB, 2006), that sought to highlight the growth of ethnic tensions within contemporary Britain. *Yasmin* was made by Loach's old production company Parallax, and produced by his erstwhile collaborator Sally Hibbin. Although shot in the north of England, it also enjoyed the backing of Scottish Screen as a result of the involvement of the Scottish director, Kenny Glenaan. Compared with *Ae Fond Kiss...*, however, *Yasmin* is much less optimistic about the state of community relations. In response to the growing prejudice around her and the heavy-handed actions of the police in the wake of 9/11, the film's central character Yasmin (Archie Punjabi) comes to reject her westernised life-style and the possibility of a romance with her white co-worker. In contrast, Casim in *Ae Fond Kiss...* does ultimately defy the wishes of (the majority of) his family by choosing his own partner. While films such as *Yasmin* and *Bradford Riots* suggest how the pressure of political events is encouraging Muslims to reject "in-between" identifications in favour of more clear-cut forms of ethnic and religious affiliation, *Ae Fond Kiss...* embraces the continuing possibility of living with new, hybrid forms of cultural identity. At the film's beginning Casim's younger sister, Tahara (Shabana Bakhsh), speaking at a school debate, denounces simplified definitions of Muslim identity and declares how she represents "a dazzling mixture... a Glaswegian, Pakistani, teenager woman of Muslim descent who supports Glasgow Rangers in a Catholic school."

It is for this reason that the production notes for *Ae Fond Kiss...* describe it as "a film that deals with identity, not just personal identity" (Sixteen Films 2004). Casim and Roisin, in this respect, represent a new kind of social settlement in which a variety of forms of cultural identification and social inheritance may coalesce (particularly as the couple involved are both, in their ways, "outsiders"). However, this "national romance" is also worked out in a particular way. In contrast to the earlier films, the drama is set amongst the well-to-do. Tariq is a self-made man whose children have, or will, all benefit from higher education. Casim is a trained accountant, and aspiring club-owner, while Roisin is a teacher (with the means to fly to Spain at short notice). The characters all live comfortably in the suburbs and many of the scenes take place in the smart new Glasgow of fashionable nightclubs and upmarket bars. The only working-class characters of significance to appear in the film are the workmen hired by Tariq to build the extension to his house. In some respects, this change of social terrain makes the point that, because the characters are not plagued by financial problems, they have the capacity to exercise choices that characters such as Joe and Liam do not. Thus, in their final confrontation, Casim is able to demand that his father "respect" the "choice" that he is making. The downplaying of material determinants may also be read as a kind of acknowledgement that ethnic and cultural tensions cannot be simply reduced to economic factors (and, indeed, that within Scotland the relatively small Asian community is predominantly middle class). However, in eliminating the issue of money that had so dominated the previous two Scottish films, the film also appears to separate off class politics from identity politics rather than investigate the ways in which these intertwine.

The separation of the economic and the cultural in this manner appears to be indicative of how the politics of Loach's films continue to be shaped by a "classic" conception of the working class in terms of white male industrial workers. This is the same group that has played a particularly important symbolic role, historically, for conceptions of Scottish identity. While heavy industry may have undergone a decline, the number of manual workers in Scotland remains substantial: forty-one per cent of the working population of Scotland were engaged in manual work in 2000 (Paterson *et al* 2004, 84). The nature of such work has, of course, changed significantly in the last thirty years. Given the demise of heavy industry, it is much more concentrated in light industry and the service sector and relies heavily on (flexible forms of) female labour. As a result, the experience of contemporary Scottish working-class experience cannot be reduced to a straightforward narrative of industrial decline and masculine crisis but is much more multi-faceted in character. As Huw Beynon suggests, commenting on the situation in Britain more generally, the "growing complex of jobs and labour contract" characteristic of contemporary forms of manual labour has combined with "gender and ethnic difference to produce a mosaic that is not easily represented in simple images" (Benyon 2001, 38). Loach and Laverty's Scottish films have provided powerful images of working-class decline and deprivation but have been rather less successful in capturing the changing character of working-class employment and the variety of ways in which the politics of class, gender, ethnicity and nationality overlap and interweave in present-day Scotland.

## Works Cited

Anon. 1998. Lottery attack by film-maker it helped fund. *The Scotsman*, May 16.

Bain, Douglas, Ouainé Bain and Gillian Skirrow. 1983. Woman, Women and Scotland: "Scotch Reels" and Political Perspectives. *Cencrastus* 11: 3-6.

Bennett, Ronan. 1995. Lean, Mean and Cruel. *Sight & Sound* 5.1: 34-36.

Benyon, Huw. 2001. Images of Labour/Images of Class. In *Looking at Class: Film, Television and the Working Class in Britain*, ed. Sheila Rowbotham and Huw Beynon, 25-40. London: River Orams Press.

Bruce, David. 1996. *Scotland the Movie*. Edinburgh: Polygon.

Caughie, John. 1990. Representing Scotland: New Questions for Scottish Cinema. In *From Limelight to Satellite: A Scottish Film Book*, ed. Eddie Dick, 13-30. London/Glasgow: British Film Institute/Scottish Film Council.

Cosgrove, Stuart. 2005. Edinburgh Lecture: Innovation and Risk—How Scotland survived the Tsunami. http://download.edinburgh.gov.uk/lectures/StuartCosgrove.pdf (accessed November 10, 2008).

Garside, Juliette. 2002. Poverty, crime, drug addiction, violence… why is cinema so obsessed with Scotland's dark side? *Sunday Herald*, June 2.

Hill, John. 1977. Towards a Scottish People's Theatre: the Rise and Fall of Glasgow Unity. *Theatre Quarterly* 7.27: 61-70.

—. 1982. "Scotland doesna mean much tae Glesca": Some Notes on *The Gorbals Story*. In *Scotch Reels*: *Scotland in Cinema and Television*, ed. Colin McArthur, 100-11. London: British Film Institute.

Loach, Ken. 2006. Director's Note for *The Wind that Shakes the Barley*, by Paul Laverty, 9. Ardfield: Galley Head Press.

McArthur, Colin. 1982. Scotland and Cinema: The Iniquity of the Fathers. In *Scotch Reels*: *Scotland in Cinema and Television*, ed. Colin McArthur, 40-69. London: British Film Institute.

McCrone, David. 1992. *Understanding Scotland: The Sociology of a Stateless Nation*. London: Routledge.

Martin-Jones, David. 2004. *Orphans*, a Work of Minor Cinema from Post-Devolutionary Scotland. *Journal of British Cinema and Television* 1.2: 226-41.

Mottram, James. 2004. In the Mood for Love. *Sight and Sound* 14.3: 22-23.

Murray, Jonathan. 2001. Contemporary Scottish Film. *The Irish Review* 28: 75-88.

—. 2007. Anywhere but here or here but anywhere? Glasgow on Screen. *Anglo-Files* 146: 33-36.

Paterson, Lindsay, Frank Bechhofer and David McCrone. 2004. *Living in Scotland: Social and Economic Change since 1980*. Edinburgh: Edinburgh University Press.

Petrie, Duncan. 2000. *Screening Scotland*. London: British Film Institute.

—. 2004. *Contemporary Scottish Fictions: Film, Television and the Novel*. Edinburgh: Edinburgh University Press.

Sixteen Films. 2004. *Ae Fond Kiss…* production notes. http://www.sixteenfilms.co.uk/films/production_notes/ae_fond_kiss/ (accessed November 10, 2008).

Spencer, Liese. 1999. Tearing the Roof Off. *Sight and Sound* 9.4: 13-14.

Turok, Ivan. 2003. Cities, Clusters and Creative Industries: The Case of Film and Television in Scotland. *European Planning Studies* 11.5: 549-565.

# SCOTLAND'S OTHER KINGDOMS: CONSIDERING REGIONAL IDENTITIES IN A GROWING NATIONAL CINEMA

DAVID MARTIN-JONES

Given the burgeoning levels of film production in Scotland post-1990, it is tempting, as with any emergent or resurgent national cinema, to seek to examine the ways in which that cinema currently constructs national identity. Yet in the case of New Scottish Cinema this is not always the most fruitful approach to take. This is so for two reasons. Firstly, it runs the risk of imposing a national label upon films that depict specific regional concerns and identities. Secondly, the three dominant myths of Scotland—those stereotypical images of Tartanry, Kailyard and Clydesidism identified in the seminal collection *Scotch Reels* as characteristic of cinematic representations of the nation—were themselves based upon specific regions of Scotland (McArthur 1982). Briefly, Tartanry expressed a romanticized view of the Highlands and Islands as a place bypassed by history; Kailyard (or cabbage patch) depicted the parochial life of isolated, Lowland rural working class communities; finally, Clydesidism constructs the myth of an "authentic," masculine, working class urban life. Focused in and around the shipyards of Glasgow in the latter decades of the twentieth century when shipbuilding began to decline, Clydesidism in cinema increasingly drew attention to the position of the disenfranchised, post-industrial "hard man", in opposition to the "feminised" middle classes (Caughie 1990, 13-20; 17).

Much New Scottish Cinema is marked by a sophisticated engagement with, or an outright rejection of, these stereotypical images of the "nation," images which potentially conflate regional imagery and identities with national equivalents. In the discussion that follows I will examine how these "national" myths are either renegotiated or rejected altogether in certain works of New Scottish Cinema, in favour of an examination of regional identities. The examples discussed are: *As An Eilean/From The Island* (Alexander, GB, 1993), *The Winter Guest* (Rickman, GB/USA, 1997) and *The Acid House* (McGuigan, GB, 1998). Such films indicate the extent to which the late twentieth-century diversification and expansion of

Scottish film production has ensured that a broader spectrum of regional identities is being constructed in features from Scotland. *As An Eilean* provides a more sophisticated examination of identity in a small island community in the Islands than those found in either Tartanry or Kailyard, whilst *The Winter Guest* and *The Acid House* both depict life in specific regional locations that are not invested with the same nationally representative resonances as those of, say, *Whisky Galore!* (Mackendrick, GB, 1949) or *The Big Man* (Leland, GB, 1990). As a consequence, recognition of the plurality of Scottish regional identities multiplies along with the proliferation of Scottish films. We can begin to examine many representations of different regional "Scotlands", rather than any one representative Scotland.

## Why Scottish National Identity?

It might seem churlish to decry so rapidly recent attempts made, in both the media and the academy, to discuss contemporary Scottish film production in terms of images of national identity. However, there is a difference between identifying a body of work examined as Scottish national cinema, and homogenising all the films within it as representations of the same "Scottish" national identity. Before I turn to analyse the films themselves, it is worth briefly examining three of the most apparent reasons why the national label has been so swiftly applied in critical discussions of New Scottish Cinema.

Firstly, that cinema's recent growth became a political issue within the larger late-'90s context of Devolution. This is especially so considering the coincidence of political Devolution with the devolution of Lottery funding for film production in Scotland in 1995, and the establishment of Scottish Screen (which eventually came to wield responsibility for distributing this funding) in 1997. As in any small nation, one way of obtaining international recognition is through the creation of a national cinematic brand. The creation of Scottish Screen—and more recently, its ongoing amalgamation with the Scottish Arts Council to produce a single new cultural development agency, Creative Scotland—emphasise the desire to see Scottish cinema identified as a national product. Moreover, for the Scottish National Party (SNP)—at time of writing the governing party in the Scottish Parliament for the first time in history, albeit with only around a third of the popular vote and forming a minority administration—representations of Scotland have at times taken on a symbolic role in their campaign for national independence. In 1995 the SNP embraced the media attention surrounding *Braveheart* (Gibson, USA,

1995), using imagery from the film in campaign literature (McArthur 2003, 126-127). More recently, MEP Alyn Smith has openly criticised what he considers to be the lack of governmental support for the industry, also noting the lucrative tourism-related benefits that potentially follow Scottish film production (Smith 2005). In such a context Scottish cinema is seen in terms of its ability to promote the nation conceived singularly.

Secondly, at a cultural level, the coincidence of Scottish cinema's growth with Devolution creates a temptation to view the former as a map of an emergent, post-Devolutionary national identity (Blandford 2007; Martin-Jones 2004). Indeed, this is not such an unusual connection to make. As Duncan Petrie demonstrates, the major cultural outpourings of the 1980s and 1990s, literary, televisual, and cinematic, can be considered a response to the widespread perception that Scotland's national interests were not being served by Westminster and the British state (Petrie 2004). Viewed in this light, recent Scottish film production is part of a larger attempt to create Scottish national identity in the cultural sphere, an undertaking that may well have continued without political Devolution, and that some date from as early as the 1920s (Gardiner 2004). From this perspective, recent Scottish cinema could be understood as an example of cultural devolution, a process accelerated by a fortuitous convergence of events in the 1990s.

Thirdly, the search in an academic context for national identity in recent Scottish cinema can be explained by the dominance of the national cinema paradigm shaping a great deal of study and publication. As happened within Scottish Literary Studies in the mid-to-late '90s (Crawford 1997; Gifford 1996; Maley 2000), Film Studies' search for representations of national identity in recent Scottish work needs to recognise the existence of multiple identities, "Scotlands" (Crawford 1997, 93) as opposed to "Scotland". The notion of "Scotlands" has major ramifications for minority identities in Scotland (be they gendered, sexual, racial, ethnic, religious, etc.) that are beyond the bounds of this particular chapter. However, one small step towards exploring this diversity of identities is to focus on the regional in recent cinema.

## The Gàidhealtachd (Gaeldom): *As An Eilean*

*As An Eilean* is a rare instance in Scottish filmmaking, a film with a large proportion of Gaelic language dialogue. Gaelic is currently spoken by less than 60 000 people in Scotland, just over 1% of the population (Macdonald 1999; Cormack 2004). Although there are concentrations of Gaelic speakers in various parts of Scotland, including a large Diaspora in and around Glasgow, Gaelic language and culture is predominantly focused around the Gàidhealtachd, an area encompassing parts of the Highlands and the Islands of Scotland, particularly the Western Isles. Despite the continual decline in numbers of Gaelic speakers, Gaelic culture has enjoyed a renaissance since the early 1980s, one due to a number of factors, the most important of which is increased British state support for Gaelic language and culture (Macdonald 1997). As information on the Gaelic Media Service website relates, this included the 1990 Broadcasting Act's establishment of a Gaelic Television Fund of £9.5m per year. This in turn led to the establishment of the Comataidh Telebhisein Gàidhlig (Gaelic Television Committee) (CTG) in 1993. In 1997 the Committee became Comataidh Craolaidh Gàidhlig (The Gaelic Broadcasting Committee) (CCG), recognising the addition of Gaelic radio to its remit in 1996. The Communications Act of 2003 replaced CCG with Serbheis Nam Meadhanan Gàidhlig (Gaelic Media Service) (GMS), and in 2007 the Scottish Executive added £3m to the annual budget to back the development of a dedicated Gaelic television channel.

During this period of development, Gaelic films first emerged. CTG, CCG and GMS played a prominent role in funding Gaelic works (the majority of which were initially designed for television), along with BBC Scotland and Scottish Screen. The short-lived Geur Gheàrr scheme enabled several short Gaelic films to be made in the mid-1990s: *An Iobairt/The Sacrifice* (Gerda Stevenson, GB, 1996), *Roimh Ghaoth A'Gheamhraidh/Before Winter Winds* (Bill MacLeod, GB, 1996), *Ag Iasgach/Fishing* (Roddy Cunningham, GB, 1997), *A'Bhean Eudach/The Jealous Sister* (Domhnall Ruadh, GB, 1997), *Dathan/Colours* (Iain F. MacLeod, GB, 1998), *Keino* (Iseabil Maciver, GB, 1998), and *Mac* (Alasdair Maclean, GB, 1998) (see Martin-Jones forthcoming). They joined predecessors *Hero* (Platts-Mill, GB, 1982), arguably the first ever Gaelic feature film, and Douglas MacKinnon's short, *Sealladh/The Vision* (GB, 1992). The last two decades also saw two full-length features, *As An Eilean/From The Island* in English and Gaelic, and *Seachd: The Inaccessible Pinnacle* (Miller, GB, 2007), the latter based on a previous Gaelic short film, *Foighidinn/The Crimson Snowdrop* (Simon Miller, GB, 2003).

Sharon Macdonald positions the "reimagining of Gaelic culture" (Macdonald 1997, xv) in the broader context of the revival of ethnonationalism in Europe. The growth of interest (state and public) in Gaelic reflects the recent recognition accorded to regional minority identities in places like Cornwall, Brittany, Catalonia and the Basque country. Thus, whilst it is possible to see the 1990s growth of Gaelic film as part of the same context that enabled the flourishing of other forms of Scottish cinema in the period, the specifically local culture of the Gàidhealtachd seen in these films should not be considered representatively "Scottish". The most apparent reason for this is of course that in such films the language spoken is that of a tiny minority of Scots. I will also demonstrate, however, the extent to which *As An Eilean* positions its island community within a global, rather than a purely national context by means other than the linguistic. By evoking the historical identity of the Gàidhealtachd as a nexus of various trade routes, *As An Eilean* represents this Scottish region as having a global/local, as opposed to a solely or purely national, identity.

Shot on Super-16mm and then blown up to 35mm for cinema release (Elley 1993), *As An Eilean* is set in the Outer Hebrides, a region closely associated with the landscapes of Tartanry. Ostensibly, the film is concerned with the clash between tradition and modernity—most clearly seen in the local minister's concern over the spiritual dangers of a young man taking a motorbike to visit his girlfriend on the Sabbath—and the dangers of internal and external exile created by a potentially ostracising close-knit island community (Myers, 1994; Kirkwood, 1998). Even so, by focusing on the community's interior mechanics, *As An Eilean* avoids the clichés associated with the Kailyard tradition. Unlike a host of films set on Scottish islands—*I Know Where I'm Going!* (Powell & Pressburger, GB, 1945), *The Wicker Man* (Hardy, GB, 1973), *The Rocket Post* (Whittaker, GB, 2004)—the film does not introduce us to the island's locals through the eyes of an outsider. Instead, positioned within the island's community, we are privy to the ongoing lives of the local people rather than being provided with a privileged external viewpoint from which to assess their relative progress in relation to the civilized 'Other'. Douglas Eadie developed the script from two stories by the Gaelic poet and novelist Ian Crichton-Smith, updating these to a contemporary setting in order to provide a realist depiction of life in the village of Carraig. This updating avoided any suggestion that a story in Gaelic was somehow synonymous with things past, thereby sidestepping the nostalgic and elegiac pitfalls of Kailyard and Tartanry.

Interwoven with this concern with community is the broader theme of the Gàidhealtachd's global positioning. At the time of *As An Eilean*'s release, director Mike Alexander argued that the film be understood not solely in a Scottish national context, but also in a wider, pan-European one:

> The outer islands are the setting … but the film has a European theme. It reflects life on a geographic edge, but it could reflect life in many parts of Europe. The outer islands are regarded as Europe's lost wilderness, the edge of things. But you're talking about a society which at one time was part of the highways of the sea—the Norse, the Celts, everybody crossed lines there. (Flynn 1993)

In fact, there is ample evidence in the film to suggest that the Gàidhealtachd's identity exists as a region of the world, rather than Europe. The very first scene shows young protagonist Callum Matheson (Iain F. Mcleod) learning French. Callum's bedroom is a mish-mash of globally signifying cultural products. His *Dandy* comic book t-shirt (Dundee) and Rangers Football Club (Glasgow) posters suggest his links to Scotland , but only as part of a cultural collage including posters for the music of the London-Irish folk-rock band The Pogues and the iconic French film *Betty Blue* (Beineix, Fr, 1986). There are in addition a number of pointed references to the Gàidhealtachd's interconnectedness with the rest of the world and the impact this has on the region's identity. Retired headmaster Charles McAllister (Ken Hutchison) posts a letter to his brother in New Zealand, thereby acknowledging centuries-long emigration from the Gàidhealtachd to various points on the globe; the enigmatic Valparaiso (Frank Wood) spent time in various parts of South America (he is nicknamed after a port in Chile) and now dreams of visiting India and South Africa; the long-awaited returning wanderer Derek (Iain Macrae) has been working in Texas. Thus when the cultural polyglot Callum becomes interested in the existence of a book of Gaelic poetry produced by Alan Ban, the great-grandfather of his school-friend Kirsty Fraser (Donna MacLeod), Gaelic history and culture are firmly positioned within a global context.

Callum and Kirsty are both about to leave the island for university, in Aberdeen and Glasgow respectively. Their stories of imminent exile are linked to that of Kirsty's great-grandfather, Ban. The latter was an illiterate Gaelic bard who emigrated to Australia, his love poems transcribed into letters by a cousin so they could be sent back to Ban's wife. Significantly, Callum first hears of this forgotten history in the schoolroom, when the literature teacher Mr McIvor (John Macneil) gives a lesson on the tradition of Gaelic love poetry that stretches from the eighteenth century (Willeam Ross) to the twentieth (Sorley MacLean). As Ban's poetry is now out of print, it is only in the mind of the schoolteacher that his position in the Gaelic canon is remembered, until this is passed on to Callum. The role of education is thus stressed in retaining the Gaelic tradition, especially when many young islanders, like Callum and Kirsty, are destined to leave the islands, forming a new generation of exiles who will take Gaelic language and culture into the world. In *As An Eilean*, then, the historical position of the Gàidhealtachd is rendered not as a Scottish periphery, but as "part of the highways of the sea." Yet the region's history can only survive if there is a concerted effort to maintain it, with those who do leave remembering their roots and spreading the influence of Gaelic language and culture.

It could in fact be argued that *As An Eilean* functions in precisely this way. The film derived a large proportion of its funding from Gaelic sources. Along with financial support from Channel 4 (£250 000) and Grampian TV (£40 000), *As An Eilean* received £500 000, the majority of its budget, from CTG, as well as additional funding from the Ross and Cromarty District Council, the Highlands Regional Council and Highlands and Islands Enterprise. *As An Eilean*'s regional identity, then, is tied directly to the national and international promotion of a regionally specific, minority Scottish language and culture. In this, it is not unique: emerging over a decade later, the Gaelic feature *Seachd* explores the power of the fantastical and the mythical in the Gaelic storytelling tradition (Martin-Jones, forthcoming). In *As An Eilean*, retired headmaster Charles McAllister (Ken Hutchinson), one of the very few non-natives on the island, diligently keeps a photographic record of the islanders' everyday lives for an exhibition he is planning with the same title as Mike Alexander's film. *Seachd* also explores the need to promote the process of recording the region's past, this time through oral history, if the unique legacy of the Gàidhealtachd is to survive. Remarkably, though made over ten years later, *Seachd* only cost £680 000 to produce, slightly less then *As An Eilean*. It replicated the earlier film's funding pattern, with GMS providing nearly two-thirds of the funding, the rest coming from BBC Scotland and Scottish Screen. Interestingly, like the character of McAllister in *As An Eilean*, *Seachd*'s director, Englishman Simon Miller, is not a native of the Gàidhealtachd, nor is the film's producer Chris Young (although he is permanently based on the Isle of Skye). This leaves a slight question mark over the future potential of this particular region to depict and promote itself from within, using film.

## The Kingdom of Fife: *The Winter Guest*

*The Winter Guest* is set in an isolated corner of the Kingdom of Fife, and as such represents an altogether different region of Scotland to those typically seen in Tartanry, Kailyard and Clydesidism. Unlike *As An Eilean*, this film does not lay claim to a regional identity in its narrative. In fact, the use of Scotland as a setting—whilst faithful to the nationality of Sharman Macdonald, author of the play the film adapts, and the film's co-screenwriter—could be seen as somewhat coincidental. Even so, despite *The Winter Guest*'s attempts to appeal to an international audience with a universal story practically devoid of nationally specific characteristics, the film still reflects life in a particular region of Scotland. It is set and shot in the now gentrified string of once-thriving fishing villages on the isolated East Neuk of Fife, particularly Crail, Pittenweem and Elie. These communities now increasingly attract permanent residents from the professional classes, including overspill populations from Edinburgh and Dundee, and a large proportion of lecturers from the nearby University of St Andrews. For this audience, in addition to its more universally appealing aspects, *The Winter Guest* also provides a recognisable image of the region.

*The Winter Guest* is a £5m US/UK co-production backed by the Scottish Arts Council Lottery Fund and the Scottish Film Production Fund. Its aesthetic corresponds to that often identified as typical of European art cinema: loose, drifting or episodic narratives (as opposed to the transparent and causal linearity of classical Hollywood narrative), "psychologically complex characters" without "defined desires and goals", and a foregrounded focus on the "dissection of feeling" amongst these characters (Bordwell 2002, 95-96). The film markets itself internationally through the star status of debut director Alan Rickman; the Oscar-winning English actress Emma Thompson and her real-life mother Phyllida Law in its lead roles; its theatrical origins; and its innovative use of special effects—created on the Quantel Domino—to suggest a frozen sea (Oppenheimer 1997; Kaufman 1998). The film uses a frozen moment in time as a metaphor for the grief of Frances (Emma Thompson), one of its adult protagonists. In this frozen moment the village where she lives becomes the location for an examination of the concerns of four different generations, when the temperature drops so low that the sea freezes over, and—apart from the unlikely service provided by one immaculately preserved 1950s period bus—normal life is entirely suspended.

As a result of its desire to be universally appealing, and to suggest through setting that Frances is locked in by her grief, *The Winter Guest* establishes its location as a paradoxical "Scottish anywhere". This is a place without clearly identifiable geographical characteristics, but which is still recognisably "Scottish" both in its isolated bleakness, and in the accents of its two youngest characters, schoolboys Tom (Sean Biggerstaff) and Sam (Douglas Murphy). This sense of location was not lost on reviewers, who repeatedly remarked upon the "Scottishness" of *The*

*Winter Guest*'s setting (Marshall 1997; Mattheou 1998; Kemp 1999). This strange identification of the film as at once set in Scotland, and simultaneously set nowhere in particular in Scotland, is perhaps a product of the "isolated wilderness" view of the nation so often constructed by Tartanry and arguably resonates with the notion of the isolated small town paradigm of Kailyard. However, it is more likely that this particular region of Scotland is not immediately recognisable to critics because it lacks the wily sense of community seen in Kailyard, the beautiful Highland and Island wilderness of Tartanry, or the focus on urban working-class life seen in Clydesidism. In other words, *The Winter Guest*'s particular Scotland has yet to be put on the cinematic map of "Scotlands." Whilst we could argue that the film creates the familiar portrayal of Scotland as a nation "lost to time", for local audiences (and here I refer specifically to those people with a knowledge of life in the present-day East Neuk), alongside the appeal of the film as taking place in a Scottish "nowhere" and "no-when", there is also the recognition of a very specific "somewhere" and "some-when," creating a cinematic reflection of the lives of its inhabitants.

The East Neuk of Fife is an hour's drive from Edinburgh, or forty minutes from Dundee. Yet in spite of this proximity to major urban centres, to many of its inhabitants it offers a life seemingly "cut off" from urbanization. This effect is reinforced by the train service through Fife linking Edinburgh to Dundee, which suddenly veers away from the East Neuk once north of Kirkaldy. Similarly, the M90—the major automobile artery through Fife—bypasses the region's entire coastline. The peninsula of the East Neuk is left to the locals who navigate its irregular and meandering byways by car and local bus. The perception of the East Neuk's isolation was reflected in media coverage of the H5N1 avian influenza "bird flu" scare of 2006, when the virus washed up on British shores in the shape of a dead swan in Cellardyke harbour. The inordinate length of time it took for the authorities to respond to the carcass hinted at the East Neuk's supposed isolation from civilization, and the British media took full advantage of this perception to allay public fears that it would spread quickly, particularly in the repeated use of a helicopter shot that demonstrated the supposed rural dislocation of Cellardyke. In this particular instance, then, a rural location south of the Highland line offers the suggestion of an isolated life in Scotland, but with the unspoken convenience of easy access to major Lowland urban centres. This has attracted a good deal of income into the area, with middle-class professionals renovating ex-fishing cottages and buying up the precious few pieces of new housing stock. It is the region's quasi-isolation and the consequently privileged life it offers to its more prosperous inhabitants that *The Winter Guest* depicts, rather than the supposedly "primitive" wilderness bypassed by modernity typically found in Tartanry and Kailyard.

The film's central protagonists are a middle-class family, professional photographer Frances, her son Alex (Gary Hollywood) and ageing mother Elspeth (Phyllida Law). Frances and Alex live in a renovated ex-fishing cottage: stripped wooden floorboards and roof beams, expensive rugs and minimalist furnishings, a converted attic, and all other mod-cons. Frances is considering emigration to Australia in order to escape her grief over her husband's death. The financial consideration of such a move never enters into the debate with her mother, presumably because her profession as a photographer makes her both financially solvent and internationally mobile. Frances' extended dialogue with Elspeth demonstrates the East Neuk's struggle with its own diminishing sense of Scottishness, brought about by the settling of the area by rootless, global middle-class citizens like her. Noticeably, Elspeth is the only character to mention specific Scottish locations. She recalls a beauty contest Frances entered as a young girl in Prestwick, and the local village of Carnoustie—not mentioned at all in the original play—is evoked as a possible alternative to Australia. Elspeth uses the locality to situate Frances's life in this specific region of Scotland, in particular by evoking memories of Frances' childhood, in order to keep her daughter from emigrating. The same struggle between the region's Scottish and global identities is played out between young schoolboys Tom and Sam, both of whom are feeling the pressure of the expectations of their middle-class parents. Whilst Sam's parents desire him to become a vet and work in a park in Africa, Tom simply wishes to settle for a local life working in a supermarket.

Frances' professional life as a photographer also reflects the contribution of the East Neuk's inhabitants to the culture and knowledge industries of Scotland, and simultaneously the distinctive artisanal, cultural and artistic production of the region. Frances' house is entirely decorated with her photographs (especially of her dead husband), and for a local audience immediately resembles the interior of the numerous houses which take part in the Annual Pittenweem Arts Festival (founded in the early 1980s), during which around thirty local artists open their homes to exhibit their work to the public.

Finally, the "anonymous" feel to the fishing village in question is undoubtedly a result of filming in various scenic locations in the villages of Crail, Pittenweem and Elie. Yet it also recreates the sense of blurred boundaries between the villages that occurs as one travels from Crail to

Cellardyke, which sprawls imperceptibly into Anstruther and then Pittenweem, before briefly travelling on to St Monans and finally Elie. Thus the film's scenic locations (from Pittenweem harbour to the Elie lighthouse) demonstrate both the natural beauty and tourist appeal of the East Neuk, and the actual backdrop against which lives are lived in the region.

In all these ways, along with its examination of universal themes such as familial relationships, life and death, youth and old age, grief and love, *The Winter Guest* also indirectly reflects a very specific, regional lifestyle peculiar to the East Neuk's scenic villages. A dual address exists in *The Winter Guest*: international audiences are courted by its universal themes and the anywhere/anywhen-ness of the beautiful locations, whilst local audiences are granted an insider's recognition of the life of the East Neuk's middle-class population. In *The Winter Guest*, the Kingdom of Fife offers an alternative representation of Scotland, another of Scotland's Scotlands, as it were, rather than a return to Tartanry, the Kailyard, or Clydesidism.

## North Edinburgh: *The Acid House*

Alongside the predominantly Glasgow-based urban features that dominate much Scottish film production and academic discussion of it, the city of Edinburgh also has a recurring presence in the history of Scottish cinema. However, Edinburgh has received somewhat less in the way of critical attention than Glasgow, due in part to repeated discussion of the Clydeside myth. *The Acid House* uses various Edinburgh locations to offer a slightly different, regionally focused perspective on urban decay from that articulated by Clydesidism.

In addition to at least two *Greyfriars Bobby* films (Chaffey, USA, 1961), (Henderson, GB, 2005), other Edinburgh-based films include *The Battle of the Sexes* (Crichton, GB, 1959), *The Prime of Miss Jean Brodie* (Neame, GB, 1969), *Women Talking Dirty* (Giedroyc, GB, 1999), *Festival* (Griffin, GB, 2005) and *Hallam Foe* (Mackenzie, GB, 2007). In the main these films draw upon the beautiful urban surroundings of Edinburgh's city centre and New Town as settings for their stories. The overarching impression is of the city's architectural distinction, cultural vitality and middle-class opulence. Yet as Duncan Petrie argued, focusing on a less well-known strand of Edinburgh horror films—*The Body Snatcher* (Wise, USA, 1945), *The Flesh and the Fiends* (Gilling, GB, 1959) and *The Doctor and the Devils* (Francis, GB/USA, 1985)—in many Edinburgh films the up-market, Dr Jekyll façade is constantly under threat from the ugly, disruptive underbelly of the murderous Mr Hyde. It is to this Gothic tradition of a city of "light and dark" (Petrie 2000, 79) that recent films like *Shallow Grave* (Boyle, GB, 1995), *Trainspotting* (GB, 1996), *The Acid House* (1998) and *16 Years of Alcohol* (Jobson, GB, 2003) belong. In all four of these recent films there is an attempt to create transnational appeal through the depiction of either young professional or subcultural identities. Even so, *The Acid House* stands out for its regionally focused depiction of the post-industrial milieu of North Edinburgh's council estates. This is the case notwithstanding the film's more universally "appealing" aspects: deliberately intrusive visual effects, narrative emphasis on crime and drug culture, and deployment of the same style of modish soundtrack as *Trainspotting*.

*The Acid House* was made on a very low budget (£900 000) by Picture Palace North Productions, who specialise in localised productions in the North of England. Made for Channel 4, the film was part-funded by the European Regional Development Fund, the Scottish Arts Council National Lottery Fund and the Glasgow Film Fund. *The Acid House* is different from contemporaneous Edinburgh films in that it examines a regional identity peculiar to the north of the city. The film's distinctive regional "accent" is provided by the source material, three short stories by Irvine Welsh, to which the film's three separate episodes adhere fairly faithfully. Welsh's original *Acid House* anthology (1994) contained stories set in London, Amsterdam, Glasgow and Edinburgh, but the three that were chosen for film adaptation are all set in the north of Edinburgh, in and around the depressed suburbs and housing schemes of Pilton and Granton. Situated slightly to the west of Leith, on the Firth of Forth, these industrial and shipping havens of the nineteenth and early twentieth centuries degenerated during the latter's second half. In this respect they are similar to certain parts of Glasgow. However, as Petrie notes when discussing Irvine Welsh's literature:

> Welsh's vivid representation of his particular stratum of Edinburgh society undermines the familiar reductive binary conception of Glasgow—the locus of an authentic, working-class Scottish identity—contrasted with an Edinburgh that is necessarily inauthentic, bourgeois and Anglo-centric. (Petrie 2004, 91)

*The Acid House*, then, recreates the post-industrial milieu usually associated with Clydesidism, but clearly locates its tales of contemporary working-class life in an identifiable region of Edinburgh, to which its inhabitants are branded, or brand themselves, as belonging. In so doing, the film questions Clydesidism's conflation of Scottish post-industrial working class identity with the city of Glasgow.

A blend of realism and surrealism, *The Acid House* focuses on the lives of several of north Edinburgh's social underclass. Parts one and three of the film are of most relevance to this discussion, the former due to its focus on Granton, the latter for the contrasts it draws between Pilton (West Pilton Park in particular) and Morningside, the upper middle class city centre area close to the public park known as The Meadows. In the film's first episode, *The Granton Star Cause*, the unfortunate hero Boab (Stephen McCole), is introduced playing football for the local team, Granton Star. Establishing shots position the pitch in the shadow of Granton's imposing housing estates. Later, when the luckless Boab is transformed into a fly by God, his initial flight enables aerial shots of the local schemes, emphasising their degraded architectural poverty. Grey, lifeless terraces stretch into the distance, their monotonous lines broken only by the occasional patch where a house has burned down or fallen into ruin. In these moments, the area's imposing landscape and Boab are shown to be inextricably linked. Despite the depressing nature of the surroundings, Boab and Granton are shown to be as one. Significantly, it is only after Boab gives up on life in Granton that his story takes its downturn, a moment symbolised by the throwing away of his Granton Star football shirt.

Boab is rejected by the football team after being replaced by a better player. Walking home from the pub, he removes his football shirt, and flings it into a fence. Shortly afterwards he is sought out by God and metamorphosed into a fly. God chides Boab for giving up on life, and letting himself slide into obesity, laziness and self-pity. In spite of the conditions into which he has been born, he is repeatedly told that it was within his power to change his life for the better. Noticeably, amongst the list of Boab's shortcomings he sets out, God notes that "you've got the power to get fit and make a more positive contribution to the Granton Star cause". Significantly, the close-up image of Boab's Granton Star football shirt hitting the fence positions the viewer on the other side of the fence that encloses the character, much as the estates previously enclosed the football pitch in the opening establishing shots of the film. As the shirt suddenly fills the screen, we are revealed as external witnesses to life in Granton, positioned along with the camera on the other side of the fence. While in the *Granton Star Cause* giving up on your regional identity is not considered to be a positive action, (Boab is punished for doing so by God), for the audience positioned on the other side of the fence, the grim conditions of the estate suggest that such capitulation may be completely understandable. It is an action akin, perhaps, to the flinging of one's prison uniform at the bars of the cell. God's refusal to take responsibility for the lives of Boab and the other inhabitants of Granton suggests that the region is in the hands of the locals; no one else—including the viewer—is in a position, or cares enough, to help. In this *The Acid House* is very similar to many Clydeside films, which seek to re-establish some sense of a united local community in the face of post-industrial socioeconomic adversity. The noticeable difference is that in *The Acid House* it is specifically Granton (rather than Glasgow or its surrounding industrial towns posing as a synecdoche for the nation) that is in the spotlight.

The film's third episode, titled, like the entire work itself, *The Acid House*, is more obvious in its identification of the local region, its working-class inhabitants and specific identity, within the larger context of the city of Edinburgh. The protagonist, Coco Bryce (Ewan Bremner) is a fan of Hibernian Football Club (Hibs, or the Hibees). Hibs' ground is at Easter Road, close to Leith, and the club, along with Heart of Midlothian FC (Hearts), is one of Edinburgh's two major football teams. The rivalry between the two clubs divides along sectarian lines, Hibs historically Catholic, Hearts Protestant. Coco constantly refers to himself in terms of the club, perpetually articulating his identity as a member of the Hibs firm (the Pilton Casuals), by repeatedly declaring himself a "Hibs Boy." He happily exists as a member of a pack. Coco's allegiance to collective cultural phenomena, football and drug culture, is at odds with the familial desires of his girlfriend Kirsty (Arlene Cockburn), and the pressures of his relationship with a physically abusive, bullying father. The Pilton Casuals have welcomed Coco as one of their own, into "the family" as one member puts it. This adoptive belonging to a regionally based sense of identity is in stark contrast to the upper middle class Morningside affluence of the thirty-something couple into whose lives Coco is magically transported when his soul switches places with that of their newly-born child.

Coco's regional identity, albeit a sub-cultural one as a football hooligan, stands out in contrast to the way Scottish identity is represented in the better-known film adaptation of Welsh's *Trainspotting*. Although *Trainspotting* is also set in the schemes of north Edinburgh, this location is never clearly articulated as such in the film adaptation. The cinematography—tightly framing characters, avoiding any attempt to establish the specific location of narrative settings—creates a sense of universalised urban outskirts, a depressed urban anyplace. In direct contrast to Coco's allegiance to Hibs, and further marking out *Trainspotting*'s international ambitions, is Mark Renton's (Ewan McGregor) professed love of Scotland's *national* football team. Although an eagle-eyed viewer might spot Hibs paraphernalia in Renton's bedroom, this is not immediately recognisable to the general viewer, and certainly not emphasised in the way it is in *The Acid House*. Rather, the footage of Renton's sexual intercourse with Diane (Kelly Macdonald) intercut with scenes of Archie Gemmell scoring for Scotland against Holland in the 1978 World Cup is *Trainspotting*'s most obvious association of Renton with the game. A post-coital Renton exclaims that he hasn't "felt that good" since he saw Gemmell's virtuoso dribble and shot back in '78. In *The Acid House*, however, the international emphasis of *Trainspotting* is replaced by the regional identity provided by Hibernian Football Club.

In Coco's case the depressed urban milieu usually associated with the Clydeside myth becomes one half of the traditional depiction of Edinburgh as a city of light and dark. Coco is reborn into affluence, and initially has difficulty coming to terms with his new environment. This is perhaps not surprising, considering he is transported into the body of a newborn baby when a lightning strike shifts him geographically from the urban periphery of Pilton to the affluent central location of Morningside. His thuggish shaking-up of a complacent upper middle-class city-centre family is contrasted with the rebirth of his physical body, which remains in Pilton, and is inhabited by the baby's soul. Girlfriend Kirsty adopts this baby Coco, and begins to manufacture him into a 'New Man' by keeping him away from drugs and his old friends in the Pilton Casuals. Although in reality the football fan and druggie Coco Bryce is obviously not a clean slate to be moulded into a more "presentable" figure, *The Acid House* does thus at least acknowledge that there may be other ways of life possible for people in the North Edinburgh schemes. Even so, as was the case with Boab, the viewer is left in no doubt that it is the lifestyle provided by the regional context that makes the man. Once again, *The Acid House*'s contrasting of wealth and class with different parts of a single city is akin to the contrasts seen in many Clydeside films. Here, however, Edinburgh, in its "city of light and dark" mode, is used to examine post-industrial working-class life in a specific urban region, rather than an image of the city being made to stand in for the whole of Scotland.

## Conclusion

As this chapter has demonstrated, the proliferation of Scottish filmmaking since the 1990s has enabled a greater diversity of engagement with regional identities in Scottish cinema. Rather than three specific regions of Scotland being isolated as nationally representative in terms of imagery and thematic concerns, numerous other regional "Scotlands" have begun to emerge in recent Scottish cinema. These "Scotlands" either complicate the traditional use of certain regions to construct representative images of national identity, as is the case in *As An Eilean*, or offer different regional alternatives in their place, as seen in both *The Winter Guest* and *The Acid House*.

## Works Cited

Blandford, Steve. 2007. *Film, Drama and the Break-Up of Britain*. Bristol: Intellect.

Bordwell, David. 2002. Art Cinema as Mode of Film Practice. In *The European Cinema Reader*, ed. Catherine Fowler, 94-102. London: Routledge.

Caughie, John. 1990. Representing Scotland: New Questions for Scottish Cinema. In *From Limelight to Satellite: A Scottish Film Book*, ed. Eddie Dick, 13-30. London/Glasgow: British Film Institute/Scottish Film Council.

Cormack, Mike. 2004. Gaelic in the Media. *Scottish Affairs* 46: 23-43.

Crawford, Robert. 1997. Dedefining Scotland. In *Studying British Cultures*, ed. Susan Bassnett, 83-96. London: Routledge.

Elley, Derek. 1993. As An Eilean. *Variety*, October 4.

Flynn, Bob. 1993. Island Stories. *The Guardian*, August 23, *G2* section.

Gardiner, Michael. 2004. *The Cultural Roots of Devolution*. Edinburgh: Edinburgh University Press.

Gifford, Douglas. 1996. The Return of Mythology in Modern Scottish Fiction. In *Studies in Scottish Fiction*, ed. Susanne Hagemann, 17-50. Frankfurt: Peter Lang.

Kaufman, Debra. 1998. Domino and the Invisible Effect. *Clips* Winter: 33-37.

Kemp, Philip. 1999. New Maps of Albion. *Film Comment* 35.3: 64-69.

Kirkwood, Holly. 1998. *Inviting the Outsider In* (1998). MLitt diss., University of Glasgow.

Macdonald, Sharon. 1997. *Reimagining Culture*. Oxford: Berg.

—. 1999. The Gaelic Renaissance and Scotland's Identities. *Scottish Affairs* 26: 100-118.

McArthur, Colin, ed. 1982. *Scotch Reels*: *Scotland in Cinema and Television*. London: British Film Institute.

—. 2003. *Brigadoon, Braveheart and the Scots: Distortions of Scotland in Hollywood Cinema*. London: I. B. Tauris.

Maley, Willy. 2000. Subversion and Scurrility in Irvine Welsh's Shorter Fiction. In *Subversion and Scurrility* eds. Dermott Cavanagh and Tim Kirk, 190-204. London: Ashgate.

Marshall, Lee. 1997. The Winter Guest. *Screen International* 1124: 24.

Martin-Jones, David. 2004. *Orphans*, a Work of Minor Cinema from Post-Devolutionary Scotland. *Journal of British Cinema and Television* 1.2: 226-41.

—. Forthcoming. Islands at the Edge of History: Landscape and the Past in Recent Gaelic Shorts. In *Cinema at the Periphery*, eds. Dina Iordanova, David Martin-Jones and Belen Vidal. Detroit: Wayne State University Press.

Mattheou, Demetrios. 1998. The Winter Guest. *Sight and Sound* 8.1: 56.

Myers, Kenneth. 1994. At the Edge of Europe: The Emergence of a Gaelic Language Media in Scotland and the Potential and Cultural Necessity for a Gaelic Cinema. MLitt diss., University of Glasgow.

Oppenheimer, Jean. 1997. Adding Chills to *The Winter Guest. American Cinematographer* 78.12: 22-24.

Petrie, Duncan. 2000. *Screening Scotland*. London: British Film Institute.

—. 2004. *Contemporary Scottish Fictions: Film, Television and the Novel.* Edinburgh: Edinburgh University Press.

Smith, Alyn. 2005. Scotland's Potential in EU Film Industry. http://www.snp.org/press-releases/2005/snp_press_release.2005-10-26.2869396727/view?searchterm=film%20industry (accessed April 20, 2007).

# ADMITTING THE KAILYARD

JANE SILLARS

## Ghosts: that which persists

During the last quarter-century of intense re-envisaging of Scotland—politically, constitutionally, and across a range of cultural forms—one of the more surprising aspects of recent cinematic production has been the relative absence of an explicit engagement with history. Instead, the past seems to function as a kind of phantom, flickering in and out of visibility on the margins. This essay addresses the consequences of these absences and presences in the cinematic imagining of Scotland. It considers how the construction of the space of the nation is skewed by the occlusion of certain voices and stories; it looks to the ways in which even self-consciously modern representations seem haunted by older patterns of imagining.

The most striking manifestation of these older patterns in contemporary Scottish cinema can be seen in the recurrent foregrounding of the idea of escape in recent films from and/or about Scotland. This escape takes physical forms in *Morvern Callar* (Ramsay, GB, 2002) and *Trainspotting* (Boyle, GB, 1996) with Morvern (Samantha Morton)'s travels across Ibiza and Renton (Ewan McGregor)'s sojourn in London. More typically, however, escape is figured as a journey into some kind of alternative state: narcotic oblivion in the abovementioned films, sexually obsessive behaviour in *Young Adam* (Mackenzie, GB/Fr, 2003), *Hallam Foe* (Mackenzie, GB, 2007) and *Breaking the Waves* (von Trier, Den/Swe/Fr/Neth/Nor/Ice, 1996), where sexual escape is combined with religious ecstasy and/or hysteria. Death becomes the final escape in von Trier's film and also in *Wilbur Wants to Kill Himself* (Scherfig, Den/GB/Swe/Fr, 2002).

Such fantasies of flight hinge on a tension between opposing conceptions of Scotland, a nation open to and connected with a changing world and/or one seen as closed, shut off and restrictive. These films chart the journeys of individuals attempting to negotiate a relationship with place, with belonging and its alternately enabling and stifling embrace. The wish for escape evokes, too, a latent desire to become liberated from the burden of Scottishness. This aspiration can contain a progressive questioning of the limits of nationhood and identity, but it can also be ingrained with deep historical (and arguably colonial) feelings of shame and inferiority. These switchbacks take us backwards, to the cultural battle that raged across the twentieth century between the confines of the Kailyard and the ejaculatory rage of anti-Kailyard. Between these forms we can find dramatised the conflict between a desire to belong and the desperation to escape; between an idealised Scotland and one left trampled in the dust; between identity seen as rooted and safe or seen as stale and stagnant; between closed and open Scotlands.

## Kailyard: longing to belong

This essay attempts to take stock of the Kailyard, to take in the heady guff of nostalgia and shame, longing and disgust which continues to eddy around this imaginary place. Out of this it offers some ways of re-imagining Kailyard's boundaries. Kailyard is, of course, the Scottish term for cabbage patch[1], your wee bit of back yard, and is also the term initially given to a school of popular literature pioneered at the turn of the twentieth century. Literary Kailyard offers sentimentalised tales of small town life, told by the moral guardians of such communities' simple inhabitants—the minister or the dominie. Typically, Kailyard novels narrate their tales in Standard English but shift into Scots for reported speech and moments of high emotion.

Early Hollywood leapt on contemporarily popular Kailyard narratives. There were numerous adaptations of the novels of Kailyard stalwarts Ian Maclaren and J. M. Barrie, including no fewer than three versions of the latter's *The Little Minister* by 1934. This extensive use of Kailyard settings, characters and mores across Hollywood and British cinema visions of Scotland made a consideration of the Kailyard a central point in the anthology *Scotch Reels,* that foundational moment in the analysis of Scottish film (see Craig 1982; McArthur 1982). The symbolic significance of the Kailyard is of nature civilised to the point of banality, a place of toil which is still only capable of producing the barest sustenance, a location bereft of beauty or pleasure. Just as the ground demands labour to prevent it running to seed, so Kailyard's inhabitants are subject to harsh moral and social surveillance. Kailyard is seen by its critics as representing a

[1] Whilst not dealt with here, the use of Scots language is highly significant within Kailyard narratives on page and screen, and is unquestionably implicated in the powerfully ambivalent emotional responses this chapter attempts to identify.

Scotland outside history, a walled-in, closed-off community. This literary and cinematic mode offers a fantasy of escape to its readers (desperate to evade the realities of the modern world) whilst denying the possibility of escape to its fictional inhabitants. Those who make the mistake of leaving its bounds variously return with regret, in disgrace or through death.

## Anti-Kailyard: "Get me away from here, I'm dying"[2]

The powerful hold that the Kailyard maintains can be seen in both the concept's spread and the affective power it commands. The term just keeps popping up, in cultural criticism, political debates, journalism and everyday discourse. The imprecision around what is evoked in no way limits Kailyard's enormous and negative affect. Its taint is used to dismiss anything from aspects of film, television, books or individuals to the entirety of Scotland's cultural production or political life. What unites such uses is the recurrence of the derogatory, the dismissive, the small, the low. The Kailyard is the holding place of all that is to be left behind, to be kept buried. But of course if there is one thing that the repressed does very well it is to return. The fear of the Kailyard haunts the Scottish imagination.

One powerful aspect of this terror which has particular relevance for Scottish film production is the fear that Kailyard may not simply be a metaphor for Scotland, but in fact a metonym for Scottishness and the Scottish community. Kailyard's ground is small, local and under-nourished; its poor soil can only support a hardy, but unappetising, native breed. The concept's latent horror, therefore, lies in the possibility that the disavowed part may just represent the whole. It's certainly possible to read the violent reaction of Scotland's film and television community in the past against moves attempting to address the structural inequities and economic marginality which that community faces—broadcasting quotas, Colin McArthur's early-'90s call for a "poor cinema" (McArthur 1993; MacPherson 1990)—as motivated in part by the fear of a kind of Kailyard production.

In some ways recent Scottish cinema's flight from the past may be traceable to the stories of national identity which worked to invigorate and to enable the beginnings of that movement. Given Scotland's classic

---

[2] The quote comes from the Glasgow band Belle and Sebastian, whose unashamed engagement with local voices and places, and playful synthesis of masculine and feminine identities, memory and change point to the kinds of creative possibilities I want to explore in this essay.

cinematic representation as a place located in the past, the desire of a new wave of filmmakers to flee from history and fling their films into modernity is understandable. The opening of *Trainspotting* gives notice of a new and different identity. Renton's flight down Princes Street is framed to exclude the prehistoric marker of Castle Rock, and is accompanied by a pounding soundtrack of newness, of elsewhere. The same production team's *Shallow Grave* (Boyle, GB, 1995) is equally self-conscious in its attempts to position its central characters, the three young, amoral inhabitants of a well-appointed Edinburgh New Town flat, as visually and ideologically separate from recognisable old Scottishness. A charity ceilidh serves as a backdrop against which these representatives of new Scotland can act out their difference and contempt, as the master of ceremonies delivers patter as dated as his Bonnie Prince Charlie-style formal dress. A Scotland of Tartanry and traditional gendered roles is heckled by Alex (Ewan McGregor) and further undermined by the willed perversity that ends his delirious Strip the Willow traditional dance with Juliet (Kerry Fox) as he licks the pointed shoe she grinds in his face. The explosion of energy which *Shallow Grave* and *Trainspotting* offered created a hunger for visions of a modern, edgy, young Scotland, at least on the part those providing funding for British film. A past hit may be no guarantee of future success, but for those working in a highly uncertain business it at least appears to offer the security of the relatively safe bet. Furthermore, the marginality of Scottish culture and the small and sporadic nature of the stream of indigenous film production can further mean that cultural gatekeepers (like cultural critics) can fall victim to a narrowly defined, univocal vision of national cultural production.

## Ghosts: things which might have been

When we consider some of the lost representations of Scotland's past however there is not only a sense of loss, but the resonance of structuring absence. The mourning for Bill Douglas, now widely (if belatedly) recognised as the poet of early Scottish cinema (Dick, Noble and Petrie 1993) was undoubtedly sharpened by the tardy understanding of what had been lost in the scripts left unfunded and unfilmed at his early death in 1991. The prospect of Douglas' screen version of James Hogg's extraordinary 1824 novel *The Confessions of a Justified Sinner*, a ghost story of shame and split identity, is one so enticing (not simply for Scottish cinema, but for a wider national culture) that its failure to come to screen is emblematic of the crushing historic material limitations of Scottish film culture.

By apparent contrast, the emergence of directors such as Peter Mullan, Lynne Ramsay and David Mackenzie in the 1990s, alongside new models of funding and support, dangled the prospect of indigenous talents being able to grow within a new Scottish cinematic ground. Yet there was a grinding sense of history repeating itself in 2005, as Terence Davies and his Scottish producers, Bob Last and Gillian Berrie, proved unable to raise funding for Davies' adaptation of Lewis Grassic Gibbon's masterpiece *Sunset Song* (1932). *Sunset Song*'s narrative of a young woman's journey to intellectual and sexual maturity within a transforming agricultural community gives voice to different identities and experiences within a national cultural landscape hardly deafened by female stories. Despite securing limited funding from Scottish Screen, the UK Film Council and Channel 4 declined to support the project (Hattenstone 2006). This sums up the most depressing limitations of contemporary British film policy, most notably the recurrent failure of public funding to recognise cinema as a significant cultural form. With crushing irony, a work which reconfigures rural Scotland as caught within the tides of modernity and global forces was condemned as something that, in the alleged words of a senior Film Council officer, "won't travel" (ibid.). The ghosts of poverty and marginalisation are inescapable. Scottish cultural institutions and creative artists lack the structures, the money, the power to make their voices heard. Different ways of seeing and speaking are invisible and inaudible within a dominant cultural settlement where the local is seen as only fit to communicate within its own borders, stuck in Kailyard's scanty ground.

Mention of Douglas and Davies' unmade projects is emphatically not meant to suggest that literary adaptations offer some kind of privileged or preferable model of national cinema. Rather, they serve as illustrations of diversity and creativity forcibly absented from the stage of filmic imagining, indictments of the limitations within which Scottish film culture is currently constituted, entangled as it is in institutional and financial structures marked by a blindspot for non-dominant forms of British culture. Questions need to be weighed, too, about persistent and disabling indigenous failures of ambition and imagination as well as unsympathetic external institutional structures. Why, for instance, was Douglas a prophet without honour in his own land? One answer lies in the relationship between the exploration of his own emotionally starved Scottish upbringing in his masterpiece, the *Childhood Trilogy* (GB, 1972-78), and that work's suggestion that the possibilities of liberation and expansion are always situated elsewhere than Scotland. The *Trilogy*'s unsparing exposure of pinched lives, savage repression and brutal hypocrisies within Kailyard's small town landscape positions it as a work expressing anti-Kailyard values. Yet Douglas' complex engagement with these earlier forms, at a point where Scottish film criticism was beginning to deploy the Kailyard as a kind of bogey, is one reason for the director's uncanny disappearance from the 1982 *Scotch Reels* volume (see Caughie 1993). The comparative lack of outrage over the failure to realise Davies' *Sunset Song* perhaps also speaks of the fear of the Kailyard: any move to address local specificity is seen as tainted, contaminated by an anxiety around being identified with the small and the marginal.

My turn away here from the newness of new Scottish cinema may appear perverse: the return to past failings and unmade projects the mere itching of an old and troublesome scab. Yet it is motivated by a belief that the present and its possibilities continue to be shaped and haunted by the stories of the past. Yes, Scottish cinema is still birthing itself, and deserves all the maieutic powers of encouragement and belief which that challenging process requires. New things require nourishment. The work of criticism, however, is also in part a kind of clearing of cultural ground, an attempt to identify not just places of potential but also those spaces still entangled. Cairns Craig has written tellingly of the terror evoked by the parochial within Scottish culture. He suggests that hostile critics faced with Kailyard and other forms of Scottish popular culture may think they mock the tawdriness of what's presented, but instead reveal:

> The profound hatred of the intellectuals for the culture they inhabited, the profound embarrassment they suffered by being unable, any more, to identify themselves with some universalist truth that would redeem them from Scottishness. (Craig 1996, 107)

I want to argue that there is another aspect of this terror: admitting the Kailyard in all its smallness and softness might collapse a national identity shored up around ideas of masculinity and hardness.

## Here come the hard men: "kicking Kailyard in the chuckies"

Despite critical attempts to corral the Kailyard by depicting it as a brief-lived, long-dead cultural form, a turn-of-the-century literary movement supposed to have been killed off by George Douglas Brown's 1901 novel *The House with the Green Shutters*, it continues to manifest itself across all kinds of cultural and political discourses today. Tom Nairn may want to claim that "the Kailyard has become a graveyard" (Nairn

2000), but it remains an ambulant ghost, sucking us back into its claggy soil. In part the life of Kailyard has been sustained by the highly generative rage it produces. Brown's *The House with the Green Shutters* is galvanised by contempt and disgust. Its gleeful reception has been more concerned with collective critical hated for Kailyard than with the merits of Brown's work. When *The House with the Green Shutters* was first published, Sir Walter Raleigh, then Professor of English Literature at Glasgow University, declared, "I love the book just for this… it sticks the Kailyarders like pigs" (Blake 1951, 100). A century later, Scotland's premier cultural listings publication, *The List* magazine, championed Douglas Brown's novel in a project designed to identify the 100 Best Scottish books, claiming "along came *The House with the Green Shutters* (the *Trainspotting* of its day), giving the Kailyard a well-deserved kick in the chuckies" (Anon 2005). This notion of literary text as agent of violent assault is striking, as is the critical orthodoxy which crosses a century and unites Edwardian literary studies with the populism of contemporary journalism. The postmodern canon embraces *Trainspotting* with ease, but the Kailyard remains beyond the pale.

Anti-Kailyard reactions use the Kailyard as a kind of dumping ground for all attitudes that are seen as redundant or unwanted in a reconfigured, forward-looking Scotland: the sentimental detritus; the gee-gaws that shame us in our new sophistication; the things we don't want the visitors to see. This defensive construction of Kailyard insists that if you're serious about your Scottishness and your intellectual standing—if in short you're a serious Scotsman (and I use the gendered term intentionally)—Kailyard is what you're agin. Ian Campbell writes that for George Douglas Brown, "the Kailyard represented a threat to Scottishness"; the gendering of this opposition can be found in Brown's characterisation of Kailyard as "sentimental slop" (Campbell 1981, 10) characterised by indiscriminate and soft liquidity, oozing of emotion, and insinuating spread. Kailyard, and any entanglement within it, poses a threat to a kind of Scottishness constructed as hardness. Kailyard threatens to unman anyone implicated within it.

Attempts to valorise anti-Kailyard as the location of a progressive national imagination ignore a troubling and insistent misogyny, whereby the idealised mother of Kailyard is shown—as in Douglas' *Trilogy* for instance—to be broken and marginal, or the agent of a repressive culture. Peter Mullan's *Orphans* (GB, 1999) works to interrogate wounded masculinities, but its comic apotheosis remains the vision of Thomas (Gary Lewis), the brother in thrall to the past, struggling alone to carry the weight of his mother's coffin, proclaiming, "she ain't heavy, she's my mother" (see Sillars and Macdonald 2008). From *The House with the Green Shutters* in 1901 to Alan Sharp's striking 1965 novel *A Green Tree in Gedde*, women are vectors of disease and weakness; they drip and rot. Though David Mackenzie's interesting adaption of Alexander Trocchi's 1954 novel *Young Adam* problematises central character Joe (Ewan McGregor)'s alienated masculinity, in the scenes of sexual abjection showing his girlfriend Cathie (Emily Mortimer)'s body smothered in custard and ketchup when alive, and dragged bloated and dripping from an industrial canal once dead, it is hard not to feel the echo of anti-Kailyard's shuddering recoil from femininity.

Yet Kailyard's stress on the feminine and domestic should not necessitate its treatment with contempt. In fact, so powerful is the effort to suppress Kailyard's feminine aspects that many critical accounts make sense only through their structuring absences: the feminised subjects, the ghostly presence of unknown women readers, the vanished women writers. In George Blake's hostile 1951 critique *Barrie and the Kailyard School*, Kailyard is presented as the creation of a trinity of men—Barrie, S. R. Crocket and Maclaren—who in turn form the basis of later accounts. Blake gives Annie S. Swan, author of 162 popular novels, two passing mentions. She and the many other women writers of Kailyard are left outside a masculine critical model of creativity. These glaring gaps are only now being filled (see Dickson 1997; Ewan *et al.* 2006).

## Beyond the Pale: Admitting Kailyard

Rather than being stalled by Kailyard, reading its apparent lack of fit with a radical industrial modernity as evidence of a failed national creative process, we might reassess the mode's ready connection with generations of audiences; we might see its evasions and absences as speaking to an experience of change, migration and trauma. Kailyard might be read symptomatically, through and beyond both the visible content of the novels and films themselves and the violent rejections of these by anti-Kailyard fiction and criticism. We need to admit the Kailyard to our critical discourse, to take it seriously. But this also is to admit to ourselves our fear and recognition of the accents that speak of home, family, belonging. We need to own the emotion generated by Kailyard and reactions to it. This means holding in some kind of balance the contempt, but also the longing, for Kailyard's familiar spaces, the contrastive qualities that make our identification with the tradition so charged and ambivalent. We must think through the ways we are implicated in the Kailyard, and the ways it implicates us. This move might enable us to accommodate the place of emotion, sentiment and even nostalgia within popular forms as phenomena other than pathological features to be violently rejected (split off for the subject's health). I am not arguing for the wholesale redemption of Kailyard: like all popular forms it contains progressive and regressive elements, successful and unsuccessful expressions. Rather, I want to suggest that there are three critical manoeuvres which can help move us beyond the condensation of myth and history, the frozen possibilities which seem to me to be as much a feature of some anti-Kailyard attitudes as they are of Kailyard itself. Firstly, to recognise the transnational nature of Kailyard; secondly, to conceive of Kailyard and anti-Kailyard not as opposites but as framing a psychic landscape which encompasses both idealised and violently negative emotion; thirdly, to put women back in the frame as subjects, producers and consumers of Kailyard culture.

## Transnational Kailyards

Kailyard speaks in distinctive accents to an audience that reaches beyond the boundaries of the nation. Kailyard's transnational status—its international audience and reach—is seldom referred to other than slightingly. The notion that Kailyard peddles pabulum to nostalgic émigrés and travesties contemporary reality in favour of fantasies of a lost home is strikingly echoed today in responses to Bollywood cinema. In both cases the relation of home and exile, of markets and marketing, and complex questions of memory, family, fantasy and lost plenitude are issues that cannot adequately be thought through by recourse to the simple equation of mass culture with impoverished product.

We need also to remember that Kailyard is transnational not just in its reception but in its production and its settings. We may have our own wee word for it, but Scotland is not unique (nor uniquely shamed) in its production of local narratives. I may feel my soul turn to cinders at the sight of the Highland-set television series *Monarch of the Glen* (BBC, 2000-2005), but were I to tune in on another Sunday night, watching instead Yorkshire-set *Heartbeat* (ITV, 1992- ) or Norfolk-set *Kingdom* (ITV, 2007- ), I would see the same tropes and values. The happy wee world of *Balamory* (BBC, 2002-2005) finds its echo in *Postman Pat* (BBC, 1981- ); *Hamish Macbeth* (BBC, 1995-1997) recalls Alaska's whimsical *Northern Exposure* (CBS, 1990-1995). Perhaps what is particular to Scottish culture is not these homely narratives, but rather the powerful and haunting (*unheimlich*) shame which they provoke?

Kailyard can be seen as a travelling culture. There has been a tendency in critical work to overplay the transaction between dominant metropolitan culture and a Scottishness presented as provincial and parochial. There are other forms of mediation at work—with domestic audience (in both senses, local and familial, feminine) and with wider diasporic communities. To see this, we need look no further than the work of Kailyard-influenced women writers such as L. M. Montgomery and Margaret Murray Robertson; the rediscovery of Aberdeenshire Hollywood writer Lorna Moon; the stunning work on Scottish migrant experiences by Canadian writers Alice Munro and Alistair MacLeod. All these examples point to the potential of ongoing and progressive reworking and translation.

Popular music also offers inspiring forms of engagement with Scotland as a rooted point of origin, but one containing diverse and shifting modes of national identification, capable of travelling and forging new connections. In particular, projects such as the Fence Collective (based in Anstruther) and bands such as Arab Strap and Mull Historical Society represent small-town Scotland as a place of emotional and creative richness. The significance of this revoiced nation can be seen in a series of collaborations between Scottish musicians and filmmakers, often on stories about reconfigured masculinity: see (and hear), for instance, the Belle and Sebastian- and Arab Strap-commissioned songs in *The Soft Touch*, one of the three shorts that make up *The Acid House* (McGuigan, GB, 1999); legendary Glasgow indie band The Pastels' cross-dressed vignette in *The Last Great Wilderness* (Mackenzie, GB/Den, 2002); the soundtrack by Aberfeldy for *GamerZ* (Fraser, GB, 2005); *Hallam Foe* (Mackenzie, GB, 2007), engagingly marketed on the back of the film's extensive utilisation of contemporary Scottish groups on its soundtrack.

The possibilities created through collaboration can be seen, too, in the ongoing cinematic experiment of the Advance Party Initiative. Advance Party seeks to extend the lessons of Denmark's Dogme95 movement through a series of Scottish/Danish feature co-productions, starting with *Red Road* (Arnold, GB/Den, 2006). Co-operation, working with your neighbours, using financial limits creatively, deploying the success of earlier projects to build on in the future are hallmarks of this initiative (Hjort 2006). These small-nation/small-town values ally the recognition of wee-ness, of modesty of means, with a tactical understanding of the ways in which such boundaries can be used to energise the imagination. This developing pattern of transnational film production, and the impressive international reception of films such as *Red Road*, illuminate but do not exhaust the possibilities of opening up new routes for Scottish cinema.

Perhaps these new directions of travel might enable a different kind of uncovering of roots, a return to a past more diverse than has been presented to date.

## Inner and Outer Landscapes

Thinking about Kailyard as a space (rather than merely an ahistorical evasion of contemporary realities) opens up a new set of critical possibilities. In accepting space as a dialectical category, Kailyard can be seen as a cultural landscape shaped by different historical and social forces. It is a space where different stories can be told, different ideological and emotional relationships can be explored, just as comedy writers/performers *The League of Gentlemen* suggest that we see *The Wicker Man* (Hardy, GB, 1973) as a remake of *Whisky Galore!* (Mackendrick, GB, 1949), humour turned to horror but an underlying narrative pattern unaltered. Kailyard and anti-Kailyard may dramatise differing emotional (and narrative) responses to the cultural landscape in question, but both are structured around a shared fascination with place, community and identity. Thinking about Kailyard as a landscape allows us to abandon the critical policing of the boundary between Kailyard and anti-Kailyard. This opposition limits our analysis of the internal contradictions which exist within both Kailyard and anti-Kailyard. It seems also to promote a critical culture where, to put it crudely, any work that suggests Scotland to be a shite-hole shows its own seriousness, whereas any work that sees the place as couthy (a term which makes the intellectuals tremble) is not worthy of consideration.

A brief survey of the depiction of space in Scottish cinema reveals some of the traditions which block less oppositional framings. The dominant screen image of Scotland is of a place locked in the past, cut off from modernity and progress. In Hollywood romanticism and the metropolitan view of British cinema there is a repeated emphasis on Scotland as remote and untouched. This imaginary Scotland, which lies outside modernity and is insulated from its cares, can then be mobilised as the setting for a journey of self-discovery—a theme seen running from *Brigadoon* (Minnelli, USA, 1954) through *I Know Where I'm Going!* (Powell and Pressburger, GB, 1945), *The Maggie* (Mackendrick, GB, 1953) and *Loch Ness* (Henderson, GB/USA, 1996). This theme becomes structured through a narrative pattern of a physical journey (played out at length in several texts) and the use of shifting *mise-en-scène*.

This imaginary Scotland emerges from a history which has seen the vast majority of films about the country funded and produced from beyond its borders. *Local Hero* (Forsyth, GB, 1983) and the *Battle of the Sexes* (Crichton, GB, 1961) offer parallel openings that introduce Scotland seen from an American corporate boardroom. Both films make great play of large maps indicating the country's apparently remote and isolated position. The visual foregrounding of American capitalism slyly comments on the representational colonialism of cinema. *Whisky Galore!*'s parodic, faux-documentary voice-over reverses the compliment by majestically locating the Outer Isles in the centre of the North Atlantic: "to the West there is nothing," modulated pause, slight disappointment, "except America". *Local Hero* works as both pastiche and the fullest expression of these visual signifiers of fantasy Scotland. Central character Mac (Peter Riegert)'s journey takes him from hyper-modern Houston, composed on screen through packed frames overflowing with fast cars, tall buildings and machinery, where the ear and eye are assaulted by overlapping telecommunications messages; via a cheap, tartanised Scottish airline (modernity and tradition battling in Technicolor polyester); to the quiet white-out of a single track road in a Highland glen where the mist has descended. Even the most basic of modern communications systems, the road, has to be abandoned in the face of this natural force.

This remote Scotland is the place where the modern world breaks down. In both *I Know Where I'm Going!* and *The Maggie*, narrative turning points hinge around the unavailability and unreliability of telephones. Again *Local Hero* echoes and amplifies this vision, through its iconic image of the red telephone box by the harbour front in Ferness, the Scottish village Mac travels from America to buy. This is the only place from which he can contact his office in the States—as long as he can borrow enough 10p pieces first. This fantasy Scotland on film is a place outside the laws of nature: villages disappear for a hundred years (*Brigadoon*), mermaids (*Local Hero*) and monsters (*Loch Ness*) pop out of its waters, curses and wishes can come to pass (*I Know Where I'm Going!*). This tension between magic and modernity has led Duncan Petrie for one to challenge some of the earlier readings that interpreted binary oppositions between the regressive and progressive, the backward looking and the forward thinking (Petrie 2000). Whilst these films dramatise an encounter between individual and landscape that becomes transformative, crucially that person travels from elsewhere to experience this healing. The emergence of cinema from Scotland offered a very different relation of individuals to environment.

Within indigenous production there persists an anti-Kailyard vision where escape is profoundly longed for but presented as an impossible dream. Here, too, certain visual and narrative tropes recur. A favoured framing shows the trapped individual staring at horizons denied to them owing to physical, emotional, financial or familial entrapment. In Bill Douglas' *Trilogy*, Jamie repeatedly stands on a railway bridge to get caught up in the steam as the engines hurtle away to the world he is shut out of: the transcendence offered is always temporary. In Ken Loach's *Sweet Sixteen* (GB/Ger/Sp, 2002), teenage Liam is repeatedly positioned by the Firth of Clyde, its waters beckoning a physical escape which his family circumstances make impossible. The spectacular mountain scenery beyond signifies escape, refuge, recuperation which Liam, shaped by his brutal urban environment, cannot access. A key moment in the new Scottish cinema shows *Trainspotting*'s junkie crew deposited at a remote Highland railway station, faced with the imposing wildness of Rannoch Moor. Clutching their cans of Tennant's lager, dressed in post-punk street style, *mise-en-scène* and framing emphasise the lads' placing outside the landscape. At a visual level the scene can be read as offering a progressive critique, through its ability to render the cliché of cinematic Scotland unfamiliar and faintly ludicrous. Yet this is undercut by an older refrain, as the film lurches into Renton's sustained and now famous rant on the "shiteness" of being Scottish. Within the anti-Kailyard, Scotland offers no space of nourishment or change. Renton can only spit out his (self) hatred, and later must journey to London to experience escape and reinvention.

In the studied stand-offs between characters and Highland scenery in *Trainspotting* and *Sweet Sixteen*—alongside Joe's journey north in *My Name is Joe* (Loach, Sp/It/Fr/GB/Ger, 1998)—there is only the sterility of confrontation. Here we see replayed the privileging of "real" urban masculinity, shut off from a landscape dismissed as fantasy, the identities of individuals and spaces fixed and irreconcilable, with no potential for movement or change.

## Femininity in the Picture

What makes Kailyard so potentially productive in the analysis of the moving image and its *mise-en-scène* is precisely the tradition's setting between the iconographically over-determined spaces of the city and the Highlands. The frequent appearance of Kailyard characters and mores within the discourses of Tartanry and Clydesidism indicates Kailyard's potential as a means of travelling between the stark representational opposition of cinema's romantic fantasies of remoteness and urban social realism.

Lars von Trier's *Breaking the Waves* locates itself in the traditional space of the Kailyard—a remote Scottish community, governed by strict

Presbyterian values. The film's plot, which centres around the subjectivity and sexuality of a young woman, turns away from the masculine trajectory usually followed in anti-Kailyard narratives, but seemingly shadows anti-Kailyard's idea of an individual journey through a landscape of repression. I want however to suggest that the shift in focus from masculine to feminine subjectivity and the ways the film speaks of this—particularly through the use of camera and soundtrack—allow a reimagining of the relationship between individual and community, a less sterile and more productive opening up of the space of the Kailyard.

*Breaking the Waves* is set in the early seventies, indicated by the use of a period Glam Rock soundtrack, the moment identified as that of the arrival of modernity in Bess' community. This is not the closed space of imaginary Scotland, but one penetrated by newness. Oil has brought the outsiders with their flamboyant clothes, their uninhibited behaviour, their implicit challenge to the repressive control of religious observance. Summoned to the church to defend her proposed marriage to Jan (Stellan Skarsgård), Bess (Emily Watson) is asked to name one good thing brought by the outsiders. "Their music," she replies. This opening, with its staged confrontation between Bess and the male elders of the church, suggests to us that Bess' body and sexuality are going to form the site of a struggle between tradition and modernity, between a community attempting to maintain its boundaries and the temptations from outside. Then something happens which disrupts this reading, with its regressive symbolic equation of woman with the land, protecting purity against penetration: Bess turns and smiles to the camera. With this break of the fourth wall and the realist enclosure of cinema we are made to understand that the means of transformation come not from without, but from within. Bess' smile speaks of her pleasure and her own desire.

The film's use of music is particularly suggestive here. Music is not used at all as a conventional background to the action, to give a raw, surface naturalism against which the breaches of realism become more visible. Non-diegetic music is restricted to the tableau sequences which break the narrative into a series of chapter headings. There it accompanies a series of digitally manipulated, hyper-real moving postcard scenes. Bess' passion for the music and her taking it into herself (flagged by a soundless sequence of her retiring under the bedclothes with her transistor radio after Jan's departure) imply that the fabulous Glam Rock fantasies of longing, desire, transgression, and outer space offer us access to her consciousness, her interior landscape. Mirroring the fantastical, pulsating digital images of Scottish scenes, this coming together of sound and image refuses the hackneyed opposition of ancient place with modern music. It speaks instead of the multi-layered meaning of landscape, its capacity to contain different experiences. This digitised and mobile spatial imagining moves away from a European tradition of Scottish landscape painting (a perspective from outside, an uninhabited wilderness, a tourist view) to explore the idea of a landscape experienced from within, one charged with the possibilities of change and transformation, not fixed but continually shifting and subject to remaking.

This idea is, of course, placed within a far from utopian tale. As *Breaking the Waves* progresses there is a grim and unremitting exposure of the limits placed on female sexuality and female agency. The crushing weight of religion, conformity, social and sexual surveillance are all made luridly visible. This darker side of the Kailyard is the object of the rage and rejection we see in anti-Kailyard narratives. Yet what is surprising and potentially fruitful is the way they co-exist in von Trier's film with a more nuanced and ambiguous presentation of place and community, rather than the scorched earth destructiveness of anti-Kailyard. The kingpins of the Kailyard—the minister and the doctor—are both represented, but in ways that perhaps confound expectation and force new engagements with place and identification, not least the semi-colonial desire to replace "primitive" belief with "civilised" rationalism. The minister (Jonathan Hackett) is a mild-mannered sort, apparently in thrall to his implacable congregation. In a nicely turned scene he stops by the iconic red telephone box to link up Bess and Jan for a breathy session (in this vision of rural Scotland the phones, communicators of modernity, actually work.) The doctor (Adrian Rawlins) at first appears as the voice of rational modernity, a voice used by Kailyard's literary narrators in a way critics suggest offers a viewpoint from which a more sophisticated audience can find comedy in local mores. This position is swiftly undermined as he is revealed as fatally compromised by his own desire for Bess and arguably by his own ignorance and prejudice. Certainly the scandalous finale of the film smashes the laws not only of realist cinema but also of Enlightenment rationalism. If we as an audience are to rescue any pleasure, or even meaning, from this film it will not be from the vantage point of knowing metropolitanism.

Lynne Ramsay's *Morvern Callar* offers an exemplary and creative engagement with some of the gaps and spaces charted in this essay. The film's content and form are poised between open and closed conceptions of Scotland, mobile and border-crossing but carrying cultural memories of the Kailyard. John Caughie sees the film as anti-Kailyard (Caughie 2007), but in keeping with the argument presented here, *Morvern Callar* can be seen as re-imagined Kailyard instead (or as well). The narrative movement of a young woman's journey out of small-town Scotland would appear to conform to anti-Kailyard's rejection of the nation's stifling restrictions; but this reading is not supported by the film's ambivalent vision. Its openness lies in a kind of shifting between inside and outside, the opacity of Morvern's inner space met by the strangeness of the outer world. She is no more at home in Oban than Ibiza, but the two spaces are not coded in opposition to one another; each carries the possibility of alienation and of fleeting moments of integration. The meaning of these landscapes is not a given but open to possibility, transformation. The emblematically Kailyard interior of Lana (Kathleen McDermott)'s granny's flat becomes infused with an erotics of intimacy as she invites the girls to share a bath. At the drug-fuelled rave at the sea loch, Morvern moves away from the party as a night-fisherman's boat passes. As he casts his light on the shore she slowly raises her skirt. This wordless and dreamlike encounter could have been a clichéd contrast between old and new identities; instead, it is freighted with the desires and the unknowability of two figures, a flicker of contact contained in a landscape filled with meanings.

This essay has attempted to use the Kailyard and the emotions provoked by its charged boundaries as a way of working through a series of oppositions highly relevant to cinematic imagining: between the local and the transnational; the individual and the space of the nation and its communities; and between masculine and feminine perspectives. Being open to the Kailyard can offer ways of thinking about the interstices of these oppositions; a more nuanced approach to nationality, place and people; and a history of a distinctively Scottish mode of wrestling with the vicissitudes and paradoxes of identity and belonging.

## Works Cited

Anon, 2005. The House With The Green Shutters. http://www.list.co.uk/article/2773-the-house-with-the-green-shutters-george-douglas-brown-1901/ (accessed November 24, 2008).

Blake, George. 1951. *Barrie and the Kailyard School*. London: Arthur Barker Ltd.

Campbell, Ian. 1981. *Kailyard: a new assessment*. Edinburgh: Ramsay Head.

Caughie, John. 1993. Don't Mourn—Analyse: Reviewing the Trilogy. In *Bill Douglas: A Lanternist's Account*, eds. Eddie Dick, Andrew Noble and Duncan Petrie, 197-204. London: British Film Institute.

—. 2007. Morvern Callar, Art Cinema and the "Monstrous Archive". *Scottish Studies Review* 8.1: 101-115.

Craig, Cairns. 1982. Myths against History: Tartanry and Kailyard in 19th-Century Scottish Literature. In *Scotch Reels: Scotland in Cinema and Television*, ed. Colin McArthur, 7-15. London: British Film Institute.

—. 1996. *Out of History: Narrative Paradigms in Scottish and English Culture*. Edinburgh: Polygon.

Dick, Eddie, Andrew Noble and Duncan Petrie, eds. 1993. *Bill Douglas: A Lanternist's Account*. London: British Film Institute.

Dickson, Beth. 1997. Annie S. Swan and O. Douglas: Legacies of the Kailyard. In *A History of Scottish Women's Writing*, eds. Douglas Gifford and Dorothy MacMillan, 329-346. Edinburgh: Edinburgh University Press.

Ewan, Elizabeth, Sue Innes, Sian Reynolds and Rose Pipe, eds. 2006. The *Biographical Dictionary of Scottish Women*. Edinburgh: Edinburgh University Press.

Hattenstone, Simon. 2006. Bigmouth Strikes Again. *The Guardian*, October 20, *G2* section.

Hjort, Mette. 2006. Homophiliac Transnationalism: The "Advance Party" Initiative. Paper presented at the Cinema at the Periphery conference, June 15-16, in St Andrews, Scotland.

MacPherson, Robin. 1990. Declarations of Independence. *From Limelight to Satellite: A Scottish Film Book*, ed. Eddie Dick, 207-220. London/Glasgow: British Film Institute/Scottish Film Council.

McArthur, Colin. 1982. Scotland and Cinema: The Iniquity of the Fathers. In *Scotch Reels: Scotland in Cinema and Television*, ed. McArthur, 40-69. London: British Film Institute.

—. 1993. In praise of a poor cinema. *Sight and Sound* 3.8: 30-32.

Nairn, Tom. 2000. Scotland, the Blair Project and the Zombie Faction: Assessing the Scottish Parliament, one year on. *Arena* 48. http://www.arena.org.au/ARCHIVES/MagArchive/Issue 48/features48.htm (accessed January 27, 2008).

Petrie, Duncan. 2000. *Screening Scotland*. London: British Film Institute.

Sillars, Jane and Myra MacDonald. 2008. Gender, Spaces, Changes: Emergent Identities in a Scotland in Transition. In *The Media in Scotland*, eds. Neil Blain and David Hutchison, 183-198. Edinburgh: Edinburgh University Press.

# NEW SCOTTISH CINEMA AS TRANS-NATIONAL CINEMA

SARAH STREET

The relationship between Scottish cinema and British cinema has been examined by Duncan Petrie in *Screening Scotland* (2000). Petrie charts the recurrence of, and a fascination with, Scottish themes in many British films. Often Scotland functioned as an "imaginary space" for audiences in films about escape, "becoming" and self-knowing such as Powell and Pressburger's lyrical meditation, *I Know Where I'm Going!* (GB, 1945) or Ealing's *Whisky Galore!* (Mackendrick, GB, 1949). There is indeed a rich British cinematic tradition here that is both dynamic and complex, but it has tended to function more from the perspective of outsiders looking in, exemplifying a tourist gaze from a heritage or social realist perspective, rather than creating an identifiably independent vision.

Films made in Scotland and those featuring Scottish themes since the 1990s, often referred to as "New Scottish Cinema" (Petrie 2000a, 153-169), represent however a rather different level of engagement with a number of national film traditions and styles. The latter include, but are not exclusively restricted to, British ones (Various 2005, 213-245). European and American influences are visible within much new Scottish cinema, in ways that result in films which are not necessarily presented as "outsider constructions". Indeed, the issues of class, identity, poverty and deprivation brought to screens by Gillies MacKinnon in *Small Faces* (GB, 1996), Danny Boyle in *Trainspotting* (GB, 1996) and Lynne Ramsay in *Ratcatcher* (GB/Fr, 1999) can be related to many different national experiences: in these films the "local" and the "global" are interrelated, appealing to a diverse range of audiences in a way that can be described as "trans-national" or even "post-national". It is now a case of insiders looking outwards, not the other way around; in the case of the three "new Scottish" films mentioned above it is notable how the central characters desire to leave their native milieu, with some of them actually doing so. Rather than offering representations of place that convey emotional security, nostalgia and self-fulfilment, these films disturb such notions by presenting far more generic, trans-national sets of visual registers.

In this chapter I want to bring into focus the uncertain national branding of new Scottish cinema, particularly in the light of debates about contemporary cinema's relationship to so-called "national" styles and economic structures. In this context the usefulness of the term "new Scottish cinema" needs to be called into question, at a time when most of contemporary film is very much a mix of styles, finance, acting talent, production personnel and locations. On the other hand (and this is not the focus of this chapter), it must be recognised that nationalist terminology does have strategic importance in film policy debates about the need for cinema to be diverse yet reflective of issues that are important to a local area with specific concerns. Indeed, new Scottish cinema as a term has gained greater currency in recent years, now that over a decade has passed since the trend began to be visible. But it is important to note that the first films in the crop were not heralded as such. When *Trainspotting* was marketed its "Scottishness" was not particularly emphasised. The film and its actors were more often discussed in terms of making a contribution to the revival of the British film industry. Indeed, the energising of the latter since the 1990s was in large part due to "the *Trainspotting* effect" (Petrie 2000, 196). The break with traditional codes of realism was appreciated as innovative, and a number of British films were clearly inspired by *Trainspotting*'s stylistic vigour and emphasis on disaffected young males, for example, *Twin Town* (Allen, GB, 1997) and *Lock, Stock & Two Smoking Barrels* (Ritchie, GB, 1998). In the USA frequent reference was made to the similarities between *Trainspotting* and intertextual British cinematic and popular cultural reference points, including James Bond, the Beatles, Britpop and Swinging London. In many ways the film can be related to 1960s British cinema, especially the "new wave" with its anti-consumerism, Angry Young Men and concern with the pressures of masculinity.

It is therefore somewhat ironic that the key film in establishing new Scottish cinema was recognised at the time of its release more as an example of a revived British film industry. Via a careful marketing campaign that de-emphasised its Scottishness, *Trainspotting* did unexpectedly well in New York and other US metropolitan cities, relating very much to a tradition of British films that "travel well" when exported (Street 2002, 206-210). Despite *Trainspotting*'s apparent regionalism it spoke to other cultures and contexts; in fact its locale was *not* particularly emphasised and could be easily understood elsewhere. As Harlan Kennedy notes,

> Boyle and writer John Hodge never characterize their story or their characters' dilemma as exclusively 'Scottish'. Drug addiction, after all, is a global franchise, and so are the petty crime, troubled love lives, and attempts by mixed-up youngsters to start life afresh. (Kennedy 1996, 31)

It is well known that Ewan McGregor fell foul of Sean Connery for his apparent lack of commitment to Scottish nationalism or cinema in interviews, perhaps because McGregor saw "Britishness" as the most suitable platform to articulate his much-publicised criticism of Hollywood. This ambivalence about contemporary life in Scotland is supported in *Trainspotting* by McGregor's character Renton's striking "anti-colonial" speech ("It's *shite* being Scottish") when he visits the Highlands with his friends. This key scene in the film serves as a defiant reminder of the co-existence of several versions of "Scottishness:" on the one hand the Highland Wilderness, heritage tradition that is subject to ironic commentary; on the other the persistent presence of urban isolationism and deprivation. The latter disconnects *Trainspotting*'s characters from "Scotland" as a Highland landscape and denies them the fantasy escape that served so well for audiences and characters in a much earlier film like *I Know Where I'm Going!* Post-1990 Scottish cinema was, therefore, a paradoxical entity. *Trainspotting* and subsequent films on the one hand contributed, in terms of theme and casting, to the forging of an independent identity from British cinema. Yet at the same time, many of the same films were heralded as contributory to a revival of contemporary British filmmaking. Clearly, a distinguishing characteristic of post-1990 Scottish cinema is that, like Scotland itself, it does not fit easily into any single national category.

The uncertain branding of new Scottish cinema can be usefully examined with reference to the turn towards the "trans-national" in European film studies. In theoretical terms there have been some significant interventions in relation to understanding the connections between diverse film traditions and cultures which provide some key perspectives on how we might re-conceptualise new Scottish cinema. Tim Bergfelder, for example, posits:

> A new turn in European film studies…a reconceptualisation of the field, which has significantly paralleled and been motivated by the wider process of political integration. (Bergfelder 2005, 316)

At the same time, of course, it could be pointed out that Scottish devolution signals an opposite direction towards separatism that is perhaps represented by the desire to 'brand' new Scottish cinema as operating somewhat out of step with these wider European developments. On the other hand, and perhaps paradoxically, it should also be acknowledged that while devolution represents withdrawal from the British state at the same time it can be seen to emphasise Scotland's connections to a pan-European culture. So, while I accept the political necessity and function of arguing for an identifiable Scottish cinema that is independent from a wider British one, the ideas about how contemporary cinema is increasingly trans- or post-national are, I believe, instructive and do not necessarily detract from the specificities of post-*Trainspotting* films. In fact it is often the case that "the national" is most pronounced when there has been historic injustice or repression of particular aspects of a cultural identity. It is not surprising therefore that the new Scottish cinema label has functioned as an expression of independence to heighten visibility and encourage specific funding initiatives.

Even so, Duncan Petrie has described new Scottish cinema as "a devolved British cinema" (Petrie 2000, 186). I would push this further to argue more positively that its trans-national elements transcend this description, that new Scottish cinema still remains bound by a particular conception of "the national" that always gets caught up in limited frames of reference. By contrast, trans-national cinema is marked by diversity in terms of its production base; funding sources; origin of production personnel and actors; variety of locations and patterns of cross-cultural reception. This should not be perceived as a negative development. As Ulf Hannerz (1996) points out, we are not talking about globalisation or internationalism, but something more localised, maintaining specific features and themes but at the same time reaching out to many different audiences. This "diversity of organisation" is represented by new Scottish films such as *Ratcatcher* (1999), *Morvern Callar* (Ramsay, GB, 2002) and *Young Adam* (Mackenzie, GB/Fr, 2003). *Ratcatcher*, for example—a UK-French co-production set in Scotland—is a prime example of a film that draws on diverse cinematic traditions, including European and American ones. Its intense visualisation of particular situations invites recognition that transcends any particular national address. Ramsay's imagery is lyrical and symbolic; framed and wild; moving and controlled. Her dialectical fascination with framing creates a dynamic address that can be described as trans-national rather than being particularly imbued with "Scottishness". Other notable co-productions which are exemplary of this strand of new Scottish cinema include *Regeneration* (MacKinnon, GB/Can 1997)—funding included the Glasgow Film Fund, Scottish Film Production Fund, Scottish Arts Council Lottery and two Canadian companies); *The Winter Guest* (Rickman, GB/USA, 1997)—Scottish

Lottery funds with input from American companies; *My Name Is Joe* (Loach, Sp/It/Fr/GB/Ger, 1998)—funding participation from five European countries; and *Ae Fond Kiss...* (Loach, GB/Bel/Ger/It/Sp, 2004)—a film again funded across five European nations.

The rest of this chapter will be concerned with how the move from the national to the trans- or post-national can be exemplified in films that have otherwise been narrowly identified with new Scottish cinema. To illustrate this point I focus on two key works, *Morvern Callar* and *Young Adam*. Working less within a conceptualisation of national cinema studies, my examples instead posit trans-national themes and structures, in particular re-location, as a key feature that characterises both narrative and form in Ramsay and Mackenzie's features. Scotland as a narrative setting is less important than its function as a place to be left, to move away from. In *Morvern Callar* and *Young Adam* Scotland is not necessarily "replaced" but rather *re-placed*, that is to say, located within a broader, trans-national perspective. In many ways the sentiments behind the films are not that different from *I Know Where I'm Going!* but in a reverse move that both illuminates aspects of Scottish life and culture, and calls them into question.

*Ratcatcher* has been identified with European art-house traditions, as well as with aspects of the Hollywood Western genre (Murray 2005, 222-224). Jonathan Murray focuses on the central character James (William Eadie)'s emotional investment in an urban relocation scheme which is figured in *Ratcatcher*'s narrative as a "utopian playground" that amounts to a "transfiguration of the local" (ibid, 222-223). In particular, Murray identifies Ramsay's use of "new frontier" iconography and framing strategies associated with Westerns—particularly frames within frames, exemplified in films such as John Ford's *The Searchers* (USA, 1956)—which on different occasions function as fantasies of escape and social memory. The latter become particularly important for audiences who remember (and still bear the traces of) the casualties of post-war urban regeneration, starkly represented in films such as *Trainspotting*. In this way, as Murray argues, *Ratcatcher* operates as a double-register of verisimilitudinous codes:

> The universalising component that makes the text legible for, and marketable to, external audiences actually facilitates the depth and resonance of the politicised national critique accessed by some domestic viewers. (ibid, 224)

When interviewed about the film Ramsay similarly emphasised its universality, suggesting that the small, observant details surrounding

James and his family could be understood by anyone, anywhere. In one interview she recalled a Latvian film festival where the film was enthusiastically received:

> Those details are kind of quite universal and actually remove it from being a film set in Glasgow, which I was trying to paint as a landscape that felt like it could be past, present or future (Bauer, 2000).

Taking this reading as a cue, I will proceed to examine *Morvern Callar* and *Young Adam* for further evidence of this illuminating, simultaneously local and trans-national address. While the films might at first appear to be quite different, I argue that they share significant themes that make them an especially interesting pair of works to analyse within a context of trans-nationality.

Adapted from Alan Warner's cult 1995 Scottish novel, *Morvern Callar* was the long-awaited second feature from Lynne Ramsay, the test of her directorial promise and of the faith put in her talent by significant funding agencies (UK Film Council, the Glasgow Film Fund and Scottish Screen). Samantha Morton plays Morvern, a supermarket worker who lives in a port town in the West of Scotland (Oban, where Warner grew up) with her boyfriend. The film opens with a striking scene of a dark room with a view through a doorway to a brighter kitchen area in the centre of the frame (another frame within a frame). In many ways this shot serves as an emblematic taster for the main theme of the film: a character seeking to escape, to adjust to disturbing events and eventually re-locate. As Linda Ruth Williams has observed, *Morvern Callar* is "a story of escape that also reflects home" (Williams 2002, 23). We see Morvern's boyfriend lying on the floor in the darkened room, the only light source a Christmas tree with pulsating, coloured lights flashing on and off. At first it is not clear that the boyfriend is dead, but the gradual revelation of his blood-stained wrists indicates suicide. This is confirmed when Morvern reads a message on the computer (signalled by a screen prompting "Read Me") which is his suicide note to her.

In subsequent scenes in a pub and then a club Morvern does not tell her friends that her boyfriend is dead but that he has "left". At home she covers him up with a sheet and then cuts up his body in the bath before burying it in the mountains. She invites her friend Lanna (Kathleen McDermott) on a holiday to Spain, paid for by money left by the boyfriend as payment for his funeral expenses. This is the first of Morvern's "escape mechanisms" in the plot, the second being her boyfriend's novel which is also on the computer for her to find ("I wrote it for you") and which Morvern sends to a publisher in her own name. Lanna and Morvern go to a

Spanish resort designed for British holidaymakers. Morvern grows tired of it and drags Lanna away so that they can see "real" Spain. The discomfort of walking in the mountains and of not having a place to stay does not suit Lanna, who Morvern leaves asleep on the roadside with some money. She hitches a lift to a town where she arranges to meet a couple from a publishing firm who are so interested in the novel that they have flown to Spain to see her. To Morvern's surprise they are prepared to pay her an advance of £100,000 for the book. The film ends with her back in Scotland, leaving the flat she shared with her boyfriend. After picking up the cheque she suggests once again to Lanna that they go away together. Lanna prefers to stay: "There's nothing wrong here—it's the same crap everywhere, so stop dreaming," she says. But Morvern does leave, and the final shots are of her walking down a dark street, case in hand, and then waiting for a train on a deserted railway platform. This is much more ambiguous than the novel's ending, which has Morvern pregnant and back in Oban after some time in Spain. In Ramsay's film, however, the ambiguity continues since the shot of Morvern on the platform is followed by a final, emblematic series of images of her dancing in a club, strobe lights punctuating the sequence (a striking formal resonance with the opening shots of the intermittently flashing Christmas tree lights) as we hear the Mamas and Papas on the soundtrack singing "Dedicated to the One I Love". Diegetic music is a striking feature of the film in the form of a tape cassette labelled "Music for You" that Morvern's boyfriend left for her. The songs on the tape are pertinent and symbolic registers of her mood in several key scenes throughout the film. This last scene is somewhat out of time—we are not sure whether it is a flashback to one of the earlier clubbing scenes, or sometime in the future.

The plot enables a structure which anticipates change and re-location from very early on in the film. On return from being out with her friends Morvern idly picks a holiday postcard off the fridge door; she tells Lanna that her boyfriend has gone away "to another country". Several scenes indicate that Morvern is different, is already living in another place in her imagination, as the music taped for her by her boyfriend forms the soundtrack for her entry to the supermarket where she works. The soundtrack (located solely with her since she is listening to the tape via a Walkman) and camerawork, also from her point of view, work to make the space strange, to render it more like an Americanised Western setting, which is similar to the imaginary affinities Murray has located as being significant in *Ratcatcher*. Morvern's character is associated with the outdoors, as she walks in the woods, relishing the open space in the scene when she has buried her boyfriend and which follows her decision to go to Spain.

The Spanish sequences are particularly interesting because they form a double address to both local and more trans-national concerns. Firstly, the scenes in the holiday resort are a painful reminder of the regimentation of leisure that such places can represent; typical of such locations, Morvern and Lanna's holiday is highly structured. When they arrive they are greeted by a cheery holiday representative and the amusements on offer are predictable, including embarrassing communal games in a swimming pool. These are all structured within the "safe" confines of the complex, which consists of high rise apartments that all look the same and where tourists behave much as they would at home, in a routine of getting drunk, going to pubs and clubs. Pleasure is highly organised, and the shots of the club are jarring, with prominent elements of the grotesque. Indeed, we have seen the same pursuits in Morvern and Lanna's home town in Scotland, creating an uncanny familiarity between "home" and "abroad". In this and other ways the holiday destination is cast as familiar, almost prison-like in scenes such as one in which Morvern sees a cockroach crawl across the floor and under the door of her hotel room. At that moment Morvern also decides to leave, the door crashing behind her in a shot that then reveals the complex as looking extremely institutional, a series of doors down a long corridor with highly polished floors. Morvern is again cast as different from Lanna when she grows tired of the resort and wants to see a different Spain. Outside the resort Lanna is clearly uncomfortable and lacks the desire to experience a change of locale. Even if Morvern's recent transformative experience has been occasioned by her boyfriend's suicide one senses that she is nevertheless destined to leave Scotland.

Once outside the complex the landscape changes as Lanna and Morvern experience the mountains, passing through a village where a fiesta and bullfight are taking place, wandering further into the countryside. This is a very different experience of Spain, one which Morvern finds exhilarating. The warm colours and sunshine of the Spanish locations (the Almeria region) form a stark contrast with the scenes when Morvern is back in Scotland, where the dominant hues are greys and blues and there is an overall impression of coldness. Again, we understand Scotland is no longer "home," the publisher's cheque ensuring that Morvern can leave in a way that is incomprehensible to Lanna, who is depicted as more rooted in the area, with a regional accent, a grandmother to look after and who is not accorded the formal devices that are connotative of Morvern's subjectivity (the soundtrack that is heard only by Morvern and the audience; shots that indicate her contemplation etc). In this and other ways the film is about moving on, about a character who dreamily connects Scotland and Spain, who searches for authenticity by travelling through landscapes that are similar yet different, as epitomised by the journeys she takes both within west Scotland and abroad. The club culture which the film documents also has internationalist perspectives, another example of a blurring of boundaries which is a typical feature of Ramsay's *mise-en-scène*. While *Morvern Callar* has its particular locales which may or may not be familiar to audiences, the film's topographies could also be identified with other landscapes, evoking a kind of shorthand familiarity that opens up the work to international audiences.

*Young Adam* is also adapted from a Scottish novel, this time by Alexander Trocchi, who left Glasgow for France in the early 1950s and then moved to the USA where he was associated with the beat culture generation of writers. *Young Adam* was first published in 1954 as a pornographic novel and was revised later for re-publication in 1966 with some of its original sex scenes cut but with the addition of a controversial scene of erotic sexual violence that also features in David Mackenzie's film. The book and film are about Joe (Ewan McGregor), a frustrated writer who works on a barge on the Union canal between Glasgow and Edinburgh with Les (Peter Mullan), his wife Ella (Tilda Swinton) and their young son. Both book and film are inflected with the existential angst that was a feature of 1950s French literature. There is also an eroticised treatment of the different sexual relationships Joe experiences with Ella and, via a series of flashbacks, with his ex-girlfriend Cathie (Emily Morton), the latter being particularly disturbing because of its violent nature in one particular scene. At the beginning of the film Joe and Les discover a partly-clothed woman's body floating in the water. We later discover that the body is Cathie's and that Joe knows how she died. This is revealed to the audience in one of the flashback sequences about half-way through the film, depicting a chance meeting between Cathie and Joe after they have parted. After talking in a café they walk to the quayside and have sex under a truck. Afterwards Cathie informs Joe that she is pregnant and would like them to bring up the child together. Joe rules this out but says that he will send her money in the future. They quarrel and she accidentally falls into the water when trying to catch up with him as he walks briskly away from her. She does not surface and instead of informing the police Joe throws her bag and clothes into the depths after her. Joe does not tell anyone that he knew Cathie or of the circumstances of her death when he and Les later bring her drowned body ashore.

This event haunts the film which is otherwise preoccupied with Joe's sexual relationship with Ella. His intimate scenes with her are often the occasion for a flashback-memory scene with Cathie, who we learn supported Joe in his failed attempt to be a writer. When Les eventually finds out about Joe's relationship with Ella he decides to leave since she owns the barge. Joe then shares the barge with Ella and her son but this does not result in a lasting relationship and Joe leaves. His lack of commitment to Ella is demonstrated when he has sex with her sister Gwen (Therese Bradley) when she visits them on the barge. The cycle of transient, risky and uncommitted relationships begins again when Joe lodges with a friend and at the same time starts an affair with his wife. The film ends with the trial and conviction of Cathie's plumber boyfriend Daniel (Ewan Stewart) who has been accused of her murder. In an attempt to salve his troubled conscience, Joe writes an anonymous note confessing that he witnessed the accident, did not report it to the police and that Daniel is innocent. He leaves the note on a desk as he enters the court but in any case the plumber is sentenced to death. Joe looks set to move on in the final scene when he throws a mirror into the water at the place where Cathie fell to her death. The mirror, which we have seen him gaze into on many occasions, is a significant object since it was a gift from Cathie, engraved with the following message: "Think of me when you look at yourself with undying love, C." The obvious symbolism of Joe trying to forget Cathie gains an ironic perspective when we know that he has been haunted by memories of their relationship, the implication in many of his contemplative interludes being that he did love her, but was unable to sustain commitment.

This representation of Joe as a transient person is similar to the central character in *Morvern Callar*. When Joe leaves Cathie he tells her he is going to China, a trip that never materialises, casting him as a dreamer who cannot even complete the period of sustained writing which life with Cathie has permitted. As we have seen, Morvern is also unable to settle and is similarly haunted by a significant death. The landscapes of *Morvern Callar* and *Young Adam* are also indicative of the move away from urban settings in a strand of new Scottish cinema, rejecting the cityscapes of *Shallow Grave* (Boyle, GB, 2005) and *Trainspotting* for pastoral, port and waterside locations that in themselves indicate points of possible departure. Both Joe and Morvern's partners die. For Morvern the death is in some ways liberating, since it allows her to travel and experience a sense of freedom, while for Joe the death results in despair. Morvern's dead writer boyfriend also links with Joe's intellectualism and authorial ambitions; in Morvern's case the novel she passes off as her own work serves as a catalyst for her escape while Joe's inability to write sends him off to seek experience on the canals, developing new relationships with people to whom he cannot ultimately commit. In a similar way Morvern's treatment of her friend Lanna has the same essence of transience. While they are clearly friends Morvern learns that she wants completely different things, not to stay and be "safe" but to use her new-found life to seek independence and new experiences. Like Joe, the people she encounters never become permanent fixtures in her life and during the film she develops a purposefulness to move on that belies her at times eccentric demeanour. In *Young Adam* Joe drifts from place to place on the barge, yet at the same time he develops a similar desire to leave the past behind, letting go of the mirror given to him by Cathie much as Morvern's personal journey to independence is inspired by the tape left for her by her boyfriend. Representations such as these, of characters who are unsettled drifters, can be seen in other examples of new Scottish cinema, including the two women in *Women Talking Dirty* (Giedroyc, GB, 1999) whose unlikely friendship is forged through a chance meeting in Edinburgh, and *The Winter Guest*, set in a Fife fishing village and which features a recently bereaved woman's desire to escape to Australia.

The characters Morvern and Joe could both be accused of demonstrating an amoral fecklessness. One review of *Morvern Callar* however argued that Morton's performance invested the character's deeds with "a kind of honour...motivated by a kind of love" (Brooks 2002, 50) for the dead boyfriend. David Mackenzie claimed of *Young Adam* that he wanted to "bring out more of what's in the novel: dare I say it, the romance" (Gilbey 2003, 19). This softening of both characters is also supported by the decision in both films to jettison the first-person narration of the novels. Rather than include voiceover narration both films are therefore more open to poetic sensibilities that link environment to character in a way that arguably absolves the protagonists from total responsibility for their actions. In Morvern's case her desire to escape is linked to the visual contrasts between Scotland and Spain while Joe's character blends in with the canals which Mackenzie explained were "decayed and often dangerous routes through cities" (ibid). In this way both characters are fundamentally linked to the landscapes they inhabit. *Chicago Sun-Times* reviewer Roger Ebert (2003; 2004) saw the class dimensions of both films as key to their presentation of convincing motivations behind the characters' actions. Other reviews of *Young Adam* made much of the visible connections between Mackenzie's film and Jean Vigo's celebrated poetic and elliptical depiction of a newly-married young couple's life on a barge, *L'Atalante* (Fr, 1934) (French 2003). While *Morvern Callar* did not invite so many direct comparisons with European cinema, the film's existentialist elements were commented upon and a review in *Variety* compared Morton's performance to that of Catherine Deneuve in Polanski's *Repulsion* (GB, 1965). Manifesting a similar desire to locate *Morvern Callar* within a European cinematic frame of reference, Linda Ruth Williams compared Ramsay's film *Morvern Callar* to Antonioni's *The Passenger* (It/Sp/Fr, 1975) for its similar themes and Spanish locations (2002: 24).

Whether these sensibilities are European and "post-national" is a consideration which invites locating *Morvern Callar* and *Young Adam* within a broad strand of contemporary cinema that also deals with characters on the move. Broadly contemporaneous British films such as Pawel Pawlikowski's *Last Resort* (GB, 2000) explore the theme of migration and the experiences of asylum seekers, as do other films produced elsewhere in Europe. Both *Morvern Callar* and *Young Adam* are co-productions, the former Anglo-Canadian, the latter Anglo-French. Despite Ewan McGregor's persistence in tagging his films with a polarised address that is "British" and anti-Hollywood (an assertion repeated again in the "Making Of" featurette contained on the DVD release of *Young Adam*), both films cannot be confined to one particular national address. Their casting is a key to their ambitions to be cross-cultural products that travel well within film festival circuits and certainly beyond Scottish or English shores. Despite his local affiliations, McGregor is an international star, known for his roles in new Scottish cinematic milestones *Shallow Grave* and *Trainspotting*, but also for US films and co-productions such as *Moulin Rouge!* (Luhrmann, Aus/USA, 2001), the second *Star Wars* trilogy (Lucas, USA, 1999-2005), and *Miss Potter* (Noonan, GB/USA, 2006). The casting of Samantha Morton in *Morvern Callar* is also highly significant for the film's trans-national sensibility. After establishing herself as a respected actress in British films and television, her work has predominantly been in American cinema and non-mainstream co-productions including Woody Allen's *Sweet and Lowdown* (USA, 1999); *Jesus' Son* (Maclean, Can/USA, 1999), *Minority Report* (Spielberg, USA , 2002) and, more recently, appearing in *Mister Lonely* (Korine, GB/Fr/Ire/USA, 2007) and *Control* (Corbijn, GB/USA 2007). Tilda Swinton's image is also related to art-house cinema, in particular her association with Derek Jarman, which creates a particular aesthetic context for *Young Adam* that helps the film easily find a home in the film festival circuit, distancing it from strands of social realist British cinema which other new Scottish films can also be seen to critique. As Christopher Meir (2007) has demonstrated, such positioning is arguably a crucial development for products of the art cinema genre, as is discussion of Ramsay's career in the terminology of classic auteur discourse.

The examples I have concentrated on in this chapter are indicative of the inherent transmutability of many images being created in, and about, Scotland in recent years. As we have seen, a Scottish setting is often the occasion for a re-evaluation of self that does not necessarily result in an affirmation of place or identity, as in older films such as *I Know Where I'm Going!* On the contrary, landscapes that might be recognisable to some are simply generic to others: one canal stretch is much like any other. The world seems smaller when landscapes merge into each other, as in the scene in *Morvern Callar* when Morvern and Lanna travel by taxi from the airport to their holiday complex in Spain. At first the mountains seem similar to those we have seen in Scotland, and it only gradually becomes clear that the topography is different when more of it is revealed, eventually (and ironically) ending up with blocks of apartments that could be anywhere. New Scottish cinema has therefore clearly represented an important shift in visibility for the cinematic representation of Scottish themes and identities. Its perceived specificity has resulted in the development of some important funding organisations and structures. Yet directors who work with Scottish themes and characters do not always remain within a confined generic identity as they operate within broad international arenas in terms of scripting, film finance and personnel. For example, Gillies MacKinnon, director of landmark new Scottish film *Small Faces*, has since worked in a variety of genres and countries, with films such as *Trojan Eddie* (GB/Ire, 1996) and *Hideous Kinky* (GB/Fr, 1998), as well as directing *Regeneration*, a historical/heritage film set in Scotland. So we must be careful that in the desire to herald a "new" style we do not slip into narrow particularism, or become blind to the ways in which the films in question look outwards to other cultures, other audiences. In this way we can perhaps begin to conceptualise the dynamism that new Scottish cinema has introduced somewhat differently, appreciating the films' diversity as they travel across borders to audiences who recognise what they are saying in more than one language.

## Works Cited

Bauer, Carlene. 2000. Interview with Lynne Ramsay. http://archive.salon.com/ent/movies (accessed February 29 2008).

Bergfelder, Tim. 2005. National, transnational or supranational cinema? Rethinking European film studies. *Media, Culture & Society* 27.5: 315-331.

Brooks, Xan. 2002. Morvern Callar. *Sight and Sound* 12.11: 50.

Ebert, Roger. 2003. Morvern Callar. *Chicago Sun-Times*, January 1.

—. 2004. Young Adam. *Chicago Sun-Times*, April 30.
French, Philip. 2003. Not bonny—but plenty of Clyde. *The Observer*, September 28, *Review* section.
Gilbey, Ryan. 2003. Written on the body. *Sight and Sound* 13.9: 16-19.
Hannerz, Ulf. 1996. *Transnational Connections: Culture, People, Places*. London: Routledge.
Kennedy, Harlan. 1996. Kiltspotting: Highland Reels. *Film Comment* 32.4: 28-33.
Meir, Chris. 2007. Underwriting National Sovreignty? Policy, the Market and Scottish Cinema, 1982-the present. PhD diss., University of Warwick.
Murray, Jonathan. 2005. Kids in America? Narratives of transatlantic influence in 1990s Scottish cinema. *Screen* 46.2: 217-225.
Petrie, Duncan. 2000. *Screening Scotland*. London: British Film Institute.
—. 2000a. The New Scottish Cinema. In *Cinema & Nation*, eds. Mette Hjort and Scott Mackenzie, 153-169. London: Routledge.
Street, Sarah. 2002. *Transatlantic Crossings: British Feature Films in the USA*. New York: Continuum.
Various, 2005. Scottish cinema dossier. *Screen* 46.2: 213-245.
Williams, Linda Ruth. 2002. Escape Artist. *Sight and Sound* 12.10: 22-25.

# *SCREENING SCOTLAND*: A REASSESSMENT

DUNCAN PETRIE

## Preamble: The Emergence of an Object of Study

As an event dedicated to the critical analysis and celebration of an identifiable object, the 2005 New Scottish Cinema symposium held at the National University of Ireland in Galway demonstrated just how far we had come in the years since a much earlier gathering, the 1988 Desperately Seeking Cinema conference held at the Glasgow Film Theatre. The latter was predicated on the question 'what kind of Scottish film-making do we want?' While responding in part to recent developments, including the production in Scotland of a handful of films such as Bill Douglas' *Childhood Trilogy* (GB, 1972-78), Bill Forsyth's quartet of features *That Sinking Feeling* (GB, 1979), *Gregory's Girl* GB, 1980), *Local Hero* (GB, 1983) and *Comfort and Joy* (GB, 1984), and a few other features funded by Channel Four, such as *Another Time, Another Place* (Radford, GB, 1983) and *Heavenly Pursuits* (Gormley, GB, 1986), the motivation of that earlier initiative was encapsulated by its title: the speculative search for a national cinema. Almost two decades on we have something far more substantive to contemplate. This is not to suggest that we have necessarily achieved the utopian goal of Desperately Seeking Cinema. Indeed Colin McArthur, whose work provided the intellectual spark for that conference, has since continued to critique with tenacity what he regards as the deficiencies and failings of Scottish cinema and its attendant institutional apparatus (McArthur 1993; 1994a; 1994b). McArthur has also been an inspiration to others. My own contribution to the serious analysis of Scottish cinema was initially in part motivated as a response to the *Scotch Reels* polemic, elaborated in the seminal 1982 edited collection of the same name (McArthur 1982) that was effectively the founding intervention in Scottish film studies. By the mid-1990s *Scotch Reels* offered little with which to make sense of the astonishing transformation of the Scottish cinematic landscape, a process that had scarcely begun at the time that book was published. The subsequent emergence of a new Scottish cinema in the 1980s and 1990s, unprecedented in terms of the number of films produced and underpinned by new funding and institutional structures, required appropriate critical recognition and engagement. This was what I attempted to provide in *Screening Scotland* (Petrie 2000) and in a more diffuse way in *Contemporary Scottish Fictions* (Petrie 2004).

Moving to New Zealand in 2004 has afforded me the opportunity to reconsider certain aspects of my conception of Scottish cinema and the challenges facing the Scottish film industry. This is not only a question of geographical distance, but also of meaningful comparison facilitated by the recent work I have completed on New Zealand, both independently and as part of a larger collaborative project on Small National Cinemas (Hjort and Petrie 2007; Petrie forthcoming). What is much clearer to me now is the way in which, despite its legitimacy as a category, Scottish cinema, like the Scottish nation, remains a devolved rather than an independent entity, embedded within the larger overarching British context and therefore subject to the same economic, political and ideological forces shaping the latter. It has also become very apparent that while the expansion of film production in Scotland has been facilitated by substantial increases in institutional funding, this remains a rather modest and limited intervention compared with the situation in other countries, as figures in recent annual reports from the New Zealand Film Commission and the Danish Film Institute indicate. For example, over the past five years in New Zealand the state has invested around NZ$86 million in film production and development through various agencies and schemes. This averages out at NZ$17.2 million a year, or the equivalent of around £6.67 million annually at current exchange rates. In comparison, Scottish Screen currently channels around £3 million per annum into the same kind of activities. Closer to home, the Danish Film Institute has in recent years invested more than four times that sum annually into around twenty feature films. The relatively generous levels of public funding for film in New Zealand and Denmark (with populations of just over 4 million and 5 million respectively compared to Scotland's 5 million) are motivated by a strong political commitment to film as a means of national expression as well as a potentially profitable industry, arguments that may be articulated in the Scottish context but without the appropriate levels of investment to back them up.

## *Screening Scotland*: A Reassessment

I concluded *Screening Scotland* on a characteristic note of optimism:

> What is clear is that Scottish film-making is entering the new millennium with unprecedented levels of confidence, achievement and ambition. The emergence of a distinctive Scottish cinema has been just one element of the rich and diverse fermentation of creativity and cultural expression in Scotland over the last quarter of a century that has done so much to forge a new culture of possibility. (Petrie 2000, 226)

This was written just after the re-establishment in 1999 of the Scottish Parliament in Edinburgh following the 1997 Devolution referendum. Eight years and two parliamentary terms later, we are now able to reflect back on a period that some commentators suggest has reconfigured the significance of "the national" in Scotland within both creative and discursive contexts. Some have argued that, having regained a level of political self-determination, there is no longer the same necessity for Scots to be preoccupied with the national question: Scottish cultural expression can therefore be resituated as primarily "from" rather than "about" Scotland. Berthold Schoene, for example, introduces an important new collection of writings on Scottish literature by calling for a more cosmopolitan reconstitution of Scottishness in critical discourse:

> Scottish culture has emerged as from a distorting mirror. No longer regarded, or led to regard itself, as exclusively Scottish and thus found or finding itself lacking, it becomes free to conceive of itself in broader terms, with reference to other cultures (not just English culture), indeed as situated within a vibrant network of independent cultural contexts. (Schoene 2007, 9; see also Bell 2004)

But the analysis of a national cinema also involves a consideration of the inter-relation of cultural and industrial questions and a thriving Scottish cinema depends on more than filmmakers embracing cosmopolitanism. It also requires the maintenance of appropriate institutional structures and functioning relationships both within and beyond a nationally-located industry. Therefore, in order to assess developments since 1999 I want to address three questions that were central to the "New Scottish Cinema" identified and explored in *Screening Scotland*. Firstly, if a film industry in Scotland has been sustained following the major institutional developments of the 1980s and 1990s; secondly, if significant filmmaking talent has continued to emerge and develop in Scotland; and thirdly, if distinctively Scottish films are still being made that express and engage with the cultural and social specificity of a changing nation in vital and innovative ways.

## A Sustainable Scottish Industry?

One of the major goals behind the institutional developments of the 1990s was to lay the foundations for a sustainable screen industry in Scotland. On one level this has undoubtedly been achieved, as Jonathan Murray, writing in 2006, acknowledges:

> Current base levels of indigenous production activity, available finance and career opportunities for domestically-based talent, as well as Scottish cinema's all-round national and international visibility, would have seemed quite unimaginable just a decade ago. (Murray 2007, 78)

Murray also notes that the infrastructure of the local industry has expanded, diversified and consolidated since the mid 1990s, with seventy three independent production companies listed in the 2006 edition of the Scottish film industry's directory *Film Bang*. But on closer examination the situation is not entirely rosy. Despite the increase in activity it remains extremely difficult for independent film producers to survive in Scotland, however experienced and industry-savvy they may be. For example, since producing the high-profile $28 million United Artists-funded *Rob Roy* (Caton-Jones, USA) in 1995, Peter Broughan has realised just one further project, *The Flying Scotsman* (Mackinnon, Ger/GB), which endured a protracted pre-production history before finally being made in 2006. The situation has been no easier for producers whose careers were effectively initiated by the upsurge in local production in the mid 1990s. After co-producing *Stella Does Tricks* (Coky Giedroyk, GB, 1996) and producing *Late Night Shopping* (Metzstein, GB/Ger, 2001), Angus Lamont has not made a feature since; former Head of the Scottish Film Production Fund, Eddie Dick, has produced only two features since setting himself up as an independent in 1997: *Blind Flight* (Furse, GB, 2003), on which he was brought in as co-producer, and *True North* (Hudson, Ger/Ire/GB, 2006); while Catherine Aitken, Dick's Head of Development at the SFPF, has also produced just one major project, *Afterlife* (Peebles, GB, 2003), in addition to being associate producer on *Wild Country* (Strachan, GB, 2005). Not only is it extremely difficult for small independents to raise funding for projects, which frequently languish in development hell for years before fizzling out, but the complex ways in which films are financed exacerbates the problem, with even low-budget productions being forced to cobble together their funding from a range of different sources. Each of the investors typically imposes their own conditions and demands. Consequently, if one piece of the financial jigsaw fails to materialise then complex deals that have take a great deal of time and effort to put in place begin to rapidly unravel. The December 2004 collapse, two weeks into pre-production of *Master of Lies*—a contemporary psychological thriller in the tradition of James Hogg and Robert Louis Stevenson for which Eddie Dick had hired the iconoclastic veteran Nicolas Roeg to direct a cast headed by Donald Sutherland, Robert Carlyle and Shirley Henderson—demonstrates the precariousness of this situation. Moreover, there are many other examples of projects that languish in limbo, unable to close their funding.

Given this, it is interesting that two Scottish producers who have thrived over the last decade have effectively diversified their activities in ways facilitated by the wider networks that bind the small and fragile Scottish film industry to larger entities. Andrew Macdonald burst onto the scene in the middle of the 1990s as the producer of *Shallow Grave* (Boyle, GB, 1995) and *Trainspotting* (Boyle, GB, 1996), the two most commercially and critically successful contributions to the New Scottish Cinema. But the London-based Macdonald then turned his sights beyond Scotland, firstly with *A Life Less Ordinary* (Boyle, GB/USA, 1997), a black comedy set in the United States, and then *The Beach* (Boyle, USA/GB, 2000), an adaptation of Alex Garland's novel about a secret slice of paradise in Thailand, starring emerging Hollywood 'A' list actor Leonardo DiCaprio. While retaining a close creative connection with Danny Boyle, who directed all four of the films noted above, Macdonald's career trajectory has also seen a significant graduation in budgetary scale: from the £1.7 million Channel Four-funded *Trainspotting* to the $12 million *A Life Less Ordinary*, backed by Channel Four and Polygram, to *The Beach*, financed to the tune of $50 million by 20th Century Fox. In this way MacDonald gradually established for himself a strong international profile and credibility, paving the way for his successful 1997 bid in partnership with fellow producer Duncan Kenworthy—*Four Weddings and a Funeral* (Mike Newell, GB, 1994), *Notting Hill* (Roger Michell, GB/USA, 1999)—for one of three Lottery franchises. Macdonald and Kenworthy's DNA Films was subsequently awarded £29 million of Lottery monies to produce a slate of British films. That slate has to date included some films with significant Scottish elements: *Beautiful Creatures* (Eagles, GB, 2000), *Strictly Sinatra* (Capaldi, GB, 2001), *The Final Curtain* (Harkins, GB/USA, 2002) and *The Last King of Scotland* (Macdonald, GB, 2006). Within this operation Macdonald has also continued to produce his own projects, including *28 Days Later* (Danny Boyle, GB, 2002), *Notes on a Scandal* (Eyre, GB, 2006), *Sunshine* (Danny Boyle, GB/USA, 2007) and *28 Weeks Later* (Fresnadillo, GB/Sp, 2007).

While also taking advantage of international opportunities, Gillian Berrie's career has a rather different trajectory. After forming Sigma Films with director David Mackenzie, Berrie produced and co-wrote the short films *California Sunshine* (Mackenzie, GB, 1997) and *Somersault* (Mackenzie, GB, 1999) before the team graduated to features with *The Last Great Wilderness* (Mackenzie, GB/Den, 2002) and *Young Adam* (Mackenzie, GB/Fr, 2003), the latter a step up into a bigger-budgeted arena which involved Berrie taking an associate producer credit. More recently Berrie has produced Mackenzie's fourth feature, *Hallam Foe* (GB, 2007), which opened the 2007 Edinburgh International Film Festival. But like Macdonald, Berrie has also involved herself in a wider range of projects involving non-Scottish partners, considerably enhancing her significance as a Scottish-based producer in the process. She has been heavily engaged in co-production activities with Scandinavian film-makers, one of the most significant recent developments in the Scottish context as Jonathan Murray among others has noted (Murray 2007). *The Last Great Wilderness* involved a co-production deal with the Danish company Zentropa, run by Peter Aalbaek Jensen and Lars von Trier. This paved the way for the two companies to collaborate on *Wilbur Wants to Kill Himself* (Scherfig, Den/GB/Swe/Fr, 2002). Berrie's role as co-producer on this Glasgow-set feature allowed Zentropa to gain Scottish Lottery investment for a project that had initially been conceived as a Danish film. Berrie then co-produced a number of Zentropa films directed by some of Denmark's pre-eminent film-makers, including *Dogville* (von Trier, Den/Swe/Nor/Fin/GB/Fr/Ger/Neth, 2003), *Brothers* (Bier, Den, 2004), *Dear Wendy* (Vinterberg, Den/Fr/Ger/GB, 2005), *Manderlay* (von Trier, Den/Swe/Neth/Fr/Ger/GB, 2005) and *After the Wedding* (Bier, Den/Swe, 2006). Sigma Films is currently a partner along with Zentropa in the "Advance Party" initiative, devised by von Trier, Scherfig and Anders Thomas Jensen to produce three low-budget features in Glasgow with first-time directors abiding by a set of rules.[1] *Red Road* (Arnold, GB/Den,

---

[1] The Advance Party rules are:

- The scripts can take their starting point in one or more characters or they may be subjected to an external drama. The characters can also participate in a form that is governed primarily by neither characters nor plot.
- The films take place in Scotland but apart from that the writers are free to place them anywhere according to geography, social setting or ethnic background. Their back-stories can be expanded, family relations can be created between them, they can be given habits good or bad, and secondary characters can be added if it is proper for the individual film.

2006), the first feature to be made as part of the initiative, won the 2006 Jury Prize at Cannes, getting "Advance Party" off to an auspicious start. In addition to all of this activity, Sigma also has relationships with the London-based company Scorpio films, which resulted in the Scottish feature *Dear Frankie* (Auerbach, GB, 2004), and with the Irish company Subotica, which led to the co-production of *Song For a Raggy Boy* (Walsh, Ire/GB/Den/Sp, 2003).

In combining personal projects with involvement in larger slates of collaborative productions, Macdonald and Berrie demonstrate in different ways the extent to which a small national cinema like Scotland is necessarily inter-connected into wider international structures. Macdonald's pre-eminent location in a British film industry with a strong preference for American models of filmmaking is a reminder of Scottish cinema's location as a devolved entity within and dependent on the UK industry: most "Scottish features" have had investments from either the BBC, Channel Four or the UK Film Council. Berrie's Scandinavian connection represents an alternative strategy facilitated by the new Danish cinema's response to the opportunities and constraints of globalization. This response, as I have noted above, has benefited greatly from levels of state support far in excess of that available to Scottish film-makers (see Hjort 2005). Fortunately, one element of the Danish strategy has been to broker new kinds of international collaboration with other small filmmaking nations, including Scotland. In addition to Berrie's projects the Scandinavian connection also encompasses other recent "Scottish" films such as *Aberdeen* (Moland, GB/Nor/Swe, 2000), *Skaggerak* (Kragh-Jakobsen, Den/Swe/GB/Sp/Ger/Fr/Switz, 2003) and *One Last Chance* (Svaasand, GB/Nor, 2004). The benefits of co-producing with other European partners has also led to closer relations with Ireland, which in addition to Sigma's involvement in *Song For a Raggy Boy* includes *The Magdalene Sisters* (Mullan, GB/Ire, 2002) (see Murray 2005) and the two features arising from Eddie Dick's collaboration with Dublin-based David Collins, *Blind Flight* and *True North*.

---

- The interpersonal relationships of the characters differ from film to film and they may be weighted differently as major or minor characters.
- The development of the characters in each story or genre does not affect the other scripts.
- All of the characters must appear in all of the films.
- The various parts will be cast with the same actors in the same parts in all of the films.

## Scottish Filmmaking Talent

Turning to the development of distinctive directorial talent, once again *Screening Scotland* ended on an overly optimistic note, in its championing of *Orphans* (GB, 1997) and *Ratcatcher* (GB/Fr, 1999) the respective debut features of Peter Mullan and Lynne Ramsay, two of the most exciting Scottish writer/directors to emerge in the 1990s. They were followed by May Miles Thomas, whose DIY digital feature *One Life Stand* (GB, 2000) suggested yet another nascent writer/director of considerable talent. But the subsequent eight years have seen each of these individuals struggle to realise just one further feature apiece: Mullan's *The Magdalene Sisters*, *Morvern Callar* (Ramsay, GB, 2002) and *Solid Air* (Miles Thomas, GB, 2003). This apparent premature stalling of careers—although admittedly Mullan's profile as an actor remains strong with key roles in *Young Adam*, *On a Clear Day* (Dellal, GB, 2005) and *True North*—echoes the fate of earlier Scottish directors such as Bill Douglas, Ian Sellar and even Bill Forsyth. Those native talents who have thrived have tended to locate and work primarily outside Scotland, such as Michael Caton-Jones, Gillies Mackinnon, Jim Gillespie and Paul McGuigan; alternatively, like Douglas Mackinnon, they have specialised in network television drama.

The two directors who have contributed the most significant body of work to Scottish cinema in the last few years are David Mackenzie and Richard Jobson. Like Mullan and Ramsay, Mackenzie came up through the ranks of short films, including those schemes initiated in the 1990s by the Scottish Film Production Fund and others specifically to identify and cultivate native talent in Scotland. Mackenzie made a range of short films including the "Tartan Short" *Marcie's Dowry* (GB, 1999)—which significantly was not a Sigma production—before graduating to his first feature, the digitally shot *The Last Great Wilderness*. He then moved into a higher budget range with *Young Adam*, a long-nurtured adaptation of Alexander Trocchi's novel, produced by the veteran Jeremy Thomas. This led to Mackenzie being hired to direct the Patrick Marber-scripted thriller *Asylum* (GB/Ire, 2005), before returning to more personal material with *Hallam Foe*. Mackenzie has undoubtedly benefited from his regular collaboration with Gillian Berrie, but he is also an assured and versatile filmmaker, demonstrating on both shorts and features an industriousness and productivity that few can match. Richard Jobson on the other hand had established careers as a musician and television presenter before moving into filmmaking, initially as a producer with the short film *Just Another Day* (Pertwee, GB, 1996), the TV drama *Tube Tales* (Various, 1999) and the DNA feature *Heartlands* (O'Donnell, GB/USA, 2002), which he also co-wrote. Jobson then wrote and directed three low-budget features in quick succession: *16 Years of Alcohol* (GB, 2003), *The Purifiers* (GB, 2004) and *A Woman in Winter* (GB, 2005), all of which he also produced in collaboration with Chris Atkins. In addition to demonstrating a remarkable ability to get work made quickly and efficiently, these films also attest to Jobson as a talented and cine-literate filmmaker drawing on a range of influences, including his mentor, the Hong Kong maestro Wong Kar-Wai, Stanley Kubrick and Walter Hill. Mackenzie and Jobson's films have continued a strong link with the tradition of European art cinema that I examined in *Screening Scotland*. However, their respective outputs also demonstrate a certain versatility and knowledge of genre film-making which undoubtedly has helped to get their projects financed, Mackenzie's at a higher budgetary level than the more iconoclastic and independent Jobson. But both filmmakers also demonstrate a profound engagement with certain thematic preoccupations that have defined Scottish cultural expression, most notably the Calvinist-inspired obsession with fear, personal responsibility and the machinations of fate (Petrie 2006).

On this cultural level Scottish cinema has certainly become more diverse and cosmopolitan, but in a variety of ways. In addition to the Scandinavian and Irish links (which as well as serving economic imperatives within the realm of low-budget production also reflect certain cultural links between countries on the North West fringe of Europe) the development of a more overtly transnational Scottish cinema is clearly apparent. On one hand, various agencies such as Scottish Screen have assisted overseas productions to be based or to shoot in Scotland, including *The Jacket* (Maybury, USA/Ger, 2005), *Man to Man* (Wargnier, Fr/SA/GB, 2005) and *Greyfriars Bobby* (Henderson, GB, 2005). Moreover, a number of high profile Bollywood productions have been shot in Scotland since the mid 1990s (Martin-Jones 2006). Elsewhere, Scottish Lottery money has gone to support a diverse range of productions, such as *Yasmin* (Ger/GB, 2004), the story of a British Pakistani woman in Yorkshire directed by Scottish film-maker Kenny Glennan; *Festival* (GB, 2005), written and directed by the American Annie Griffin and set against the overtly cosmopolitan backdrop of the annual Edinburgh Festival; *Nina's Heavenly Delights* (Parmar, GB, 2006), a cross-cultural romantic comedy set among Glasgow's Asian community that relates directly to the work of Gurinder Chadha and Hanif Kureishi; and *The Last King of Scotland*, based on Giles Foden's book about a fictitious Scottish doctor who becomes personal physician to the Ugandan dictator Idi Amin. This phenomenon of transnationalism has been discussed by Jonathan Murray, who suggests that devolution has allowed Scottish cinema to relax the terms of its apparent obsession with national identity:

> At the end of the twentieth century the notion of 'devolution' applied to Scottish cinema implied a process of distanciation from specific models of national identity and national cinema: unitary British ones.....Yet perhaps over the early years of the 2000s the concept of 'devolution' has come to mean something different. It might now be more accurate to say that, both in terms of international working and co-production arrangements and the representational content of much contemporary local feature work, what Scottish cinema is devolving itself away from is the notion that it must automatically be framed and best understood within any framework of national specificity at all. (Murray 2007, 90)

## Economic and Cultural Issues in British and Scottish Cinema

The globalisation of the motion picture industry, of which the above developments are clearly a part, and the creation of what some have termed "The New International Division of Cultural Labour" (Miller *et al* 2005), have had major implications not only for the organisation of industrial strategies but also Government policy in support of national film production. Since coming to power in 1997, the cultural policy of the British Labour government has been driven by a Creative Industries agenda that regards the value of culture in primarily economic terms. The Creative Industries are defined by the government's Department of Culture, Media and Sport (DCMS) on its website as those which "have their origin in individual creativity, skill and talent and which have a potential for wealth and job creation through the generation and exploitation of intellectual property". The justification for this conceptual transformation of the arts (including film) into creative industries has been couched in terms of the advent of a new phase in advanced capitalism—the so-called "creative economy"—in which the increased circulation of cultural products places a new emphasis on the symbolic content of commodities and on the experiential desires of consumers. This in turn has had major implications for the role of public support for culture and cultural activities, as John Hartley notes:

> The 'creative industries' idea brought creativity from the back door of government, where it had sat for decades holding out a tin cup for subsidy—miserable, self-loathing and critical (especially of the hand that fed it), but unwilling to change—around to the front door, where it was

introduced to the wealth-creating portfolios, the emergent industry departments, and the enterprise support programmes. (Hartley 2005, 19)

While cinema has traditionally been treated as an industry by the British government, there have also been more culturally-inspired avenues of state support for film, including the British Film Institute, the English Regional Arts Boards and the Scottish Film Production Fund. In recent years, however, guided by the wider Creative Industries approach of New Labour to culture, UK film policy has been predominantly driven by a concern with economic and commercial issues. This was reflected in the 1998 report of the Film Policy Review Group, *A Bigger Picture*, and has guided the operations of the UK Film Council since that body's inception in 2000 (see Ryall 2002). The clearest indication of this mission was articulated by the Film Council's Chairman, Sir Alan Parker, in his "Building a Sustainable UK Film Industry" speech in November 2002. Here Parker advocated the repositioning of British cinema as a creative film hub—in other words a service industry for international (i.e. Hollywood) production—in order to help it compete more successfully in the world marketplace. He also called for the redefinition of what was for official purposes taken to constitute a "British" film, in order to allow a wider range of productions to qualify for Lottery funding and fiscal incentives such as tax breaks.[2]

Over the past ten years serious public support for film in Scotland has been largely administered to local productions through the Scottish Lottery Fund. This source of money came on stream in 1995 and was initially overseen by the Scottish Film Production Fund (1995-1997) on behalf of the Scottish Arts Council. The Fund was subsequently moved back under the auspices of the SAC in 1997, and then to Scottish Screen in 2000, where it currently remains. In its operations the Lottery Fund has attempted some kind of workable integration between economic and cultural concerns through nurturing a local screen production industry, developing Scottish filmmaking talent, and promoting cultural expression

---

[2] Since then a new test for defining a "British" film has been introduced that assigns projects points for their cultural content, cultural contribution, cultural hubs (location of services) and cultural practitioners (residency of key individuals involved). The position adopted by Parker and the DCMS represents an unequivocal endorsement of the New International Division of Cultural Labour, which among other things emphasises the ways in which national film industries and governments have been complicit with the interests of the powerful players (i.e. the Hollywood majors) in their attempts to obtain a competitive advantage in the global market.

through the production and distribution of cinematic narratives and images. This broader mission has been supported through shared production initiatives with the major Scottish broadcasters BBC Scotland and the Scottish Media Group, brokering another kind of integration between public service and delivering popular programming to an audience. While the first transfer of responsibility for the Lottery Fund from the Scottish Film Production Fund to the Scottish Arts Council was as a result of investigations into accusations of cronyism after substantial production awards were made to projects in which Lottery Panel members had major interests, the subsequent shift of the Lottery Fund to the more industry-focused Scottish Screen can clearly be understood in terms of broader policy shifts. An economic rationale for funding film had been previously established in Scotland in 1993 with the inception of the Glasgow Film Fund, an initiative involving the Glasgow Development Agency, Glasgow City Council, Strathclyde Regional Council and the European Regional Development Fund. The GFF was motivated by factors such as inward investment, local production spend and the promotion of Glasgow through the city's appearance on large and small screens around the world. Any returns on investments would be used to boost the pot available for subsequent productions. But the kind of films to which the GFF made a contribution, including *Shallow Grave*, *Small Faces* (Mackinnon, GB, 1996), *My Name is Joe* (Loach, Sp/It/Fr/GB/Ger, 1998), *Orphans* and *The House of Mirth* (Davies, GB/Fr/Ger/USA, 2000), can be more readily accommodated within a tradition of cultural rather than commercial filmmaking.

The cultural and the economic have always been tightly bound up together in the sphere of small films and modest budgets within which the new Scottish cinema has been nurtured. This point has been persuasively articulated by those involved in funding such innovative low-budget cinema, whether inside or outside Scotland. Thus, in an account of a decade in charge of the Irish Film Board, Rod Stoneman recalls the recognition on the Board's reconstitution in 1993 that it needed to adopt:

> A more complex and adept negotiation of audience expectations: requiring the reshaping of auteurist visions in relation to the very powerful forces of the market and the complex financial machinery that underlies contemporary cinema processes. (Stoneman 2005, 251)

The problem arises when only one side of the equation is considered, generating either a solipsistic conception of a creative process in which the audience plays no meaningful part, or one in which second-guessing the market is the only motivation. Neither has anything to offer a sustainable small national cinema.

The Creative Industries agenda has impacted on funding initiatives in Scotland, but arguably in a less direct fashion than that suggested by the rhetoric of the UK Film Council (which was itself re-branded from the original Film Council which was *de facto* considered to be an English-focused body). Moreover, the operations of the Scottish Screen Lottery Panel, which I was a member of from 2001-2003, reflected a balance of economic and cultural considerations in that body's decision-making. While the Panel's composition reflected a strong industry orientation, comprising independent producers, directors, television executives, distributors and exhibitors, some of these individuals were also strongly associated with a cultural conception of film. The process appeared to work very well from the inside, but tensions began to develop between Scottish Screen and independent producers in Scotland over the transparency and efficiency of the decision-making. In part this was a consequence of the inevitable gap between heightened expectations and limited funds, but unfortunately it also exposed the organisation to damaging criticism, precipitating the resignation of the Panel Chair, Jim Faulds, at the end of 2003 and paving the way for disbanding this body a year later. While this was regrettable, it is useful to note that similar funding panels such as the BFI Production Board have tended to function in such a way as to justify a more culturally-informed approach to funding, compared to the executive model adopted by British Screen and Channel Four, where decision-making has been defended more robustly along business lines. Given the general climate change in British film culture, this shift to a process in which greater decision-making was invested in the officers of Scottish Screen, albeit with the assistance of a smaller group of hand-picked industry consultants, was probably inevitable.

But the damage to Scottish Screen's credibility also contributed to the departure of Chief Executive Steve McIntyre and the ushering in, under his successor Ken Hay, of a new agenda aligned much more clearly with the Creative Industries discourse. Since devolution in 1999 the Scottish Executive had also enthusiastically embraced a version of New Labour's Creative Industries agenda in guiding its formulation of cultural policy. This has been examined by Jonathan Murray, who reveals a rather disquieting lack of engagement with questions of culture among Scottish politicians:

> The first term of Devolution was one in which most local politicians insisted on seeing Scottish cinema almost wholly as an area of *industrial* activity, one minimally defined by issues of economic development and

> entrepreneurship, and very secondarily, by 'quality of life' considerations, including adequate leisure and cultural provision and access to cinema screens showing a diverse range of films across the country. (Murray 2006, 68)

The economic value of cultural activity coupled with social inclusion (via the jargon of "cultural rights for the Scottish citizen") were subsequently the major issues guiding the 2005 comprehensive review of public funding for culture in Scotland by the Cultural Commission, which recommended the establishment of a new funding and development organisation, Creative Scotland, to replace existing institutions, including Scottish Screen and the Scottish Arts Council. It is unclear how the commitment to the moving image will be affected by the establishment of Creative Scotland, an institutional reconfiguration whereby arrangement the film production sector will have to compete with the other arts for financial and associated forms of support. Scottish Screen's *2006/09 Corporate Plan*, published in March 2006 and clearly written as a means of influencing the future objectives of Creative Scotland, adopts a textbook Creative Industries discourse that begins by acknowledging the significance of the Scottish Screen Archive (but noting the plan to transfer this to the National Library of Scotland) and Education. The document then labels Scottish Screen's other priorities under the headings "Enterprise and Skills" (dealing with training and infrastructure), "Inward Investment and Communications" (attracting overseas productions and marketing local productions), "Market Development" (exhibition) and "Talent and Creativity' (production). Moreover, rather than talking about films and programmes the document refers to "screen-based content and formats," a reflection of the increasing emphasis on interactive media and computer games alongside cinema and television within the "screen industries". While this may simply reflect changing realities driven by new technologies and patterns of consumption, both the strategic interests of a Scottish film industry and any concerns with cultural engagement and expression have either been driven to the margins or excluded altogether. Moreover, any institutional commitment to a Scottish national cinema seems to have evaporated in the process. It is also instructive to compare the discourse of the public funding institution in Scotland with that of the New Zealand Film Commission, which, while also operating in a political environment in which the Creative Industries agenda holds sway, is far more concerned to articulate both the necessary interdependence of cultural and business imperatives and the centrality of feature films to the Commission's remit. Indeed in the Commission's *2005/06 Annual Report* the goal stated as guiding the organisation's activities in the financing of feature film production is:

> To maintain the number of New Zealand films including larger budget films; to support diverse, culturally-specific New Zealand films which reflect New Zealand's multicultural society.

The Danish Film Institute, on the other hand, still talks on its website of a responsibility to "support and encourage the art of film-making" as part of the wider role of "the national agency responsible for supporting and encouraging film and cinema culture and for conserving these in the national interest." While the advocates of the Creative Industries discourse in Scotland and Britain may regard this terminology as outmoded or inappropriate, the commitment of the Danish to a viable national cinema is overwhelmingly vindicated by its current levels of success.

## Conclusion: The Challenge for Scottish Cinema

Despite the rather chastening tone of this essay, I still believe that over the last decade Scottish filmmaking has followed literature in playing a key role in the reawakening of a sense of national self-awareness and cultural confidence. The predominant screen images of the nation have been transformed: a rural and remote setting for romantic or unsettling encounters has given way to a greater focus on an urban post-industrial environment framing narratives concerned with various aspects of contemporary experience and social change. Rural depictions are still in evidence, but these tend to eschew romance in favour of darker, more unsettling preoccupations. Moreover, given the close associations between culture, tourism and "the national brand" at the heart of the Creative Industries agenda, it is significant that many Scottish films continue to posit a critical engagement with the negative aspects and limitations of contemporary society and identity. In this way the new Scottish cinema functions as an important component of a national conversation that weaves together tradition and innovation, past and present, inside and outside, local and global. This sense of the permeability of categories or borders is particularly important. As the Australian film scholar Tom O'Regan asserts, national cinemas "are not alternatives to internationalisation, they are one of its manifestations...vehicles for international integration" (O'Regan 1996, 50-51). Similarly, Mette Hjort suggests that the impact of global forces has generated new ways of considering small national cinemas, including the potential for forging new collaborations and connections among such cinemas and the imagination of alternative globalisations. One key example of this is provided by the Danish-initiated Dogme95 phenomenon. Described by Hjort as “a small nation’s response to Hollywood-style globalization” (Hjort 2005, 32), Dogme95 is a concerted attempt to generate an alternative and oppositional aesthetic which is international in application while remaining closely associated with its nationally-specific origins. Similarly, in the Scottish context the more overtly cosmopolitan configuration within which Scottish filmmakers are patently operating does not diminish the national dimension of their work.

But the sustenance of small national cinemas remains a major challenge. Despite the success and visibility of several recent Scottish films and filmmakers, the smallness and fragility of the independent sector in Scotland has ensured that independent producers face a continual struggle for survival. A related problem is the high cost of producing films in the UK. New digital technology is providing one way in which production costs can be reduced, with Richard Jobson’s films a case in point. But the problem is far from resolved and we are left with the conundrum of where to draw the line between over-inflated costs and exploitation. Micro-budget production, particularly when the result is a *One Life Stand* or a *16 Years of Alcohol*, is a very seductive strategy. But a sustainable industry also requires fair rates of pay, rather than endless deferrals. However, at the same time a low-budget mentality is the only viable way forward for the new Scottish cinema, affording a greater opportunity for innovative, difficult and locally engaged films to be made. This also reinforces the key point about the integration of culture and the market, as Steve McIntyre noted more than a decade ago in an essay setting out the challenges for a putative Scottish film industry:

> If there is one defining characteristic of low budget film-making it is that it dissolves the distinction between commercial film-making and cultural film-making—it is a meeting ground. (McInytre 1994, 106)

This brings me back to the consideration of the central role of public funding. The dictum that a cinema which is productively engaged with questions of national specificity is necessarily a dependent cinema retains a certain truth. But we need to avoid a reductive conception of films as either solely subsidised or commercial entities. The reality is that most of the productions that make up the new Scottish cinema have combined funding from the Lottery, broadcasters, pre-sales to distributors, tax shelter investment and bank loans against unsold territories. However, the public element of this—Lottery funding—remains crucial. In most cases Scottish

Screen has provided the all-important development funding and then committed a key chunk of the production budget, allowing producers a much better chance of raising other sources of money. The reduction or removal of this life support system, or its bland reconfiguration in Scottish Screen's *2006/09 Corporate Plan* as the "development and production of screen-based content and formats," will have serious consequences for future Scottish film production. The new Scottish cinema has given us much to celebrate, but we have reached another moment of transition with the advent of Creative Scotland. The time has come for Scottish filmmakers, policy makers and intellectuals to embrace a common cause and combine their efforts in advocating the value of a small national cinema in Scotland. It behoves all of us to do what we can to ensure that the very real gains of recent years are not lost and that Scottish cinema continues to develop and thrive.

## Works Cited

Bell, Eleanor. 2004. *Questioning Scotland: Literature, Nationalism, Postmodernism*. Houndmills: Palgrave.

Hartley, John, ed. 2005. *Creative Industries*. Oxford: Blackwell.

Hjort, Mette. 2005. *Small Nation, Global Cinema: The New Danish Cinema*. Minneapolis: University of Minnesota Press.

Hjort, Mette and Duncan Petrie, eds. 2007. *The Cinema of Small Nations*. Edinburgh: Edinburgh University Press.

McArthur, Colin, ed. 1982. *Scotch Reels: Scotland in Cinema and Television*. London: British Film Institute.

—. 1993. In praise of a poor cinema. *Sight and Sound* 3.8: 30-32.

— 1994a. The Cultural Necessity of a Poor Celtic Cinema. In *Border Crossing: Film in Ireland, Britain and Europe*, eds. John Hill, Martin McLoone and Paul Hainsworth, 112-125. London/Belfast: British Film Institute/Institute of Irish Studies/University of Ulster.

—. 1994b. Tartan Shorts and the Taming of First Reels. *Scottish Film* 9: 19-20.

McIntyre, Steve. 1994. Vanishing Point: Feature Film Production in a Small Country. In *Border Crossing: Film in Ireland, Britain and Europe,* eds. John Hill et al, 88-111. London/Belfast: British Film Institute/Institute of Irish Studies/University of Ulster.

Martin-Jones, David. 2006. Kabhi India Kabhi Scotland: Recent Indian Films Shot in Scotland. *South Asian Popular Culture* 4.1: 49-60.

Miller, Toby, Nitin Govil, John McMurria, Richard Maxwell and Ting Wang. 2005. *Global Hollywood 2*. London: British Film Institute.

Murray, Jonathan. 2005. Sibling rivalry? Contemporary Scottish and Irish cinemas. In *Ireland and Scotland: Culture and Society 1707-2000*, eds. Liam McIlvanney and Ray Ryan, 144-163. Dublin: Four Courts.

—. 2006. (D)evolution in Reverse? The Scottish Executive and Film Policy, 1999-2003. *Edinburgh Review* 116: 57-70.

—. 2007. Scotland. In *The Cinema of Small Nations*, eds. Mette Hjort and Duncan Petrie, 76-92. Edinburgh: Edinburgh University Press.

O'Regan, Tom. 1996. *Australian National Cinema*. London: Routledge.

Petrie, Duncan. 2000. *Screening Scotland*. London: British Film Institute.

—. 2004. *Contemporary Scottish Fictions: Film, Television and the Novel*. Edinburgh: Edinburgh University Press.

—. 2006. Hard Men and Justified Sinners: The Dark Side of Contemporary Scottish Cinema. *Edinburgh Review* 116: 71-82.

—. Forthcoming. New Zealand Cinema: Negotiating the Local and the Global. In *Cinema at the Periphery*, eds. Dina Iordanova, David Martin-Jones and Belen Vidal. Detroit: Wayne State University Press.

Ryall, Tom. 2002. New Labour and the Cinema: Culture, Politics and Economics. *Journal of Popular British Cinema* 5: 5-20.

Schoene, Berthold. 2007. Going Cosmopolitan: Reconstituting 'Scottishness' in Post-Devolution Criticism. In *The Edinburgh Companion to Contemporary Scottish Literature*, ed. Berthold Schoene, 7-16. Edinburgh: Edinburgh University Press.

Stoneman, Rod. 2005. The Sins of Commission II. *Screen* 46.2: 247-264.

# NOT MADE IN SCOTLAND: IMAGES OF THE NATION FROM FURTH OF THE FORTH

DAVID STENHOUSE

As explored elsewhere in this volume, many Scottish film critics and producers take the absence (whether historic or contemporary) of Scottish film as a given. Our missing film industry, in the sense of a home-produced cinema which would draw on Scottish production and acting talent and address Scottish themes and concerns, has been seen for much of the last century as an embarrassment to Scottish culture. It is another Caledonian gap, omission or absence to be set alongside *lacunae* like the perceived disruptions to the nation's musical and theatrical traditions. Worse, cinema, unlike theatre, which was boosted by the creation in 2003 of the National Theatre of Scotland, has for a variety of structural and financial reasons proved much harder to sponsor at a national level. The trans- or supra-national nature of much film production, the high capital costs of filmmaking and the pressure to seek international audiences have often seemed to act against the apparently enabling, downward pressures exerted by technological innovation. It may be easier to edit a feature film in Glasgow or Inverness than it ever has been before but that fact has not lead to an exponential growth in the number of edits overlooking the Clyde or the Ness.

But complicating this picture of structural neglect is a sense in which the *presence* of one kind of Scottish film, as opposed to the absence of another, can also be an embarrassment. Even if the filmmaking tradition within Scotland has been fragmented or unsatisfactory—itself a debatable proposition, and one interrogated in this volume—that clearly does not mean that there has ever been a lack of films made *about* Scotland. Indeed, since the very beginning of cinema there have been thousands of films made about the country or on Scottish themes, by filmmakers predominantly working outside Scotland's borders. Yet far from being welcomed, as I will explore below these films have often been subject to the harshest censure by domestic critics and filmmakers. This essay is concerned with the kinds of films about Scotland which are more often excluded from, rather than included in, any canonical list on the subject; films that for a variety of reasons and in many different ways are often considered to be "wrong".

It is not difficult to draw up a Scottish film list of shame: there is a persistent kind of movie which is guaranteed to drive Scottish film critics (of both the academic and the journalistic varieties) into despair, scorn, even genuine anger; a category of films which, in the words of one film critic, "borrowed Scottish scenery and plundered Scottish history and then made up the rest" (Pendreigh). It is not hard to come up with a stereotypical definition of the Wrong Kind of Scottish Film: it would have an elastic, inexact sense of Scottish history; it would cast a high profile outsider (David Niven, Liam Neeson, Mel Gibson) as a Scottish hero with the wrong accent; it would sample promiscuously from Scotland's natural landscape, often rejecting the real thing because, in the famous words of producer Arthur Freed after scouting for physical Scottish locations in which to shoot *Brigadoon* (Minnelli, USA, 1954), "nothing...looked like Scotland" (Hardy 1990, 1). The Wrong Kind of Scottish Film may also lean heavily towards sentiment, pawky humour, the couthily conventional and the emotionally cloying. Ironically, and infuriatingly for those championing the development of the Scottish film industry, the Wrong Type of Scottish Film is usually more successful internationally than the domestic product, thus perpetuating the "wrong" kind of image of Scotland abroad, dooming those who desire a viable Scottish film culture to work in the shadows of what they see as a distorted or debased version of "Scottishness". Each generation of Scottish film lovers has had their favourite version of the "wrong" kind of Scottish film. For film audiences in the 1920s it may have been the Lillian Gish vehicle *Annie Laurie* (Robertson, USA, 1927), a film discussed below. For many Scots at the end of the 20th century it was *Braveheart* (Gibson, USA, 1995).

This chapter proposes an alternative way of viewing Scottish film, one that breaks down the reductive binary division between "good" and "bad" movies, and challenges the distinction between "authorised" and "unauthorised" versions of the nation, its history and iconography. This chapter will also suggest that, despite their marginalised status, stigmatised individual examples of the Wrong Type of Scottish Film do relate very closely to the broader critical and industrial debates about Scottish cinema. In particular, I want to propose that such films have been deliberately set in a falsely antithetical relationship with an idealised and broadly unrealised vision of Scottish cinema which emphasises values like documentary relevance, reality or at least realism, and aesthetic or geographical proximity to the subject being depicted. The Wrong Type of

Scottish Film also poses a vision of "Scottish cinema" which is not focused exclusively on production, funding structures and institutions, but instead on product, aesthetics and a sometimes wilful, sometimes joyful, sometimes naïve sense of narrative play. It is useful to focus on such an approach not least because the dominant mode of thinking about Scottish film has tended to be institutional or productionist.

When Jim Hickey wrote a short chronology of Scottish Film Culture for the volume *Scotch Reels* (Hickey 1982) his starting point was the founding of the Glasgow Film Society in 1929. In a different sense, the relationship between film and Scotland had begun a good two decades earlier. From 1908's version of Shakespeare's *Macbeth* (Stuart Blackton, USA) through *The Chieftain's Revenge, a Tragedy in the Highlands of Scotland* (McDougal, USA, 1908)—"the story is laid in the Scotch mountains about the middle of the 15th century" boasted the playbill—to another *Macbeth*, this time produced in Italian in 1909 (Calmettes, Italy), then *Kenilworth*, after the Walter Scott novel of the same title (Mullin, USA, 1909), *The Bride of Lammermoor, A Tragedy of Bonnie Scotland*, (Blackton, USA, 1909), *The Bottle Imp* (Neilan, USA, 1917) based on Robert Louis Stevenson's short story, and various *Lochinvars*, tumbling Scots acrobats, Highlanders and *Mary Queens of Scots* produced from French, Italian, and mostly American studios, Scottish themes were early favourites for filmmakers. By 1913 there had been three separate films of *Rob Roy*, including one that was even scouted and shot in Scotland (see McBain 1990).

There are distinct reasons for this early cinematic fascination with Scottish themes, but they have common threads. In the United States the popularity of Scott and Stevenson as writers was an important element. North American interest in Scottishness was stirred up by a series of Harry Lauder tours of the North Eastern States and Canada between 1907 and 1914. Such developments helped to prime the pump amongst cinemagoers in the large cities of Chicago, Boston, New York and Toronto, much as the rising American interest in Scottish identity in the 1990s helped supply audiences for the US releases of *Trainspotting* (Boyle, GB, 1996), *Rob Roy* (Caton-Jones, USA, 1995) and *Braveheart*. In Italy, historical interest in the figure of Macbeth, reflected in and then further encouraged by Verdi's opera of 1847, and, in France, an abiding fascination with the French-speaking Mary Queen of Scots, made these two Scottish monarchs attractive box office. Take too the influence of music hall on early film reels and the explanation for the tumbling, drunk and/or broad Victorian-stereotyped Scots who populated American silent comedies becomes obvious. In silent film the Scot had a distinct advantage over, say, the

Welshman: an instantly recognisable iconography of hill, kilt, bagpipe and claymore, one established as early as the 18th century in paintings and popular engravings and easily translated to the moving image. It is noticeable how familiar many of these film images are even when viewed for the first time; the flickering frame of the film cel echoes the static ones of eighteenth- and nineteenth-century oil paintings of the Scottish landscape, of farmers, Highland Clansmen, cattle or pretty female peasants. For those who wanted to represent "the Scots" on screen in cinema's early decades there was a pre-existing visual iconography to hand, one supplied by the historic fascination with Scottish landscape, dress, customs, musical instruments and the rest. For cinema audiences this shorthand promised romance, exoticism and a set of stable narrative conventions grounded within a broadly familiar emotional, tonal and cultural space. Even if you missed the film's title, it was clear that you were looking at a work about "Scotland," if not Scotland.

Though numerous, these early Scottish-themed films remain little examined by Scottish film critics. Writing in 1982 Colin McArthur noted that "the history of these representations remains to be written" (McArthur 1982, 42). It still does, although the more general question of how Scots are represented in cultural products from outside the country has been approached by Alan Riach who has recently discussed at length representations of Scottishness in international popular culture (Riach 2005).

Yet for all that Scottish-themed films made outside the country have received little sustained critical attention from within it, they go to the heart of many of the representational issues which have perplexed and vexed many Scottish critics over the last century. Many of the images of Scotland produced in foreign-made films are popular, abiding, and broadly conservative, in the sense that they are content to echo, enforce and enlarge upon, rather than interrogate their subject matter. Because of this, such images have too often been seen as part of an undifferentiated mass of material—tea cosies, album covers, tartan memorabilia—which is interesting for sociological or historical reasons, but has little to detain critics of cinema for long. Early representations of Scots and Scottishness have tended to be stigmatised and dismissed by Scottish critics rather than being closely read: too often there has been a core assumption that the image presented is banal and kitsch, and therefore unworthy of close study. The films have been quickly labeled a product of Tartanry, Kailyard or both. For reasons I will return to, it is worth interrogating this comfortable assumption.

Nor is this just an academic blind spot. Journalists are particularly prone to falling for the easy copy possible in exploring the gap between "real" Scotland and the cinematic version of the country. Just as Scots have been portrayed in cinema made outside Scotland since the beginning of film, Scottish critics have been complaining about the nature of that portrayal from the moment of its emergence. Forsyth Hardy in his pioneering 1930s film columns for *The Scotsman* newspaper often complained about the way in which Scots were depicted in the films he reviewed: one early commentary on *The 39 Steps* (Hitchcock, GB , 1935) took exception to the way that Scots were portrayed in the film as "pawky peasants," though he later admitted, "when I first saw the film I reacted disproportionately to a sequence set in a Highland crofter's cottage which seemed to underline the charge of meanness so often brought against Scots" (Hardy 1990, 17). Over the years, Hardy was able to compile quite a collection of complaints; his list of shame included the 1927 Hollywood version of *Annie Laurie*, a film which conflated the Burns heroine with the Massacre of Glencoe, and in which she was serenaded in a song written some years after her death. Hardy also despaired of *The Secret of the Loch* (Rosmer, GB, 1934), which has Seymour Hicks playing a scientist trying to persuade London journalists at Invermoriston that the Loch Ness Monster was half-Brontosaurus, half-Diplodocus and hatched from a prehistoric egg preserved from decay by the unplumbed waters of the loch. He touches on other delights such as Katherine Hepburn in John Ford's *Mary of Scotland* (USA, 1936), Laurel and Hardy's *Bonnie Scotland* (Horne, USA, 1935), Walt Disney's *Rob Roy* (Masters, USA, 1953) and *Greyfriars Bobby* (Chaffey, USA, 1960), Orson Welles in *Trouble in the Glen* (Wilcox, USA, 1954), Errol Flynn in *The Master of Ballantrae* (Keighley, USA, 1953), and *The Ghost goes West* (Clair, USA, 1935). This last film has much to be said for, and about it. It is concerned with a feud from 1745 between the Glouries and the MacLaggans which will end only when a MacLaggan is forced to admit that a Glourie is worth seven of his clan. The ghost is the double of the contemporary Glourie who, in order to settle his debt, sells the castle to an American who dismantles it stone by stone and transports it, complete with ghost, to Florida, where a rival businessman turns out to be of MacLaggen blood. Viewed today it is a life-affirming film, but Hardy didn't like it.

Hardy distilled many of his thoughts about Scottish films and films made about Scotland in his broadly autobiographical 1990 book *Scotland in Film*. In it, he wrote:

> The motivation for the making of all the films I have described did not come from within Scotland. They formed part of the pattern of film making

> [sic] in London or Hollywood, items in production schedules. They were made because someone somewhere thought that an idea in a novel or play, or a character from history would result in a film which audiences all over the world would want to see. (Hardy 1990, 29)

It is interesting that the final point is presented as a lament. Is there no pleasure to be taken in the fact that audiences all over the world respond so warmly to films about Scotland? The number of films occurring on Hardy's watch which drew on Scottish themes, settings and tropes was remarkable. Despite recent policy-driven efforts to sell the nation as a location to film movies, post-devolutionary Scotland has, to date, proved rather less appealing as a setting for films attempting to attract an international audience. It is an interesting irony that between them Walter Scott, Macbeth, Robert Louis Stevenson and Nessie have inspired more Scottish films that Donald Dewar, Henry McLeish, Jack McConnell and Alex Salmond combined.

Hardy grudgingly concluded his introduction to *Scotland in Film* by concluding of foreign films on Scottish topics that, "some at least of these approaches by Englishmen and Americans have been genuine efforts to achieve authentic and credible portrayal" (ibid, 5). Authenticity, fidelity to the real, was Hardy's watchword. True to that credo he preferred documentary, or feature films which had elements of documentary to them, to outright fiction film. There is, incidentally, an irony here. When one looks at the large numbers of Scottish films which look towards Scottish novels for their narrative structure—the many different versions of *Kidnapped*, *The Strange Case of Dr Jekyll and Mr Hyde*, or even the movie version of *Trainspotting*, for example—such movies are leaning on a cultural form—the Scottish novel—which is not in fact predominantly realist but has always had very strong fantastical elements and aspects of freewheeling narrative play. As Duncan Petrie notes (Petrie 2004), the bias towards documentary realism Hardy exhibited represents only one tradition, and not even the dominant one, in Scottish narrative.

It is worth questioning why the representation of Scotland by external agents has been a source of such domestic anxiety. The internationally recognised iconography of nation referred to above (kilt, caber, bagpipes) is uncomfortable territory for many Scottish critics, because it is clearly pre-modern, romantic (if not Romantic) and clichéd. It is also stubbornly persistent, and seemingly impervious to all attempts to replace it. As such, the classic iconography may be an international calling card of Scottishness, but it is one which has, many modern Scots feel as they look down to read it, misspelled their name. Because of this discomfort, Scottish critics have tended to see partial, particular takes on Scottishness from external producers, directors or performers as distorting, constraining, restricting, and controlling: a cultural version of the imperial land grab. Perhaps responding to a familiar Scottish sense that the nation's reality is always in danger of being overwritten by a more powerful neighbour, the need to enforce indigenous norms of representation has felt like an imperative. This has led in turn to a desire to police images of Scottishness, a tendency which will be discussed in greater detail below.

In early twentieth-century film culture the obvious way to police images of Scottishness was to take control of the means of production. For Hardy and many of his generation, the solution to perceived misrepresentation of Scots, Scotland and Scottishness was clear: Scotland must have the means to produce film images of itself, specifically, through a Scottish National Film Studio. The campaigning pamphlet "Scotland on the Screen", produced by the fledgling "Scottish National Film Studios" in 1946, explicitly cited misrepresentation by outside filmmakers - implicitly Hollywood – as an argument for Scotland having its own film studios:

> Hollywood and London, with few exceptions, have presented the Scot as a bibulous comic in small parts. In fact, however, no country produces human individuals with sharp characteristics more naturally or more abundantly than Scotland. This is indeed a feature of the Scottish nation! (Bruce 1990, 75)

Behind this there was a core assumption that only Scots working in film production in Scotland, not Americans (or Scots-Americans) in Hollywood, or English filmmakers in Laing or Shepperton—though of course there were many Scots working in Laing or Shepperton—could interpret Scotland correctly.

I have discussed Hardy, though he is a figure seldom referred to in academic film criticism (see Caughie and McArthur 1982 for a notable exception), at some length for a number of reasons. The first is that he represents an unusual figure in the Scottish context, an expert film journalist interested in the whole process of film production; not just a film critic in the sense of a reviewer of completed movies, but someone who could be found on location, quizzing people as they worked, with excellent contacts within the industry, and a sophisticated feel for the whole process from conception to screening. Secondly, his intellectual position, and the blind spots in it, seem entirely representative of a certain critical orthodoxy which still exists in Scotland, and is not confined to the world of film criticism.

The division between acceptable and unacceptable images of Scotland and Scottishness encompasses cinema but also many other art forms. This is because much twentieth-century Scottish cultural debate was dominated by a MacDiarmidian-inspired school of criticism in which tough, masculine, modernistic art is preferred to a feminine, fantastical, romantic equivalent. Within this school facts are prioritised over fantasies and exterior readings of Scottish culture are strongly resisted as, by definition, misrepresentations. MacDiarmid also bequeathed another powerful, and, I would argue, destructive belief to Scottish culture, the idea that art could be willed into being by a sufficiently determined critical elite. This belief, which ran through many of the critical interventions published in the influential socio-cultural magazine *Cencrastus* during the 1980s, can be characterised as an assumption that the critic can serve as the vanguard movement of a new national art. This Leninist vision of cultural policy led in the late 1980s to the determined championing of writers and artists—the Alasdair Gray of *Lanark* (1981), James Kelman—who seemed to fit the need for demanding, hard, modernistic work. Subsequently, the same vision drove the determined neglect of writers emerging in the late '90s and early '00s—Ian Rankin, Alastair McCall Smith, J. K. Rowling—who, because they wrote in nonliterary genres (crime, children's fiction), could be quickly dismissed until they became too successful to be ignored any longer.

In film criticism the *Scotch Reels* volume is the most significant intervention in this respect. That enduringly influential publication represents a clear attempt to divide acceptable images of Scotland and Scottishness from unacceptable ones. The backdrop to this book was an event held at the Edinburgh Film Festival in August 1982. There had been related events before, like *Cinema in a Small Country* (1977) and Murray and Barbara Grigor's *Scotch Myths* (1981), the latter, an analysis of Scottish kitsch souvenirs and art. *Scotch Reels* was important, however, because it expressed a very strong statement of aesthetic judgement, one which quickly became a default position for Scottish critics, and which, in important ways, remains in place today. *Scotch Reels* also came to enshrine a particular form of modernist film criticism at its intolerant best, confidently and comprehensively announcing that most images of Scotland produced from outwith the country were "deformed and 'pathological'" (McArthur 1982, 5). *Scotch Reels* was focused on various representations of Scottishness, providing a critique of the way such images had been made into familiar, tradeable symbolic goods in an international market. The three great representational traditions Scotch Reels identified were Tartanry, with Culloden as a central trope, Kailyard, its central trope the Great Disruption of the Church of Scotland in 1843, and Clydesidism, concerned with heavy industrial urban life and late-twentieth-century decline.

As the *Scotch Reels* organisers acknowledged, their whole intellectual enquiry had its roots in Tom Nairn's investigation in his *The Break-Up of Britain* (1977) into the idea of the useable past in Scottish culture and politics. For instance, Cairns Craig's complaint in *Scotch Reels* adopted Nairn's earlier theoretical position full on:

> The problem that these mythic structures have left to twentieth century Scottish art is that there are no tools which the artists can inherit from the past which are not tainted, warped, blunted by the use to which they have been put. (Craig 1982, 14-15)

The modern critic's role was to create, or at least put a keen edge on, the artists' tools so that a new Scottish (cinematic) art could be born. But, as I have already discussed, *Scotch Reels* also built on a longstanding view within the Scottish film community about the inability of external voices to articulate anything other than inaccurate, willfully ignorant or (un)consciously parodic versions of Scots, Scotland or Scottishness. So, to anatomise the dominant critical position which determines much discussion of film made in and/or about Scotland:

1. There are authentic and inauthentic ways to portray Scotland, and the number of inauthentic portrayals greatly outweighs the authentic.
2. The inauthentic ways of portraying the county are unworthy of detailed analysis and are instead to be disparaged and disowned as "debased, deformed and pathological".
3. Inauthentic versions of Scotland mostly originate from outside the country, though not exclusively. Inauthentic images which originate from inside the country can be attributed to false consciousness, and those which originate from outside to ignorance.
4. An authentic Scottish cinema is yet to be born but can be created as long as the critical elements which will be around to appreciate it are kept polished and ready for the new birth.
5. (Implicitly) the only appropriate task for a Scottish cinema is the authentic depiction of Scottish life.

I want to argue that these ideas have long ceased to be useful, and that their persistence has hobbled the development of Scottish film criticism and culture in a number of different ways. I see these critical assumptions behind the neglect of films which, though they are shot and set in Scotland, are non-canonical because unserious, romantic road movies like *Hold Back the Night* (Davies, GB, 1999) or horror movies like *Urban Ghost Story* (Joliffe, GB, 2000), with its juxtaposition of Glasgow council estates and poltergeist activity.

Moreover, such non-authorised, ironic, kitsch or marginal films don't necessarily have to come from outside Scotland. They can also be made by Scottish filmmakers who in a variety of ways are seen to be outside the mainstream funding or critical structures which manage and define the Scottish film industry as it currently exists. Richard Jobson's features, drawing on themes and styles as diverse as Hong Kong Kung Fu films, pop videos and serial killer movies, and utilising funding from unconventional sources, are often situated in the category of The Wrong Kind of Scottish Film. Even more excluded are the hardcore porn films of Gazzman, "The Highlander of Porn," whose film *The Scottish Loveknot* (GB, 2003), featuring a sex-starved ghost in a Highland castle, was supposedly the first commercial hardcore feature shot in Scotland. In 2004 it won two "porn Oscars" in Las Vegas.

Such films are at least shot (whether wholly or partially) within recognisably Western film traditions. Films which come from different cultural traditions and use Scottish actors or settings are also often excluded from consideration as part of the national film tradition. The Bollywood film *Pyaar, Ishq aur Mohabbat* (Rai, Ind), shot in Glasgow in 2001 and premiered in Govan, or the Jet Li action vehicle *Unleashed* (Leterrier, Fr/GB/USA, 2005), set in Glasgow because the filmmakers appreciated its "Gotham City" feel, would qualify for exclusion here (see Martin-Jones forthcoming).

Excluded too from the category of "Scottish film" are Scottish filmmakers who chose to make their films outside the country or on topics which are either non-Scottish or tangentially Scottish. Characters like Mike Myers' Scots-American Charlie McKenzie in *So I Married an Axe Murderer* (Schlamme, USA, 1993), with his manic Scottish dad who spends his time shouting "Heid" or "move yer massive Cranium" to Charlie's ginger-headed brother, are seen as comic turns, not meaningful additions to the parade of Scottish identities presented onscreen. And with McKenzie's father we should also include Fat Bastard from the *Austin Powers* sequence of movies, another character who is Scottish perhaps for no other reason than his creator's desire to self-identify with Scottish nationality.

As the profile of Scotland rose in the United States during the 1990s, a range of central and more minor onscreen characters started to be ascribed

Scottish identity. Recent appearances of Scots on American screens include Caleb McDougal, the Scottish Groomsman at Charlotte's wedding in series 4 of *Sex and the City*, whom Samantha beds though she doesn't understand a word he says: "[she] thought if his tongue could do that to his 'r' s what could it do to her?" It's important, too, to state that the pleasures of such moving image works aren't purely kitsch or postmodern. There are issues to be legitimately explored in such texts, not least that they disprove one of the most sacredly held prejudices of modernistic Scottish cultural criticism: the belief that traditional tropes of Scottishness are exhausted and destined to redundantly self-repeat to the point of extinction. In fact, recent years have proven the images in question to be remarkably perky: re-imagined traditional Scottish tropes have proven to be the most creative, fecund source of ideas for outsiders who want to give their takes on Scots, Scotland and Scottishness. The popularity of cultural productions which draw on "debased" romantic or traditional images of Scotland gives the lie to the idea that the kitsch past is unusable rubble. In fact the rubble contains a number of ideas which remain so beguiling to outsiders that they are constantly drawn back to revisit and rework them.

To give an indication both of the fact that this critical prejudice runs across art forms in Scotland and that it represents a fantastically wasted opportunity, I want to give an illustrative example from another art form. In 2004, after returning from working in the United States I wrote an article for the *Sunday Times* about the extraordinary growth in Scottish-themed romance writing in the US (Stenhouse 2005). The topic was fruitful because these Romances enjoyed enormous success in the US though they had grown up without anyone in Scotland noticing, and, rather like some of the films under discussion here, they were dismissed as unserious art, read not just by women, but by the wrong type of women, romantic women. "Romance is an extremely lively genre at the moment", Karen Kosztolnyik, the senior editor at Warner Books in New York explained to me then: "It makes up nearly 40 % of sales in the mass paperback market" (ibid.). The facts indeed spoke for themselves. Romance sales brought in an astonishing $1.4billion (£750m) in 2003. One in 50 American readers gets through more than 100 romances a year, and discerning fans have a bewildering array of settings to chose from. But though historical romances concocted among the ranks of the Pilgrim Fathers or set in the exotic South Pacific have their adherents, in 2004 the popular port of call for writers was Scotland. "It's the kilts", explained Sue-Ellen Welfonder, the author of the bestselling *Devil in a Kilt*, "that or the men that fit in them. Scottish men are unbelievably sexy" (ibid.). There is indeed no shortage of Scottish sexiness in Welfonder's book. Bosoms heave, lips are crushed, and, in one memorable scene, a caber is caressed. “Scottish men are so passionate and uncontrollable,” one online fan told me: “Just the thought of trying to tame one makes me feel weak at the knees” (ibid.). “And the warriors!" agreed another: “the thought that one could seize you and take you back to his Highland castle in the Borders (sic)” (ibid.).

*Devil in a Kilt* (it hasn’t yet been filmed; an opportunity for any Scottish production company) is set entirely in the past, but a key trope in American cultural production—novels, films and television—about Scotland is time travel. The film (Mulcahy, USA, 1986) and then the TV spinoff of *Highlander* (1992-1998), with its sexy, time-travelling northern noble savage, inspired Diana Gabaldon’s *Outlander* literary saga, in which plucky nurse Claire Randall, married to a cold fish of a don in 1945 Inverness, is projected back 200 years to 1745, where she finds a Highland lad to ignite her passion (this in turn provokes an interesting moral discussion as to whether sexual intercourse with another 200 years before you meet and marry your husband qualifies as adultery). In the successful novels of Karen Marie Moning, the time-travelling Scotsman appears again, his primordial sexual power emphasised in a way that would make Queen Victoria blush. These new and (to Scottish eyes, extraordinary, unsettling or surprising) cultural forms have three things in common. They are subgeneric, they are “about” Scotland and Scottishness though they have been developed far from Scotland itself, and they have flourished almost without anyone in Scotland noticing. They almost certainly fall into the *Scotch Reels* category of “debased, deformed [and] pathological.” But they are also extremely creative, extremely popular, and they indicate that assertions about the sterility of popular images or conceptions of Scottishness, as far as the ability of such phenomena to continue generating novel versions of themselves, are demonstrably mistaken.

And this wholesale re-examination of Scottish tropes is not just happening in books. Diana Gabaldon’s novels were informed by repeated viewings of *Highlander* and of old re-runs of Patrick Troughton’s late-’60s *Dr Who*: Jamie, the Doctor’s assistant rescued from the aftermath of Culloden was a strong influence. It is clear that sub-generic influences work across art forms, covering television, film, literary writing, online blogs, fan fiction and the rest. Just as Scotchtoberfest, the entirely fictional Scottish event dreamed up by Principal Seymour Skinner in an episode of *The Simpsons* (1989- ) to catch out Bart Simpson, is now celebrated in an ironic spirit by American and Canadian Scots, it is clear that many of these cultural manifestations of interest in Scotland are playful, celebratory and exploratory, rather than reductive or definitive statements about Scottish identity. That there is a mismatch between these forms of cultural production, and the set of critical expectations that we have traditionally used in Scottish film criticism to respond to images of Scotland produced around the world is, I hope, now obvious. By applying strict criteria of "responsibility" or "aesthetic integrity" to time-travelling Scotsmen whose arrival in the present brings much needed sexual passion into the lives of frustrated twenty-first-century women—see the plot of Karen Marie Moning's novel *Kiss of the Highlander* (2001)—we run the risk of crushing a plaid butterfly on the wheel of critical judgment.

These (literally) "outlandish" versions of Scotland also challenge us in other ways. Because of our default critical position, it is often assumed that in some ways anyone who makes a film or writes a book that uses Scotland in non-authorised or non-canonical ways is somehow doing so in a parodic spirit; that they are insulting their subject. In order to approach this problem it may be worth quoting Michael Korda, who describes *Bonnie Prince Charlie* (Kimmins, GB, 1948) with David Niven as:

> A semi-fictionalised retelling of an event with very little emotional significance, except to the Scots themselves. Who were bound to be bloody-minded and nit-picking about any movie based on the life of their hero. (Hardy 1990, 77)

This is a useful quote to bear in mind when thinking about *Braveheart*, a film which was both an enormously popular international version of Scottishness (particularly in the US, where it remains a favourite at Highland Games and Scottish gatherings) and a clear embarrassment to Scottish film critics. Colin McArthur described it to the *Sunday Times* as a "f*cking atrocious film" in 2005 (Rifkind and Farquarson 2005). But whatever its aesthetic strengths or weaknesses, *Braveheart* is emphatically not an attack on Scotland or the Scots. On the contrary, it is an act of piety, produced by Randall Wallace, a man who self-identifies as Scottish and who wanted to pay tribute to a historical figure he sees as a pre-eminent national hero. To argue that *Braveheart* is somehow a "joke" which denigrates Scotland is to miss the point entirely; it is no more or less a joke than Blind Harry's pietistic epic poem *Wallace* (c. 1477).

Similarly, it is important to note that many of the Scottish-themed film or TV dramas discussed above are not parodic in the normal sense of the term, that is, they do not challenge the premise or aim to send it up. Rather, they aim to celebrate it, though in forms which have riled Scottish intellectuals and critics. The proliferation of such images is itself a sign that "policing" Scottish-themed iconography is a wasteful critical enterprise; instead we should celebrate the idea that national and transnational culture is a conversation, an endless coining and re-coining of images, tropes and iconography, and that sometimes the direction which that conversation takes may astonish us. But there is another challenge for Scottish critics and film makers, and that lies in realising that Scots-based arts practitioners do not have a monopoly, or even necessarily a privileged position, in deciding what is an acceptable image of Scottishness or not. It may feel "natural" for Scots in Scotland to pass judgement on the way Scots are presented on film, but in the global market place no-one may care what we think.

Our current critical position, sceptical, occasionally hostile or scornful, always on the lookout for the next "incorrect" image of Scotland to come along from abroad, prevents us from using the resources, experiences, and perspectives of the Scots Diaspora communities in the way that we have to in order to navigate the future. In general Scotland's decision-making elites (political as well as critical) have been poor at drawing on the Diaspora. This is partly because of a disagreement about what we want from them, and partly because there is a prevailing prejudice (as outlined here) about the kind of images of Scotland they produce, and a concomitant misunderstanding of their "seriousness" about engaging with Scottish culture. Consider, for example, the thinly disguised scorn of much of the Scottish media towards Tartan Week in the US, which provoked derisive hooting at the idea of Scottish pipe bands and kilt-based fashion shows in New York timed to coincide with the anniversary of the Declaration of Arbroath (1320). The idea that Tartan Week was not actually a celebration of Scottish culture in the US, but was instead intended to celebrate Scottish-American culture didn't seem to register in Scotland, but it is a vital distinction.

I would argue that Scottish closed-mindedness towards such cultural experiments cuts us off from a full engagement with the possibilities of global national identity. To give a parallel example: one of the greatest musical and dance hits of the last two decades is *Riverdance*, a pseudo-Irish confection dreamed up by Michael Flatley, a Chicagoan of Irish ancestry. *Riverdance* emerged from a seven-minute intermission performance in the 1994 Eurovision Song Contest and went on to become a global hit, performing to packed houses in Dublin and other European capitals. Flatley's latest venture is *Celtic Tiger*, a show which explores the history of Irish emigration to the US. These dance spectaculars are by no means aesthetically pure or authentic; they are show-business hybrids of traditional dance and glitzy spectacular. Yet even in Dublin they received a warm, if sometimes wry, reception. There is of course no Scottish *Riverdance*, despite the fact that Scottish dance remains popular throughout the US through the avenue of a thriving network of Highland Games. The reason for the absence, I would suggest, has nothing to do with the inherent appeal of Irish versus Scottish dance, or the absence of a Scottish-identifying Chicagoan dance guru to compare to Flatley, but everything to do with the attitude to Scottish critics to external representations of Scottish culture. When American Scots dress up in kilts and celebrate innocent reinterpreted traditions like the Kirking of the Tartan, eminent Scottish historians line up to inform them that they have made it up and are celebrating a fake. The impulse to police and control representations of Scottishness, to devalue external versions of ourselves is profound but also profoundly restrictive. Historically, it has added up to nothing less than the policing of Scottish Culture. To fully engage with the future it may be time to disband the police force.

## Conclusion: *Brigadoon*, New York and Scotland

*Brigadoon*, the movie which Arthur Freed filmed on a Hollywood lot after he had rejected everything which the Scottish landscape had to offer, began life as a musical performance in the Ziegfeld Theatre in Midtown Manhattan on March 13, 1947. Today the Ziegfeld Theatre is a cinema, and a block away an adult education college runs a thriving evening class on learning the bagpipes. Like Scotland, New York too is regularly portrayed in movies, though the city of around 5 million souls (Scotland-sized, in skyscrapers) wastes little anxiety worrying about how it is portrayed. In his "biography" of the city Michael Pye argues that,

> New York was usually built somewhere else [in the movies] which means it was always distilling some idea of the city... Actual New York was just too hard to see—too tall, too busy. (Pye 1991, 23)

Pye goes on to list a series of NYC-set movies, from Woody Allen's *Manhattan* (USA, 1979) to *Saturday Night Fever* (Badham, USA, 1977) to *King Kong* (Cooper/Schoedsack, USA, 1933) and *Tarzan's New York Adventure* (Thorpe, USA, 1932). Since his book was published, thousands of new movies have been filmed or set in New York, up to and including *Sex and the City* (King, USA, 2008) and *The Wackness* (Levine, USA, 2008). Pye takes the number of films made about New York, and the myriad different versions of the city these present, as a tribute to the multiple faces of the metropolis itself. He implies that the city is always ahead of its representations, so that each imagined version of New York is only partial, incomplete. It is an attractive idea, because it makes each film only a small "take" on an infinitely more complex reality. Yet in Scotland we view the same phenomenon, films made about Scotland by outsiders, as an oppressive ideological land grab, rather than a tribute to the endless, fascinating power of Scotland and Scottishness.

We are now in a position that critics of twenty years ago could only dream of. The idea that Scottish culture is cowering, fearful, yet to fully emerge, beset by problems and the rest has been blown away, not least because of the buoyant confidence of Scottish Diasporic communities. Negotiating our relationship with those groups, in film, novels, dance and other creative forms, is one of the challenges facing us in the next thirty years. We are faced with a unique historical opportunity which has been created by a combination of factors: a resurgent Diasporic community anxious to coin its own, sometimes unsettling, images of Scotland and Scottishness; the efforts of the devolved Scottish government to attract foreign filmmakers here to make films which often rebound against traditional images of the nation; the fact that technological change and the fracturing of cultural authority into fissiparous parts means that there are more and increasingly varied "takes" on Scottishness from within and without the country. To get anything meaningful from these emergent and expanding processes, we need to dismantle the explicit and implicit assumptions of a critical community which is still, despite nuancing, clinging to essentially modernist assumptions about authenticity, history and seriousness. As *Brigadoon* and an ever-increasing number of other popular cultural works show, there is more, and less, to Scotland than that.

## Works Cited

Caughie, John and Colin McArthur. 1982. An Interview with Forsyth Hardy. In *Scotch Reels: Scotland in Cinema and Television*, ed. Colin McArthur, 73-92. London: British Film Institute.

Craig, Cairns. 1982. Myths against History: Tartanry and Kailyard in 19th-Century Scottish Literature. In *Scotch Reels: Scotland in Cinema and Television*, ed. Colin McArthur, 7-15. London: British Film Institute.

Hardy, Forsyth. 1990. *Scotland in Film*. Edinburgh: Edinburgh University Press.

Hickey, Jim. 1982. Scottish Film Culture: A Chronicle. In *Scotch Reels: Scotland in Cinema and Television*, ed. Colin McArthur, 70-72. London: British Film Institute.

McArthur, Colin, ed. 1982. *Scotch Reels*: *Scotland in Cinema and Television*. London: British Film Institute.

McBain, Janet. 1990. Scotland in feature film: a filmography. In *From Limelight to Satellite: A Scottish Film Book*, ed. Eddie Dick, 233-255. London/Glasgow: British Film Institute/Scottish Film Council.

Martin-Jones, David. Forthcoming. *Scotland: Global Cinema*. Edinburgh: Edinburgh University Press).

Nairn, Tom. 1977. *The Break-Up of Britain: Crisis and Neo-Nationalism*. London: New Left Books.

Pendreigh, Brian. No date. From *Brigadoon* to *Trainspotting*. http://www.iofilm.co.GB/scots/briefhistory.shtml (accessed November 28, 2008).

Petrie, Duncan. 2004. *Contemporary Scottish Fictions: Film, Television, and the Novel*. Edinburgh: Edinburgh University Press.

Pye, Michael. 1991. *Maximum City*. London: Sinclair Stevenson.

Riach, Alan. 2005. *Representing Scotland in Literature, Popular Culture and Iconography: the Masks of the Modern Nation*. Basingstoke: Palgrave.

Rifkind, Hugo and Kenny Farquarson. 2005. Braveheart battle cry is now but a whisper. *The Sunday Times*, July 24.

Stenhouse, David. 2005. America is turned on by kilt-ripping yarns: Sales of Scottish romance novels are rocketing in the US, where readers lust for a Highland fling. *The Sunday Times*, March 27, *Ecosse* section.

# CHASING CROSSOVER: SELLING SCOTTISH CINEMA ABROAD

CHRISTOPHER MEIR

## Introduction

This chapter will be concerned with Scottish cinema's international circulation. It focuses specifically on how Scottish features have been packaged for overseas consumption through a comparative study of two films which occupy sharply different places in the canon of Scottish cinema: *Local Hero* (Forsyth, GB, 1983), a somewhat infamous example of the influence of foreign markets on indigenous filmmakers, and *Young Adam* (Mackenzie, GB/Fr, 2003), one of the films of the "new" Scottish cinema, a movement whose perceived success is part-predicated on the ways in which films reached international audiences. My goal is to document how Scottish films have been presented to non-Scottish audiences since 1979, and in so doing to ask whether there are patterns of continuity or difference to be found in this period. To this end, the chapter will conclude by commenting on a number of other Scottish films, including recent international successes and failures.

Besides looking for patterns in the marketing and promotion of Scottish cinema, this chapter seeks to broaden the scope of Scottish film scholarship to incorporate international circulation, while also removing some of the pejorative connotations that "international success" has accrued in Scottish cinema historiography. I look to bring a descriptive, not prescriptive, perspective to the relationship between Scottish films and international audiences. A brief overview of Scottish cinema criticism's traditional ideas about international audiences illustrates the necessity of the approach I adopt here.

Given Scotland's small population and the capital-intensive nature of film production, it was perhaps inevitable that the success (or lack thereof) of Scottish films abroad should loom large in the minds of film producers. The "international market" (within this chapter, mainly referring to North America, the other British nations and sometimes continental Europe) has also held a prominent place in critical accounts of Scottish cinema. For many of the earliest Scottish film critics, the international marketplace played the role of villain (see McArthur 1982; Michie 1986). The culturally deleterious forces of global capitalism were personified by figures such as producers Michael Balcon and Louis Freed, the Scottish-themed films they made demonstrating the fact that the commercial demands of the international marketplace dictated that only the most simple, stereotypical images of Scotland could appear in films. This critical stance is typified by Colin McArthur's warning that:

> The more… films are consciously aimed at an international market, the more their conditions of intelligibility will be bound up with regressive discourses about your own culture. (McArthur 1994, 119-120)

Analysis of this kind has placed historical emphasis on, variously: the American sales of Tartan and Kailyard novels in America (Craig 1982; Nairn, 1981); Spaghetti Westerns ensconced in plaid (McArthur 1982a, 40); surreal marketing materials such as the tartan knickers used to promote *Brigadoon* (Minnelli, USA, 1954) (McArthur 2003, 101). Colin McArthur's work in particular analyses the discourses found in promotional materials, "useful evidence as to how the company involved viewed the film at the time" (ibid., 80), in order to buttress its ideological critique of the Scottish-themed films being promoted.

The breakthrough success of *Shallow Grave* (Boyle, GB, 1995) helped usher in a new era in Scottish film history, one in the international viability of indigenous films became the central mark of their perceived success. Duncan Petrie claimed that "new Scottish cinema" represented an unprecedented moment because Scotland was now producing films that were reaching audiences at home and abroad (Petrie 2000, 184). In a similar vein, Jonathan Murray claimed that

> *Ratcatcher*'s remarkable *domestic and international critical successes* constituted proof positive that productive Scottish cultural and industrial appropriations of a US precedent can form one aspect of the ongoing consolidation of a progressive national film culture and a viable production base. (Murray 2005, 221; emphasis added.)

For Petrie, Murray and many others, it seems that internationally visible Scottish films after *Shallow Grave* represented "an outpost for serious, demanding independent cinema" (Blandford 2007, 77) rather than the traditionally perceived tartanised embarrassment of "old" Scottish cinema. This sort of international success—variously compared to the overseas reception of European cinema (Petrie 1996; Petrie 2001) or American

Independent film (Murray 2004)—is now seen as implicitly "better" than the kind sought and achieved by earlier films. The ways in which historians have treated the two films which are the main focus of this chapter demonstrates the extent to which this is so.

*Local Hero*'s place in Scottish film history is an infamous one. Crucially for my concerns here, much critical antipathy towards the film stems directly from the latter's international orientation, though its domestic marketing has also drawn criticism (Caughie 1983). Attacks on *Local Hero*'s international orientation began even before the film was released, Colin McArthur presupposing on the basis of a plot summary and the casting of Burt Lancaster that the film had fallen into the trap of Kailyardism (McArthur 1982a, 66). Several years later, McArthur took issue specifically with the ways in which *Local Hero* was "produced and packaged by David Puttnam" (McArthur 1994, 119) for the international commercial marketplace. Other writers have followed suit: Tom Milne's contemporary *Monthly Film Bulletin* review proclaimed that,

> If one didn't already know, one would have little difficulty in guessing that [*Local Hero*] was Bill Forsyth's first venture into the big time from the way his script has been broadened for commercial consumption. (Milne 1983, 87-88)

More recently, Duncan Petrie's *Contemporary Scottish Fictions* locates the film within director Bill Forsyth's career as "a temporary retreat into a more stereotypical representation [of Scotland] for mass consumption" (Petrie 2004, 61), an example of "market-driven distortions" (ibid., 209) that Petrie's book deliberately chooses to omit from the canon it constructs of important late twentieth-century Scottish cultural production.

In contrast to *Local Hero*, *Young Adam* has received less direct commentary from Scottish cinema critics. Despite the film's generally high public profile at the time of its release and its relatively successful international box office performance, *Young Adam* has yet to attract any thoroughgoing academic analysis, the most extensive comment on it being two paragraphs in a survey of post-devolutionary British film and theatre (Blandford 2007, 83). Here, Steve Blandford situates *Young Adam* as a paradigmatic example of laudable, internationally successful post-*Shallow Grave* Scottish cinema, and presents the film as evidence of the predominance of art cinema models with Scottish film culture of the period. Though there is a paucity of further critical work on the film, *Young Adam* is nonetheless routinely cited as an example of the "impeccably 'European art-house' fare" (Murray 2007, 84) held to be typical of the most significant achievements of new Scottish cinema. We can thus reasonably conclude that the assumption within the field is that the film reaches international markets in what is implicitly the right way when compared to films such as *Local Hero*. But before assessing the manner in which *Young Adam*—and by extension much post-*Shallow Grave* Scottish cinema—reached international audiences, we should look more closely at how *Local Hero* actually went about navigating the overseas market.

## *Local Hero*, High Concept and Kailyard

If one were to scrutinize the marketing and promotion of *Local Hero*, at least in its early stages, it would be possible to come to similar conclusions as those McArthur draws the marketing and promotion of *Brigadoon*. Those involved in marketing *Local Hero* (i.e., producer David Puttnam and distributors Warner Brothers and 20th Century Fox) drew on many stereotypes about the Highlanders and the Highlands, encouraging readings of the film that would be generally in line with Tartanry and Kailyard. Take, for instance, some conventional marketing devices, such as the trailer for *Local Hero*'s North American theatrical release. Here, as flute and drum music plays slowly on the soundtrack, we see Mac (Peter Riegert) in Happer (Burt Lancaster)'s planetarium. As the roof of the latter opens we hear that omniscient, gravel-voiced narrator (who seems to only exist in film trailers) start to intone a monologue interspersed with clips from the film (narration in bold, images in brackets):

> **There is a place where the Northern Lights transform the sky**... [Happer tells Mac to watch the sky and to phone him about what he sees]... **Modern mermaids spring from the sea**... [Cut to Marina (Jenny Seagrove) meeting with Danny (Peter Capaldi) on the beach]... [Cut to Ben (Fulton Mackay) saying to Mac and Gordon (Dennis Lawson) that he finds amazing things every two or three weeks]... [Cut to Mac and Danny's car in the mist]... **The land breathes with an ancient mystery**... [Cut to Mac in the car saying 'Where are we?']... [Cut to Mac watching the meteor shower]... **And all who witness its wonders come to believe in its magic**... [Cut to Happer receiving Mac's call about the Northern Lights]... [Cut to Mac in the phone booth watching the lights trying to explain them to Happer]... [Cut to the villagers on the beach seeing the light of Happer's helicopter in the sky; it is never made clear in this clip that this is Happer's chopper and instead the impression created is that of a divine light in the firmament]... **This is the new film from the producer of *Chariots of Fire*: *Local Hero***... [A montage of images summarizing the oil company's plan to buy the town and Mac as its agent; Gordon is shown dancing on the chair saying "We're gonna be rich"]... **Peter Reigert and Burt**

> **Lancaster**... [Montage now shows Mac's desire to stay in the town, offering to swap lives with Gordon. Cut to a shot of Danny, from behind, running into the water to Marina. The editing makes it appear to be Mac running into the water, "going native"]... ***Local Hero***... [Cut to Ben laughing in front of the fire]... **The story of an ordinary man who cared enough to do something extraordinary**... [Cut to a continuation of Danny swimming to Marina, the implication, though, being that it is Mac the audience is seeing]... ***Local Hero***.

As Lisa Kernan argues of trailers generally, that for *Local Hero* "accentuates the film's surface of cinematic spectacle, displaying the film's shiniest wares, or most attractive images, positioning it as a commodity for sale (Kernan 2004, 10). Such "wares" here include creative personnel (stars and producer) but also the sometimes laughable clichés generally associated with Tartanry and Kailyard: the Northern Lights, "modern mermaids", a land that "breathes with an ancient mystery" and so on. The images selected for the trailer likewise emphasise *Local Hero*'s stereotypically Scottish aspects: meteor showers and the *Aurora Borealis*, Scotch mists, Mac apparently following cinematic forebears in movies like *Brigadoon* and *The Maggie* (Mackendrick, GB, 1954) in appearing to "go native," even more than he actually does in the film.

Other promotional materials for *Local Hero* use similar strategies. The film's main advertising poster is a painted picture of Mac and Happer in full business suits except for shoes and socks wading in the water of a Highland bay: seagulls circle overhead and mountains are visible in the distance. In a memo to David Puttnam, Allan Manham, the poster's illustrator, describes the image as showing "the contrast between the smart and sophisticated world of international business and the refreshing values of the little community" (Puttnam Collection, box 7, item 36). Alternative poster images for the film—including Mac in the phone booth with the villagers surrounding it peering in, and another featuring a stretch limousine parked on the beach outside Ben's shack—offer variations upon this Kailyard theme.

In addition to these standard marketing devices, as John Caughie notes, *Local Hero* also had domestic tie-in promotions with the Scottish Tourist Board and John Menzies Outfitters, a retailer specialising in outdoor clothing and supplies (Caughie 1983, 45). Shoppers at Menzies could win tickets to see *Local Hero* and some would be eligible for an all-expenses-paid Highland holiday (ibid.). David Puttnam arranged special screenings all over Scotland for school children on the pretext of showing them what the Highlands were like (Puttnam Collection, box 7, item 35). Special screenings were also arranged for radio disc jockeys in an attempt to market Mark Knopfler's Celticised original soundtrack, which featured arrangements of traditional ceilidh music as well as swelling romantic compositions to accompany many of the film's landscape shots. Newspaper articles, such as one in an Aberdeen publication, offered accounts of the film's production making much of the rascally behaviour of the inhabitants of Pennan (the Scottish village where *Local Hero* was shot) as they played "Kailyardic" tricks on the film's producers in hopes of getting more money out of them (Puttnam Collection, box 9, item 41; see also Goode 2008). Such examples underscore the degree to which Kailyard discourses were used to promote *Local Hero* within Scotland as well as without.

The ideological slant of such marketing is by now very clear. It constructs precisely the sort of exoticised Highland environment that many critics accused *Local Hero* itself of offering. But this does not tell the whole story: there are two points which must be borne in mind in order to fully appreciate the nature of the film's position in the international market. Firstly, in some ways the marketing campaign for *Local Hero* is historically specific to the early 1980s; the former's crude usage of Kailyard can be attributed to the "high concept" approach to film marketing which was at its peak in terms of influence and usage during this period (Wyatt 1994, 15). Such an approach places emphasis on presenting films in simple terms, with the ideal being a film plot that can be summarized in one sentence, with that summary used consistently from the original pitching of a project to a studio through to a finished film's marketing to audiences (ibid., 9).

## *Local Hero* and Longer Term Marketing

> I remember on occasions being very glad the film-maker wasn't there to hear me as I distorted his complex vision with a few, simple, descriptive strokes. *Local Hero*, for example, became a quirky comedy about a giant American oil company, which, in trying to buy a small Scottish village, is confronted by the apparently principled opposition of the stalwart villagers, who, in reality, are only stalling to push up the price. Of course, it's a far more complicated film than that, but for the purposes of selling to Hollywood that's what you have to say. (Former Head of Goldcrest Films, Jake Eberts, quoted in Eberts and Illot 1990, 32)

The second point to make regarding the selling of *Local Hero* is that the film was not marketed solely in simplistic, "high concept" terms. Though the marketing materials described above constitute the opening stages of the film's marketing campaign, the promotion of the film did change over time as it remained on release. Later posters and trailers, such as a March 1983 advertisement in the New York publication *Village Voice*, incorporated critical praise from reviewers in quality newspapers, praise which framed the film in Kailyard terms—"entrancing comedy"; "warm and wacky"—but also described it as "thoroughly original" and offering "breezy social commentary". A later cut of *Local Hero*'s US trailer is particularly illuminating in this regard. While retaining the overall shape seen in the original cut described above, the later trailer also features an inserted section quoting leading critics who laud the film's generic pleasures but also extol the "surprisingly complex tones" and "assured artistry" of "a thoroughly original film".

Despite all that has been said in Scotland and Britain about Forsyth pandering to the American market, *Local Hero*'s US reception was not characterised solely by naivety or simplistic embrace. Leading American critics such as Andrew Sarris and Pauline Kael advised their readers that Forsyth's film was not just another formulaic small-town comedy. Sarris praises *Local Hero*'s "exquisitely modernist melodies and bittersweet half-notes" and expresses a reluctance to provide a plot summary lest his reader come to "anticipate a series of cute highland flings and picturesque poses of facile anti-materialism" (Sarris 1983, 55). Kael likewise takes on genre directly, writing that Forsyth's "style is far more personal and aberrant than that of the popular British comedies of the 1950s" (Kael 1983, 116).

Such marketing and reception is in keeping with the *Local Hero*'s distribution strategy, which included a long stay in theatres and a reliance on positive word of mouth to promote the film. To this end it opened in selected cities on February 17 1983, was still playing as late as July 11 that year in Scotland and was intended to be re-released in early 1984 to cash in on any Oscar nominations it may have garnered (see Puttnam Collection, box 6, item 34). Such a distribution strategy (gradual release of the film, reliance on word of mouth publicity, extended theatrical run) indicates that *Local Hero* circulated in a manner akin to prestigious art films rather than "high concept" commercial movies, which generally look to generate most of their revenue at the box office in the opening few weeks of a wide simultaneous release (see Lukk 1997).

## *Young Adam*, Low Concept and Controversy

Like *Local Hero*, *Young Adam* was at the time of its release something of a Scottish event film, featuring a "local hero" of its own: *Trainspotting* (Boyle, GB, 1996) actor-cum-international star Ewan McGregor returning to indigenous Scottish production. McGregor took centre stage in the press surrounding the film's production. Unlike the somewhat genial terms on which *Local Hero* was launched, however, *Young Adam* was at the focal point of a number of acrimonious contemporary controversies related to censorship and public funding priorities. These would end up shaping how the film was received in both the US and Britain. Also contrasting sharply with *Local Hero* were the terms in which *Young Adam* was initially pitched to audiences: these stressed what could be described as the "low concept" elements of the latter film. But before exploring the more normative devices that were used to promote *Young Adam*, the wider controversies it became embroiled in, and which in and of themselves promoted the film to audiences in very specific terms, are worth looking at in greater detail.

The first major controversy encountered in the UK related to the role that the UK Film Council played in *Young Adam*'s production. Producer Jeremy Thomas had gained enough financial backing for the film to have a £4m production budget, an arrangement which included support from the Film Council as well as Scottish Screen. When one of *Young Adam*'s backers pulled out just before the start of shooting, Recorded Picture Company (Thomas' production company) approached the Film Council to fill the hole left in the film's budget. The Council refused to do so and the filmmakers faced a delay of over six months while additional funds were sourced. Recriminations aimed at the Film Council for its role in delaying the completion of the film began with its promotional press conference at Cannes in 2003. One trade press report tells of a heated argument backstage between Alan Parker—then Chair of the Film Council—and Thomas after Ewan McGregor and co-star Tilda Swinton dedicated part of their post-screening question-and-answer session to attacking the Council's decision not to intercede when the production was in trouble (Minns 2003, 10). This was just the beginning, however, as McGregor in particular continued to use publicity interviews for *Young Adam* to criticise the Film Council, accusing it of penny-pinching and general philistinism when it came to "important" works such as this film. In some cases these attacks rather than the film itself became the main story, a fact evinced by headlines such as: "McGregor Rages at Film Fund's Agenda" (Gibbons 2003, 7) and "McGregor in Attack on 'Betrayal' of British Films" (Alberge, 2003, 11). The broadsides found in these articles often combined critiques of the kind of cinema that the Film Council supposedly favoured with claims that its funding policies were not acting in the interest of national culture, Scottish and/or British.

*Young Adam* was a film that the Film Council needed to support, McGregor claimed, precisely because it was not an easily marketable work. Such a position can be seen in a newspaper article in which the case of *Young Adam* is considered alongside that of the Hanif Kureishi-scripted film *The Mother* (Michell, GB, 2003), another film which featured explicit sexual content and faced similar difficulties getting Council funding. The comparison is used as a springboard to inquire sceptically into the values of the British filmmaking establishment:

> Their triumph [that of *Young Adam* and *The Mother*] will reignite the debate on whether Alan Parker's Film Council is too ready to spend its pot of lottery money on middle-brow, commercial projects rather than daring scripts. (Gibbons 2003, 7)

The piece then goes on to quote McGregor as saying:

> Had I gone to them [the Film Council] with a romantic comedy there would have been no problem… We went to all the British film funding people and they all said no. We used to have a reputation of being able to do anything in British film. And I was lucky to be involved in two films that opened the door to that, *Shallow Grave* and *Trainspotting*. But the door has slowly closed behind us. (ibid.)

McGregor's positioning of *Young Adam* is one in which the film is the opposite of less substantial or important genre production appeals more easily (in theory) to mass audiences. Leaving aside the issue of the role that public funding bodies should play in film production, what it is significant for our current purposes is how actors' polemics (Pearce 2003) on this issue acted as a source of promotional discourse for *Young Adam*, a discourse which framed the film in very specific terms relating to national importance, and implicitly, difficulty, complexity and originality.

Many of these qualities were also stressed in the promotion of *Young Adam* through reference to the 1954 novel on which it was based and the author of that book, Alexander Trocchi. One central promotional strategy revolved around sparking public curiosity and interest the figure of Trocchi and his place within the Scottish literary canon. To this end *Young Adam*'s press pack includes a section entitled "The Life and Work of Alexander Trocchi," and a large portion of the "making of" featurette included as an extra on the DVD release of the film is devoted to explicating Trocchi's life and work of Trocchi; another extra is a recording of McGregor reading passages from the *Young Adam* novel. Several members of the film's creative team gave interviews in which they discussed their personal interpretations of Trocchi's life and work, while director David Mackenzie in particular described his great passion for the novel and for Trocchi's work generally.

Yet much of the publicity generated by this promotional strategy was curious in tone regarding Trocchi himself. Mentions of the author and his work in press surrounding *Young Adam* are conflicting in their accounts of his legacy. Some refer to Trocchi as a "countercultural hero" (Hodgkinson 2002); others describe him as "virtually forgotten by the time of his death" (Cumming 2003). One particularly unkind commentator called Trocchi "little more than a footnote in the history of the Beat Generation" and stated that, despite the publicity generated by *Young Adam*'s production, "his name still means little or nothing outside of the world of the counter-culture anorak" (Burnside 2002). While the latter comments overstate the case somewhat—a retrospective of Trocchi's life and work was published in 1997 (Campbell and Niel) and reviewed in *The Sunday Times* (Horovitz 1997) and other mainstream publications—"obscure" was nonetheless the right word to describe Trocchi in 2003. His name is not to be found in mainstream anthologies and textbooks on the Beat movement, and what was written about him to coincide with *Young Adam*'s UK theatrical release tended to dwell on his wasted potential and life spent in obscurity. To appreciate the significance of the strategy of foregrounding such an obscure literary figure, one need only think of the innumerable inconspicuous adaptations that are to be found throughout film history. Since *Young Adam* Mackenzie has himself made two such films, *Asylum* (GB/Ire, 2005) and *Hallam Foe* (GB, 2007), in which even though the source novel is well known there is little use made of it or its author in the promotional discourses surrounding the film. The very different strategy used in the promotion of *Young Adam* lent that film a degree of prestige as a work of something like public service scholarship, rediscovering a seemingly lost artist and attempting to reintegrate him into public life, all the while gaining attendant free publicity from upscale newspapers keen to cater to the chattering classes.

One final element that I would like to discuss here which contributed to *Young Adam*'s consciously constructed reputation as "serious" and "important" cinema relates to the role that censorship, or its spectre, played in the film's reception. Upon its UK release *Young Adam*'s graphic sex scenes were a major talking point in journalistic reviews, with some foregrounding the film's "custard scene" to the point of including it in headlines (see Andrews 2003; Romney 2003; Sandhu 2003a). Meanwhile, the film's North American release was held up by difficulties with the Motion Picture Association of America (MPPA), who informed distributor Sony Pictures Classics that they would need to remove a number of sexually explicit scenes in order to avoid an NC-17 rating, something which Mackenzie, with the blessing of McGregor, refused to do.

Before exploring the ramifications that these particular controversies had for the promotion of *Young Adam*, it is important to appreciate that such scandal is something that those promoting the film actively sought to cultivate, even seeming in some instances to bait censors. In introducing the custard scene, the film's press kit claims that "there's one particular sex scene in the film certain to cause a stir" and later says of McGregor that he "is in no doubt that the film's sex scenes will cause a stir," as well as quoting him comparing his role to that of Marlon Brando in *Last Tango in Paris* (Bertolucci, It/Fr, 1972). The promotional signposting of this scene, with its unorthodox and graphic erotic content, potential to incur controversy and possibly censorship, presents it as one that could potentially attract curious audiences and contribute to making the film a *sucès de scandale*.

In keeping with the branding of *Young Adam* as important and serious, the film's press pack is also quick to assert that the movie's sexual content is not there for the sake of titillation. Its usage is instead portrayed as an integral part of *Young Adam*'s aesthetic and thematic design. Producer Jeremy Thomas, for instance, argues that,

> Sex is a crucial element in the film… If you're making adult films, it's bound to be a central theme… sex acts as emotional punctuation to the story. Joe is trying to lose himself in sex.

Elsewhere, the filmmakers' commentary track on the DVD release of *Young Adam* features Tilda Swinton discussing the ratings controversy in the US and criticising the "prurience" of American audiences. In this way sexual content and attendant issues pertaining to artistic freedom and integrity serve to further brand *Young Adam* in high art terms. But artistically high-minded exploration of sexual boundaries is not all that such promotional discourses promised viewers. Realising the full extent of what was at stake in this aspect of the film's promotion offers yet another way of conceptualising the selling of *Young Adam*.

## Genre and Marketing: *Young Adam* as Noir Erotic Thriller

The prominence of sexuality in the promotion of *Young Adam* did not simply cast the work as high-minded art cinema. Rather, the use of sexuality can also be seen as an indirect way of inviting less rarefied forms of consumption. Some promotional materials for the film were less than subtle in their pursuit of audiences searching for titillation. *Young Adam*'s North American trailer, for example, features extracts from two of Joe and Ella's sex scenes as well as two shots of Mortimer topless and several others of her dressed only in her petticoat (the UK trailer featured no nudity and concentrated instead on a generic presentation of the film as thriller). The emphasis on sexuality is in keeping with European art cinema's traditionally perceived alignment with soft-core pornography, an alignment that helped to popularise the mode of production with American audiences during the last days of the Hays Code in the late 1950s and which has remained in place with films such *Last Tango*, *Bad Timing* (Roeg, GB, 1980), *Crash* (Cronenberg, Can/GB, 1996) and others (see Lev 1993, 8-14; Bordwell 2002, 95-96).

Besides aligning *Young Adam* with the sort of sexually explicit art cinema production that has proved popular with international audiences in the past, those promoting *Young Adam* also sought to present the film in closely related generic terms, namely, as an erotic thriller. The film's press pack describes it as a "moody, sensual thriller" and several British reviewers subsequently picked up on this terminology (Christopher, 2003; French 2003; Sandhu, 2003b). Such promotional and reviewing discourses participate in depicting the film in terms that bridge the art cinema/popular cinema divide: parts of *Young Adam* such as the "custard scene" can be read equally as art cinema sex or as erotic moments familiar from thrillers such as *Jagged Edge* (Marquand, USA, 1985) or *Basic Instinct* (Verhoeven, USA, 1992), films which often attempt a stylistic imitation of film noir (see Williams 2005, 1-76; Dyer 2007, 120-125). Film noir is significant to the promotion of *Young Adam*: the term appears in the film's press pack, the filmmakers' commentary track on the DVD release (here Tilda Swinton compares *Young Adam* to French film noir to accentuate the film's European credentials), and the North American theatrical trailer.

## Selling *Local Hero* and *Young Adam*: Critical and Commercial Promises

This range of marketing and promotional materials suggests that *Young Adam* was presented not only as serious art cinema but also as a work which promised a number of (perhaps baser) generic pleasures. This process of broadening the film's appeal finds a crucial parallel in the ways in which *Local Hero* was presented as something more complex than simple Kailyard. As described above, Bill Forsyth's film was pitched at first in the "high concept" terms fashionable within the international marketplace during the early '80s, and the early stages of the marketing campaign therefore accentuated *Local Hero*'s kailyard aspects. But even before the film's international theatrical release, producer David Puttnam had plans to market the work in a way that fostered positive critical word of mouth, an attempt to emulate the kind of success he achieved with *Chariots of Fire* (Hudson, GB, 1981). *Local Hero* thus remained on release for longer than most commercial films at the time and began to incorporate critical praise into its marketing materials the longer it stayed on release. In contrast, *Young Adam* was presented from the very start as a complex, challenging and important art cinema work. At the same time, however, the film was also presented in terms which would appeal to mass audiences: a noirish erotic thriller with transgressive sexual content.

Despite the disparity between depictions of *Local Hero* and *Young Adam* in their respective marketing campaigns (whimsical comedy as opposed to dark thriller), there are some points of continuity between these two case studies. Both films sought to present themselves at various points as both prestigious art cinema works *and* genre films accessible to mass audiences. Though these two categories are not inherently or completely incompatible, each does tend to bring with it a different set of film cultural and industrial consequences, be they critical prizes or box office profits. Within Scottish film criticism *Local Hero* and *Young Adam* have each been classically aligned with *one only* of the broad categories of "art" and "genre". Yet the contemporary marketing for these films attempted to situate them in *both* categories, hoping to achieve a synergy of critical acclaim and mass appeal, attempting to generate a crossover critical and commercial success in international terms.

## Crossover Filmmaking in Scotland

In their pursuit of the crossover ideal *Local Hero* and *Young Adam* are quintessential examples of post-1979 Scottish cinema. Ken Loach's late-'90s and early-'00s Scottish films, for instance, continually strike a balance between leftist didacticism and the generic pleasures built into melodrama and romance in order to draw audiences. *Ae Fond Kiss...* (Loach, GB/Bel/Ger/It/Sp, 2004) was marketed in such a way to make the film seem like a variation on *Bend It Like Beckham* (Chadha, GB/Ger/USA, 2002), with British and European trailers focusing on Tahara (Shabana Bakhsh)'s speech about multiculturalism, a peroration which culminates in her changing into a Glasgow Rangers football top in front of a predominantly Roman Catholic audience of schoolchildren. *Mrs Brown* (Madden, GB/Ire/USA, 1997) located itself self-consciously within the inherently crossover-oriented framework of heritage cinema. *Trainspotting* was the clearest case of deliberate crossover marketing, promising variously as it did the (potentially incompatible) pleasures of social realism, a sensual and kinetic exploration of club and youth culture, and an adaptation of an acclaimed contemporary Scottish novel with a loyal following (Finney 1996, 173-182; Street 2003, 207-210). *Morvern Callar* (Ramsay, GB, 2002) attempted to mimic the *Trainspotting* marketing campaign, complete with modish marketing tie-ins with Warp Records and Vintage publishers. *The Last King of Scotland* (Macdonald, GB, 2006) is the latest Scottish-related film to fall roughly within the overall crossover mould: its dependence on American star Forrest Whitaker for production, promotion and critical esteem parallels the role that Burt Lancaster played in the production of *Local Hero*. The creatively marketed crossover film has been the model to which nearly all internationally successful Scottish features of recent years have adhered. Moreover, understanding the market logic of new Scottish cinema in these terms would also account for a number of critically and/or commercially unsuccessful projects. *On a Clear Day* (Dellal, GB, 2005) or *Nina's Heavenly Delights* (Parmar, GB, 2006) clearly imitate prior English crossover successes—*The Full Monty* (Cattaneo, GB, 1997) and *Bend it Like Beckham* respectively; *One Last Chance* (Svassand, GB/Nor, 2004), like *Local Hero*, tries to emulate the Ealing comic tradition; *The Acid House* (McGuigan, GB, 1999) attempted to repeat the success of *Trainspotting*.

## Conclusion: Scottish Cinema History and the Crossover Film

All the recent Scottish films listed above attempt to deploy the same marketing and promotional strategies as the two films I have analysed in detail here, the critically respected *Young Adam* and the derided *Local Hero*. This fact tells us much about Scottish cinema in a global context but it also leaves questions unanswered about the relationship between Scottish films and the international markets they increasingly rely upon. In their attempts to simultaneously reach out to audiences as examples of genre *and* art cinema, Scottish films are not alone, attempting as they do to tap into the same market niche that the majority of British films target. Despite the occasional blockbuster success, British films in the last two decades have depended on a mix of high-end and generic marketing discourses to reach overseas audiences. To expand the frame of reference even further, such dependency can be found in nearly all national cinemas that for financial reasons must seek to sell their films abroad. As Tom O'Regan has argued with reference to Australian cinema, all national cinemas require a semblance of prestige to circulate successfully outside of their national borders (O'Regan 1996, 111). At the same time, art films since the early 1990s have been characterized by increasing accessibility as they pursue larger international audiences (Polan 2001, 17). It is in these conditions that Miramax became the leading international distributor of non-American cinema in North America, and it is their brand of filmmaking and marketing, both of which can be broadly described in terms of an attempt to crossover from the art house to the multiplex, that has become the international industrial standard. Within such a context, Scottish cinema can be seen as a typical present-day non-American cinema. Indeed, it is therefore not surprising that Miramax should be the distributors for two of the biggest new Scottish cinema successes of the last decade or so, *Trainspotting* and *Mrs Brown*. While these two films locate themselves at opposite ends of the taste spectrum they are united by the precisely constructed terms of their international market positioning. Much has been made of the so-called "*Trainspotting* effect" on Scottish cinema, but perhaps we should start thinking of the Miramax effect, which still saw its most perfect realization in that landmark film, but which was felt as early as 1982 with *Local Hero* and as recently as 2006 with *The Last King of Scotland*.

Once we come to appreciate the market position of Scottish cinema over the last fifteen years or so a significant question remains. Has this collective, consistent attempt to crossover at the levels of marketing and promotion translated to similar strategies being employed in textual terms? In other words, have pressures related to the necessity of international marketing actually affected the shape of new Scottish films themselves? This is, after all, the real concern of the Scottish cinema critics whose work this chapter has sought to engage with. These are questions for further research, but hopefully this chapter demonstrates that the pressures exerted on Scottish films by the international market are more complex than a simple demand to "dumb down". Those marketing *Young Adam* felt the need to play up the generic, potentially sensationalist aspects of that film; yet those promoting *Local Hero* felt an equally strong need to portray Bill Forsyth's feature as something smarter than mere Kailyard. Given the pressing question of how markets actually affect Scottish film production, as well as the reliance on assertion and generalisation that exists in the scholarly field, further research into the production of individual films is still needed. Such research will need to move away from generalising claims as to the inherently European, American or British nature of

Scottish cinema and instead appreciate the complexity of new Scottish cinema's place within the global film economy, a phenomenon outlined in this chapter.

## Works Cited

Alberge, D. 2003. McGregor in Attack on "Betrayal" of British Films. *The Times*, May 19.

Andrews, Nigel. 2003. Custard, Ketchup and Sugar Leave a Bad Taste. *The Financial Times*, September 25.

Blandford, Steve. 2007. *Film, Drama and the Break-Up of Britain*. Bristol: Intellect.

Bordwell, David. 2002. The Art Cinema as a Mode of Film Practice. In *The European Cinema Reader*, ed. Catherine Fowler, 94-102. London: Routledge.

Burnside, Anna. 2002. Sex, Drugs and Murder, He Wrote. *The Sunday Times*, February 3.

Campbell, Allan and Tim Niel, eds. 1997. *A Life in Pieces: Reflections on Alexander Trocchi*. London: Rebel Inc.

Caughie, John. 1983. Support Whose Local Hero? *Cencrastus* 14: 44-46.

Christopher, James. 2003. A Marvel from the Mean Streets. *The Times*, August 14, *Times2* section.

Craig, Cairns. 1982. Myths against History: Tartanry and Kailyard in 19th-Century Scottish Literature. In *Scotch Reels: Scotland in Cinema and Television*, ed. Colin McArthur, 7-15. London: British Film Institute.

Cumming, Tim. 2003. Mean Streets. *The Guardian*, August 8.

Dyer, Richard. 1997. *Pastiche*. London: Routledge.

Eberts, Jake and Terry Illot. 1990. *My Indecision is Final: the Rise and Fall of Goldcrest Films*. London: Faber & Faber.

Finney, Angus. 1997. Trainspotting. In Finney, *The State of European Cinema: A New Dose of Reality*, 173-182. London: Cassell.

French, Philip. 2003. Film of the Week. *The Observer*. September 28, Review section.

Gibbons, Fiachra. 2003. McGregor Rages at Film Fund's Agenda. *The Guardian*, May 19.

Goode, Ian. 2008. Mediating the rural: *Local Hero* and the location of Scottish Cinema. In *Cinematic Countrysides*, ed. Robert Fish, 109-126. Manchester: Manchester University Press.

Hodgkinson, Will. 2002. Menace a Trois. *The Guardian*, May 17.

Horovitz, Michael. 1997. Wasted Genius. *The Sunday Times*, September 7.

Kael, Pauline. 1983. Local Hero. *New Yorker*, March 21.

Kernan, Lisa. 2004. *Coming Attractions: Reading American Movie Trailers*. Austin: University of Texas Press.

Lev, Peter. 1993. *The Euro-American Cinema*. Austin: University of Texas Press.

Lukk, Tiiu. 1997. *Movie Marketing: Opening the Picture and Giving it Legs*. Los Angeles: Silman-James Press.

McArthur, Colin, ed. 1982. *Scotch Reels: Scotland in Cinema and Television*. London: British Film Institute.

—. 1982a. Scotland and Cinema: The Iniquity of the Fathers. In *Scotch Reels: Scotland in Cinema and Television*, ed. McArthur, 40-69. London: British Film Institute.

—. 1994. The Cultural Necessity of a Poor Celtic Cinema. In *Border Crossing: Film in Ireland, Britain and Europe*, eds. John Hill, Martin McLoone and Paul Hainsworth, 112-125. London/Belfast: British Film Institute/Institute of Irish Studies/University of Ulster.

—. 2003. *Brigadoon, Braveheart and the Scots: Distortions of Scotland in Hollywood Cinema*. London: I. B. Tauris.

Michie, Alastair. 1986. Scotland: Strategies of Centralisation. In *All Our Yesterdays: 90 Years of British Cinema*, ed. Charles Barr, 252-271. London: British Film Institute.

Minns, Adam. 2003. A Very Public Affair. *Screen International* 1415: 10-11.

Murray, Jonathan. 2004. Convents or Cowboys? Millennial Scottish and Irish Film Industries and Imaginaries in *The Madgalene Sisters*. In *National Cinema and Beyond: Studies in Irish Film I*, eds. Kevin Rockett and John Hill, 149-160. Dublin: Four Courts.

—. 2005. Kids in America? Narratives of Transatlantic Influence in 1990s Scottish Cinema. *Screen* 46.2: 217-225.

—. 2007. Scotland. In *The Cinema of Small Nations*, eds. Mette Hjort and Duncan Petrie, 76-92. Edinburgh: Edinburgh University Press.

Nairn, Tom. 1981. *The Break-Up of Britain: Crisis and Neo-Nationalism*. 2nd Edition. London: Verso.

O'Regan, Tom. 1996. *Australian National Cinema*. London: Routledge.

Pearce, Gareth. 2003. She's Gone from Jarman's Art-House Muse to Hollywood Heroine. *The Sunday Times*, August 17, *Culture* section.

Petrie, Duncan. 1996. Peripheral Visions: Film-Making in Scotland. In *European Identity in Cinema*, ed. Wendy Everett, 93-102. Exeter: Intellect.

—. 2000. *Screening Scotland*. London: British Film Institute.

—. 2001. Devolving British Cinema: The New Scottish Cinema and the European Art Film. *Cineaste* 26.4: 55-57.

—. 2004. *Contemporary Scottish Fictions: Film, Television and the Novel.* Edinburgh: Edinburgh University Press.

Polan, Dana. 2001. *Jane Campion*. London: British Film Institute.

Puttnam, David. n.d. Collected Papers. British Film Institute Reading Room, London.

Romney, Jonathan. 2003. Dirty, Damp and Bone-Chilling. And Let Us Not Forget the Bowl of Custard. *Independent on Sunday*. September 28, *Review* section.

Sandu, S. 2003a. Existentialism and Messy Sex. *Daily Telegraph*, September 26.

—. 2003b. Going Out. *Daily Telegraph*, September 27.

Sarris, Andrew. 1983. Local Hero. *Village Voice*, February 22.

Street, Sarah. 2003. *Transatlantic Crossings: British Feature Films in the USA*. New York: Continuum.

Williams, Linda Ruth. 2005. *The Erotic Thriller in Contemporary Cinema.* Edinburgh: Edinburgh University Press.

Wyatt, Justin. 1994. *High Concept: Movies and Marketing in Hollywood.* Austin: University of Texas Press.

# WHAT'S THE POINT OF FILM SCHOOL, OR, WHAT DID BEACONSFIELD STUDIOS EVER DO FOR THE SCOTTISH FILM INDUSTRY?

ALISTAIR SCOTT

In 2005 the Scottish Screen Academy was established in Edinburgh, a joint venture between Napier University and Edinburgh College of Art, and one of a network of seven Skillset Screen Academies across the UK. At last there was an institution established in Scotland with proper funding to train filmmakers of the future. Among comments recorded on the Scottish Government website from Screen Academy Scotland's official launch, Scottish First Minister Jack McConnell declared, "what we need to do now is to encourage even more Scots to be successful behind the camera," while Napier University's Vice-Principal, Professor Joan Stringer added: "no longer will Scotland's film talent have to head to London to seek a comprehensive education in film and television."

As Stringer was at pains to indicate, for the previous three decades many aspiring Scottish filmmakers had made the journey south in order to gain a precious film school experience, even though very often the films made by such students brought them back to Scotland. This chapter will examine the experience of Scots at the National Film and Television School (NFTS) in Beaconsfield (created in 1970) and that institution's influence on the Scottish film industry. It traces the trailblazing career paths of role models for today's Scottish film school students and investigates what such trailblazers' early student films tell us about their subsequent filmmaking styles and careers. This examination of the relationship between Beaconsfield and Scotland contributes to debates about how best to develop the full future potential of the Scottish Screen Academy and promote the most effective training for filmmakers north of the border in the twenty-first century. In some ways this project might be described as a kind of retrospective ethnographic study, since the author was a postgraduate student in the documentary department at the NFTS in the early 1980s, with first-hand knowledge of what life at Beaconsfield was like for a student arriving from Scotland.

In the critical discourse on Scottish cinema first launched by the 1982 *Scotch Reels* event and publication (McArthur 1982) it can sometimes seem that films are viewed with incomplete consideration of their educational and institutional histories and antecedents. The influential polemical approach pioneered by *Scotch Reels* does chronicle the history and progress of Scottish cinema and it examines contemporary feature films in relationship to those that preceded them. Often, however, a full investigation of the institutional influences which shape how *that* particular director reached the point of departure in order to start work on *this* particular project is lacking. In Duncan Petrie's comprehensive account (Petrie 2000) there is more detailed context given for individual Scottish filmmakers, but the importance of the NFTS and the connections between key personnel that it facilitated is not analysed. The 2005 Scottish cinema dossier in published in *Screen* (Various 2005) is structured by an implicit assumption, given the relatively recent provenance of the particular films it discusses, that Scottish cinema's rejuvenation dates only from the middle of the 1990s. Now that a Scottish Screen Academy has been established, it seems relevant to review an earlier period and to unpick how the film school experience was already starting to act as a catalyst to help bring about radical change within Scottish film culture in the 1980s. That said, the work of four Scottish Beaconsfield graduates has received some critical attention in the recent discourse on Scottish cinema: Michael Caton-Jones, Gillies MacKinnon, Lynne Ramsay and Ian Sellar. This chapter will pay close attention to the importance of film school in shaping the work of these filmmakers. The NFTS studies of all four became a starting point from which they set out as professional feature directors, and which was crucial in shaping their future work.

First, some historical context: the environment for any would-be filmmaker starting out in the 1970s, '80s, or even '90s, was very different to that which exists today. There have been seismic changes in technology, institutional structures and practices, audience, and ideology. In 1970s Scotland there was a small community of filmmakers based around the Scottish Freelance branch of the ACTT (Association of Cinema and Television Technicians) trade union. In order to work in the industry at that time it was essential to become an ACTT member. The loose-knit group of filmmakers constituting the ACTT's Scottish Freelance branch had three principal aims: to create a network which could publicise their skills and talents, thus generating new opportunities for professional filmmaking; to campaign for the establishment of a Scottish film studio; and to lobby for the local provision of suitable training and education which would enable new entrants to start to make their way in the film industry. The idea of access to a film school experience was always a crucial part of this collective strategy.

Today any would-be filmmaker can start to make movies and learn their craft using relatively inexpensive, readily available digital video equipment. The cameras are simple to use and computers come pre-loaded with editing packages which can provide a wide range of filmic effects simply and at reasonable cost. The 1996 launch of the DV camcorder and the accessibility of home editing packages such as Apple's iMovie (1999) and Microsoft Windows' Movie-Maker for PCs (2000) have had an impact on filmmaking which might be compared to that of the introduction of the Kodak Box Brownie on photography in 1900. Suddenly the basic tools are affordable and accessible to all. Kodak's simple $1 snapshot camera brought photography to the mass market and, one hundred years on, something similar is happening with filmmaking. Not only are the tools accessible, but since the 2005 launch of YouTube's Broadcast Yourself facility, there is a free means of exhibition and distribution via the internet. Of course, this "box brownification" process doesn't mean that there is easy access for would-be filmmakers to make feature-length work for cinema or television. It does, however, have enormous implications for the curriculum required for training new filmmakers. Back in the 1970s a key attraction of a film school course was to get "hands-on" experience: to learn a craft, to gain access to necessary tools—the film cameras and lenses, the cutting rooms and editing equipment—without being constrained by the demarcation of the craft-guild structures of relevant trade unions. Of course, outside of a film school context there were a few amateur enthusiasts with Super 8 cameras or wind-up 16mm Bolex cameras and also some determined filmmakers, who would go on to form the political and experimental independent production sector, who gained access to "reel to reel" black-and-white ½-inch Portapak videotape recorders in educational institutions and community projects. Nevertheless, for those wanting to join the commercial mainstream industry it was the gleaming film kit, otherwise virtually impossible to access, that in large part constituted the attraction of film school. If a mainstream professional career was one's aim, there were, unlike today, very few alternatives to film school. As the 1980s progressed, the creative energy associated with this enthusiasm for the film school ethos contributed to the revitalisation of the Scottish film industry called for in *Scotch Reels*, albeit in terms of professional filmmakers training outwith Scotland, rather than the expansion of an indigenous film and video workshop movement that the *Scotch Reels* project identified as the main priority (see, for instance, McArthur 1982a and 1982b).

Institutional arrangements in the 1970s and '80s were also more rigid than today. The British film industry (alongside ITV) operated with a closed shop union agreement and all directors and technicians had to be members of ACTT. There were several ways into the ACTT, for example, joining as an assistant in a specific department such as camera, sound or editing, and then making progress by learning the craft and working one's way up. The completion of a film school course, however, was an alternative way of gaining union membership. As well as rewarding the graduating student with a diploma, more importantly the job-seeking graduate gained their essential union ticket. Without the latter it was impossible to work in the industry; moreover, successful film school graduation could lead immediately to union membership in the grade of 'Director'. This was another reason why film school training was so attractive for so many.

There were always strong connections between Scotland and the NFTS. Colin Young, the School's founding Director was a Scot who emigrated to California in the early 1950s to make his way in the film industry in Los Angeles. Within a few years he was lecturing at the University of California, Los Angeles; by the mid 1960s he was Chair of the Department of Theatre Arts and Head of the film school at UCLA. Young was a UCLA Faculty member when maverick young filmmakers such as Francis Ford Coppola were graduating from the university. Although Young was particularly involved with new approaches to documentary led by filmmakers such as Fred Wiseman, Richard Leacock and D.A. Pennebaker, and his own principal focus was on ethnographic film studies, his position in UCLA meant an involvement across all genres of film (MacDougall 2002, 81-88). At the same time in Britain, Harold Wilson's Labour Government was taking a number of radical steps in establishing new educational institutions such as the Open University, created in 1970. As an additional new venture, Jenny Lee, then Minister for the Arts, argued for the establishment of a national film school. In 1970 Young was head-hunted by ministerial aides and enticed to relocate to Beaconsfield.

From the time of his appointment Young established close links with the emergent Scottish filmmaking community. In 1970 US producer Roger Corman came to Edinburgh for an event which celebrated independent American cinema. The Director of the Edinburgh International Film Festival (EIFF) at the time was film producer and director Murray Grigor, who quickly realised that Young could play an important role as a link between the filmmakers of the New American cinema and those in Scotland. Young knew how important exposure at film festivals such as

Edinburgh would be for his students. He remained actively involved in the EIFF after Lynda Myles took over from Grigor, throughout her period of office 1973-1980 and during the time of her successor, Jim Hickey (see McArthur 1990).

At the NFTS Young was starting from scratch: attempting to gain support and funding from the industry as well as government; putting together a team of staff who could teach (and who looked as though they had some industrial and creative credibility); recruiting students with talent and ambition. In 1971 the first student intake gathered in the huts around the old Crown Film Unit studios in Station Road, Beaconsfield. Among their number were several Scots: Bill Forsyth, Steve Morrison and Michael Radford from Edinburgh. Morrison became the first NFTS graduate, taking his documentary about the occupation of London's Centre Point office block for transmission on Granada TV's series *World in Action* (1963-1998) in 1974. Morrison spent a long and successful career at Granada, eventually becoming the company's Chief Executive. During his time at Granada he was Executive Producer on a number of feature films, including *My Left Foot* (Sheridan, Ire/GB, 1989). In 2003 Morrison set up the independent conglomerate All3media, now one of the UK's largest production companies.

Bill Forsyth, by contrast, wearied by the commute up the M6 and was one of the earliest drop-outs from the NFTS. Forsyth was already in partnership with Charlie Gormley in Tree Films, a small Glasgow-based independent production company specialising in sponsored documentaries, and had to keep that business running. Colin Young remained a keen supporter of Forsyth, however, as the latter established himself as a feature film writer/director with *That Sinking Feeling* (GB, 1979). After a second feature, *Gregory's Girl* (GB, 1981), won the 1982 BAFTA award for Best Screenplay, Young remedied Forsyth's drop-out status by making him the first Honorary Graduate from the NFTS.

Prior to film school Mike Radford had been teaching at Stevenson College, Edinburgh. He returned to Scotland after his time at Beaconsfield to work with the department of Music and Arts at BBC Scotland and forged there a close relationship with Scottish writer Jessie Kesson. Radford directed an innovative documentary drama based on Kesson's memoir of growing up in Elgin in the 1920s, the daughter of an alcoholic mother forced into prostitution. *The White Bird Passes* (GB, 1980) combined poetic dramatisation with an extended interview with Kesson. Radford and Kesson made such a strong connection that the former's first feature was made from a script based on a WWII-set novella by the latter. *Another Time, Another Place* (GB, 1983), set and filmed entirely on the

Black Isle around Cromarty, was one of the earliest Channel 4 feature film commissions with a Scottish subject (Petrie 2000, 161) and the start of a prolific feature directorial career for Radford.

This small cohort of Scots in the first year of operation at the NFTS was followed by a line of other students throughout the 1970s, as graduates from both Edinburgh College of Art and Glasgow School of Art also went south to continue their training. Sandy Johnson returned to his home city of Glasgow to make his graduation film, a pastiche film-noir, *Never say die!* (GB, 1980). Ian Knox used his NFTS graduation film (and its screening at the EIFF) to raise funding from the Scottish Arts Council for his next project, *The Privilege* (GB, 1983), an adaptation of a George Mackay Brown story about *Droit de seigneur* in Scottish feudal society. Johnson and Knox, along with another Scottish contemporary, Brian Ward, have had successful directorial careers in British television since graduation from the NFTS. Johnson has directed episodes of many classic TV dramas, from *The Comic Strip Presents...* (Channel 4, 1982-1992; BBC, 1992-2005) to *Inspector Morse* (ITV, 1987-2000) and *Jonathan Creek* (BBC, 1997-2004). He has worked in England almost exclusively, with the exception of a couple of episodes of the BBC Scotland television series *Monarch of the Glen* (2000-2005). In the 1980s Knox directed a number of landmark BBC Scotland television films written by Peter McDougall, bringing an austere and distanced aesthetic to the latter's scripts (Petrie 2004, 24). *Shoot for the Sun* (1986) was a story of Edinburgh drug-dealing with Brian Cox and Jimmy Nail. *Down where the Buffalo Go* (1988), starring Harvey Keitel, was set in Greenock, focusing on men stationed at the US nuclear submarine base at the Holy Loch and their impact on the local community. Like Johnson Knox has since been confined to shaping blue-chip network TV dramas. Brian Ward has worked with BBC Scotland Children's department devising and scripting the fantasy series, *Shoebox Zoo* (BBC, 2004- ), a Canadian co-production.

Another Scot at the NFTS during the late 1970s was writer Paul Pender. At film school he wrote *The Game*, about two fans following the television coverage of Scotland's final match in the 1978 World Cup in Argentina. The script wasn't made into a film at Beaconsfield, but, after a Fringe First-winning theatre debut at the Edinburgh Festival, Granada Television bought the rights and produced it as a play for television. Pender developed his contacts at Granada, writing for their drama series *Crown Court* (1972-1984). Since then he has worked as writer, script editor and producer. He wrote *The Bogie Man* (Gormley, GB, 1992), a one-off drama for BBC Scotland based around the idea of a comic book hero loose on the mean streets of Glasgow. Now based in Los Angeles,

Pender wrote and co-produced the international co-production *Evelyn* (Beresford, Ger/Ire/USA/GB/Neth, 2002), a star vehicle for Pierce Brosnan. Dennis Crossan was another Scottish NFTS student who subsequently spent much of his professional career working in the US. Crossan trained as a lighting cameraman and shot a number of fellow students' NFTS graduation films, including *Fall from Grace* (Wyse, GB, 1984), filmed on location in the West Highlands and telling a comic but brutally realistic version of Bonnie Prince Charlie's flight after the 1746 Battle of Culloden. After graduation Crossan gained his first feature film credit as lighting cameraman on the Berlin Silver Bear-winning Scottish feature *Silent Scream* (Hayman, GB, 1990), a work based on the life and writings of Barlinnie Special Unit inmate Larry Winters.

Despite such notable successes, however, the NFTS was not the only film school to have an impact on Scottish filmmaking in the 1970s. Operating prior to the establishment of the NFTS was the privately-funded London International Film School. Two notable Scottish graduates from the latter have had a lasting impact on Scottish cinema: writer/director Bill Douglas and producer, Iain Smith. Douglas' unique vision and passion secured support from the BFI Production Board to return to Scotland to make his seminal Childhood Trilogy of autobiographical films: *My Childhood* (GB, 1972), *My Ain Folk* (GB, 1973) and *My Way Home* (GB, 1978). Smith gained early professional experience as production manager on these films. Knowing the importance of their respective student experiences, both Douglas and Smith became very closely associated with the NFTS, Douglas as a regular visiting tutor up to the time of his death in 1991 and Smith as a member of the NFTS Board of Governors.

By 1980 five students out of an annual intake of 25 were Scots. Through the '80s the impact of the NFTS on films made in Scotland was most profound. Ian Sellar was one of the 1980 group. He had previously studied photography at Napier College and design at Bournemouth, but his main inspiration came after he was recruited by Iain Smith to work on Douglas' *My Childhood.* At the NFTS, influenced by Douglas, Sellar wrote *Over Germany* (GB, 1983), a semi-autobiographical story of a young Scottish boy, son of a World War II bomber pilot and Jewish refugee, whose eyes are opened to the real impact of war. Staying with his German grandmother in Hamburg, he gains insights into the complexity of family identity (Petrie 2004, 197). Sellar was able to take a sabbatical from Beaconsfield to work on this project after it was funded by German broadcaster ZDF and the newly established drama department at Channel 4. After *Over Germany* screened at the EIFF and on television, he returned to the NFTS where for a number of months he laboured unsuccessfully on a new Scottish-set project, graduating eventually with an adaptation of a David Cook short story, *Albert's Memorial* (GB, 1985).

Sellar's *Over Germany* came to the attention of a first-time Scottish producer, Chris Young. Young was developing a film script written by Christopher Rush, based on the latter's 1985 novel *A Twelvemonth and a Day*. Sellar was drawn to the themes of the story, that of a rural Scottish fishing community viewed through the eyes of a young boy, but his prior experience of adaptation led him to believe that Rush's script required substantial revision, telling the present author in a February 2008 interview that, "the key thing about film school was that it gave me the confidence to have faith in my own vision and argue for changes and revisions." The result was *Venus Peter* (GB, 1989), funded by Channel 4 and the BFI, an elegiac, Fordian story of a boy growing up amid a changing world, learning about nature and life from the community, and especially from his grandfather (Richards 1998, 204; Petrie 2000, 163-164). The setting, story and characters of *Venus Peter* were distilled from Rush's book, but we can trace the influence of Sellar's previous work in the way he infuses the finished film with a poetic visual style. The "look" of *Venus Peter* was also influenced by another NFTS graduate, Mexican lighting cameraman, Gabriel Beristain, and, as in *Over Germany,* the film's narrative was defined by a young male central character's point of view. Sellar shared with Rush a determination to make a film which celebrated life and affirmed a strong sense of individual identity through imagination and childhood memory (Rush 1990, 115-132). The representation of Scottishness in Sellar's films is always rooted in the particular, in a personal story inseparable from the central character. He later returned to the themes of individual identity and recent European history in a second film produced by Christopher Young, *Prague* (GB/Fr, 1992), starring Alan Cumming.

Another 1980s NFTS film depicting Scotland through the eyes of a young boy was *The Riveter* (Caton-Jones, GB, 1986), filmed in Glasgow and the Western Isles, a collaboration between two Scots who had come to Beaconsfield in 1984, scriptwriter John Kerr and director Michael Caton-Jones. The story of *The Riveter* was rooted in Kerr's experience, but the behaviour of an errant father seen through the eyes of a young teenage boy was brought to life through Caton-Jones' *mise-en-scène* and in sensitive, revealing performances from Andrew Barr and Ewen Bremner. Perhaps more than any other Beaconsfield-trained Scot, Caton-Jones' career approximates to the original 1960s dream of how film school might open any door. After a second NFTS short, *Leibe Mutter* (GB, 1986), made before he graduated, Caton-Jones was hired by Scottish independent producer Gareth Wardell to direct *Brond* (1987) for Channel 4. This was a three-part television drama series set in Scotland and based on the menacing 1984 novel by Frederic Lindsay. *Brond*'s associate producer, Paddy Higson, had been a mentor to several film school shoots in Scotland and had spotted Caton-Jones' talent and bravura style. With *Brond* Caton-Jones demonstrated his directorial skill, using a flamboyant camera style to maintain the tension in this dark thriller. This was his first time working with a full professional crew which included other NFTS graduates and students (e.g., Richard Greatrex, Joke Van Wyk). Caton-Jones also consolidated his NFTS-created reputation as a director with an ability to cast and work with relatively unknown young actors (here, John Hannah fresh from graduation at the Royal Scottish Academy of Music and Drama) as well coping with the egos of established stars such as Stratford Johns, a veteran of years of British television police dramas. *Brond* led to Caton-Jones' feature debut *Scandal* (GB, 1989). This led in turn to a major international co-production, *Memphis Belle* (GB/Jap/USA, 1990), and the start of a prolific Hollywood directorial career.

Perhaps because he has worked in mainstream genres and does not write the scripts for the films he directs, Caton-Jones' contribution to Scottish cinema has rarely been addressed to anything like the same degree as those of fellow NFTS graduates such as Ian Sellar, Gillies MacKinnon or Lynne Ramsay. But he was brought back to Scotland to direct (and act as Executive Producer) on *Rob Roy* (USA, 1995), a film seen by most critics as a striking contrast to the European art house production model generally asserted to have characterised 1990s Scottish filmmaking (Petrie 2004, 202). It was perhaps inevitable that *Rob Roy*, a tale produced many times since the days of two-reel silent movies (McBain 1990), should be in the Hollywood tradition. From the outset of the project producer Peter Broughan sought out Scots who had established reputations within American studio cinema. He travelled to New Zealand to commission expatriate Alan Sharp to write the script. Sharp's background as a Scottish writer with US studio experience and an intimate understanding of American films led to a new style of historical film which resuscitated the Classic Hollywood genre of the Western in an eighteenth-century Scottish setting.

Like Caton-Jones, Gillies MacKinnon received his first feature directorial opportunity after NFTS graduation on a Channel 4-funded project by Gareth Wardell's Jam Jar Films. *Conquest of the South Pole* (GB, 1990) was based on the 1988 Edinburgh Festival Traverse Theatre production of Manfred Karge's play. MacKinnon had arrived at Beaconsfield with a wide range of experience. After graduating from

Glasgow School of Art in 1968 he left Scotland and worked in London as a teacher and later as a cartoonist and illustrator. He travelled in North Africa and then returned to London. Employed there as a detached youth worker, MacKinnon began to use video and storytelling as tools in his work with teenagers. While studying at Beaconsfield he knew he had a personal film he wanted to both write and direct and he worked closely with script tutor Shane Connaughton on his screenplay. *Passing Glory* (GB, 1986) is about an unemployed Glasgow teenage girl who is appalled at how her grandmother's Communist background and involvement on the Republican side in the Spanish Civil War seems forgotten at her Mayday funeral. Together with her boyfriend the girl takes action to honour her grandmother's radical past. The film celebrates the Clydeside tradition of political activism through a story centred on young people and is full of iconoclastic surprise and humour. *Passing Glory* can be seen as a work that takes on the challenge outlined in the *Scotch Reels* volume for Scottish film work to engage with the history and legacy of Red Clydeside (Caughie 1982, 121). At the same time, MacKinnon's film produced a complex story about modern Scotland which defied genre stereotypes and was naturalistic yet full of symbolism.

*Passing Glory* was also important in consolidating the link between the NFTS and the Scottish Film Production Fund, then the major source of indigenous production finance in Scotland. To enable the complex student shoot to come to the country, money from the SFPF supplemented the level of budget available to a student film. In return for this support the NFTS film utilised participants in a local training scheme, the Scottish Film Training Trust, in lead roles in a number of different departments. This flexible arrangement, which also allowed MacKinnon's brother, Billy, to produce *Passing Glory*, benefited all parties and delivered a polished and powerful final production. The film won a 1986 EIFF award, was picked up for terrestrial broadcast on Channel 4, and brought MacKinnon to the attention of a range of metropolitan agents and producers, including George Faber at the BBC. By the time *Conquest of the South Pole* was completed, MacKinnon's link with Faber had led to directorial work on the television dramas *Needle* (GB, 1990), scripted by Jimmy McGovern, and *The Grass Arena* (GB, 1991), based on the novel by John Healy. Subsequently, MacKinnon's former NFTS script tutor, Shane Connaughton, developed a feature script set in Ireland which he wanted his ex-student to direct. *The Playboys* (USA/GB/Ire, 1992) was funded through the Sam Goldwyn Company, and the success of the film led to an invitation from Steve Martin for Mackinnon to direct the

Hollywood film *A Simple Twist of Fate* (USA, 1994), a present-day adaptation of George Eliot's 1861 novel *Silas Marner*.

As with Caton-Jones, after an early-'90s Hollywood sojourn MacKinnon wanted to return to Scotland to make a film, a more personal project drawing on his memory of the late twentieth-century Scottish urban experience and one which would enable him to work again with his brother, Billy. The siblings collaborated on the script for *Small Faces* (GB, 1996), incorporating a number of semi-autobiographical themes which facilitated fresh examination of certain well-established Scottish cultural stereotypes, such as the hard man, working-class family life, and the violence of Glasgow's notorious teenage gang culture (Petrie 2000, 201-204). The intimate yet unsentimental portrait of family life in *Small Faces* harks back directly to *Passing Glory*. MacKinnon directed another 1990s Scottish feature, *Regeneration* (GB/Can, 1997), based on the WWI novels of Pat Barker. He continues to have a prolific career in both film and television.

The Scottish filmmakers trained at the NFTS in the 1970s and 1980s would appear from this account to be exclusively male. The institutional gender imbalance was not so extreme, however: the NFTS did attract many talented women filmmakers in the 1970s and 1980s, although not from Scotland. This situation changed in the late '80s, and throughout the 1990s. Amy Hardie arrived at the NFTS as a playwright with an award for her Edinburgh Festival Fringe production *A Precarious Living*. At Beaconsfield she focused on documentary and together with Arthur Howes made *Kafi's Story* (GB, 1989). This film about a Sudanese boy's survival in time of war, won the Joris Ivens Award for feature documentary in 1991. Since 2000 Hardie has co-ordinated the Doc-Space project and teaches at Edinburgh College of Art. Alex Mackie also arrived at the NFTS in the late 1980s. At film school she honed her editing skills and formed links with rising stars such as American student Danny Cannon. When Cannon took his feature *Judge Dredd* (USA, 1995) for post-production in Los Angeles Mackie was onboard as editor. Since that time she has worked in both the British and US industries and been nominated for Emmy awards for her editing work on the US television series *CSI: Crime Scene Investigation* (CBS, 2000- ) and the television film *RKO281* (Ross, USA, 1999). Other female Scottish NFTS students in the 1990s included writers Aileen Ritchie and Eirene Houston. Since graduation Ritchie has worked on a number of projects, directing *The Closer You Get* (GB, 2000) while Houston has written scripts for television series including *This Life* (BBC, 1996-97) and *Monarch of the Glen*.

In 1990 Andrea Calderwood and Kate Swan, two women who would be important for the development of Scottish cinema later in the decade, became closely involved with the NFTS without ever becoming full-time students. The link between the NFTS and the SFPF, forged through Gillies MacKinnon's *Passing Glory*, had successfully opened the door for further collaborations with the Scottish Film Training Trust. This led Calderwood, a SFTF production trainee, to gain extensive experience on a number of Scottish films by Scottish NFTS writer/directors including: *Ashes* (Douglas Mackinnnon, GB, 1990) and *Tinned Fish* (Murton, GB, 1990). Calderwood acted as Producer on the latter, a contemporary story about the consequences of contamination of the Holy Loch linked to incidents at the US submarine base. Such ambitious NFTS student films could be shot in Scotland because of SFPF supplementary funding. This high-level apprenticeship was an important element in Calderwood's success in becoming Head of Drama at BBC Scotland in 1994 (a post she held until 1997) at the young age of 28. At the BBC she was responsible for commissioning Paul Murton's television ghost drama *The Blue Boy* (GB, 1994). She went on to support other NFTS graduates, most notably Lynne Ramsay, when later Production Head at Pathé Films. Most recently, through her own independent production company, Slate Films, Calderwood was Executive Producer of the Oscar-winning *The Last King of Scotland* (Macdonald, GB, 2007).

Kate Swan was first involved in the Scottish film industry as the administrator of the Celtic Film Festival in 1987. Like Calderwood she gained production experience on Scottish NFTS student work, such as *Alabama* (Shields, GB, 1990) and went on to be producer of *The Blue Boy* and later Director of the SFPF. *Alabama*'s director, Jim Shields, has worked on a range of TV dramas, establishing a reputation as a director of soap operas including *Eastenders* (BBC, 1985- ) and *River City* (BBC, 2002- ). The flexible, *laissez-faire* approach of both the NFTS and the SFPF in the early '90s led to lasting benefits not just for Calderwood and Swan but for the wider Scottish industry, kick-starting the professional television careers of a range of SFTF production trainees and graduating NFTS students.

In the early 1990s a number of new developments in Scotland led to changes in the relevance and importance of a film school experience for aspiring Scottish filmmakers. The preeminent, elite position of the NFTS in identifying new professional writers and directors was undermined. The 1992 establishment of Tartan Shorts, a short film production scheme funded by BBC Scotland and the SFPF (and from 1997 by Scottish Screen), meant that there was now another, locally available way for would-be filmmakers to make a "calling card" film geared toward entry into the mainstream film and television industries. Moreover, Tartan Shorts was open to a wider field rather than just film school graduates; indeed, current full-time students were ineligible to apply. The success of this scheme and other Scottish and British successors meant that producers and broadcasters looked not just to the NFTS graduation films when scouting for new talent; novice directors were increasingly expected to win their spurs in the explicitly competitive environment represented by initiatives like Tartan Shorts (Petrie 2000, 180; 228). This development meant that the kind of leap straight to feature-length drama possible for Sellar, Caton-Jones, MacKinnon and others of their generation is unlikely to happen again. At the NFTS itself, Colin Young retired in 1992 and the new director, Henning Camre, brought a more strictly delineated approach to training. From the early 1990s the NFTS aimed to deliver training more focused on all the different departments and there was an expansion of short courses tailored to deliver teaching targeted at the needs of continuing professional development, as opposed to a less precise, more formative individual film student experience. Also, a number of other industry-linked training schemes such as EAVE (the European Audio-visual Entrepreneurs scheme) and Moonstone gained prestige, becoming sought after because they offered a different style of intensive training which did not rely on becoming a full-time student. It was now possible to get the film school experience part-time and in places other than the NFTS.

Some notable Scottish filmmakers did still benefit from full-time study at the NFTS in the late '90s, however. Lynne Ramsay took up her place at Beaconsfield as a full-time cinematography student. Despite the more rigorous demarcation now in operation at the NFTS, Ramsay was determined to pursue a flexible, individual approach, writing and directing rather than being restricted to camerawork. For her graduation film she returned to Glasgow to film *Small Deaths* (GB, 1995), a personal story about secrets within a working-class family viewed through the eyes of a little girl. Casting non-professional actors and family members, and developing the narrative through a sequence of short epiphanies, Ramsay produced an atmospheric, visually arresting, intense and melancholic story. The film was selected for the 1996 Cannes Film Festival where it was awarded the Short Film Jury Prize, an unprecedented honour for a student work. Nevertheless Ramsay, unlike, say, Michael Caton-Jones a decade earlier, did not make an immediate move to feature-length work and continued making shorts. She went on to work professionally with the same team of ex-NFTS students who collaborated with her on *Small*

*Deaths* on the short projects *Gasman* (GB, 1996), funded through Tartan Shorts, and *Kill the Day* (GB, 1997). As with a number of other new Scottish directors who gained notice in the late 1990s, Ramsay's Tartan Short was crucially important in demonstrating her talent post-film school. Her first feature, *Ratcatcher* (GB/Fr, 1999), was encouraged and nurtured through BBC Films (and Pathé) by Andrea Calderwood, who acted as Executive Producer. *Ratcatcher*'s use of non-professional actors, emotional landscape, poignant images and a pared-down aesthetic (all facets of Ramsay's work originally developed during her time at film school) brought widespread critical acclaim for her unique approach (Williams 2002, 22-25; Kuhn 2008). As with Ian Sellar, Caton-Jones and Gillies MacKinnon, Ramsay's preferred themes and individual directorial approach are clearly established in her film school work. In the case of all these directors, the freedom to experiment at an early stage of their creative and professional development proved fundamental to their eventual individuality as filmmakers. With each new project Ramsay has continued to work with the same close-knit creative team first established during her time at the NFTS: co-writer Liana Dognini, Director of Photography Alwin Küchler, and editor Lucia Zucchetti (Macdonald 2002). This team was involved in Ramsay's feature adaptation of the 1995 Alan Warner novel *Morvern Callar* (GB, 2002).

Ramsay's career trajectory is indicative of the extent to which, from 1992 onwards, progression into features has been dominated by the need to impress with short films made after, rather than at, film school. Even with the Cannes prize for *Small Deaths*, Ramsay did not get a feature commission until after two further shorts. Although some Tartan Shorts were made by NFTS graduates, many of the successful films associated with the scheme came from talented directors who had not taken the Beaconsfield route. The Macdonald brothers (Andrew and Kevin) worked together on television documentaries such as *Shadowing* (GB, 1991) for Scottish Television before their first short, *Dr Reitzer's Fragment* (GB, 1992). Andrew then had rapid success as a producer with *Shallow Grave* (Boyle, GB, 1995) followed by *Trainspotting* (Boyle, GB, 1996). Directors such as Peter Mullan—*Orphans* (GB, 1997), *The Magdalene Sisters* (Ire/GB, 2001)—Kenny Glenaan— *Yasmin* (Ger/GB, 2004), *Summer* (GB, 2008)—and Alison Peebles—*Afterlife* (GB, 2003)—are all actors whose experience directing short films led to a progression to feature work. David Mackenzie also made a full slate of varied shorts in the late '90s before his first feature, *The Last Great Wilderness* (GB/Den, 2002). Two other recent Scottish directors went to overseas film schools before making a directorial impact with short projects. Shona Auerbach completed her training at the Polish film school in Lodz before her internationally distributed feature debut *Dear Frankie* (GB, 2004). Andrea Arnold studied at the American Film Institute in Los Angeles before making a number of shorts, including the Oscar-winning *Wasp* (GB, 2003), as a prelude to her Cannes prizewinning feature debut *Red Road* (GB/Den, 2006). The most recent feature debut by a Scot trained at the NFTS was Douglas Mackinnon's *The Flying Scotsman* (Ger/GB, 2006), a biopic of the champion cyclist Graham Obree. After graduation from Beaconsfield Mackinnon directed the Gaelic short *Sealldh* (GB, 1992), funded by the CTG, and then spent fourteen years working in a wide range of television genres before his first feature was made.

In the early years of the twenty-first century the role of film schools everywhere is continually changing. This chapter has focused mostly on the Scottish directors who have progressed to feature work, though many film school students concentrate on gaining different specialist skills and training. Film school is certainly not a conducive environment for would-be auteurs only. Since accepting its first students in 1971 the NFTS has made an important contribution to Scottish film. Now Screen Academy Scotland is part of a wider training network and will work alongside various bodies, including the NFTS, to educate emerging Scottish filmmakers. The challenge is to create an environment which in addition to providing craft skills can also instill ambition and confidence so that new directors and writers can pursue their passions and emulate important predecessors such as Sellar, Caton-Jones, Mackinnon and Ramsay. For those four Scottish directors the experience of film school enabled them to develop and articulate a distinctive filmmaking approach from the very outset of their careers. Today, however, it can seem as if there is a log-jam of new trained entrants to the film industry who wait year after year to move forward from the world of short film competitions to longer, more commercial projects. The industry in Scotland and beyond needs to work harder at creating opportunities for the talented new writers, directors, producers, and editors graduating from Screen Academy to have a real chance to progress into sustainable careers in film and television.

## Works Cited

Caughie, John. 1982. Scottish Television: What Would It Look Like? In *Scotch Reels: Scotland in Cinema and Television*, ed. Colin McArthur, 112-122. London: British Film Institute.

Kuhn, Annette. 2008. *Ratcatcher*. London: British Film Institute.

Macdonald, Fraser. 2002. Interview with Alwin Kuchler, Jane Morton, Lynne Ramsay and Lucia Zucchetti. In *Projections 12: Film-makers on Film Schools*, eds. John Boorman, Fraser MacDonald & Walter Donohue, 101-123. London: Faber & Faber.

MacDougall, David. 2002. Colin Young, Ethnographic Film and Film Culture of the 1960s. *Visual Anthropology Review* 17.2: 81-88.

McArthur, Colin, ed. 1982. *Scotch Reels: Scotland in Cinema and Television*. London: British Film Institute.

—. 1982a. How to spend £80 000 on film-making. *Glasgow Herald*, July 17.

—. 1982b. Cinema needed to represent truly the Scottish people. Glasgow *Herald*, November 3.

—. 1990. The Rises and Falls of the Edinburgh International Film Festival. In *From Limelight to Satellite: a Scottish Film Book*, ed. Eddie Dick, 91-102. London/Glasgow: British Film Institute/Scottish Film Council.

McBain, Janet. 1990. Scotland in feature film: a filmography. In *From Limelight to Satellite: a Scottish Film Book*, ed. Eddie Dick, 233-255. London/Glasgow: British Film Institute/Scottish Film Council.

Petrie, Duncan. 2000. *Screening Scotland*. London: British Film Institute.

—. 2004. *Contemporary Scottish Fictions: Film, Television and the Novel*. Edinburgh: Edinburgh University Press.

Richards, Jeffrey. 1998. *Films and British National Identity: from Dickens to Dad's Army*. Manchester: Manchester University Press.

Rush, Christopher. 1990. Venus Peter: from Pictures to Pictures. In *From Limelight to Satellite: a Scottish Film Book*, ed. Eddie Dick, 115-132. London/Glasgow: British Film Institute/Scottish Film Council.

Various, 2005. Scottish Cinema Dossier. *Screen* 46.2: 213-245.

Williams, Linda Ruth. 2002. Escape Artist. *Sight and Sound* 12.10: 22-25.

# SHAPE-SHIFTERS: INDEPENDENT PRODUCERS IN SCOTLAND AND THE JOURNEY FROM CULTURAL ENTREPRENEUR TO ENTREPREURIAL CULTURE

ROBIN MACPHERSON

## Introduction

> There is a certain wine bar in Glasgow's West End where, I swear, all you have to do is open the door and throw in a tangerine and you are guaranteed to hit an aspiring screenwriter who has received funding from Scottish Screen. Should that tangerine then ricochet it would hit a relative who has also had funding. (Lister 2001)

> The history of this rash of cultural industries developments—of the shifts and re-directions of the arguments, of the increasing attenuation of the first half of the culture/industry couplet, and of their success or failure (on whatever grounds)—still has to be written. (McIntyre 1994, 88)

The rather scathing comment reported by David Lister on the seemingly incestuous world of Scottish film, made at the height of alleged profligacy in allocating Lottery funds to feature production at once reveals and obscures a certain truth about cinema in Scotland today. Paradoxically, despite arguably enjoying never greater credibility as part of the economically and politically ascendant "Creative Industries," the apparently tight-knit Scottish film community has largely failed to articulate any shared vision of Scottish cinema's future beyond a rather fragile economic case for continued public subsidy. This essay asks why this should be so when Scotland appears to be enjoying a renewed self-confidence in other areas of the arts and cultural industries, and a resurgent politics of national identity. In attempting to answer this question I hope also to partially redress the historical deficit noted nearly fifteen years ago by former CEO of Scottish Screen, Steve McIntyre, in the second quote beginning this essay. The explanation for both absences—that of a convincing contemporary definition of Scottish cinema's future on the part of those responsible for making it and that of a full historical account of the evolution of the "Creative Industries" concept—can in large part be found in the very success of Scotland's screen producers in mobilizing the rhetoric of "Creative Industries" in the public sphere. This success has been dependent upon the muting of precisely the kinds of cultural, social and political arguments for a national cinema that, were they still "in play," could broaden the terms through which filmmaking in Scotland is understood and pursued as an object of public policy. Such a wider frame of reference would help make Scottish cinema less vulnerable to attacks from those who have lost (or perhaps never had) confidence in the economic arguments for public subsidy of film production. As we shall see, Scottish filmmakers today face increasing scepticism about the return on investment they received over a decade of significant public largesse from the mid-1990s on.

Of course this is not to deny either the material significance of the creative economy or the continuing importance and necessity of mobilising the economic arguments for public investment in film. However, the equally important social, cultural and political dimensions of cinema's contribution to Scottish life have been excessively marginalised in public policy debate. A wider understanding of cinema's place in civil society is thus confined to the realm of *post hoc* analysis of filmmakers' work. Such analysis is in most instances authored or edited by officials of the public film agencies, academics seeking to define "Scottish cinema" as a whole, with occasional forays into public discourse by filmmakers themselves—in which category I include writers, producers, actors and others and not just directors (see Hardy 1990; Dick 1990; Bruce 1996, Broughan *et al* 1997; Petrie 2000). By succumbing to the economic doctrine of "Creative Industries" discourse (Schlesinger 2007), Scotland's filmmakers and policymakers have exercised a form of self-exclusion which removes social, cultural and political concerns from the arena of "legitimate" film policy discussion. This is to the detriment not just of Scottish cinema, but of our national cultural life as a whole.

It is beyond this essay's scope to explore in detail the extent to which this apparent disavowal of cultural politics represents either a conscious avoidance of any argument that might be deemed too close to political Nationalism or a desire to articulate a politically "neutral" case for film that could be endorsed equally by all parties. What I will seek to argue, however, is that there is a price to be paid for several disappointing developments. The first is the effective evacuation of the terrain of "cultural politics" by filmmakers and the wider filmmaking community. The second is the muting of any national (with a small "n") aspiration that is not first and foremost grounded in economic terms. Following on from the previous two, the third is the consequent denial that there are significant policy issues which arise as a result of the historically specific national configuration in which filmmaking in Scotland finds itself. The price of such developments is, in a word, confidence—the confidence to assert the importance of non-economic values in the institutions and structures of public policy making as they relate to film and in the wider "conversation" concerning cinema's role in national life. A more balanced approach would empower decision-makers to take risks in pursuit of a distinctive national cinema. This cinema would be one which accepts its responsibility to engage with the life of the nation without being subservient to it, and which also accepts its commercial, entrepreneurial, global dimensions without abandoning a sense of accountability to its "home" audience. Promoters and policy-makers seem entirely comfortable with such a position when it comes to, say, theatre, publishing or television. Yet they have somehow become deeply suspicious of it when dealing with cinema.

## Some historical background

One might summarise the development of the Scottish independent film and television production sector over the last twenty-five years thus: a shift from endeavouring to be taken seriously as part of the nation's culture to being perceived as a serious part of the nation's economy.

The dominant Scottish professional filmmaking discourse of the 1970s and 1980s revolved around questions of access to resources, largely equated with increased public funding. Such access was demanded in order that Scottish stories, representations and concerns could be made more widely accessible to audiences inside and outside the nation. Despite considerable internal differences in ideology, aesthetics, and industrial priorities, a shared sense of impoverishment allowed a relatively united front around the objective of injecting greater public funding into Scotland's filmmaking infrastructure. Shared hopes for "a better future" came by the mid-1990s to be fervently projected onto the new national screen agency, Scottish Screen.

Since the 1970s independent producers and cultural commentators alike had invoked concerns with national identity in calling for measures to foster a Scottish cinema (Eadie 1973; McArthur 1976). Following the creation of Channel 4 in 1982, the importance of securing a "proportional" space for Scottish television production on the UK's networks became a closely related concern (Taylor 1987). The economic and industrial dimension of film and television production was not entirely overlooked during this period, but the predominant justification for investment or regulatory intervention appealed to questions of national cultural and socio-political entitlement—what we might for convenience term "expressive entitlement". As some noted at the time (McArthur 1982) this "expressive entitlement" was generally characterised as the right to participate in UK, or indeed global, structures of production, distribution, exhibition and consumption. This contrasts notably with the focus on the "internal market" in the contemporaneous Welsh situation. In Wales, the political, linguistic and cultural imperative was first and foremost the pursuit of an autonomous national space for cinema or television, manifested in the successful campaign to establish a Welsh fourth channel. Despite the reticence of Scottish filmmakers to pursue a comparably nationalistic agenda, questions of culture, identity, and representation remained an important theme in public discourse (Grigor 1976; Caughie 1983; McArthur 1983; McGill and McInytre 1983). During the 1970s and for a good part of the '80s, questions of what cinema/television might be *for* (ends) therefore maintained a reasonable degree of purchase in the periodic debates about structural, investment and regulatory priorities (means) within the public bodies that influenced the development of Scotland's audiovisual landscape.

During the late '80s and early '90s, however, the language of entitlement gave way to an increasingly hegemonic discourse of "economic opportunity" (see Taylor 1987; Scottish Development Agency 1989). A twofold shift took place: from expressive to economic concerns, and from a rhetoric of entitlement to one of opportunity. Policymakers and institutional personnel shifted their focus from a *distributive* economic model to an *entrepreneurial* one. With one eye on the resources that might be tapped from industrial development coffers they argued that, once historical market distortions (Metropolitan commissioning bias, brain drain, lack of infrastructure investment, distance from market, and so on) were removed, Scotland's screen producers would be able to secure both their economic and cultural viability by achieving accelerated growth through unfettered access to a growing and diversifying national (and international) audiovisual market.

This shift in discursive emphasis from subsidy to investment was neither arbitrary nor solely an accommodation to the broader contemporary shift in public discourse towards neo-conservative economics following the impact of recession, Thatcherism, and the restraint of public arts and cultural spending. Even the most hardened cultural activists were forced to adapt to the *realpolitik* of the 1980s and the need to couch arguments for public intervention in terms of either economic benefit or amelioration of the social fallout from monetarism's effects. In the 1990s Scotland's screen community as a whole changed in composition and outlook. It moved ever closer to an economic view of its own significance as independent television production matured into a recognizable business sector. Moving into the 2000s, 2003 saw the creation of a new and, so far, highly effective lobby group, the Screen Industries Summit Group (SISG), following the publication of an extremely influential report, *An Audit of the Screen Industries in Scotland.* Such recent developments further crystallise and help sustain a longer-term process in which Scottish screen industries have increasingly prioritised entrepreneurial rhetoric as a way of defining, maintaining and enhancing their public credibility. The Summit Group's perception of the central "weakness" of Scottish *film* (as opposed to television) is revealing: "the current system of subsidies in the film industry is working against growth and entrepreneurship, with Scotland yet to discover a business model for profitable films" (Screen Industries Summit Group 2004, 5). The expansion of the UK independent television sector as the overall market grew on the back of production quotas imposed on the BBC and ITV precipitated a growing number of mergers, acquisitions and the emergence of the "super-indie". The 2004 stock market flotation of the largest indies symbolised independent television production's coming-of-age of as a "serious" sector of the creative economy. The 2005 £13m sale of Scotland's largest indie company, Ideal Wark Clements, to "mega indie" RDF media, the latter also paying £10m in 2006 to acquire the Comedy Unit, Scotland's second largest indie, set the seal on local perceptions of independent television production as a potentially profitable growth sector of the national economy.

The reconstitution of the identity of Scotland's screen community around the television business helped to further marginalise attempts within that community to self-define in more cultural, social or politicised terms. This phenomenon is vividly reflected in the words of the Scottish spokesperson for film and television trade association PACT, speaking at the first major event organized by the SISG in 2003:

> We need to embrace the commercial realities of the marketplace. We fear that companies seem to be restricted in what they can produce in Scotland. They seem to be restricted to attaining funding for projects on cultural criteria. (Mcdougall 2003)

It is important to state here that I am not implying that one group or faction within Scotland's screen community actively marginalized another over the last three decades or so. What the brief historical survey offered above does demonstrate, however, is that since the 1970s there has been a clear and progressive narrowing in the shared sense of what were and were not legitimate forms of appeal in debating, formulating and communicating screen policy ideas in Scotland. Today, questions and considerations of national identity and expressive entitlement are no longer admissible in public discourse to anything like the degree they once were.

## Lines of force

Perhaps the deeper reason for this significant shift lies in the intersection of three distinct lines of force. These combined to decisively alter not just the dominant *concerns* of the independent production sector, but also the sector's very *composition*. The effect of this was to decisively place the figure of the "independent producer as entrepreneur" at the very heart of public policy discourses concerning cinema and television in Scotland.

The three lines of force which produced this decisive shift were as follows. Firstly, the triumph of "creative industries" rhetoric as the primary discursive context in which film and television are recognised as legitimate objects of public policy and investment. Secondly, the emergence of independent television production, unlike film, as a genuinely profitable sector, allied to the emergence of convergent/new media as a growth sector in the latter's own right. Thirdly, the consequent emergence of profit-driven large, and in many instances publicly quoted, production companies such as All3Media, RDF, Tiger Aspect and Endemol UK as the hegemonic voice in the independent production sector. While these three forces operated at a UK level they each have had a particular and arguably even greater impact in the Scottish context. This is partly because of the Scottish sector's smaller size and relative "weakness" in comparison to the metropolitan centre, partly because of the historical dominance of film *vis-à-vis* television in Scottish public policy and partly because of the relative historical weight of cultural and social agendas in the articulation of Scottish producers' concerns to public agencies and the wider public.

From the mid '80s the increasing prevalence of "Creative Industries" as a concept uniting arts with economic policy can be seen in a number of influential UK policy documents and commentaries (Greater London Council 1985; Mulgan and Worpole 1986). A clutch of reports on the future of Scotland's screen industries (Taylor 1987; Myerscough 1988; Dovetail Management Consultants 1988) reveal how rapidly cultural industries discourse spread. It would take longer, however, for that spread to be manifested operationally in the restructuring of the public bodies charged with promoting screen culture and industry: Scottish Screen, established through the amalgamation of the Scottish Film Council, the Scottish Film Production Fund, Scottish Screen Locations and Scottish Broadcast and Film Training, did not emerge until 1997. By the latter date, however, the shift was unmistakable and, it must be said, in many ways productive: it enabled Scotland's screen sector to secure for the first time access to non-cultural funds from bodies such as the Glasgow Development Agency and Scottish Enterprise. It also helped independent film production companies to be taken seriously as part of the emerging "creative economy".

In the television sector the benefits of a "fairer" share of network commissioning in terms of company growth, employment generation, opportunities for talent etc. were relatively easy to articulate. As a result "Nations and Regions" production quotas have become progressively enshrined in policy and regulation. The 1990 Broadcasting Act required the BBC to source 25% of its programmes from independent producers; the 1994 Hatch Report set internal BBC targets for "out of London" commissioning; the 2003 Communications Act requires the Office of Communications (OFCOM) to police regions and nations production and to report regularly on outcomes. In an environment where all of the major channels currently have public service obligations which commit them to nations and regions *production* to a greater or lesser degree there is a clear focal point for debate and a tangible set of parameters—share of network hours, spend, and so on—around which discussion can take place. Following a long period in which broadcasting was neglected in Scottish policy circles, the Scottish National Party administration elected at Holyrood in 2007 appointed a Broadcasting Commission with a fairly wide-ranging remit, turning television in Scotland into a high profile subject for debate.

Compared to independent television production's apparent economic dynamism, Scottish film producers have had greater need of cultural benefit arguments to support their case for public funds. Until very recently the film community has, nonetheless, focused on *economic benefits*, stressing film's capacity to promote tourism, generate multipliers on location spending and promote Scotland's attractiveness as a place to live and work. But recently it has become increasingly difficult to make a coherent argument for indigenous film production (as opposed to visiting location shoots) as a direct generator of economic benefit. The commercial returns of public investment in film (there is effectively no other kind in the Scottish context) have been so unequivocally poor that even a small proportion of its investment being recouped has been presented by Scottish Screen as a "positive" return on investment. From 2000–2005 Scottish Screen invested £17m of Lottery funds into indigenous feature production and recouped just under £2m. Things have improved in recent years, but only relatively. A peak return of £0.9m from awards was reached in 2004/5 but this must still be seen against average annual investment in the region of £3m (Scottish Screen 2005). Of course, these figures represent the return to Scottish Screen alone; other investors will have seen income from Scottish-produced films, but few if any of them will have been Scottish-based. We should note, however, that in *public* funding terms, as opposed to a commercial context, Scottish Screen's return on investment compares favourably with other national agencies' general rates of between 5% and 10%.

Domestic private finance, long sought after as the key to securing a step-change in Scottish film production, remains as elusive as ever. The Glasgow Film Fund's announcement of a private-sector partnership $2.4m film fund at the 2000 Cannes film festival did not translate into the anticipated chorus of investment. A variety of other attempts to interest venture capitalists and other city investors in funding baskets of Scottish films have, without exception, all failed. Scotland's venture capitalists, fund managers and banks, despite being more numerous in Edinburgh than anywhere outside the City of London, share a sceptical view of the risk/reward ratio in Scottish film production. The film sector's arguments remain more or less wholly targeted on the direct financing role of the public film bodies and the domestic broadcasters, BBC and Channel 4. These public patrons remain disproportionally critical to the health of UK film production in what is popularly considered to be a commercial, theatrically-led medium.

This state of affairs leaves Scotland's film producers facing a far more entrenched set of economic problems and a much less coherent set of solutions than their colleagues in television. At a UK level independent television producers have already won the key battles: overall production quotas, retention of rights and access to commercial capital. Film producers by contrast have no "local market" equivalent to either UK network production or the (admittedly declining) opt-out commissioning of the BBC and STV on which to build a business base. They also have no equivalent of the longer-term revenue stream from returning series upon which to grow their business and build development capacity. In film there is little prospect of a gradual upward trajectory comparable to that of Scottish companies like Ideal Wark Clements, from the foothills of lower value regional/off-peak/digital channel series to the high peaks of network commissions and indeed eventual stock market flotation or sell-off.

The independent Scottish film producer faces a far more canyon-esque prospect: long periods toiling in the tributaries of short films (a talent- and credibility-developing loss leader), ultra low-budget feature production (generally a loss leader, too, although from time to time one project may at least turn a profit) and successive development-deal dead ends. Occasionally a Scottish producer may find a route through the brush onto the high ground of a completed financial package. This sees a modestly budgeted film produced, recent examples including producer Chris Young and director Annie Griffin's *Festival* (GB, 2005) producer Peter Broughan and director Douglas Mackinnon's *The Flying Scotsman* (Ger/GB, 2006), producer Gillian Berrie and director David Mackenzie's *Hallam Foe* (GB, 2007). Of *The Flying Scotsman*, one trade press report noted: "this is a movie that never got greenlit, never had a completion bond, never closed its finance, went into administration (the U.K. equivalent of Chapter 11) during post-production and still hasn't paid half its bills" (Dawtrey 2006). But for those few projects that make it this far, fewer still achieve theatrical distribution or a significant audience and a tiny proportion secure a financial return to the producer from distribution, as distinct from whatever fees can be clawed back from the production budget, (monies that in any case are often deferred just to get the film made). The Scottish television sector, given a healthy overall demand, identifies systematic obstacles to commissioning Scottish-based producers or a lack of commitment to delivering regional quotas. The local film sector, however, cannot articulate a comparable "solution" to the seventy years-plus domination of theatrical distribution by Hollywood and the absence of a consistent audience for British film. Even if the audience was more consistent, the brute commercial truth is that the UK market is too small to sustain an indigenous production sector except at the very lowest end of the budget scale. International distribution is a prerequisite of successful financing. The Scottish producer has, perforce, to play in the international marketplace or perish.

The high-risk and generally low reward nature of UK/Scottish film production and producers' lack of influence on demand from "aggregators" (i.e., the distribution and exhibition sector) has focused filmmakers and public film bodies on "supply-side" issues in an attempt to increase the "hit rate" of projects, producers and companies. Scottish Screen's delegation in 2006 to Skillset of £800,000 over a two year period "to support freelancers, small production businesses and training providers" (Scottish Screen 2006) is a good example of the increasing emphasis on skills and "workforce development". Screen and enterprise agencies have thus become increasingly preoccupied with supporting researcher and executive producer development programmes, slate-fund investment, networking with commissioners, rather than direct production funding investment in a single feature project. In the fields of television and interactive media this kind of intervention is also increasingly focused on company development. Growth and consolidation in the sector and, at least in England, a growing number of publicly quoted companies, calls for an increasing emphasis on managerial skills, in other words, an enterprise- rather than a project-focused approach.

In the Scottish film context, however, much more attention is necessarily focused on projects and individuals. Firstly, there are in effect almost no sustainable film "businesses" in the country into which enterprise-focused funding can be ploughed. Secondly, the complexity and costs of individual project development/financing are often much greater and their significance (in terms of anticipated if not realized economic/cultural value) much higher than in television (with the exception of something like a long-running series drama or soap). Moreover, given the residual importance of cultural criteria in project investment decisions by bodies like Scottish Screen, the emergence of a single-mindedly business-focused approach to the support of film production companies remains problematic. Frustration at this state of affairs from some parts of both the Scottish film and enterprise communities is evident, for example, in PACT's submission to both the Cultural Commission set up by the 2003-07 Labour administration at Holyrood and both it and Scottish Enterprise's evidence to the current Scottish Government's Broadcasting Commission. It is instructive to consider the comments of Jack Perry, CEO of Scottish Enterprise, to the Broadcasting Commission at some length:

> We operated a Glasgow Film Fund for a few years. … Every single one of those films lost its shirt, I mean big time. Even the most successful were serious commercial failures. The proposition was made, ah, but it's employing loads of people, and you know, this is preserving talent in Scotland and creating production jobs and those kinds of things; but every single one of those jobs was destroying value. They had negative value to the economy. Now it might have been a perfectly legitimate thing for the government to do in saying, 'Look, these are important things that we want to preserve and develop in Scottish culture'. So it might be entirely legitimate for government to do that but as an economic development agency, it was very hard for us to defend the destruction of value in the Scottish economy. So we cannot do this any more. If Scottish Screen or someone else wants to take it on that's fine but we cannot do it. (Scottish

Broadcasting Commission 2007)

The fact that for over a decade almost the only source of film investment in Scotland—Lottery funding—has been predicated on *both* economic *and* cultural ends has placed both the distributor (Scottish Screen) and its clients (Scottish film producers) in an uneasy position. Rationalising the distribution of public monies to support film production has to involve a routine mobilisation of the importance of economic sustainability and the need to attach industrial development criteria to investment decisions. Simultaneously, however, both Scottish Screen and its clients need also maintain that funding decisions (indeed, the very existence of public funding for film as a whole) have to be seen in a wider, more nuanced context in which crude measures of economic success have to be circumscribed. To take a representative example from 2001, then Scottish Screen Chairman James Lee was forced to perform just such a balancing act in defending an emergency financial package to support Peter Mullan's film *The Magdalene Sisters* (GB/Ire): "the market is not yet ready to back Peter Mullan as a director, but he is undoubtedly one of Scotland's most accomplished talents" (McGregor 2001). In the event, *The Magdalene Sisters* turned out to be an international commercial and critical success, but the rationale advanced by Lee to support the film's production in the first place, could not depend on that fact.

All of this leads to the Scottish film producer inhabiting a space where, much as some may desire to discursively foreground considerations of "economic opportunity" rather than those of "expressive entitlement", there really is no option but to maintain both arguments simultaneously, emphasising whichever seems more opportune at a given place and a given time. Unfortunately, this fact gives rise to an element of confusion if not contradiction in public and policy discourse around Scottish film. This is particularly so in the film production community's attitude towards the role of Scottish Screen and its successor, Creative Scotland. In somewhat belatedly expressed outrage at Scottish Screen's planned dissolution into the new Creative Scotland, local filmmakers accusing the former of "voluntary suicide" (McGregor 2006). The core of the filmmakers' concern was that Scottish film would no longer have a prominent, internationally recognisable champion that could maintain engagement by overseas filmmakers in Scotland. No less significant, however, was their concern that television, interactive and other screen media would displace film's pre-eminent place once Creative Scotland was up and running, a reflection of the latter sectors' greater economic significance than indigenous feature production.

What is most revealing about this intervention is that it is principally concerned with the organisational structure of the new Creative Scotland and its accessibility to overseas producers because: "[Scotland] is crucially dependent on co-productions, we need an agency whose structures and personnel make sense to the international film community" (ibid.) But at the same time the filmmakers argue against the role of domestic broadcasters or distributors in influencing the funding decisions of the new agency:

> If development funding from the public purse is tied into dependence on matching funding from broadcasters or distributors, it means that the rights to projects are going to continue to be taken from the independent production company. This makes the film company dependent rather than independent, culturally as well as financially. (ibid.)

Here, then, the filmmakers are simultaneously attempting to mobilise a market-led argument for having a dedicated screen agency and an anti-market case for not being subject to "excessive" influence by two of the biggest sources of film investment in the UK, Channel 4 and the BBC. However, if we look more closely we can see that the argument against broadcaster influence is actually based on a case for the *independence* of Scottish film producers within the UK. In other words, the filmmakers are concerned at Scotland being subordinate to the UK film market. The implication is that Scottish Screen or its mooted replacement should function to protect Scottish film producers from the distorting influence of UK institutions. Exactly why overseas co-producers are not seen as a distorting force and Channel 4/BBC are is not exactly clear. In essence, the filmmakers, recognising their vulnerability as undercapitalised businesses in an industry with high upfront costs, argue Scottish Screen's fundamental role should be to underwrite the retention of producers' intellectual property rights, control of which they would otherwise risk losing. This is a perfectly understandable and coherent goal, but it also reveals the limitations of the filmmakers' case. Virtually no Scottish based-producer (with the possible exceptions of those noted in passing above) has in the past two decades been able to demonstrate a sustainable business in feature film production. It is highly questionable whether that sad fact is primarily due to producers ceding Intellectual Property rights to external investors.

Another revealing illustration of just how central industrial development "levers" had become to the film community's concerns can be found in submission of the film and television producers' association PACT to the Cultural Commission in October 2004 (PACT 2004). The submission's opening statement suggests a robust concern for cultural well-being:

> A country can define itself and have a sense of its own identity through how it represents itself on screen. Film, television and other screen content are therefore key indicators of the cultural health of the nation. (ibid.)

However, subsequent paper itself makes it abundantly clear that PACT believes Scottish Screen or a future successor should "shake off old assumptions" and not have an editorial role in project decision-making, instead concerning itself with putting in place "simple and automatic measures to level the playing field for Scottish-based producers":

> Rather than setting itself up as yet another editorial gate-keeper (creating enemies for itself at every awards round and critics among the film-making community), the agency could devise a system linked to international market criteria. (ibid.)

In other words, PACT is explicitly citing the supremacy of market forces as the basis for determining the allocation decisions of a public body which has both cultural and industrial obligations. This is despite the fact that international market forces have, over the past 70 years or longer, systematically frustrated the sustainable development of anything approaching a representative Scottish cinema. Throughout Europe, precisely because of the failure of the free market to ensure a level global playing field, consistent demands have been and continue to be made for a different relationship between culture and commerce. No individual European country, big or small, has been able to demonstrate a viable alternative to some form of "cultural exception" for its domestic film industry: the most successful European film industry (that of France) is also the continent's most interventionist. Likewise, despite the best efforts since 1991 by the European Union, its various MEDIA programmes and other interventions such as the Council of Europe's EURIMAGES, there is still no coherent European market able to challenge the hegemony of Hollywood in European cinemas. Producers, distributors and exhibitors remain, as they have since the 1940s, reliant on state subsidy, tariffs, quotas or other mechanisms to stay in business.

## The present moment

The unexpected failure of Scotland's minority SNP administration in June 2008 to pass the legislation establishing Creative Scotland, replacing both Scottish Screen and the Scottish Arts Council, was a significant moment in the history of screen industry policy in Scotland. The very fact that the Bill fell largely because of questions over the limited extent of the new body's proposed economic development role (reflecting a deeper internecine conflict over the transfer of Scottish Enterprise resources to Creative Scotland) emphasises just how mainstream the concept of creative industries has become. By the same token, the emergence of something approaching a national debate over the form and functions of the new body dangles the tantalising possibility of a new and broader discursive space with the potential to allow a wider range of interests to interrogate and influence the relationship between economic, cultural and democratic goals in creative industries policy.

Equally significant, perhaps, is how slow the film community has been to fully engage in the debate—reflecting in part the very fragmentation of what was once (in the late 1970s and early 1980s) a much more unified and articulate grouping. Scotland's filmmakers rather belatedly expressed concern at Scottish Screen being subsumed into the new "all art forms" body, raising the alarm some time after the political decision had been made and by means of an *ad hoc* coalition of concerned filmmakers rather than via PACT, the body ostensibly representing filmmakers' interests, but from which they had become increasingly estranged.

It is rather ironic that, having secured independent television producers' economic "breakthrough" in wrestling back programme rights held by the broadcasters, the same broadcasters then withdrew their subsidy of PACT, leading to the closure of its Scottish office just when film and broadcasting policy issues in Scotland were heating up. In a context of revived devolutionary politics, in April 2007 PACT took the decision to centralise its "Nations and Regions" function and in effect dismember its Scottish policy group. The position of the Scottish film lobby has been further undermined by the increasingly negative perception of film production within the enterprise community, and indeed within PACT itself, when compared to the relatively buoyant, if far from untroubled, television sector.

Over the past twenty-five years filmmakers in Scotland have benefited from a protected support system which has privileged their claims to both cultural subsidy and direct financial investment in screen content. That situation is changing rapidly, as television, games and new media producers demand equal status in the subsidy game, basing their claims on economic, cultural and democratic grounds. The arguments are in many respects sound—the ecologies of film and television drama in Scotland *are* intimately intertwined; the case for third-party subsidy of "quality" television, as commercial broadcasters retreat (aided by OFCOM) from their public service broadcasting obligations *is* increasingly persuasive; and the "success" (by whatever criteria you choose to employ) of thirteen years of Lottery investment in film production *is* very debatable. John McVay, CEO of PACT and former Director of Scottish Broadcast and Film Training, put the case "against" film to the Broadcasting Commission thus when discussing the benefits of post-1995 Lottery monies:

> The obsession with film was a big mistake. It should never have been assessed by film it should be assessed by Scottish content and particularly television and building up to Scottish drama because my argument was if you build up Scottish drama you build up Scottish film…you know there's hardly any film producers in Scotland, while there's always been lots of TV people and I think you know, if people….if you look at what is possible, quickest and where the markets are to develop your talent, then telly is better for you because it's quick…cinema is not a good business, it takes years to finance anything if you can, and it doesn't give you any return. (Scottish Broadcast Commission 2007).

Nonetheless, as Scotland continues to redefine its relationship to the politics and policies of the British state we face a significant opportunity to redefine both the terms of the national screen discourse and the relationship between cultural, industrial and social objectives in making the case for public support for cinema. This can only happen, however, if the current debates surrounding the establishment of Creative Scotland, and issues raised by the Scottish Broadcasting Commission, are sustained and enlarged to address the wider aspirations of Scotland's image makers and the audiences they serve. Scottish cinema needs to provoke a debate which can "think the (currently) unthinkable," that is, that there are different but equally sound reasons for public intervention in Scottish filmmaking beyond the once liberating, but now increasingly limiting discourse of "Creative Industries."

What has been conspicuously missing from the past ten years' debate (such as it is) around Scottish film is any sense of a broader vision of the cinema that a multicultural society of over five million people might reasonably expect in ten, twenty or thirty years time. Where and how should indigenously produced film make (if at all) its contribution to national life beyond the economic sphere? In an increasingly globalised, technologically convergent world what should the role of government and public bodies be in addressing not just the old but the new kinds of market failure, cultural exclusion and "claims of right" to creative expression and representation? Given the inevitability of "outcome measures," "balanced scorecards" and all the other paraphernalia of sound administration and "auditability," what should be the success criteria structuring film policy?

Such issues have become urgent matters for debate in the arena of television, as long-cherished but increasingly derided notions of public service broadcasting obligations—funding of the BBC by license fee, regulation of content and advertising, protection of privacy etc.—are challenged by an increasingly vocal lobby calling for a free market in all forms of media. The specific needs of Scottish film as both a cultural and economic practice are in grave danger of being eclipsed by a creative industries doctrine that suppresses discussion of inconvenient cultural or economic truths.

Perhaps it is finally time to accept that for the foreseeable future there is no prospect of a commercially viable, unsubsidised cinema in the UK, far less Scotland, and to engage properly with what that means for public policy and funding north of the border. As a consequence we also need to accept that there cannot be a clear distinction between "commercial" and "subsidised" filmmaking because any intervention to address market "imperfections" is a form of subsidy and all support for "film as art" is also a potential investment in economic outcomes.

In a sense, then, we come full-circle to the discourse of "creative industries" but with a pressing need to wrest power to define the terms of that discourse away from an economistic, technocratic and inevitably self-serving elite, however well meaning. We need to re-invest the "creative industries" concept with a larger set of cultural and social values. Cinema is too important to the identity, imagination and conscience of Scottish society to be left to dwindle away on the margins of a global media industry, at the far end of the "value chain" contributing little more than a few multiplexes-worth of profit to the Hollywood behemoths.

## Works Cited


Broughan, Peter *et al.* 1997. Scottish Stand. *Glasgow Herald*, May 24.

Bruce, David. 1996. *Scotland the Movie*. Edinburgh: Polygon.

Caughie, John. 1983. From 'Scotch Reels' to the 'Highland Fling': The Fourth International Festival of Film and Television in the Celtic Countries. *Cencrastus* 13: 40-42.

Dawtrey, Adam. Flying Scotsman' Defies Gravity. *Variety*, July 23.

Dovetail Management Consultants (1988) *Commercial Opportunities for Scottish Film, Television and Video*. Unpublished report.

Eadie, Douglas. 1973. We can't say meanwhile any more. *Scottish International* September: 25-27.

Greater London Council. 1985. *State of the Art or the Art of the State* London: Greater London Council.

Grigor, Murray. 1976. Editorial. *New Edinburgh Review* 34.2: 2.

Hardy, Forsyth. 1990. *Scotland in Film*. Edinburgh: Edinburgh University Press.

Lister, David. 2001. Scottish Lottery board members 'gave themselves funding for films'. *The Independent*, June 15.

McArthur, Colin. 1976. Politicising Scottish Film Culture. *New Edinburgh Review* 34.2: 8-10.

—. 1982. Introduction. In *Scotch Reels: Scotland in Cinema and Television*, ed. Colin McArthur, 1-6. London: British Film Institute.

—. 1983. Tendencies in the New Scottish Cinema. *Cencrastus* 13: 33-35.

Mcdougall, Liam. 2003. Producers told: Dump Arthouse Movie Flops. *Glasgow Herald*, November 11.

McGill, Brian and Steve McIntyre. 1983. Scottish Film Culture: the High Road and the Low Road. *Cencrastus* 13: 36-37.

McGregor, James. 2001. Lee defends Lottery Film Investment. http://www.netribution.co.uk/news/northern_exposure/67/6.html (accessed August 13, 2008).

—. 2006. Don't let our film industry go down the pan. http://www.netribution.co.uk/2/content/view/681/182/ (accessed August 13, 2008).

McIntyre, Steve. 1994. Vanishing Point: Feature Film Production in a Small Country. In *Border Crossing: Film in Ireland, Britain and Europe,* eds. John Hill et al, 88-111. London/Belfast: British Film Institute/Institute of Irish Studies/University of Ulster.

Mulgan, Geoff and Ken Worpole. 1986. *Saturday Night or Sunday Morning? From Arts to Industry-New Forms of Cultural Policy*. London: Routledge.

Myerscough, John. 1988. *Economic Importance of the Arts in Glasgow*. London: Policy Studies Institute.

PACT Nations and Regions. 2004. An Approach to Screen Production in Scotland.
http://www.scotland.gov.uk/culturalcommission/cultural/files/Ph1%20186%20pact..pdf (accessed August 13, 2008).

Petrie, Duncan. 2000. *Screening Scotland*. London: British Film Institute.

Schlesinger, Philip. 2007. Creativity from Discourse to Doctrine. *Screen* 48.3: 377-388.

Scottish Broadcasting Commission. 2007. Transcript of Oral Evidence, 7 December.

http://www.scottishbroadcastingcommission.gov.uk/Resource/Doc/4/0000394.pdf (accessed August 13, 2008).

Scottish Development Agency *et al.* 1989. *Report of the Scottish Film, TV and Video Working Party*. Glasgow: Scottish Film, T.V. and Video Working Party.

Scottish Screen, 2005. Scottish Screen's response to the DCMS request for information about National Lottery awards. http://www.culture.gov.uk/images/consultations/ScottishScreen.pdf (accessed August 13, 2008).

—. 2006. Skillset Scotland Training Fund http://www.scottishscreen.com/content/sub_page.php?sub_id=152&page_id=30 (accessed August 13, 2008).

Screen Industries Summit Group. 2004. Submission to Phase 1 of Ofcom's Review of Public Service Broadcasting. http://www.ofcom.org.uk/consult/condocs/psb/responses/q_z/ssi.pdf (accessed December 2, 2008).

Taylor, Doreen. 1987. *Scottish Film, T.V. and Video: Survey and prospects for development*. Glasgow: Scottish Film, T.V. and Video Working Party.

# LIST OF CONTRIBUTORS

**Cairns Craig** is Glucksman Professor of Irish and Scottish Studies at the University of Aberdeen, and Director of the AHRC Centre for Irish and Scottish Studies there. He was General Editor of the four-volume *History of Scottish Literature* (Aberdeen University Press, 1987-9). His books include *Out of History* (Polygon, 1996), *The Modern Scottish Novel* (Edinburgh University Press, 1999), *Associationism and the Literary Imagination* (Edinburgh University Press, 2007) and *Intending Scotland* (Edinburgh University Press, 2009).

**Fidelma Farley** has held posts in the Film Studies Departments at University College Dublin, the University of Aberdeen and the National University of Ireland, Galway. She has written about Irish cinema, with a particular focus on gender and post-colonialism, including *This Other Eden* (Cork University Press, 2001), *Anne Devlin* (Flicks Books, 2000) and, most recently, articles on Irish and Scottish cinema, and Irish-language cinema.

**John Hill** is Professor of Media at Royal Holloway, University of London. He was a contributor to *Scotch Reels* (British Film Institute, 1982) and, more recently, was the author of *British Cinema in the 1980s* (Clarendon Press, 1999) and *Cinema and Northern Ireland* (British Film Institute, 2006).

**Robin MacPherson** is Professor in the School of Arts and Creative Industries at Napier University in Edinburgh and has been Director of Screen Academy Scotland since it was established in 2005. A film and television producer since 1989, he has produced a wide range of documentary, current affairs and drama for BBC, Channel 4 and international broadcasters. He received a UK BAFTA nomination in 1996 for his first drama production and a Scottish BAFTA nomination for best documentary in 2004. From 1999 to 2002 he was in charge of Script and Project Development for the national screen agency, Scottish Screen.

**Colin McArthur** has written extensively on Hollywood cinema, British television and Scottish culture. His publications include *Underworld USA* (Secker and Warburg/British Film Institute, 1972), *Television and History*

(British Film Institute, 1978), *Dialectic! Left Film Criticism from* Tribune (Key Texts, 1978), *Scotch Reels: Scotland in Cinema and Television* (British Film Institute, 1982; contributing editor) and *Brigadoon, Braveheart and the Scots: Distortions of Scotland in Hollywood Cinema* (I. B. Tauris, 2003). He has also written books on individual films: *The Big Heat* (British Film Institute, 1993), *Casablanca* (Half Brick Images, 1992), *Whisky Galore! and The Maggie* (I. B. Tauris, 2003). Formerly Head of the Distribution Division of the British Film Institute, he is currently a stallholder in a London antiques market, a role he struggles to render compatible with that of independent scholar.

**David Martin-Jones** lectures in Film Studies at The University of St Andrews. He is the author of *Deleuze, Cinema and National Identity* (Edinburgh University Press, 2006), and of the forthcoming *Scotland: Global Cinema* (Edinburgh University Press, 2009). He has published articles in a number of international journals, including *Cinema Journal, Screen, The Journal of British Cinema and Television* and *CineAction.*

**Christopher Meir** is Lecturer in Film at the University of the West Indies, St. Augustine in Trinidad and Tobago. He completed a PhD project at the University of Warwick on film policy and Scottish cinema and has published research on Scottish cinema, documentary film-making and Canadian cinema. He is currently preparing a manuscript based on his doctoral thesis and working on a comparative study of the film industries of the nations of the Commonwealth.

**Neil Mulholland** is Director of the Centre for Visual & Cultural Studies and Reader in Contemporary Art Theory at Edinburgh College of Art, Scotland. He is the author of The Cultural Devolution: Art in Britain in the Late Twentieth Century (Ashfield, 2003) and curator of a wide range of recent exhibitions, including *Ye Ye* (French Institute, Edinburgh, 2007), *Young Athenians* (Athens Biennial, 2007) and *Strategic Art Getts* (The Embassy, Edinburgh, 2005.

**Jonathan Murray** is Lecturer in Film and Visual Culture at Edinburgh College of Art. He is the author of *That Thinking Feeling: A Research Guide to Scottish Cinema, 1938 - 2004* (Edinburgh College of Art/Scottish Screen, 2005), *Discomfort and Joy: the Cinema of Bill Forsyth* (Peter Lang, forthcoming), *The New Scottish Cinema* (I. B. Tauris, forthcoming) and the co-editor of *Constructing The Wicker Man: Film and Cultural Studies Perspectives* (University of Glasgow Crichton Publications, 2005) and *The Quest for The Wicker Man: History, folklore and Pagan perspectives* (Luath Press, 2006).

**Sarah Neely** is a member of the Stirling Media Research Institute and a Lecturer in the department of Film, Media & Journalism at the University of Stirling. Her research focuses on Scottish and Irish film and literature. She has also written on a number of areas of film adaptation including the heritage genre, adaptations of Shakespeare, and the use of classic literature in the teenpic.

**Duncan Petrie** is a Professor in the new department of Theatre, Film and Television at the University of York. He is the author of six books: *Creativity and Constraint in the British Film Industry* (Macmillan, 1991), *The British Cinematographer* (BFI, 1996), *Screening Scotland* (BFI, 2000), *Contemporary Scottish Fictions* (Edinburgh University Press, 2004), *Shot in New Zealand: The Art and Craft of the Kiwi* Cinematographer (Random House, 2006) and *A Coming of Age: 30 Years of New Zealand Film* (Random House, 2008) and editor or co-editor of a further ten, including *The Cinema of Small Nations* (Edinburgh University Press, 2007), co-edited by Mette Hjort.

**Alan Riach** is a poet and Professor of Scottish Literature at Glasgow University. Currently President of the Association for Scottish Literary Studies, he is also the general editor of the *Collected Works* of Hugh MacDiarmid (Carcanet), the author of *Representing Scotland in Literature, Popular Culture and Iconography* (Palgrave Macmillan, 2005) and co-author with Alexander Moffat of *Arts of Resistance: Poets, Portraits and Landscapes of Modern Scotland* (Luath, 2008). His fourth book of poems, *Clearances* (2001), follows *First & Last Songs* (1995), *An Open Return* (1991) and *This Folding Map* (1990). His radio series *The Good of the Arts*, first broadcast in New Zealand 2001, may be visited at http://www.southwest.org.nz

**Marilyn Reizbaum** is Professor of English at Bowdoin College. Her scholarship is in the areas of Modernisms, contemporary Scottish and Irish literatures and culture, and Jewish cultural theory. She is the author of *James Joyce's Judaic Other* (Stanford University Press, 1999), and numerous essays on Joyce; and she is coeditor with Kimberly Devlin of *Ulysses: En-gendered Perspectives—Eighteen New Essays on the Episodes* (South Carolina University Press, 1999). Her current book project is titled *The Inversion of the Jews: Scientism and Modern Arts.*

**Alistair Scott** is Senior Lecturer in Film and Television at Napier University, Edinburgh. After a career as a television director and independent producer he began teaching at the University of the West of Scotland in 2005. His documentaries include *Raploch Stories* (2001 and 2007, BBC Scotland); *Postcards from Sighthill* (2001, Scottish Television); *Execution at Camp 21* (1999, Channel 4); *Children under fire* (1993, Channel 4); *Leithers* (1987, Channel 4); *Two Painters Amazed* (1986, BBC). He was a postgraduate student at the National Film and Television School in the early 1980s.

**Jane Sillars** is Teaching Fellow in Film and Media and the University of Stirling. She has published work on questions of nationality and identity, particularly in relation to film and television in Scotland, gender, sexuality and Scottish film, and postcoloniality and European cinema in journals such as *Studies in French Cinema* and *Screen* and edited collections including *The Media in Britain: current debates and developments* (MacMillan, 1999) and *The Media in Scotland* (Edinburgh University Press, 2008).

**David Stenhouse** is a Senior Producer at BBC Scotland, Visiting Professor of Journalism and English Studies at the University of Strathclyde and the author of *On the Make: How the Scots took over London* (Mainstream, 2004).

**Rod Stoneman** is the Director of the Huston School of Film & Digital Media at the National University of Ireland, Galway. He was Chief Executive of Bord Scannán na hÉireann/the Irish Film Board until September 2003 and previously a Deputy Commissioning Editor in the Independent Film and Video Department at Channel 4 Television. He has made a number of documentaries including *Ireland: The Silent Voices* (1983), *Italy: the Image Business* (1984) and *12,000 Years of Blindness* (2007) and written extensively on film and television. His most recent book, *Chávez: The Revolution Will Not Be Televised*, was published by Wallflower Press in 2008.

**Sarah Street** is Professor of Film at the University of Bristol. Her publications include *British National Cinema* (Routledge, 1997 and second, expanded edition, 2008), *Costume and Cinema: Dress Codes and Popular Film* (Wallflower Press, 2001), *Transatlantic Crossings: British Feature Films in the USA* (Continuum, 2002), *Black Narcissus* (I. B. Tauris, 2005) and (co-authored with Tim Bergfelder and Sue Harris), *Film*

*Architecture and the Transnational Imagination: Set Design in 1930s European Cinema* (Amsterdam University Press, 2007). She is a co-editor of the *Journal of British Cinema and Television* and of *Screen.*

VERMONT CO
MONTPELIER, VT
P9-CDK-499

# LEARNING HOW TO LEARN

# LEARNING HOW TO LEARN

AN AMERICAN APPROACH TO MONTESSORI

*by Nancy McCormick Rambusch*

*Foreword by* Dr. George N. Shuster

*A Montessori Bibliography of Materials in the English Language, 1909-1961*
*Compiled by* Gilbert E. Donahue

HELICON BALTIMORE — DUBLIN

Helicon Press, Inc.
1120 N. Calvert St.
Baltimore 2, Maryland

Helicon Limited
53 Capel Street
Dublin, Ireland

*Library of Congress Catalog Card Number: 62-13977*



2nd Printing
February, 1963

*Photographs by* SUZANNE SZASZ
*Courtesy of* THE SATURDAY EVENING POST

PRINTED IN THE UNITED STATES OF AMERICA
BY GARAMOND PRESS, BALTIMORE, MARYLAND

# Foreword

Here is a book which says in effect that common sense in education has been uncommon. It is right about that. Teachers had devised a bright formula that read pretty much as follows: if we fill a room with little Susans and Johns and start them doing things together, they will acquire the art of "social adjustment" which in turn will insure the vitality of our democratic society. By now it is evident that the formula has worked out only too well. Our youngsters are so well adjusted that by the time they reach maturity they are as much alike as the dressing tables the Navy bought during the War for the WAVES.

Mrs. Rambusch, in seeking to reestablish the right of the child to be himself or herself, starts with Maria Montessori in the center of her scheme of things but does not assume that everything knowable about children was in the mind of that remarkable woman. But it is good to have her back. Many people retain the erroneous impression that in the Montessori world a child did what it pleased. What she said may be very briefly and no doubt too crudely stated as, a child will want to find out what it can do provided it can be helped to do so. This means—and to some ears will sound relatively horrendous—it will actually be anxious to *work*.

That learning to read at three can be for some children as exciting as stringing beads or jumping was news to a certain school of pedagogy until experiment began to prove it was the truth. We have, in short, been wasting a lot of the nation's time. But this is only the beginning. You can help young people of four

or five to make choices, to determine whom they wish to be like. Moreover, as the author says, "competence breeds confidence." I like this very much.

Perhaps the best thing about Mrs. Rambusch's discussion of the Montessori approach to education is that, for all the profound and exultant faith in that method which it professes, it is solidly aware of much that has been found out and written by others. You can pick this book up almost anywhere and find somebody being quoted who has something useful to say. And what the sum-total of this is may perhaps be distilled in the judgment that the Montessori world is one in which the teacher acquires new meaning. She does not merely take the place of a parent. Nor does she merely whistle tunes from a rule book. She—and I quote with delight—protects the child's "right to learn." That should be the most inalienable of rights.

George N. Shuster

# Preface

SCHOOLS HAVE existed for three thousand years, but children have been around for a lot longer than that. Any discussion of educational improvement must give at least equal emphasis to who is to be improved and what will improve him. How much of what young children by nature possess needs proving—and how much improving—is the subject of this book. The complex history of progressivism in education provides the background for educational soul-searching, and the genesis of books like this one. Theoretically, a generation of argumentative, articulate and critical adults should provide an audience.

A re-evaluation of the theories of Maria Montessori is inevitable in a decade of educational discussion presaged by Bernard Iddings Bell's *Crisis in Education.* Montessori was a doctor of medicine, and a pioneer in psychiatry, child development and educational theory. Her work spanned the first half of our century—she and John Dewey died in the same year.

Montessori's ideas are challenging on two counts. She anticipated many trends in current early learning research. She conceived of an early education in many respects dramatically unlike the present stereotyped American nursery and kindergarten. Montessori believed that social adjustment was integrally related to a strong sense of accomplishment. She viewed the years between three and six as those years in which both the habits and the bases of learning were established.

Montessori's view of the child is too vast to be encompassed in any description of her separate ideas. She saw the child as Savior

of Man. She saw in his freedom to construct himself the transformation of a new adult generation better able to solve the dilemmas of an adult world. One need not accept uncritically Montessori's notion of anthropometrics; one need not imitate the adulation of Montessori's uncritical admirers who state flatly that the ills of the world would have been solved had she been heeded, or will be solved if she now is heeded. An innovator of Maria Montessori's stature needs neither the assent of the world to every particle of her thought nor the defense of zealots who panic at any form of criticism directed against her. If Montessori has a message for America in the nineteen-sixties, it is because of those of her ideas and methods which relate to present preoccupations and techniques in early education.

In an effort to find more effective solutions to learning at all levels, can Americans do less than look again at Montessori?

NANCY McCORMICK RAMBUSCH

January 6th
1962

# Table of Contents

# LEARNING HOW TO LEARN

# Introduction

THE CHILD emerges into society through his family, modified by it and by the educational opportunities provided both by the family and by the larger world. Depending on environmental emphasis, the child moves toward conformity, adjustment and acquiescence or toward individuality, autonomy and awareness. The child become adult may choose to submit uncritically to the forces that have molded him, or he may protest constructively against them. If adults are not themselves aware of the forces that have shaped *them,* how can they hope to free their children from their own limitations?

As Americans we pay lip service to the notions of freedom and liberty. In the abstract, we believe in both. But as qualities to be engendered in our children, awareness of freedom and liberty have become increasingly difficult to transmit. Why is this so? What is the chemistry of these responsible virtues? Has the reason been glimpsed in such recent polls as the "Study of American Adolescents" reported in the *Saturday Evening Post* (December 23, 1961), where the researchers lamented the preponderance of "nice kids" and the probable consequences of being "nice" as stated by Leo Durocher: "Nice guys finish last"?

Part of the difficulty in the transmission of values to today's children comes from parental and cultural confusion concerning what education ought to be doing. Education is not simply a method for the imparting of a standard knowledge of correct behavior. It is the provision of "good habits and sound principles as to help (the child) to take cognizance of his human nature,

and to furnish him with the elements of knowledge and the lines along which he may most fully discover how to adapt himself to his condition."[1]

Margaret Mead believes that we place altogether too much confidence in the educational process. "Not until we realize that a poor culture will never become rich, though it be filtered through the expert methods of innumerable pedagogues, and that a rich culture with no system at all will leave its children better off than a poor culture with the best systems in the world, will we begin to solve our educational problem. Once we lose faith in the blanket formula of education, in the magic fashion in which education, using the passive capacities of the children, is to create something out of nothing, we can turn our attention to the vital matter of developing individuals, who as adults can gradually mold our old patterns into newer and richer forms."[2]

American education has placed emphasis on activity rather than passivity for the past two generations. The current adult generation has lost faith in the blanket formula of education. Yet how can we now achieve those "new and richer forms" of which Mead speaks?

Parents are understandably confused about what conditions promote the development of individuality in children. How can that which makes a child *different* be protected and nurtured, but in such a way that he is also capable of working with his fellows? There is a distinction that must be made here between a need of others, and a need to be something to others. In a society apparently oriented toward conformity and oversocialization among its young, one can legitimately wonder *who* cares enough (to do anything about it) that today's children be free, autonomous and ruggedly individual?

Schools have been as timid as parents in recognizing the importance of the child as an individual. The shift in emphasis away from the group has begun only within the last decade, in American education. Social adjustment, "getting along with others," had become a goal on a par with intellectual learning, the once traditional goal of the school. Robert Lindner has excoriated the "adjusted," parents and children, thus: "Adjustment, that synonym for conformity that comes more easily to the

modern tongue, is the theme of our swan song, the piper's tune to which we dance on the brink of the abyss, the siren's melody that destroys the senses and paralyzes our wills. But this is known only to the few who have penetrated its disguises and glimpsed the death's head beneath; for many, adjustment is the only way of life they know . . ."[3]

There are critical rumblings throughout the land, presumably from those adults who have escaped "adjustment," those refusing to be supine in the face of group pressure. One sizable group now wondering "out loud" is comprised of college-educated parents. Many of them are better educated (in terms of content, if not method) than those teaching their children. But those parents not content to accept uncritically the nostrums of educators are not yet numerous, though their ranks do appear to be growing.

At present there is no organized underground ready to rise, armed with McGuffey Eclectic Readers, to revamp the schools. There is, however, precedent that just such a thing could happen in the history of the Progressive Education Association. In 1918 Stanwood Cobb spoke of the then emergent group: "I had a vision of the vast numbers of mothers, heartily dissatisfied with the present methods of education, reaching out for newer and better methods—a splendid potential material upon which to form an educational reform movement."[4] Those mothers, long gone, are being replaced by vaster numbers, equally anxious.

Young mothers are concerned with education at the "optional" level (that is, below the age of six) as well as at the formal level. They see their young children attempting to learn but, paralyzed into non-intervention, they let their children founder until the first grade. The source of many a parental trauma is to be found within the ranks of nursery and kindergarten teachers, within a group which expresses resistance, and frequently hostility, to certain kinds of learning experiences among young children (principally experiences leading to academic learning). Many a child eager to begin reading at three or four is being re-routed into bead-stringing and block play by teachers completely convinced that the child is not "ready" to learn, when frequently it is the teacher who is not "ready" to teach him.

Dr. Omar K. Moore's work at Hamden Hall in teaching children of two-and-a-half and three to read (which has precedents in the work of Locke and Montessori), simply leaves this group unmoved. The criteria of much early education continue to be predicated, for them, exclusively on social adjustment. What does it merit a five-year-old to *read*, one is told, if he doesn't *jump* satisfactorily? These teachers find repugnant the notion that children actually derive pleasure from the exertion involved in what is to them "work." On seeing children so intent on a structured sensory-motor activity that they frown in concentration, the adult reaction is as often one of pity as of pleasure. To see young children "work" means to many teachers of the young a return to the crueler aberrations of the pre-Industrial Revolution. The hypothesis that the nursery-age child, as an individual, is more important than that child as a member of a group (which in fact is largely teacher-oriented), is an unsettling one. The thought of children learning early some of the "ground rules" of later academic life disturbs many teachers, who see the "preschool" education of the child as quite discontinuous with his later school life—despite the fact that as Americans we agree quite largely with the proposition that education should be continuous with life.

The crisis of discontinuity in early education is best seen in those children who reach "school age" without having reached the appropriate measurable level of intellectual or social or emotional maturity. In the lockstep arrangement of American formal education, the child's developmental gears must be meshed by age six if he is to put his foot firmly and competently on the first rung of the academic ladder, as it has been designed. If he is unready in one of these areas of development, it is "back to kindergarten—to cutting, pasting, and reading-readiness." In the event that he is the victim of an adult misjudgment and is in the first grade, where he does not "belong," there is no other course open to him but the repetition of the year. In a culture priding itself on flexibility and ingenuity in dealing with practical problems, why so little headway has been made in American schools in the proper placement of children between five and seven remains a significant question.

Maria Montessori advanced the notion of what has come to be called the "ungraded primary class" sixty years ago. She recognized that the child might easily function at different levels of development in the three areas of intellectual, social and emotional maturity. In a class with a three-year age span the child would be able to work at one level intellectually and socialize at another. Dr. Paul Woodring's recent espousal of this pattern, despite the practical problems of programming that it raises, heralds an educational breakthrough.[5] Montessori carried the idea of grouping children in three-year age spans below the age of six. Her concept of the first class (not called the "pre-school") was of a group of children from three to six, obviously representing varied stages of development.

As a matter of fact, the word "school" is understandably vague to most three-year-olds. Often it is associated with the notebook, paper, pencils and lunchboxes of older brothers and sisters. Many American three-year-olds are "ready" for school. But reliable data on the number of mothers of three-year-olds "ready" to have them leave home are more difficult to obtain. The attitude of the parents to the new adventure does much to affect the child's entry into that world outside his own family circle. The first school experience of the young child forms a vestibule between the little world of family and the larger world of life. There are elements of both worlds in it. Many young children associate school with learning, and learning with reading, writing and computation; they reject certain activities as "babyish" and espouse others as suitable for "big" boys and girls.

If, as Montessori has suggested, the environment "should reveal the child and not mould him," this real interest in academic learning at an early age deserves a sympathetic hearing on the teacher's part. Granted, one does not teach a three-year-old as one teaches a six-year-old. But it is quite another thing to say that a three-year-old is not capable of the beginnings of so-called "academic" learning through materials designed to motivate and stimulate him through sensory-motor activity. It is one that Montessori attempts to answer in the larger context of helping the child to construct himself. The task of helping children achieve confidence and competence as learners depends to a greater

degree on his first rather than his last teachers. We have for the most part been content to offer children the illusion of achievement rather than the fact, through practices designed to make all children participants in group activity on an identical level, despite individual differences.

In the complex and competitive culture of the next decade, the goals of early education must be related to terminal educational goals. Yet Robert Maynard Hutchins points out that although "Now, we confront new problems, the solution of which is crucial to us and to all civilization. . . . *Nothing is more striking than the absence of connection between the basic problems of America and the education program of America.*"[6] A culturally relevant educational pattern for young children will respond to the increased emphasis on academic achievement throughout American life. "Never for a moment has Montessori envisaged the taking of the growing child out of its century, or the adapting of it to any state of civilization except that to which it is born."[7]

A culturally relevant educational pattern for young children will also take cognizance of Jerome Bruner's words on the content of learning: "We begin with the hypothesis that any subject can be taught effectively in some intellectually honest form to any child at any stage of development. It is a bold hypothesis and an essential one in thinking about the nature of a curriculum. No evidence exists to contradict it; considerable evidence is being amassed that supports it."[8]

In discussing early education, one faces a two-fold problem. What are the aims of education for the young, and what methods appear most effectively valid in implementing these aims. Maria Montessori specified both the aims and the means of early education. The Montessori approach to learning (and it is an approach rather than a method) consists in the application of a certain set of principles regarding the child, his will and his need to learn. They are utilized by all those working with him. These principles in their "working out," their articulation, must take into account not only the culture in which the child finds himself, but the expectations of that culture for the child as an adult. In certain cultures the boys need only to fish and hunt and the girls need only sew and tend the fire. In others, such as ours, the

demands of literacy alone complicate the task of early learning. By the time an American child is six and in the first grade, time is already running out for him.

The idea of teaching the very young through their own activity is not a recent one. Long before "learning by doing" was dreamt of by John Dewey, Aristotle had recommended it. His views were seconded by Montaigne and Rousseau, who believed in "teaching the very young with real things." The burning question in an activity-oriented school is how much should the children *do*, and for how long. An understanding of the way in which children appear to learn makes the use of structured learning materials relevant when they are small and irrelevant when they are old enough to dispense with them. Motor thinking cannot be substituted for abstract thinking too long, if the child is ever to think abstractly.

There were many "educational toys" designed by Maria Montessori as one component of an approach to learning admirably suited to the disposition, talents and development of the young child. They constitute an aid to learning at an age when the child cannot communicate ideas verbally to adults. The Montessori approach to learning reflects the child's immediate need to know and the development of dispositions (attitudes) in him which make learning possible and pleasurable to him. Lest this statement be construed as meaning that "learning" and "fun" are interchangeable words, one must say that the words which Montessori interchanges are "learning" and "work" (even though the sense of work in the young is different from that of the adult).

A positive attitude toward the challenge and inevitability of working to learn can be engendered in children at a very early age. If children perceive early the equation between effort and accomplishment, they are being realistically prepared for a life of learning. If they do not perceive this equation and are allowed to persist in their early years in a "learning" situation quite discontinuous with one they will be expected to enter at the age of six, then early education is doing more to unfit them for the reality of school life than to prepare them for it.

In speaking of the "old-fashioned" basic education he received some forty years ago, Clifton Fadiman mentions what that edu-

cation gave him: "A foundation on which later on, within the limits of my abilities, I could erect any intellectual structure I fancied. It gave me a wherewithal for the self-education that should be every man's concern to the hour of his death."[9] The process of education is not bounded by the nursery school and the college diploma, though the process of instruction may be. The disposition to learn comes not only from the interest of what is to be learned but from the value assigned by society to learning in the first place. Children who are avid readers generally come from families of avid readers. What is engendered in the child by the example of the adults with whom he is most closely associated will form the basis of his values.

Young children will learn no matter what adults may do or not do—the question is, *what* will they learn. The world of the television screen with its cartoons and patronizing EmCee's doling out behavioral advice about crossing streets and drinking chocolate milk "like all the other kids" does provide instruction in these twin arts. Yet, the belief that the noisy, inane world of animation corresponds to the interests of the child only promotes hyperactivity in him. Restlessness, institutionalized in many nursery schools and kindergartens, makes it increasingly difficult for him to settle down and focus on tasks requiring attention and energy. We know children are capable of prodigious concentration, if we have watched them practicing tying their shoes or repeating incessantly some activity, apparently meaningless to an adult.

This ability to concentrate and develop an "attention span" is part of the expected human skills a child needs to learn. Assuming that whatever learning he is presented is accessible to him at his particular stage of development, the habit of working is still one he must *develop.* If he does not develop the work habit when he is small, he will not survive an education that continues to be so much fun that little is demanded of him, or an education that makes tremendous demands he is unable to meet because he has been ill-prepared through earlier school experiences. Children must, in short, *learn how to learn.* This is an acquired, not a natural skill, and if it is not learned before the age of six, it is questionable whether many children will ever learn it. Among

the many insights that fifty years of unremitting labor in the service of the child brought Maria Montessori was her discovery of the child's need to "accomplish" himself through work. By work, Montessori did not mean work for the sake of achievement, but work for the sake of self-development.

The pendulum of American education has swung away in the past few years from the well-adjusted illiterate. In a culture whose minimum academic requirement is literacy, the millions of children who *do not read,* either because they have not been effectively taught or because of their own incapability, are a growing national concern. If children can be set early on the path to learning those skills which will be demanded of them, inexorably, in the early years of elementary school, they will be free to use the skills for the acquisition of knowledge. Early learning, too long optional in our culture, needs to be regarded from a new perspective. Can we, as a nation, afford to promote illiteracy in the guise of an early learning so socially oriented that it frequently unfits children to sit down to the serious business of the three R's?

The amount of research on how children learn is mounting rapidly. But the lag between the research and the classroom practice in nursery school and kindergarten is staggering. From the time Montessori's "new" children appeared in her first Casa dei Bambini in 1907, they showed themselves capable of attitudes hitherto unseen in young children. It was not their performance (which was precocious, but a byproduct), but their ability to work with relish, that struck those adults who saw them. The revolt against the excesses of the over-disciplined child is over. The revolt against the under-disciplined child is gaining momentum. Self-learning is the key to that inner discipline so necessary for anyone who will educate himself to the hour of his death. If American education does not accept the key, having found it, educational reforms at higher levels will benefit only those children who already know how to learn. Those who have never *learned how to learn* will be no more than another generation of "hollow men."

PART I

# The Child

CHAPTER I

# Montessori and the Casa dei Bambini

Maria Montessori's view of the role of the child was too vast to be encompassed in any description of her merely pedagogical ideas. She saw the need for a new adult attitude toward the child. If the adult could free the child to realize his true, though hidden, potentialities, the child would be transformed, and as an adult would in turn transform this world. The child could then fulfill the role for which he was created, to be the Hope of Man. She questioned the foundations of an education that had been producing "results" rather than co-creating whole human persons, for Montessori saw the child as the creator of himself. What he would become—the pallid reflection of necessarily limited parents, or a mature adult transcending the previous generation—depended on the adults' ability to free him so that he might become truly himself. She questioned the efficacy, in its then present form, of the "main, though not the only instrument of education . . . an odd invention three thousand years old, the school."[1]

Montessori made no claim to absolute originality of thought. A doctor, she drew inspiration from the work of two French predecessors, Jean Marc Gaspard Itard (1775-1838) and Edouard Seguin (1812-1880). Itard, whose work with the "savage of Aveyron," a wild boy discovered by hunters in the South of France, reared away from man, had made an effort to determine what the education of such a person of "apparent idiotism" would involve.

Edouard Seguin, the foremost teacher of mental defectives of

his day, developed a method of "physiological education." He had perceived clearly that the brain is not an organ existing and functioning independently of the nervous system of which it is a part. He appreciated that body and mind in the human being constitute an organic unity. He realized that the function of education is to complement the organic development of the child. Seguin believed the condition called "idiocy" was largely the effect of causes producing retardation of physical and mental development, and could be partially and often completely cured by an education of the muscular, sensorial and nervous systems. Seguin's work, "as early as 1842-43, was known to Horace Mann and George Sumner; they were familiar with our personal labors at Bicêtre, on which they wrote approvingly, sending over the seeds which soon rose from American soil."[2] In his opinion, the two areas most crucial to development are muscular and sensorial. Studying the work of Seguin, one sees the obvious influence that it exerted on Montessori. She was to say later that the work of these two great men, representing forty years of their labor, was seconded by a ten-year period of her own personal investigations with all kinds of children, abnormal and normal, and this half-century of cumulative activity gave rise to her hypotheses on education.

In 1907, when Maria Montessori initiated her first *Casa dei Bambini* (Children's House) in a tenement of Rome's San Lorenzo district, it was a matter of understandable speculation why she should turn her attention to this humble level of learning. She was by then Professor of Anthropology at the University of Rome, and an external University Examiner (together with Luigi Pirandello, the playwright). However, her previous work in medicine, psychiatry and "special education" had prepared her admirably for the work she was unknowingly beginning. A Housing Association, desirous of protecting its investment, offered Montessori some space in one of its buildings to provide custodial care for the young tenement children with a view to preventing vandalism.

For this initial work, Montessori chose two untutored young women who were able to carry out her wishes uncritically. She remarked later that had they been school teachers, conventionally

trained, they would probably not have been able to do this. Montessori had been given some toys by her wealthy philanthropic friends for the children, and also introduced to them the "apparatus" of her own making which she had previously developed from her studies and in her work with defective children in the Orthophrenic School which she had directed.

She discovered that the children were more attracted to the materials she provided than the toys, and that they seemed to evidence a joy in order and a pleasure in work which she had not foreseen. The children delighted in the performance of the simplest household tasks. "Education," Montessori said, "is a work of self organization, by which man adapts himself to the conditions of life. We find the beginnings of self organization for the child in the works which by us have been considered to be the humblest and lowest forms of work—the exercises of practical life (those tasks of a generally domestic nature)—the putting of the environment in order. These things co-ordinate the mind and fix the attention in a simple manner. They are a necessary preparation for subsequent constructive work."[3] But Montessori's statement of the apparently simple did not derive from any ignorance of educational theory. "If in the end I have put aside the complicated and come down to the simple, surely anyone ought to see that it is because, after a lifetime of study, I am finally convinced that the simple things which have hitherto been neglected are the most vital."[4]

CHAPTER 2

# Insights

## *The Child's Rhythm of Life*

It is often possible to distill from an original thinker the principle animating a whole complex thought structure. Students of Montessori would acknowledge her principle to be the fundamental difference between the child and the adult: *The child is in a constant state of growth and metamorphosis, whereas the adult has reached the norm of the species.* One is reminded of Ortega y Gasset's comment that "every life is, more or less, a ruin among whose debris we have to discover what the person ought to have been."

The emphasis on the child as a being in the *process* of metamorphosis reflects the biological analogies made by Montessori to the transforming nature of growth in the child. The child ends other than he began. Although he anticipates his final form genetically, environment greatly modifies his capacity for self-realization. The adult *is;* the child *is free to become.* Montessori's notion of the prepared environment, of "liberty within limits," of the periods of sensitivity, and the rest, can be subsumed in the governing notion of the child's transformation.

It is the child who *constructs* himself. He masters himself and his environment through the help given him by adults, not *through* adults. The child "is" before he knows that he "is," and the discovery of himself absorbs much of his early energy. Then comes the discovery of that larger world of sensation and idea which he masters on the way to becoming a communicative, social and intelligent person.

The child, rational by virtue of his nature, wants to learn. As Gardner Murphy has recently expressed it: "It is the responsibility and privilege of the teacher to encourage, to give freedom, to swing wide the gates wherever the child's or adolescent's mind wants to explore, to make contact, to know, to grasp, to assimilate the new. This involves three steps. First comes encouragement of the child's sheer *sensitiveness* to the charm, the challenge, the mystery of this wonderful world and protection of the warm response to sensory, motor and cognitive challenge. Second, aid to formation of strong canalizations on sensory, motor and cognitive content and the forming of positive canalizations upon the self as creator. Third, the freedom to move from infantile, direct wish fulfilling fantasies (Freud's primary process thinking) to a controlled and ordered thinking in which cravings are fulfilled by dealing with reality (secondary process)."[1]

Bearing in mind the fundamental difference that Montessori noted between children and adults, we can see that the attitude of a child to his activity provides a dramatic illustration of this difference. An adult works to complete a project. He bears in mind that time is passing as he is working. He works for profit rather than pleasure. Frequently, adults forget the different rhythm of the child and do not allow enough time for children to act unhurriedly. Children are taught to "speed up" their performance by an emphasis on completing a task or test accurately within a fixed time. The young child has, in his own view, all the time in the world. And he needs this time. The number of perpetually harassed mothers who tell their children to stop dawdling and get it finished, whether "it" be supper or dressing, is legion.

Many a mother whisks a three-year-old into a snowsuit over his vociferous protest and plea to do it himself. She has not considered that if he is to dress himself he needs more than the five minutes allotted him by her. Any thirty-year-old adult can zip a snowsuit in seconds. Few three-year-olds can. *Nor are they inclined to.* A young child is quite prone to unzip himself after he has finished zipping. He does not have the supermarket in mind as he gets into his snowsuit. He is much more absorbed

in the business of the immediate present. Consequently, he could spend a happy half-hour zipping and unzipping his suit.

The role of repetition in the child seems related to his tremendous "inner" energy. G. K. Chesterton writes of the role of repetition in man and nature: "It is supposed that if a thing goes on repeating itself it is probably dead. . . . People feel that if the universe was personal it would vary; if the sun were alive it would dance. . . . The sun rises every morning. I do not rise every morning; but the variation is due not to my activity but to my inaction. . . . The thing I mean can be seen for instance in children, when they find some game or joke that they specially enjoy. A child kicks his legs rhythmically through excess, not absence, of life. Because children have abounding vitality . . . therefore they want things repeated and unchanged."[2]

One of the most interesting results of the work pattern of the child, as observed by Montessori, was the absence of fatigue that it engendered. This may seem difficult to believe for American parents of young children. In Montessori classes children are offered the possibility of stopping their work at any time. Yet it is common for them, at the ages of three to five, to work uninterruptedly for two hours, sometimes changing activities but continuing in the pattern of purposeful work.

Montessori believed that the reform of education would need consideration on a far vaster and more fundamental scale than mere curriculum reform. The very structure of the school would need to be called into question. The solution for constructive education would be *more* rather than *less* work for young children as restlessness and inactivity, both promoting eventual intellectual sloth, begin in early childhood as do industry and interest. The adult working with children needs to respect, not despise, the capacities within the child.

## *The Absorbent Mind*

Montessori refers to the period of life between birth and three as one in which not only the intelligence but all the psychic faculties are being formed. "It is the period of creation; because before, nothing existed; since the individuality starts from zero. Here

we are confronted, then, not only with something which is developing, but with a creation that starts with nothing (except of course a potentiality). To accomplish this miracle, the newly born infant *must* possess a different type of mind from ours, endowed with different powers . . . there is no consciousness in the small child, no will; both have yet to be created . . . if we call our type of mind conscious, then we must describe that of the child as unconscious."[3]

As an example of the way in which the child's mind works "unconsciously," Montessori chooses the development of his skill in the use of language simply through living in the environment in which it is spoken. If more than one language is found in the environment, the child assimilates them all. With Whitehead, she realized that children master apparent difficulties with ease. "It is not true that the easier subjects should precede the harder. On the contrary, some of the hardest must come first because nature so dictates, and because they are essential to life. The first intellectual task which confronts an infant is the acquirement of spoken language. What an appalling task, the correlation of meaning with sounds! It requires an analysis of ideas and an analysis of sounds. We all know that the infant does it, and that the miracle of his achievement is explicable. But so are all miracles, and yet to the wise they remain miracles. All I ask is that with this example staring us in the face we should cease talking nonsense about postponing the harder subjects."[4]

Montessori underscores the relation of mobility to development. "When the child begins to move, his absorbent mind has already taken in the world unconsciously. Now, as he starts to move, he becomes conscious. If you watch a child of two, or even one, he is always manipulating something. This means that—while he is manipulating with his hands—he is bringing into consciousness what his subconscious mind had already taken in before. It is through this experience of objects in his environment, in the guise of playing, that he goes over again the impressions that he has already taken in with his conscious mind. It is by means of this 'work'—for it is as much work as play—that he becomes conscious and constructs himself. He develops himself by means of his hands, using them as instruments of human intelligence."[5]

The importance of *all* the stages of movement preparatory to walking—creeping, crawling, and standing—as neurologically constructive, accompanies this first phase of development. It is the way the child is constructing himself as an instrument of learning. In the period between three and six, as the child becomes more aware of himself, he acts on the environment through movement. Though he is in society, he is not a consciously social being for some time.

The task of the adult in these early years of learning is to help the child in the construction of himself. Direct intervention in his activity by an adult will not do for him what he can do for himself, by himself. The genesis of Dr. Montessori's notion of the "prepared environment," the learning and living situation designed for the small child, is a reflection of her understanding of the adult role: to dispose to learning, not to impose it. It is also in the light of this role for the adult that Montessori's insistence on the untapped riches of the pre-adolescent child must be understood. At approximately that point at which the child is able to think abstractly, he passes into a new phase of growth. The child shows an interest in morality; he begins to make judgments; he is aware of cause and effect relationships; he is capable of accumulating masses of information. This is the age at which Montessori believes that reservoirs of knowledge should be tapped, when children should be taught as much as their voracious appetites demand. "All other factors sink into insignificance beside the importance of feeding the hungry intelligence and opening up vast fields of knowledge to eager exploration."[6]

Montessori recognized that the young child absorbs almost all of his early learning from the environment in which he is placed. He absorbs the attitudes of his parents toward him and toward each other, without any need to recognize their adult patterns of speech. He constructs language, grammar and syntax from the environment in which he hears language used, first at the level of tonality and then at the level of meaningful speech. Any observant adult could chart the progress of a child from the moment of the articulation of his first sound to the point at which he is able to use the personal pronoun "I" correctly and to generate sentences apparently learned unconsciously. Dr. Bruner has recently

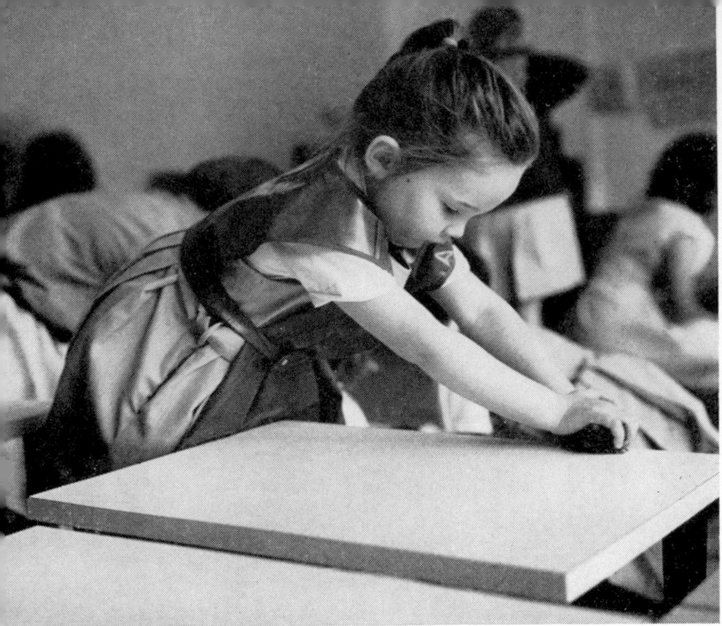

This little girl is washing a table according to a complex ritual designed to satisfy the child as much as to clean the table.

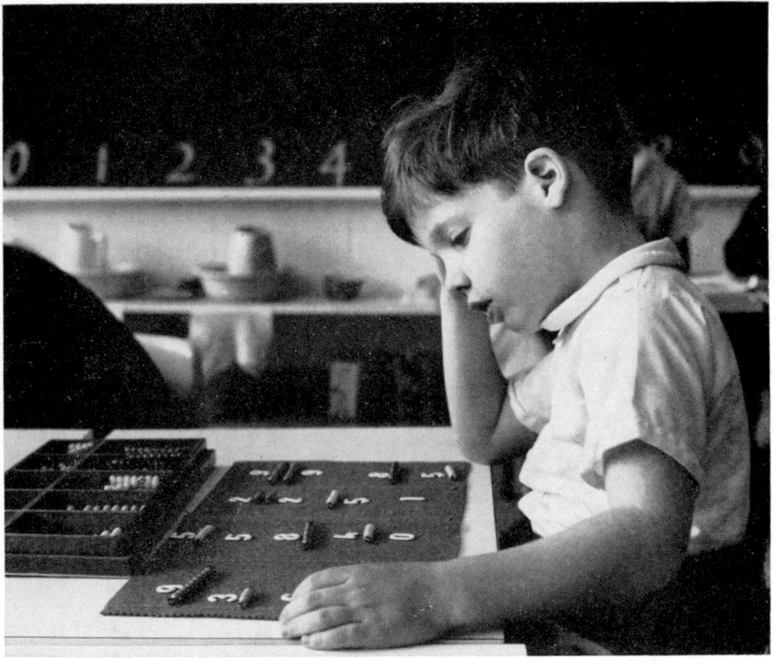


This child is matching two sets of symbols—groups of beads representing number and numerals.

These children are working with plane geometric forms, laying out cards on which the appropriate forms will be placed.

Putting away a tray of geometric insets is part of the activity of working with them.

reaffirmed this: "The often unconscious nature of learning structures is perhaps best illustrated in learning one's native language. Having grasped the subtle structure of a sentence, the child very rapidly learns to generate many other sentences based on this model though different in content from the original sentence learned. And having mastered the rules for transforming sentences without altering their meaning—'The dog bit the man' and 'The man was bitten by the dog'—the child is able to vary his sentences much more widely. Yet, while young children are able to *use* the structural rules of English, they are certainly not able to say what the rules are."[7]

Montessori states that "the child of six who has learned to speak correctly, knowing and using the rules of his native tongue, could never describe the unconscious work from which this has come. Nevertheless, it is *he*, Man, who is the creator of speech. He does it entirely by himself, but if he lacked the power, and could not spontaneously master his language, no effective work would ever be done by the world of men."[8] Recognizing the enormous educational process of the first six years of life, she commented on the fact that official educational curricula, whether or not they made adequate provision for the first phase of education (3-6) nonetheless recognize that at about the age of six children enter into a developmental phase during which they can be taught the elements.

"There are many who hold, as I do, that the most important period of life is not the age of university studies, but the first one, the period from birth to the age of six. For that is the time when man's intelligence itself, his greatest implement, is being formed. . . . If we call our adult mentality conscious, then we must call the child's unconscious, but the unconscious kind is not necessarily inferior. An unconscious mind can be most intelligent. We find it at work in every species, even among the insects. They have an intelligence which is not conscious though it often seems to be endowed with reason. The [young] child has an intelligence of this unconscious type, and that is what brings about his wonderful progress."[9]

What does a young child, scarcely separate from his mother, bring to the dramatic task of mastering himself and his environ-

ment? He brings a need to grow and a need to move. To dismiss lightly the tremendous learning tasks of the young child is to lose sight of the fact that whether or not children are taught anything formally, they continue to learn. It is not from the words of adults, but from their actions and attitudes, that young children learn about the world in which they have been placed. This world, no matter how "natural" it may appear to the parent involved in the family, is both a natural and an artificial situation. Many of the attitudes that parents have towards their children are only reflections of the attitudes of their parents towards them. There are constant judgments intruding on the child's apparent freedom to grow physically as nature intended.

The modern world is full of hazards for the young child. To protect him from drafts (and his mother from a strained back), he is placed in a cage called a "crib." To protect him from aggressive older children (or the furniture from him), the young child is often placed in a playpen, and thereby denied the opportunity to creep and crawl in the process of learning to walk. Despite his need to move and to master movement by the achievement of co-ordinated mobility, the American child is frequently carried and caged when he needs most to explore this atmosphere from which he will draw his early learning experience. Yet, even caged, the child will learn.

Conventional education has long equated immobility with virtue. In many American schools, teachers are silently warning themselves to "watch that one—he's moving." Despite the fact that early nursery education allows the American child tremendous mobility, by the time he reaches the calendar age of six and is "ready" for school, presumably he is also ready to sit still. In a culture that has, in the post-Sputnik era, become increasingly performance-oriented, there is a correspondingly great anxiety about mobility. If children need to move in the service of learning, and if mobility plays the large part in child development that we acknowledge it to, then its importance as necessary rather than optional ought to be considered.

"It is high time that movement came to be regarded from a new point of view in educational theory. . . . As a part of school life, which gives priority to the intellect, the role of movement

has been sadly neglected. . . . One of the greatest mistakes of our day is to think of movement by itself, as something apart from higher functions. We think of our muscles as organs to be used only for health purposes. When mental development is under discussion, there are men who say 'How does movement come into it? We are talking about the mind.' And when we think of intellectual activity, we always imagine people sitting still, motionless. But mental development *must* be connected with movement and dependent on it."[10] These statements, made by Montessori the physician in 1949, point up the problem facing educators of young children in their assessment of the importance of movement.

The unfortunate equation of mobility with "progressivism" in education has supplied many of the immobile traditionalists with ammunition to keep the children stationary. This is occasioned surely both by a lack of understanding of the importance of the sensory-motor foundations of conceptual learning, as indicated for example by the Swiss psychologist Piaget, and by a misunderstanding of the valid role of what Lyman Bryson characterizes as "motor thinking."[11] Though no substitute for "abstract thinking," which occurs at a later stage of development, motor thinking has a very important place in early education.

"The child learns through movement." The way in which brain and hand work together in the tasks of early education demonstrates the importance of providing sensory-motor activity for young children in a culture so strongly oriented toward verbal activity. Montessori told her teachers to show the children, not to speak to them. If the child is shown he watches the teacher's hands, if he is spoken to by the teacher, he watches her mouth.

The role of movement in early education (in America) has usually been restricted to what could be called gross motor activities. Important as these are, and omnipresent as they are, found in every nursery school throughout the country (opportunities to pull, push, climb, vault, scale, etc.)—the small muscles, particularly those of the hand, get relatively little emphasis. The ability to oppose thumb and finger, in that gesture which will be necessary later on in the grasp of a pencil, pen, or crayon, is a human ability. The ability to use a pencil is an acquired human

skill, one the child will need to know on the fateful day he enters first grade, or shortly thereafter. Society no longer concerns itself with whether or not the six-year-old likes learning; its only concern is that he learn in the time allotted him by his culture and the tax budget.

Through the opportunities allowed the child to move, and in so doing to learn, Montessori offers the child in the school situation true liberty. The child who never moves except on the initiative of the teacher is less in control of his movements than the child who is free to move within the social group that is his class as long as he respects certain rules regarding movement. The greater the child's interest in the work at hand, the greater the likelihood that he will become immobilized through interest rather than through adult coercion. The acquisition of controlled movement is, for the young child, a point of arrival, not a point of departure. The freedom with which he moves in a controlled manner is one of the tasks of his early learning.

The attitude of adults toward movement will be absorbed by the child. The punitively viewed moving child will be timid, the child allowed to move in order to learn will be confident. The allowance made for children's mobility on the part of the adults with whom they find themselves, is the child's index as to whether the moral judgment made about movement is positive or negative. Why we should place our children in the position of suspecting that movement as such is bad, is a dilemma traditional educators have neither resolved nor faced.

### *Liberty Within Limits*

One of the most dramatic ways in which the child is free in a Montessori class is seen in his ability to move. Both John Dewey and Maria Montessori revolted against the nineteenth-century practice of keeping children "pinned like butterflies" to their desks. The historical equation between immobility and learning, and immobility and virtue, was, Americans thought, decisively invalidated with the advent of progressive education. However, no one could have foreseen the anxiety which movement is causing the American parent. Currently there is a re-

action in the lower elementary grades in many performance-oriented communities against allowing the children to move. Many parents believe that if the children are sitting at their desks, somehow they are learning more effectively than if they are sitting on the floor or sitting in groups or appearing to enjoy learning wherever they may be.

Montessori, as a pioneer in the field of child development, realized that children learn through movement when they are small. There is no point in a young child's life at which one can be certain that if he is absolutely still he is learning anything. One cannot, of course, be sure that if he is moving he is learning either. Nonetheless, the muscles of the young child appear to require constant flexing. Affording the child a chance to use his muscles and to stretch and sit and squat and kneel, and generally experiment with all kinds of body movement, appears a valid aid in interesting the child in learning, and in focusing his attention. In a Montessori class the children are free to move. They are free to work alone; they are free to work together.

A key concept of Montessori can be characterized by her expression, "Liberty within limits." What Dr. Montessori developed as a learning situation and called the "prepared environment" is the triad composed of child, teacher, and physical surroundings in which a child is motivated, stimulated and encouraged to choose his work and execute it to his own satisfaction. At the same time, he is afforded the protection of a loving, accepting adult who will not intrude on the child's need to act by himself. By *liberty* we mean the freedom to choose between things which are in themselves good, so that the child is never endangered either by a choice that is detrimental to him or by a choice that he is actually incapable of assessing.

There are certain "ground rules" in the so-called prepared environment which insure for the child and for other children true liberty. "A system has been devised which accords a remarkable degree of freedom to the individual children of the Montessori schools. A contrast between the Montessori school and the kindergarten of the more formal and traditional type may serve to give a clearer picture of the Montessori procedure, and consequently of the Montessori conception of liberty as it appears

in practice. The kindergarten [teacher] is clearly the center and arbiter of the activity in the room. The Montessori directress seems, on the contrary, to be at one side. The kindergartner contemplates at each moment the whole of her group; the directress is talking usually to one alone—possibly to two or three. The kindergarten children are engaged in some form of directed group activity; each Montessori child is an isolated worker, though one or more comrades may look on and suggest. . . . The directress perchance will not interpose in the slightest throughout a whole period . . . on the whole, the children work as busily as ants about a hill."[12]

The "prepared environment" is prepared for the child, in advance, by the adult. Like all other school situations, of course, it is artificial. In the classroom, the adult orders the physical environment in a certain way. She establishes those rules by which the child relates to other children, so that at all times he has the maximum security of knowing where everything is, where everything belongs, what everyone's rights are. From the moment he comes into the class there are certain things upon which he can rely, unalterably.

Part of the preparation of the environment for the child's learning involves the establishment of ground rules of human behavior. These provide the limits for the group and for the individual. A child may not touch another child while that child is working. A child may not touch another child's work while the other child is working. These rules are designed to develop in the child who is free to observe at any time what other childen are doing, a respect not only for the work in progress, but for the worker. Children are free to invite others to share their work, but they are also free to refuse participation on the part of another child if they are so minded.

The usual adult attitude toward choice involves snatching a toy away from one child to give it to another, and then telling the child from whom the toy is taken to share it. This is not sharing. This is physical coercion—frequently, at a very base level. In order that a child share, he gives not only some object, but he gives himself. He must be capable of making this gift of self before an adult can reasonably expect it of him. In order that he

be free to give, he must also be free to retain. In this way a child must accept the verdict of another that he may not be invited to work with a second child.

Among other ground rules that are taught in a Montessori class are such simple things as learning how to care for oneself; learning how to open and shut a door; how to move a chair quietly; how to excuse oneself when walking in front of someone else; how to carry a pitcher of water without spilling it; how to button up one's own coat; how to do, in short, for oneself those things which one needs to know in order to be free—to be free from adult interference, and also to be free from the dependence on adults which young children find extremely irksome. A child is not helped by the teacher until he asks for help or until the teacher sees that he is in need of it although he may not be aware of it himself.

One of the principles of the Montessori environment is that much of what children learn is learned through incidental teaching and through observation. If it is the job of the teacher to put the children in direct contact with what they are learning, then it is further her job to free them and let them alone once they begin to learn, and not to intrude herself constantly upon what they are doing. She is there to help the children. She is there to answer their questions, to stimulate them, to straighten out their mistakes when they are viewed by the young children as mistakes. She is not there to learn for them or to substitute her will for the child's will, because if the child is not free to choose, he will never choose. One of the great emphases in American education of the young seems to be over-groupiness. When a teacher claps her hands and says "let us dance," "let us sing," "let us go to the bathroom," she is not reflecting the so-called "felt needs of the group"; she may well be reflecting her own felt needs, because among a group of children of ages three to six it is highly questionable whether or not any or all would be capable of articulating any particular need for the group.

Piaget, the Swiss psychologist, in his book *The Language and Thought of the Child*, makes the statement, "There is as we have said no real social life among children of less than seven or eight."[13] This statement will no doubt be traumatising to Ameri-

can Educators. The notion of the education of the young as primarily an education of socialization is something that is highly debatable. In contradistinction to socialization, there is the notion (which is very deep-seated in Montessori as well as in child development) that the child has to learn who he is; and he has to, in some measure, learn to get along with himself before he is capable of getting along with anyone else—or indeed before he is even capable of being aware of the existence of anyone else. Many of the insights of Montessori and the hypotheses upon which she based her work with young children are echoed in contemporary American thought. One need not read *into* Montessori things which were not consciously present to her. One can simply juxtapose certain of her ideas to those of contemporary workers in fields related to education.

## *The Child's Social and Emotional Development*

The child reacts and learns totally. The separation of thought into affective and cognitive elements for the sake of discussion may be justified. But in working with living children, particularly young children, it would be difficult to sort out the emotional reactions from learning situations since the child acts and reacts as a total entity. When he hears a loud noise he jumps; if another child punches him he may be moved to anger. He is reacting emotionally as well as learning in these situations.

To a frequently posed question, "What provision does Montessori theory make for emotional and social development?" there can be but one answer: the same provision that is made for cognitive development, since the emotional, social and cognitive are parts of a whole. From the moment a child is born, he is a social being in so far as he is in society. He is dependent from birth on others. There is no point at which he stands alone in early childhood. Whether it be in the family or in the class, the child is in a social environment, with a substratum of expectations and taboos. Social development is a necessary condition of learning.

Social awareness appears to be a developmental phenomenon. The child goes from isolated play to parallel play to social play.

"The beginnings of play are closely associated with motor behavior, and at the two- and three-year-old level, especially with much manipulation of objects. During the child's second year language often becomes an important part of play, although children differ widely in the amount they use. . . . As children grow older, their solitary play patterns become more complex and more directed toward some goal. . . . In the pre-school years the child develops from individual play to parallel play to a few beginnings of social play."[14]

If one were to substitute "work" for the word "play" in this passage, using it in the context in which Dr. Montessori uses the word (i.e. to indicate activity meaningful to the child and directly implicated in his construction of himself), the Montessori approach would be seen as providing the same developmental opportunities socially as the conventional nursery and kindergarten. True, there are no group tables, which impose a "social" situation on the children juxtaposed at them. There are individual tables, which the children are free to group as they choose. There are numerous children in the group, thus providing for activity at isolated, parallel and social levels.

It is at least as organic, and possibly more so, to provide the child with the possibility of socializing on his own terms, rather than to insist on an adult-oriented concept of grouping as a necessity for children who have neither the need nor the inclination for this in their early development. The very life of the child in the Montessori environment provides for that emotional development found in any situation in which the child is free to explore.

The choice of activities in a Montessori class appears somewhat different from that of a conventional nursery class. The emphasis on sensory motor development is very frankly present; not only the large muscles but the small ones involving such cortical functions as thumb-finger opposition (leading to the ability to hold a pencil and write) are provided for. The Montessori materials have the appearance of toys, but they are unlike those toys with which the children will be most familiar, standard equipment in home and nursery school alike: blocks, puzzles, wheel toys, dolls, etc.

In her initial work in the slums of San Lorenzo, in her first Casa dei Bambini, Montessori recounted that the children were offered both toys and the materials she had designed. The children, according to her, preferred the work materials to the toys. Of course, the material in the Montessori classrooms differs from culture to culture, as does the furniture. In India, provision is made for spinning and weaving in some village schools. In France, Montessori schools reflect a precision of small movement expected of the very young, where a child of seven is expected to make a clean copy of his work in ink in a bound notebook. In English Montessori classes there appears to be less emphasis on such rigid hand control, despite the fact that between the ages of four-and-a-half and six in any Montessori class the children are most likely to be fascinated by writing.

The children in a Montessori class are free to pursue their activities according to their own taste for solitude or companionship. There is a great deal of "incidental" learning occurring as they ask others for help or are freely corrected by more knowledgeable peers who see inaccuracies in their performance which they themselves do not see. As the children are obliged to wait their turns to use some of the materials, they are introduced at the beginning of their life in the class to the importance of respecting each other as workers as well as respecting each other's work. Since the rhythm of individual children varies so greatly, and since in a class that is in essence ungraded because it numbers children in a three-year age span, the bulk of the morning's activity takes place on an individual rather than a group level—in the context of each child respecting the work of the others. When invited to do so, a child may join in the work of another. But if the child already working refuses any assistance, the child who wants to work with him must abide by this judgment. The teacher does not intervene to persuade the solitary worker to allow the other child to join him. She too abides by the child's decision.

Group effort is the natural outgrowth of much of the Montessori activity. In an effort to multiply 15,698 by 12, with symbolic material and numerals, a child will naturally look for help because the physical layout of the problem involves the as-

sembling of fifteen *thousand* cubes, six *hundred* squares, nine *ten* bars and eight *unit* beads in twelve separate piles preparatory to the combination of these quantities. Their final expression requires the changing of all the units in excess of nine for tens, the tens in excess of ninety for one-hundreds, the hundreds in excess of nine hundred into thousands, etc. Such a "problem" could well occupy three five-year-olds for a few hours.

A characteristic of the Montessori class is the tremendous concentration noticeable on the faces of some of the children. This concentration seems incapable of being destroyed despite the fact that in working the children face every conceivable kind of normal distraction: children walking past and engaging others in conversation, children working out loud at something a few inches away, possibly a lesson being given by the teacher to other children within earshot. It is the interest with which the children attack their activity and the pleasure they find in it which must provide the clues for this concentration. It is not uncommon for observers to consider the children unduly solemn, failing to distinguish the fierce active attention that characterizes a child absorbed in something he himself is interested in from the passive attention accorded a teacher who is directing a group activity. The children in the Montessori class are the agents of their learning. They are active, and are acting upon their environment. Even as fond parents frequently deny that their hyperactive child may be a neurological problem, so many nursery teachers judge the efficacy of a social environment for the young by the amount of noisy confusion produced in it.

Much of the activity of the American nursery classes has become sacrosanct through usage. Such activities as "Show and Tell," though perfectly fine activities, do not necessarily stunt children's emotional growth by their absence from the school curriculum. Block building, a legitimate activity in the preschool, has suffered the fate of uncritical acceptance by teachers who do not possess Carolyn Pratt's insight, and the mere mention of its absence causes a shudder of consternation to pass through many a nursery teacher. Why should this be? Whatever the social and emotional implications of block play *may* be, how can the nursery school in the United States have become so non-

susceptible to new forms of activity which may be equally beneficial (or rather "other" forms, in as much as Montessori activity goes back sixty years and could hardly be considered new)? The question so often asked, "What do you substitute for block play?" should first be restated as "What do I hope to achieve through block play?" in order eventually to elicit a satisfactory answer.

In an effort to expand rather than contract the frontiers of knowledge of young children, it would seem incumbent on American educators to consider forms of activity other than those to which we are historically committed. Is it the consensus of teachers that American children between three and six can do nothing other than the things they now do? Or is it possible that given an opportunity to attempt other approaches to learning and different things to be learned—such as early reading, writing, and spelling—they might prove themselves capable of more, earlier and other learning?

Recent research on the role of the responsive environment, on the capacities of children for early learning, on the need for the creative personality to work alone rather than in a group, on the limited response of the young child to the verbal onslaught of the adult—all of this underscores new directions in early education. The fact that techniques in child study and educational psychology have frequently been at polar opposites, and that research in child development has been conducted far from actual nursery and primary classes, heighten the possibility for a "new" look at the substance of the early years of learning.

Americans, with their deep-seated eclectic penchant, will not necessarily accept uncritically the ideas of Montessori, nor ought they. That her ideas bear a striking relation to other varied though related insights in education and child development makes them worthy of consideration.

One of the Montessori ideas that might well be further investigated in the United States is her belief that the inner life of the child develops apace with his perception. At the same time as children are "constructing" themselves from their environment, Montessori advanced a notion of development relating to those fugitive periods of sensitivity in the child which, once passed, would not return. She drew analogies from biological research

to make her point. Hugo de Vries, the Dutch biologist, has discovered that a certain butterfly *(Porthesia)* laid its eggs precisely at the juncture of trunk and branches of a tree. The small caterpillars hatched from the eggs could nourish themselves only on the tenderest leaves, which grew at the tips of the branches, far from the newborn caterpillars. However, the sensitivity to light manifested by the newly-hatched caterpillars drew them to the tips of the branches where their nourishment waited. As they grew stronger and could go elsewhere for food, their sensitivity to light disappeared. They did, however, possess it at the time that it was important for their very survival.

The apparently "irresistible" urge of the caterpillar Dr. Montessori saw mirrored in the young child. "Children pass through definite periods in which they reveal psychic aptitudes and possibilities which afterwards disappear. That is why, at particular epochs in their lives, they reveal an intense and extraordinary interest in certain aspects of their environment to the exclusion of others . . ."[15] Montessori points to the need for order as an illustration of this sensitivity. Order to the young child means finding things in the same place and counting on repetition and ritual. Almost every young child has a blanket, or teddy bear, or pillow he drags around the house, from which he will *not* be parted. All readers of Charlie Brown know of Linus' blanket. All parents of young children recall those periods in which a story had to be repeated verbatim, and the light in the hall had to be left on. Montessori counsels young mothers and those taking care of babies to aid this emergent sense of order by conscious repetition of action—by passing the same landmarks in taking a child walking, for example, to enhance this disposition to order.

Montessori makes a distinction between the apparent need the young child has for order and the more arbitrary need of the adult. The adult generally likes things to be orderly and tidy because he equates order with comfort, or because he cannot function as effectively in disorder. Montessori believes that order is indispensable for the fullest development of the young child precisely because he learns from the environment what the environment provides. The greater the confusion in the environ-

ment, the more difficult for the child to derive order from it. The particular sensitivity to order occurs in children from the age of two and seems most marked around the age of three. Many of the repeated activities which give children pleasure in Montessori classes, particularly those involving household activities, could be related to their interest in what amounts to a ritual in the performance of simple tasks.

As sensitive periods are fleeting, the possibilities they offer for refinement of movement are very great. The child, for his own pleasure, will continue to perfect a movement long after the adult thinks he has adequately mastered it. "If this perfecting of movement is introduced at the *creative moment* (two-and-one-half to four years of age) it not only tends to the normal development of the mind but also affects the whole personality, bringing contentment, concentration and inner nourishment . . ."[16] The introduction by the teacher of what Montessori calls the *motive of perfection* stimulates the children to refine their movements by making them aware that there is an even more interesting way of doing something than the way they have learned. Setting a chair down, placing one leg in contact with the floor at a time, is a way of controlling the chair. Undertaking the same action as quietly as possible introduces a refinement of the action. The satisfaction that the children derive from the expenditure of this extra effort must be observed to be believed.

If an approach to learning in young children emphasizes acquisition of percepts through sensory-motor means, if the activities are structured in so far as they follow a sequential pattern, the inference is frequently made by Americans that structure precludes creativity in the child and that emphasis on the child's use of the class for reality testing impoverishes his fantasy life.

The activity of children tracing what are called the "metal insets" in a Montessori class, mistaken for artistic structuring, has been understandably criticized by those who see little connection between this and Montessori's statement that "the free hand is the educated hand." What the children are engaged in is an indirect preparation for writing, which promotes the necessary skill required to hold a pencil, develops a forward moving wrist motion and a "light touch" of the pencil on the paper.

"There can be no 'graduated exercises in drawing,' leading up to an artistic creation. That goal can be attained only through the development of mechanical technique and through freedom of the spirit. That is our reason for not teaching drawing directly to the child. We prepare him indirectly, leaving him free to the mysterious and divine labor of producing things according to his own feelings. The drawing comes to satisfy a need for expression, as does language; and almost every idea may seek expression in drawing. The effort to perfect such expression is very similar to that which the child makes when he is spurred on to perfect his language in order to see his thoughts translated into reality. This effort is spontaneous; and the real drawing teacher is the inner life, which of itself develops, attains refinement, and seeks irresistibly to be born into external existence in some empirical form. . . . The sensory and manual preparation for drawing is nothing more than an alphabet; but without it the child is illiterate and cannot express himself . . ."[17]

This passage does not make a necessary distinction between purely manipulative activities and creative ones. Very young children enjoy the manipulation of paints, clay, etc. and frequently decide after the fact what it is they have produced, as opposed to children who consciously create by the intentional impression of their ideas on matter.

Obviously, the ability to express oneself varies from child to child and from one developmental stage to another. It is certainly a matter of agreement that children should be exposed to artistic materials in order to manipulate them and create with them. The emphasis that a Montessori teacher might make would be one of demonstrating technique in order to assure the child a maximum success in his use of the material—something as simple as showing him (*not* telling him) that by wiping the brush on the lip of the jar, the drips are minimized in transferring the paint to the paper. This demonstration might give rise to the objection that the child is being deprived of the chance to discover the cause and effect relationship between too-full-brush and drips-on-paper by this prior demonstration. If the point at issue is using the paint to express something else, the controlled use of it will lead to a more successful execution of the child's idea

with a resulting reduction of frustration from inept technique. Any artist would show his apprentice this; it seems a most justifiable way to free the child to express himself without any direct intervention on the part of the adult in the act of expression.

Sir Herbert Read was understandably confused by Dr. Montessori's reference to "horrible daubs" carefully collected in the common schools as evidence and "documents" of the child mind. Montessori contended that they showed only that the eye of the child was uneducated, the hand inert, the mind insensible alike to the beautiful and the ugly, blind to the true as well as to the false.[18] As Montessori provided no samples of "horrible daubs," it is difficult to know just what she had in mind, unless it would be a failure to distinguish between the manipulative and creative impulses in the children's finished productions. In any case, there is a valid argument for demonstration of technique (as Victor Lowenfeld has emphasized),[19] though not necessarily implying thereby an abandonment of the discovery of the uses and limits of various media.

Read's own definition of art bears a striking relation to the emphasis of activity in the Montessori class. "That [art] has been so elusive is explained by the fact that it has always been treated as a metaphysical concept, whereas it is fundamentally an organic and measurable phenomenon. Like breathing, it has rhythmic elements; like speech, expressive elements; but 'like' does not in this case express an analogy; art is deeply involved in the actual process of perception, thought and bodily action."[20]

What has been said concerning art also applies to the early development of pitch and rhythm through exposure to these in a school environment. There is evidence to support the contention that children are able to sing tones and intervals, and are able to identify them with practice even at three and under. Rhythmic reactions tend to depend on individual children, but exposure to rhythm does evoke a response in many young children and provides them with a means of expression.

That a great deal is still to be learned about the nature and nurture of creativity is demonstrated by recent research at the University of Minnesota which shows that there is no necessary correlation between high measurable intelligence and creative

ability. That there are latent creative powers in children, we know. That they deserve an opportunity to make themselves known, we know. Any school for young children must conscientiously make provision for this vital facet of expression.

In Montessori classes, there is an environmental emphasis on reality. While fairy and folk tales are pleasurable for children who are able to distinguish fact from fancy, they can be disturbing to children unable to make these distinctions. There are opportunities for expression of fantasy through writing and painting, and free play in Montessori classes. These opportunities are less marked than those of many conventional nursery schools, though of course they vary from culture to culture.

CHAPTER 3

# Corollaries

## *The Sense of Self*

When we consider the child at birth, we see a being who is still integrally related to his mother. As an infant he is participating in her very life, and he is continuously learning. Montessori states that *the greatness of the human personality begins at birth.* The personality itself begins then. The mother, when dealing with the child, needs an awareness of the tremendous task the baby is setting himself. "The concept of an education centered upon the care of the living being alters all previous ideas. . . . The education of the newly born becomes suddenly of the first importance."[1]

By considering the other elements in the child's life that contribute to his development, the mother is in no way relinquishing her continuing role. However, as the child grows, crawls, observes and walks, he develops a sense of power which is for and of *himself*, and not his mother. The sense of self which the young child possesses not only delights him but motivates him to try progressively more difficult tasks. At this point at which the child feels distinct from his mother, the point at which he is able to stand on his own two feet and walk away from her (when he is about eighteen months old), in the sense that he is now physically independent of her in a limited way he is beginning to orient himself toward a larger world.

Erik Erikson points out that in the development of ego-identity, which is an integral part of the healthy personality, there are three phases which the child must go through. These are basic trust, autonomy, and initiative.[2] A baby may show something like

autonomy from the beginning, for example, in the particular way in which he angrily tries to wiggle his hand free when tightly held. During each phase of development, the child passes through a kind of crisis; autonomy becomes a subordinate instead of a dominant principle, and then comes up again.

The most important ingredient that a child receives from his mother is a basic trust. This trust extends, ultimately, to his relation to everyone else. If a child, at the age of about eight months, is deprived of his mother's presence traumatically this can, we are told, cause a real problem later on. At that particular time, when trust was the most important element the mother could afford the child and it was not forthcoming, certain disturbances which will make him a non-trustful person can develop. After the child has developed a sense of trust he moves on to what would be considered autonomy in so far as he is now aware that he exists as independent of his mother, and wants to assert himself. But, it is at this point that he requires from adults firm handling so that he is allowed to become both firm and tolerant with himself. This development occurs at about three years of age.

The importance of allowing a child to do for himself, which is one of Montessori's prime principles, appears to be integrally related to a child's sense of his own worth. Everyone who has ever been exposed to children has heard them say, "Do it myself." Every child, once he believes himself capable of attempting something, wants to try it without help. The teacher, working with young children, needs a sound judgment to expose the child to a gradual progression of simple tasks, at which he can succeed. The child takes pleasure in whatever he does, successfully feeling confident because he has proven himself competent. All simple tasks, well-fulfilled, whether they are represented by buttoning one's coat, polishing one's shoes, opening or closing a door, following an instruction, reinforce for the child a sense of his own worth.

In *Continuities and Discontinuities in Cultural Conditioning* Ruth Benedict cites the case of a three-year-old Indian child asked by the elders of the tribe to close a door. "The tasks [the child] is asked to perform are graded to its powers and its elders

wait quietly by, not offering to do the task in the child's place. . . . Dr. Ruth Underhill tells me of sitting with a group of Papago elders in Arizona when the man of the house turned to his little three-year-old granddaughter and asked her to close the door. The door was heavy and hard to shut. The child tried, but it did not move. Several times the grandfather repeated, "Yes, close the door." No one jumped to the child's assistance. No one took the responsibility away from her. On the other hand, there was no impatience, for after all the child was small. They sat gravely waiting till the child succeeded and her grandfather gravely thanked her. It was assumed that the task would not be asked of her unless she could perform it, and having been asked the responsibility was hers alone just as if she were a grown woman."[3]

Benedict, Montessori, and Erikson are all cognizant of the extra dimension of the child's action, of a human action not beyond the competence of a three-year-old. The action has merit above and beyond the actual physical fact of the child's accomplishment. It has the merit of allowing the child to participate in the society in which he finds himself, not at the level of an adult, but at the level of an emergent adult. The importance of a strong sense of self can be seen when one considers the tasks which will be demanded of an American child of three in a few short years. The ability to work independently, to continue to accomplish, whether or not the adult is physically present at one's elbow at all times, the ability to initiate work because one has had previous successful experience, are important learning skills for a child. Many children are so conditioned by adults that they will refuse to attempt anything new until they have been given either explicit directions by an adult or, what is more frequent, explicit approval to do so by an adult.

In a Montessori classroom motives for activity, which are nothing other than objects with which the children can work, through which they can unite the activity of hand, eye and brain, are everywhere apparent. They can be books, they can have the appearance of visual aids or educational toys. They do, however, provide for the child the ability to work independently, to achieve a limited goal with success through manipulation,

through repetition, through reinforcement, and contain certain "felt" corrective aspects, which when the child is more aware, will make it possible for him to move on to the next task. One of the simplest tasks in a Montessori class is the manipulation of the graded cylinders.[4] The obvious object of the manipulation of the cylinders is threefold: it gives the child a sense of discrimination in comparing the various cylinders; it makes him aware of dimensional differences; it also in their manipulation affords him a chance to utilize the small muscles he will ultimately need for writing. All this is helpful for the development of a sense of self. First of all, the child is given something he can do. This is very basic. One does not give a child a Greek translation when he is three. It means nothing to him. One gives him not only something that he can do, but something from which he can derive pleasure, something that has a beginning, a middle and an end. The kind of structured activity that is characteristic of a Montessori class is a series of tasks involving the child's hand, eye and brain, which gain momentum through repetition, rather than through complex operation.

Another good example of a motive of activity is the study of continents and countries, oceans and land masses through large maps of the various continents in which each country is a physically separate puzzle piece surmounted by a small knob necessitating the same kind of finger grasp. The children start working with the maps, gradually learn the names of the countries, gradually learn to read the names, gradually free themselves from the necessity of reassembling the map in the outline form in which it is first found, so that ultimately they become confident and competent in locating geographically on a globe or on a Mercator projection map all the countries of the world. This may seem irrelevant to those who begin with the assumption that the child's world consists only of those objects most immediate to him. If one considers the local fireman or policeman of paramount interest to the young, and then orients the entire learning program around this, the child, in a sense, never leaves home.

The ability of the child to identify correctly geographical places which occur in the news, on the television, in conversation —and to find pleasure in his knowledge—is surely of as great

immediate value as knowing what will be demanded of him at a slightly later age. Knowledge of geography is basic to our culture, and a child learning his geography effortlessly and pleasantly, literally absorbing it at an early age, is a freer child in terms of eventual geographical judgments than the child who learns at a later age with less interest.

In terms of the development of self from such an activity it is obvious that the child is learning something in which he can take pride, because it corresponds to knowledge in the real world, his parents' world. There are any number of areas of activity which will feed the child's sense of pride and the sense of himself, but the main components of such activity appear to be that the child views his activity as work rather than play, and that the child takes real pleasure and pride in what he is doing, that he does not need adult reinforcement for either the initiation of the task or its completion.

The child learns at an early age with his whole being. He throws himself into his activities. He does not learn intellectually. To understand the emphasis placed on sensory motor activity, the joint action of "hand, eye and brain," in the Montessori class, it is important to relate the perceptual knowledge such activity provides to the more abstract thinking we generally associate with intellectual learning. The emphasis of the early years is on perception rather than on intelligence, following the distinction supplied by Piaget. "Perception is the knowledge we have of objects or of their movements by direct and immediate contact, while intelligence is a form of knowledge obtaining when detours are involved and when spatio-temporal distance between subject and objects increases."[5]

Piaget does not categorically divide motor thinking from abstract thinking. "A perception, sensory-motor learning (habit), an act of insight, a judgment, all amount in one way or another to a structuring of the relations between the environment and the organism. We shall refer to them as cognitive functions in the wide sense (to include sensory-motor adaptation)."[6] Piaget later states that the use of the term "intelligence" precludes a determination of where it starts; its origins are indistinguishable from those of sensory motor adaptation. The structured activities

in the Montessori class provide for percepts acquired through sensory motor means and through mobility. The importance of neurological organization and of the extension of sensory motor activity can be seen in the gradual development of abstract thought. One may draw from Piaget an inference that activities of the type found in a Montessori class, providing sensory motor stimulus, should enhance the later stages of learning.

The child absorbs from the world of sights and sounds all manner of impressions and gradually classifies them to the level of his own needs. A "Montessori" child, a little four-year-old who was learning to dance, is said to have exclaimed one day in tremendous amazement, "I told my hand to do it, and my hand did it." This awareness of the component parts of the body is something that comes as a tremendous surprise to the children, who first are, in a sense, undifferentiated blobs of protoplasm, and then gradually become aware that they themselves are no longer to be referred to in the third person but they have an "I" to talk about. Because of the tremendous emphasis that is placed upon bodily movement in Montessori classes, that is, moving with grace, balancing, walking on a line, opening and shutting a door, setting a chair down quietly, carrying juice without spilling it, such a child is constantly harnessing his whole physical being in the service of an activity or of an interest that he has. It is precisely for this reason that Montessori believes that the child has to learn with his whole body at this age if he is to learn at all. "Movement is the conclusion and purpose of the nervous system, Montessori tells us, without it there can be no individual. . . . Scientific observation shows that intelligence is developed through movement; experiments in all parts of the world have confirmed that movement helps psychic development, and that development in turn expresses itself in further movement, so there is a cycle, which must be completed, because mind and movement belong to the same unity."[7]

Emotions play a very important part in this whole awareness of self. It has been said by detractors of Montessori that there is no emotional provision in the Montessori approach to education. To say this is to completely misunderstand what Montessori is talking about. Socialization occurs when a child who is aware

of himself then becomes aware of another person and is capable of some kind of relationship with another or with others. A child is constantly expressing himself through his emotions. Teaching him to work with his whole person, however, also teaches him unconsciously some of the controls that are necessary for living in a society where the rights of others are as important as his own rights. It has been said, and truly said, that the limitation of a child's liberty in a Montessori classroom is the liberty of the whole group. A child is free to do whatever is not harmful to anyone else, and he is free to do anything not contrary to the good of the whole group. If a child has his sense of self strongly developed, he is then organically capable of taking his chances within the group, as opposed to the child who has no sense of himself—a child lost, alone, and lost in the group. If, as Piaget says, the child is not really a social being until he is seven, American elementary schools (and this is as true of Montessori schools as any other) need have no fear of isolationists. By the time a child is socialized, he will form into a group automatically. The Montessori child is left to learn himself only as long as it is important for him to establish himself as a person. At the point at which, culturally, he must take his chances competitively, he must be inserted into the pattern of the culture in such a way that he is able to utilize what he has learned, "on his own." Montessori would caution against placing children in highly competitive situations *before* they are ready to have their performance tested. "Never let a child risk failure until he has a reasonable chance of success." We are all familiar with first grade classes of non-readers in which some of the children do not know how to read as well as other children do not know how to read. These groups may be variously designated as Dodgers and Braves, Navajos and Sioux, Butterflies and Earthworms, but the children *always* know who the best and the worst of the non-readers are!

### *Self-Mastery*

Montessori said that the educated hand is the free hand. Self-discipline is a point of arrival for the child, not a point of departure. In developing in the child a sense of true liberty (as

opposed to anarchy or to a false liberty in which the adult will is continually substituted for the child's will), the Montessori environment provides for the child a chance to achieve control over himself and his environment which is unique in the development of the young. The way in which this self-discipline is induced in the child derives from the preparation of the environment to receive him. If we view the same Montessori classroom with its various elements, its opportunities for the child to learn to wash and comb and dress, to polish and scrub and shine, to count, to read, to write, to sound, to dance, to sing, etc. we see that the ability to shift from activity to activity (as the child is free to do) necessitates on his part an ability to initiate, carry through and complete activities in such a way that the balance of the environment is not disturbed each time the child shifts his attention to a new object or a new action.

Among the first things a child is taught in a Montessori class, as much through the attitude of the teacher as through any specific form of her activity, is that there is a way to do almost everything. There is a way to open and shut a door, not the "only" way, but a way, which if carefully followed will result in success and will allow the door opener to move on to another task. One of the basic ingredients of self-discipline is the awareness that the child has of his own competence. A child is not disciplined who is unable to be quiet.

A child develops a concept of work, initially through the attitude the teacher has toward work, ultimately through the satisfaction that his activity affords him. The child works because it pleases him, not because of any external aim. He apparently identifies the satisfaction of his activity with the notion of work, as opposed to the notion of play. Work is activity with purpose but child purpose, not adult purpose. Work is more than the "curse of the fallen." It is a means of achieving self-respect. The distinction between play and work is one that only a child can make. To the adult a specific activity may look like play; to the child engaged in that activity it may be work because it is invested with a conscious or unconscious purpose which only the child feels. Therefore, many activities in which children engage are not only worthwhile activities, but they are also controlling

activities, because the motivation for their completion is within the child and he will persist and perfect something when to adult eyes he has already perfected it sufficiently to stop.

This needful repetition is also a very real part of self-discipline because only a child can determine when he has worked with something a sufficient number of times. This is true in all of the activity found in a Montessori classroom. A child who has very carefully washed a table (and washing a table is a very elaborate process, where a child fetches water, sets out his equipment, soaps the table one way, washes it another, wipes it, folds all the cloths up and puts them away), and when he has gotten the last thing put away and has taken his apron off and hung it up may then turn around, take the apron, put it on again, and go back and repeat the whole thing in sequence. Now this may appear ridiculous to an adult, or at very least, meaningless. The child was not washing the table to get it clean, in the first place; he was washing the table because that was a pleasurable activity for him, and consequently the repetition of this task had for him an unconscious purpose not accessible to the adult. Montessori's notion of the periods of sensitivity, those periods between three and six which are fleeting in nature but during which children focus on certain sensory perceptions for a brief period of time before moving on to others, reinforces the need to capitalize on the child's sensory interests in an ordered way.

A child in control of himself is also freer in his contacts with others. An observer in a Montessori class once said, "I have been here an hour and a half, and I haven't seen any of the children fighting, and I wonder why?" All the children were very busy; and, as they were not constrained to stay at tasks longer than the tasks had meaning for them, they were not bored. Boredom and restlessness are integrally related to fighting and tussling. A child who is kept constructively busy is usually a child minimally aware of those around him. Between the age of three and six the child is often juxtaposed to other children rather than interacting with them. One discovers the kind of activity in a Montessori classroom whereby a child is working by himself, and only periodically impinging on his consciousness are the activities of other children or other children themselves. He will

stop his activity, he may reconsult with another child, discuss something, then come back to what he is doing. There is no hard and fast rule for socialization at this age, but the fact that he is focusing on his own work does not prevent him from being interrupted and re-orienting his attention either to the needs of an individual child, or, in certain cases, to the requirements of the whole group which would be articulated by a teacher who might say, "Well, we will soon be eating lunch; I'd like everyone to know so that if you are almost finished with your work, you will be ready to tidy up."

Montessori believes that the cultivation of silence is the fruit of the young child's self-mastery. She would not define silence as cessation of speech, but as the attention of one's whole being. A child is not disciplined who is kept quiet only because of the fearful presence of an adult. But a child who through concentration on an activity gradually achieves an attention span which makes it possible for him to focus his whole being on work, and to become not only verbally but muscularly quiet, is a child for whom silence has more than a superficial meaning.

There is no good reason for a child to be silent if by speaking he can communicate something that is to him worthwhile. He is a better judge at this stage than the teacher would be. The point and times at which a child would be asked to be silent would be sufficiently few and far between, and for sufficiently short periods of time, that the teacher would not be projecting on the child any unrealistic demands. The children themselves from one end of the year to the other become more capable of sustained periods of silence as they become more attentive to their activities. They also become more capable of self-direction.

A traditional fallacy in the education of young children is best exemplified by the teacher who dominates the class totally. The same teacher, when she leaves the classroom, in nine cases out of ten will have all hell break loose behind her back, because she carries within herself not only all the motives for discipline, but all the discipline itself. When the child is exposed to this type of discipline, he will work when the teacher is watching him and will not work when she is not, because he takes all of his cues

from her. In a Montessori class, the child is working for his *own* benefit. From an early age he is very aware of this. He is not working to please the teacher, he is not working to be the best. He is working because work pleases him, and satisfies him. The only worthwhile motivation for the young child to work derives from the fact that work is recognized as a good thing. Whether or not one is best or worst, it is a good thing to learn. Montessori teachers discourage the children from these intermediate motives for learning which only confuse the child in the long run and fail to provide him with long range goals for sustained academic effort.

If one were to discuss the present American system of education at the level of its two polarities—the most permissive kind of public education on the one hand, and the most rigid kind of private education on the other—it could be said that in neither of these extremes is self-discipline truly found. A child who is exposed to anarchy is not a free child, nor is a child who is exposed to rigidity. One of the difficulties of progressivism in education has been the methodological difficulty on the part of adults structuring the work of the child in such a way that the child be respected and at the same time that he be disciplined. The choice has been made frequently between discipline and respect, with respect at the expense of discipline triumphant. At the opposite polarity, the teacher protests both love and respect for the child, but uniquely on her terms. The teacher's identification with higher authority makes her unaware frequently of the need to give the children a sufficient measure of freedom to enable them to incorporate freedom and discipline in themselves. If the child is passed from hand to hand with this kind of adult attitude, it is not until he becomes an adult himself that he realizes he has no self-discipline at all. The discipline has *always* been extrinsic to him, it has resided principally in those people in authority who have dealt with him.

There is definitely a carryover between self-mastery at home and self-mastery in the school. Montessori children, from the time that Dr. Montessori first worked in the slums of San Lorenzo, sixty years ago, bring home an interest and a need for order that is a surprise and a delight to their parents, who may or may not

have felt this need. American culture does not place a high value on order. Our vision of the Victorian family is one in which the father sat at the head of the table and the mother at the foot and the children sat around and waited their turn to speak, or they waited for their piece of chicken selected by father. We have gone from what was possibly a hyper-rigid form of family structure to an informal form to an amorphous form. If one believes that order ought to be a high social value in terms of developing attitudes in the child and does not provide means to achieve it, a very real conflict can result. The school, being a sub-cultural situation, can induce order in the child in a very simple way, by ordering the physical environment of the school and respecting and reinforcing the order once established.

The problem of inducing structured behavior is a real one in teaching young children to achieve self-mastery. If the only way in which the group protoplasm is held in place is through the adult, the minute the adult turns his back the cell walls expand and the children are "all over the place."

Montessori says that when something occurs in the classroom that requires adult attention or intervention, the adult should intervene, even decisively, to prevent the good of the group from being impinged upon. Obviously, in giving the child a choice in terms of self-discipline, the adult must know whether the child is capable of choice. The child shows himself capable through the adult's observation of him. Gradually the child is given a choice between two things. Very gradually the choice is expanded, always to those things a child can do, always to those things which are good in themselves, always to those things which are related to the good of the entire group. There are controls built into the whole notion of choice that make the self-discipline a very safe mechanism for the development of the child. The teachers exert an authoritative presence; they may also exert authority in certain circumstances. But the discipline resides in three areas in a Montessori classroom: it resides in the environment itself which is controlled; in the teacher herself who is controlled and is ready to assume an authoritarian role if it is necessary; and from the very beginning it resides in the children. It is a three-way arrangement, as opposed to certain types of

American education in which all of the authority is vested in the teacher, or where, in the caricature of permissive education, all of the authority is vested in the children.

## *The Sense of Responsibility*

As the child masters himself, knows himself, and is able to function to his own satisfaction, he is ready to move out and to socialize. To discuss the relationship between self-discipline and a sense of responsibility involves a shift from what Erikson calls autonomy to what he calls initiative. "Having found a firm solution to his problem of autonomy, the child of four or five is faced with the next step and with the next crisis. Being firmly convinced that he is a person, the child must now find out what kind of person he is going to be, and here he hitches his wagon to nothing less than a star: he wants to be like his parents, who to him appear very powerful and very beautiful although quite unreasonably dangerous."[8] Then Erikson goes on to say, "One may ask what are the criteria for an unbroken sense of initiative . . . the child seems to be more himself, more loving, more relaxed and brighter in his judgment . . . he seems to be as it were self activated; he is in free possession of a certain surplus of energy which permits him to forget failures quickly and to approach what seems desirable with undiminished and better aimed effort."[9]

This really relates to the transition between the self-discipline which gives the child the necessary controls over himself and the sense of responsibility which, after all, is a more social reaction and helps the child in his mastery over his environment. One could well ponder in what sense a child of this age is responsible. A child of five can, for example, be taught to cross the street. However, this type of learning is for him a terminal thing. Once he has mastered crossing the street, there is no greater or more profound use to which he can put this knowledge. Crossing the street is a specific lesson which contains in it all the child needs to know to form a pattern of safety. A child is responsible when he is aware of himself and, to a certain degree, of his own needs, and when he is also aware of others and

the needs of others. Responsibility is related to social response. There must be something or someone or some stimulus to which he is responding. The minute a child is born into a family he is in a social setting. Does the child have any sense of social structure? He seems to have a very strong sense of his own rights, and he can, through exposure to other children, become aware of their rights as other selves, which is one of the ways in which he seems to function.

There also is a kind of group pattern which a child becomes subject to in a Montessori situation, in which he finds himself with his peers and with an authority figure. When a child has finished his work he is free to put it away, he is free to initiate new work or, in certain instances, he is free to not work. But he is not free to disturb or destroy what others are doing. If the day is arranged in such a way that at a certain time the teacher must demand of the children that they arbitrarily finish what they are doing—if it is lunch time, or recess or whatever—the child must accommodate himself to the demand of the group. It is largely a question of balance. In a Montessori class the teacher does not delude herself into believing that her manipulation of the children represents their consensus of what they would like to do. If she is manipulating them insofar as she is determining arbitrarily that this must be done at this time, she is cognizant of what she is doing, which the child may or may not be.

However, before a child can successfully relate to other children, it would seem, as Erikson, Piaget and others tell us, that he must have a strong sense of himself, a sense of basic trust. When he has this, he is ready to go out into the larger world and take his chances. To the young child of three or four the larger world in this case is really the world of the classroom, which is the next step removed from the family which has loved him and protected him and uncritically accepted him. The school situation will not uncritically accept the child. The child must measure up at certain levels, to certain social tasks, though the measuring up is not the prime reason for his activity in the class. He is still learning because it is pleasurable to him, and not because society demands it of him. Conscious motives are not of much use to the child at this age at all. A child must be

responsible first to himself, and then to the situation in which he finds himself, which in this case is social. In the family, the child is so intimately linked to the mother prior to the age of three that other people in the family are not as relevant to his development. The children in the classroom will be relevant to his development once he begins to emerge into an awareness of socialization.

It has become an American commonplace to say that the reason we send young children to school is for socialization. They learn how to get along with others, how to follow instructions; they learn how to walk in a line, how to paint, how to clean up—they learn all of these things. There is a great deal of socialization in a Montessori class which one could call incidental socialization, being incidental in so far as it relates organically to, but does not replace, the importance of the child emergent as a self. As the child progresses, as he becomes older, as he becomes more responsive to verbal communication, there is less need for him to work independently and individually; there is also less need for him to focus all of his attention on his own activity to the exclusion of the activities of everyone else. Group learning and classroom participation are all steps in his recognition of the fact that he belongs to the larger world. But it is not merely for this social recognition that a child comes to a Montessori class.

Social learning is an organic by-product of the emphasis that this type of learning places on the child's personal growth. Self-mastery is to the young child power. He sucks his thumb because it pleases him. He sucks candy because it pleases him. And he also works in the school because it pleases him. Any adult who does not understand the power of the pleasure principle in dealing with young children is very much deluded. Piaget, for example, shows us in fact that "the child's mind is woven on two different looms, which are as it were placed one above the other. By far the most important during the first years is the work accomplished on the lower plane. This is the work done by the child himself, which attracts to him pell-mell and crystallizes round his wants all that is likely to satisfy these wants. It is the plane of subjectivity, of desires, games and whims, of the *Lustprinzip* as Freud would say. The upper plane, on the contrary, is built up little by little by social environment, which presses more

A "group" lesson, which is alternated with the periods of individual activity. The Montessori teacher does not abandon all facets of "traditional" teaching.

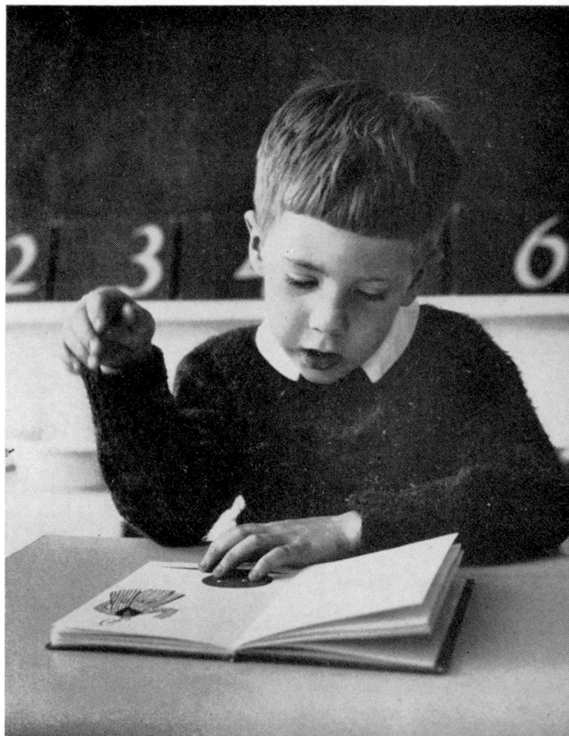

An "early" reader absorbed in a beginner's book.

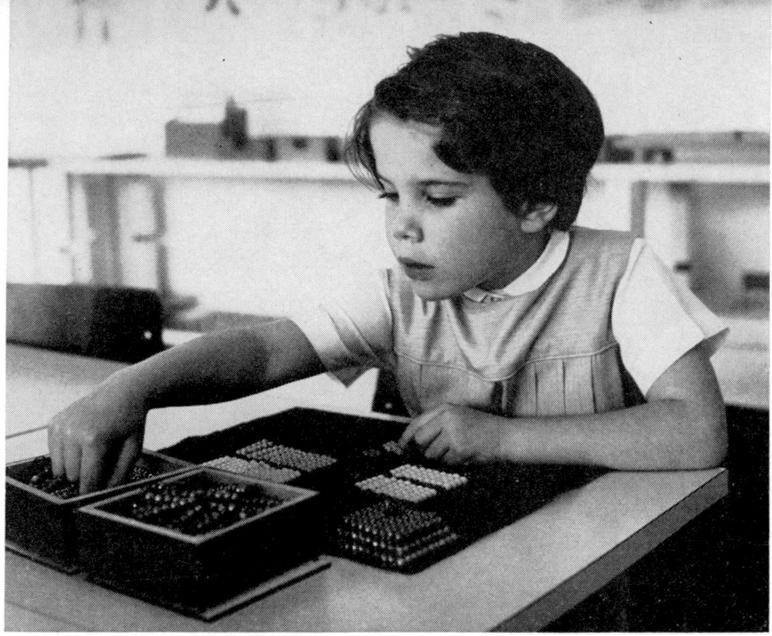

This child is composing squares of rows of bead bars and comparing them to ready-made "squares."

This child is doing a multiplication "layout" in bead bars expressing the multiplication combinations of $1 \times 1$ to $5 \times 4$.

and more upon the child as time goes on. It is the plane of objectivity, speech and logical ideas, in a word the plane of reality."[10]

Taking a four-year-old aside and telling him that it is good for his soul to do this or that, has absolutely no relevance for the child, because he is incapable of seeing beyond the pleasure principle. It is possible to start from this principle and bypass a lot of other less noble but very commonly utilized principles such as "it would make mother so happy, dear," or "we all want you to be the best in your class." These are all ignoble motives for promoting the accomplishments of children, and yet they are commonly used. The mechanism of shaming is very common in certain cultures, including our own, developing in the child a sense of guilt through invidious comparisons which should not be made between children all of whom have not achieved the same norm of accomplishment. To say to a child who does not know how to read, "come and compete with another child who does not know how to read" is foolish; one waits until a child knows how to do something before asking him to perform. At that point he can hardly wait to demonstrate his activity.

Competence breeds confidence. The sense of responsibility that competence develops in a child is remarkable. In a Montessori classroom, as soon as the child knows how to do something, he can hardly wait to show other children. When a child is in some difficulty—he does not know how to pronounce a word, or he does not know how to do an addition problem—his first recourse is to another child. When the other child cannot supply the seeker with the right answer, then the teacher will be asked. There is built up an inter-action of mutual self-help among the children that comes about because the children themselves realize that their presence in the classroom, like the teacher's, is to enhance the learning of all.

Ideally, we give answers to the children as well as questions, because we want to reinforce learning patterns that are correct. It used to be a matter of conjecture as to whether five times three was fifteen or not. Now we give children the answer 5 x 3 is 15 because we want to build up that learning pattern. The Montessori environment affords the child not only the opportunity for

the child to become responsible to himself and responsible for his own work, but it affords him the opportunity to become responsive to the needs of others, in a way in which he can handle. Not the needs of the group, but the needs of first one other child, then perhaps two others, until perhaps eventually he can accommodate a sufficient number of children to feel some sense of a group. It undoubtedly does take two or three years of exposure in a social situation for the child to begin to make an identification with a group situation. The importance of this sense of responsibility for the work of others as well as one's own work is an important factor when we consider what the nature of the school is.

The nature of the school would indicate that it is a place to learn. The teacher should not test to find out what the child does not know, but to find out what the child does know. Therefore, what any individual child knows should be constructively placed at the service of all the other children. A positive approach to learning is something the children can develop at an early age.

Children absorb from adults what the adults are rather than what they say or do; responsible adults communicate to children unconsciously a sense of responsibility. An adult who does not fail a child is a responsible and dependable adult. The parent who says, "I am going to the store and I'll be back in a little while" and does come back, (as opposed to the one who says "I'm going into the next room" and then goes away for the week-end) is a responsible adult. There is a great deal of irresponsibility in the adult treatment of children in our culture which makes children both mistrustful of adults, and also unaware of what true responsibility is. The only sense of responsibility a child can get comes from the adult patterns with which he is presented. If a child is responsible about closing a car door, his parents have initiated him into two levels of responsibility. First of all, they have shown him or indicated to him, perhaps through the vehemence of their words if not through their actions, that it is extremely important that one close a car door carefully; then they have shown him *how* to close a car door carefully.

Adults are often sporadic in their emphasis on children's re-

sponsibilities, frequently failing to teach them the responsible gestures. If children prove responsible accidentally, we congratulate them, as we scold them if they do not. Little thought is given to the communication involved in teaching a child to become responsible. If a child is to keep a younger sibling from crossing the street, he must know at least two things. He must know that crossing the street is in some way dangerous, because this is the only motivation that will keep him from allowing the littler one to go across; and he must have an awareness that the child with whom he is dealing, who is younger than himself, is less capable of judging in this situation than he is.

In the *Inner World of Childhood* Frances Wicks comments on the fact that what children literally do absorb from their parents and others in the place of parents, (and this would apply to teachers of the young), is much more Being than anything else. If one is absolutely fair and responsible with the child, he will absorb fairness and responsibility rather than anything that one can communicate verbally to him. A Montessori environment provides maximum security for the child; it provides something as simple as finding his work in the place in which he left it. If a child must leave the room—to go on an errand, to go to recess, or eat his lunch—he will come back, absolutely certain that his work will be found in the condition in which he left it, that no one will touch it. This certainty breeds in the child a sense of responsibility, because he has had shown him that which he must then show others. It is the job of the adult working with children to safeguard the child's rights.

## *Motivation*

Motivation in the child comes from a number of sources. We know that motivation can come from the child's desire to emulate his parents, to be big, to grow big, to do what his father does. Therefore the notion of work is integrally related to the notion of motivation because a child does not think that the fact his father works is a negative thing; he thinks of it rather more positively. Many children play at working because they realize in some obscure way that they are imitating their parents by so

doing. The desire to grow, to be big, to be a man is an underlying motivation in a great deal of the child's learning. When a child goes to school, he feels he is placing his foot firmly on that path that will lead to maturity and he is right in assuming this.

The child who is overly indulged by his mother for one reason or another is the child who, in shaking off her loving hand, is attempting desperately to do for himself what he can. Erikson tells us that the child whose hand is held too tightly while crossing the street is exerting a kind of reaction against this constant shepherding even when he is still two years of age. His only ability is a capacity to rebel and he rebels, because he wants not only to be himself, not to be dependent on his mother, but he also wants to make his own way, he is motivated to grow.

In terms of interest, if a child does not derive pleasure from an activity, he will not persist in it. In the complex timetable of acculturation, one could spend a great deal of energy and thought on the ways to render pleasurable certain steps in the development of a child toward socialization which must inevitably take place. Some of these we know take place almost automatically. The child learns to control his temper frequently, because lack of control of temper brings unpleasant consequences. Also, he associates control with certain forms of adult approval. Toilet training is an example of this. In American middle-class society, frequently children who are not trained by a certain age are shamed by their mothers, and this act is a powerfully motivating force to training. This is interesting in view of the fact that many cultures are not the least bit concerned whether or not children are or are not toilet trained by the age of three, though in American culture three seems to be the age at which children are expected to control their bladders and bowels, and the child who is unable to do this is often considered incapable of entering nursery school effectively.

One of the most important aspects of motivation present in the education of the young child is related to the pleasure the child derives from objective accomplishment. Many studies on reading have been undertaken in the past generation to prove and disprove the contention that it is a good thing for children to learn

to read at a tender age. Critics of early reading state their case in approximately the following terms. If it is in no way detrimental to the child to learn to read at an early age, why then is it beneficial for the child to learn to read early? By the time the child is about fifteen he will probably not be reading any more efficiently than children who learn to read much later than he.

Motivation plays an important role in the continuing learning process of the child. The child who learns to read at three (if he is ready to learn to read at three) will be reading effectively and pleasurably at fifteen because at every stage of his learning career he found reading pleasurable and accessible. He could be contrasted to the child who is eager to read, but instead was detoured into cutting and pasting until such time as the teacher felt his eye balls had matured or she felt she could determine when he was "ready." The tendency to place children in the lockstep educational system which predicates its judgments on norms of maturity rather than actual children has caused many casualties in the American educational system.

It is to avoid this type of thinking that Montessori respects the rhythm of the young child. The young child does not develop in an unbroken vertical line. There are periods of ascent and periods of reinforcement in the growth pattern of the young child. It is difficult for an adult to assess adequately the value or importance of continual repetition of an activity by a child after the child appears to have mastered the activity. However, as each stage of growth contains within it the seeds of the following stage and consolidates the preceding stage, frequently, the marking of time at a certain point in the child's life will occur before significant gains dramatically reveal themselves. Continuing motivation toward learning is not only the specific task of the school but also a necessity for the child who is to take his place in this culture.

A child is not only motivated to perform; he is motivated to perform for a certain purpose. The child who performs because he enjoys doing so, because he is confident that his performance is adequate for his needs and that it will stand the test of scrutiny is the child who will ultimately be able to take his place in a

culture where sheer force of numbers forces any but the most competent towards the bottom of the heap.

To reinforce the child's sense of his own worth and to interest him in continual challenges, of which the only apparent value will be his own sense of satisfaction is also an important task of the teacher of the very young. There comes a time in every child's life when the adult can honestly say to him, "You don't have to like it, you just have to do it." But saying this to the young child before he has had an opportunity to like what he is doing, is to place in his mind an identification of what is necessary with what is unpleasant or undesirable.

Montessori and Dewey share a belief that the child's immersion in experience will give him a firsthand view of learning that all the talking of the teacher will never do. At the same time, by the emphasis on individual work which Montessori makes, she frees the child to work at his own pace, in his own way, on his own project, unhurried by adults, and outside the realm of competition with other children. This individual activity is in itself a powerful motivating force for many children who would otherwise remain passive in the face of bigger, brighter, or more competent companions. The child is always given the choice of joining or abstaining, of holding back or letting go. In this way the child who does not move with the group is not judged antisocial, but is allowed to continue independently of the group, and at the same time recognizes the rights of the group to exist and to work without him.

Motivation in learning is made up of many things, but a large measure of competence is necessary for a child to continue to learn. By teaching children what they need to know early in life, they may be better able to cope with the problems of their culture than by learning late the basic rules when little time is allotted for their mastery. Knowing what we do of young children, and what we do of the complex, competitive demands of our culture, it seems astounding that Americans pay so little heed to the development of the young child in view of the academic cycle into which he will very quickly enter. If the end results of education can be judged by the fullest use of a child's individual capacities, then it behooves a culture to capitalize on the child's

gifts from the moment they begin to emerge. First grade is far too late to develop motivation, as a separate skill, in children. By the time a child is six, he is either motivated or not, depending on his previous experiences which for American children are mainly non-academic.

The only way for a child to learn to choose is to choose. The only way for him to make a decision is to decide, and in a child-serving culture, such as ours tends to be, we are constantly choosing for the children, substituting our ideas for their ideas, and then jollying them into thinking it was really their idea all the time. A child who is never allowed to exert his own judgment, does not trust his judgment. The fact that so many American children are incapable of vocational choices, may reflect their lack of opportunity to make small choices that would have strengthened their ability to choose. A Montessori classroom allows the child to see that he *has* to make a choice. He must choose constantly; he must choose consciously; he must accept or refuse.

Motivation in a Montessori class is built up in two ways. First of all, there is the very ordered, structured way in which children are presented with certain tasks so that the child does not risk failure due to ignorance of the preceding steps in any given task. Second, when the teacher asks him whether or not he would like to attempt something new, he is free to accept or refuse. If he refuses to embark on some new task, and it is well to bear in mind that time is in his favor because he is being initiated in tasks which ordinarily would not come for two or three years, no time factor enters in. If he is not interested in doing the given thing, the teacher offers him something else to do instead. She does not make any judgment that he is a poor sport, or that a big boy of his age ought to be doing this or that. These are irrelevant judgments for a young child. She works uniquely on the principle of capturing his interest.

The expression "normalization" occurs in the thought of Montessori to indicate that state of true normality achieved by once disturbed or deviant children. True normality is rarely seen, because many of the manifestations of disturbance are accepted as normal behavior. Hyperactive children, restless bored children,

chronic complainers, spoiled children all represent a sort of deviation which will impede enjoyment of self-expression through work. The key to "normalization" is found in the first moment of spontaneous concentration shown by the child. The teacher may have been vainly attempting to interest him in all manner of activities and been refused each time. Once she succeeds in presenting him with one thing which interests him, he has made the first contact with normalization. From a brief spell of concentration, he will develop the ability to concentrate more spontaneously and expand his interest.

The "normalized" child loves to work, and loves the order that work involves. He works well alone, but will suffer companionship. He seems completely absorbed in his tasks and yet will be willing to share information and experience with others. He will enjoy being obedient, yet will not lack initiative. This hypothetical child *does exist* in Montessori classes. He manifests a set of learning skills not often associated with the young in American schools. Because he enjoys working, he is no less normal than the child playing in the conventional nursery school. He is simply freer to demonstrate a form of behavior that is usual for him in an environment that is tolerant of work.

In American education, the motivation to excel is certainly a real one. It is best exemplified by coaches who say, "I don't field a team to play, I field a team to win." If we examine in depth such social phenomena as the Little League, we see that the intrusion of parents in the Little League is directly related to the American goal of the best team winning. Participation becomes secondary to an objective accomplishment. Any culture makes certain demands on its members at a certain time. There is a cut-off point, by which time children must know how to do certain things; but prior to that time the greatest latitude ought to be afforded children to learn each at his own rhythm so that by the time a child is eight, for example, he is able to read, and that it is of no great disastrous consequences whether he learned at three or whether he learned at seven and a half.

By introducing what one might well call ignoble motives—such as making mother happy, etc.—into learning at an early age, children begin to learn for all the wrong reasons, and frequently

the right reasons never occur to them simply because they are never introduced with as much force as the wrong reasons. For Americans of any age, judgment of one's peers is a very potent force. Parents seem to be as impressed with peers as the children are, so even young children are frequently expected to accede to norms of group behavior that may not be congenial to them as individuals but that are representative of what a group of their peers is doing. "Parents and other adults come to value the child in terms of his ability to live up to the group's expectations and to wrest popularity from it," says David Riesman in speaking of the childhood of the "other-directed."[11] The Montessori approach to motivation is precisely to interest the child first through the attraction to the activity and through the pleasure he derives from it, and from that point on to enlarge the field of motivation to include the objective good of the activity, so that a child would learn to read because it pleased him, and quite soon he would look around to see his mother and father reading and would even see that reading is a good thing. Reading to please the teacher or to be a better reader than someone else or to be a butterfly when his friend was an earthworm, a kind of motivation that is very common, does not have very much to do with the child's relation to learning, because the young child knows all grown-ups read, but he is not too aware that he too, one day, is going to have to learn.

## *Notion of Experience*

The child begins with himself—the most real thing to him is himself, his own greatest production—and though he is functioning in a world of sights and sounds, a world that is chaotic and from which he must derive order, still his great awareness of that world does not seem to occur until he is aware of himself. Montessori begins with the young child, and she considers education as beginning with birth; therefore, she is aware of the child's needs from the moment he leaves his mother's body—she is focusing on the child, at all times.

It has been said of Dewey, that his is a child-centered rather than a subject-centered kind of education, which is true. It is

also true that Montessori, focusing on the child, does not forget the subject. She never loses sight of the child's great work of *constructing* himself. One might wonder why, after discussing the child in his various aspects of responsibility, motivation, self-awareness, the last category to be discussed would be that of experience, rather than the first. Were one to compare the thinking of Montessori on this point to that of John Dewey, one would discover that Dewey believes that experience is the environment stimulating the individual to modify the environment. "The organism does not stand about Micawber-like, waiting for something to turn up. The organism acts in accordance with its own structure upon its surroundings."[12]

Learning by doing has been a capsulization of the Dewey approach to learning. Critics of this have said that it is better to learn by thinking than to learn by doing, failing to distinguish the levels of activity. But learning by abstract thinking is a form of learning not readily accessible to the young child, precisely because his intellectual perceptions run far behind his sensory motor perceptions. Before a child is able to interact consciously on the environment, to simulate or modify the environment, he must contain within himself a sufficient awareness to act at all. In assuming that the role of education begins at birth Montessori underscores the dramatic activity that occurs within the child before he reaches the point at which he emerges into society as a person capable of acting upon it, stimulating it, or modifying it. Possibly Lyman Bryson's comment in Riesman's book, *Constraint and Variety in American Education*[13] points up the fact that Montessori began at the beginning—the perceptions of Dewey with respect to the nature of experience tend to begin at a higher level of child development. Dewey may well be speaking of the first grader where Montessori speaks of the toddler. For this reason, though the role of experience is similar in both educators' thought, the relation of the individual to experience is somewhat different. "It [progressive education] too generously substituted motor thinking, which the child usually loves, for abstract thinking which he has to learn to do."[14]

There are many things a young child learns not through doing but through being. He learns through the attitudes of his parents

and those to whose care he is entrusted. There is much in the relation of the child to the adult encompassed in the expression "learning by doing," if one imitates what the adult does. However, Montessori points out that putting a child in contact with experience through the imitation of adult action is one way of insuring success for him. In a Montessori classroom a teacher will demonstrate to a child how something is done, not by talking about it, but by showing the child, and then the child will feel free to do this. The similarity of outlook on the role of experience in Dewey and Montessori can perhaps be best seen in their mutual conception of the role of the classroom as a "learning situation." The irrelevance of school desks in rows with the teacher poised at the top of the class becomes obvious when we analyze the fact that a number of children with various interests and abilities should be able to be doing different things at the same time. The content of study, the notions of discipline, and the role of the teacher are all affected by this idea of experience. School studies, Dewey says, should be continuous with the child's environment. They should utilize the child's everyday experience.

The child's parents are real to him, but what is most real of all or what must become real is himself. The antithesis that used to exist between discipline and interest should theoretically disappear when experience is called in to the learning complex. If a lesson was interesting it was without value in traditional education. Conversely, what was unpleasant to learn appeared to be more valuable than what was pleasurable. The importance of the responsibility in selecting matter for the child to learn is placed in the hands of those adults who are aware of what the culture will demand of the child and who are able to "program" learning in such a way that what is suitable for the child's age and stage of development is also learnable and pleasurable to him. Both Dewey and Montessori feel that interest and discipline are connected and not opposed. Dewey himself decried unrestrained freedom of action in speech, in manners, and lack of manners. He was, in fact, critical of all those progressive schools that carried the thing they call freedom nearly to the point of anarchy. Criticisms of Montessori could then be related

to a misunderstanding of some of the Dewey *dicta.* Dewey says, "when there is a genuine control and direction of experiences, that are intrinsically worthwhile by objective subject matter, excessive liberty of outward action will also be naturally regulated. Ultimately it is the absence of intellectual control through significant subject matter which stimulates the deplorable egotism, cockiness, impertinence, and disregard for the rights of others apparently considered by some persons to be the inevitable accompaniment if not the essence of freedom."[15] The concept of experience, then, involves interest, individual work, and discipline, all self-corrective mechanisms in terms of character development. It is not surprising that considering the child from the Montessori point of view, one would take experience last in order to utilize it as an exemplification of all of the controls that liberty within limits offers the child.

PART II

# The Environment

CHAPTER 4

# The Prepared Environment

---

## *The Problem Stated*

ANY SCHOOL situation is highly artificial. Many cultures have successfully educated their young to the tasks of the culture without the need for or the organization of education into complex, formalized school patterns. Any teacher who enters a class of children brings not only the sum of herself and her personal attitudes, she brings conscious ideas about what ought to be placed in the environment in order that certain reactions be assured in the children with whom she is working. Margaret MacMillan believed that the upper middleclass schoolroom situation of Victorian England would give young English children the best opportunity for development of social and intellectual virtues deemed desirable; Carolyn Pratt believed that through the use of block play certain specific goods in the realm of manipulation and socialization would be forthcoming; Froebel believed in his "gifts," Montessori believed in the "prepared environment," and alone among educators was lucid enough to admit from the outset that her environment *was* prepared.

The motives for activity that are placed within the classroom provide opportunities for the children to act individually, to interact or to act as a group. It is no accident that play equipment in Russia is designed in such a way that it requires the combined strength of groups of children to manipulate it effectively. Group activity and group solidarity go hand in hand. Montessori's insistence on the rights of the individual child makes

many Americans—who have never analyzed the importance that organized education accords to group responses—uneasy. There is much talk of individualization within the group in American schools. Yet, rarely has anyone queried either the advisability or the inevitability of children being instructed in bunches as opposed to being instructed alone. Despite the fact that the monitorial system of Lancaster and Bell is little more than one hundred years old, and that as Americans we profess allegiance to the notion of Mark Hopkins on one end of the log with the students on the other, American education for the young has always assumed that the life of the individual child is the life of the group. The fact that this emphasis on the group is often meaningless for the young child keeps many children out of nursery schools whose avowed aim is "getting along." That the child can come to the life of the group, in fact recognize the existence of the group largely through an awareness of himself—though this has been known for at least two generations—appears to be one of the better kept secrets of early childhood education.

If the child is to merge with the group in some form of activity let it be a conscious act on his part; let it reflect his desire to do so. The present American pattern of large, tightly spaced families coupled with group education is depriving many children of "lebensraum"; the physical limitations of small servantless homes are cramping the child physically as well as emotionally, because there are frequently *no provisions made for him to get away from others.* Split level houses seem to have no hiding places in the attic—indeed they have no attics. The delightful eccentrics of the present-day grandparents' generation are disappearing. Such social chroniclers as Edwin O'Connor attest to this fact. Where are the Skeffingtons and Charlie Carmodys of the present? They are gone surely as much because of the conformity-oriented education of the past sixty years as for any other reason. It matters little whose were the original assumptions upon which much educational patterning is based. In fact, succeeding generations of teachers, who were technicians but no educational theorists, have implemented half-digested ideas with no notion that it was somebody's conscious intent to place a certain activity in the classroom in order to achieve a conscious and specific child response.

Maria Montessori combined a sharp clinical eye with the mind of an educational theorist. Her first work was to observe children, as they showed themselves to be, in as free an environment as she was able to create. Then, having induced from her observation certain principles, she consciously constructed a "prepared environment," which would ensure certain of the child-responses. Montessori need make no apologies for such a procedure, though many of her critics appear to find it disconcerting.

"The education of our day is rich in methods, aims and social ends, but one must still say that it takes no account of life itself." This statement was made in *The Absorbent Mind* in 1949. As Americans we pride ourselves on our emphasis on education not only for life, but for life in a democratic society, education that foresees and hence ideally forearms the men and women of tomorrow against the problems they will be called upon to face and to resolve. Granted the complexity of the American educational task, granted the option for universal education of all, regardless of native endowment, granted the laws governing compulsory school attendance—inorganic in the case of so many restless adolescent non-learners—granted all this, are we coming close to achieving effective education for more than a slim minority of our hardy, aggressive, better endowed children who may well be learning despite the "system" rather than because of it? American education has lofty aims, enormous problems, and immediate challenges. Yet, happily, never have Americans been more concerned both with the techniques of education and the ends of education.

For the first time in American history, two generations after the waves of immigrants of the late nineteenth century brought in force the hewers of wood and the drawers of water, a generation of young parents has risen up, sassy, articulate, and critical of educational practice. In many instances, they are better educated than those teaching their children, and sophisticated in their knowledge of Freud, Jung and Spock. Medicine has experienced a similar situation. Doctors are frequently being told by interested patients of the latest developments in medicine. Perhaps teachers and doctors dislike this turn of events. But there is little that can be done about it. The mystical aura of education and medicine has faded. Such groups as the Council for Basic

Education have consistently criticized the flabby, vacuous rationalizations of the educational "establishment."

The entire educational framework is being reassessed. How many years are necessary for elementary learning? What should be learned? How long should it take? How long should children be in school? When should they have completed professional studies? How do they learn? Of what they are taught, how much do children learn? Does classroom instruction proliferate error? How can the individual child be put in direct contact with content without it passing through the teacher? How important is verbal teaching? What is the role of motivation in learning? These and literally dozens of other questions are being asked by expert and layman alike.

In this long look at education, it seems imperative that we face the assumptions of children's early development. To speak of educating the child with revised concepts of social studies and to ignore both the manner in which he obtains information concerning the formation of judgments (whether from peers or adults), as well as the fact that from the moment he toddles in front of the television screen in his own home he is being assaulted by someone else's judgments, is to prolong the fiction of education beginning "seriously" at the age of six. If American education is to capitalize on the resource represented by the nation's children, then it can do no less than the child is forced to do—begin at the beginning and, upon each successful accomplishment, build the next stage of development. Until early education is made respectable in its own right, and not merely "readiness" for the lockstep supposedly *real* education which begins at six, there will be a continued waste of human potential and a corresponding need to build into existing school programs more remedial than preventive emphasis. It is ludicrous to consider the revamping of American education without a thoughtful glance at the origins of learning and of learning how to learn.

## *The Theory of the Prepared Environment*

The "prepared environment" of Dr. Montessori, like the "responsive environment" of Dr. Moore, is designed by an adult in

advance of a child's entry into it. It is the physical and psychological situation made ready for the young child in order to enhance his opportunity to learn through experiences provided him. Obviously all of the experiences of life are not present in the Montessori class situation. It is not designed to duplicate the child's home environment. It is not designed to afford the child all of the experiences that life itself, outside the few short hours the child is in the class, will provide. The "prepared environment" is designed to help the child achieve a sense of himself, self-mastery and mastery of his environment through the successful execution and repetition of apparently simple tasks which are nonetheless linked to the cultural expectations the child faces in the context of his total development. Montessori stresses that the child does not work in the way the adult works: the adult works for profit or from necessity; the child works to *create himself.* The simplest activities of the baby, creeping and crawling, underscore the validity of Montessori's view. The research of Carl Delacato, in the establishment of laterality (sidedness) in children, provides rich evidence that the child is creating himself as an instrument of learning in the early years.[1]

"The foundation of development and growth lies in progressive and ever more intimate relations between the individual and his environment: for the development of individuality, and of what is called the freedom of the child, can be nothing else than his progressive independence of the adult, realized by means of a suitable environment in which he can find the necessary means of evolving his functions. This is as clear and simple as the fact that in weaning a baby we prepare baby food from cereals, fruit juices and vegetables, that is to say, by using the products of the outer world in place of mother's milk. . . . The preparation of the environment is part of the science of education, just as the preparation of baby food is part of the science of health."[2]

Physically, the "prepared" Montessori environment resembles a nursery or kindergarten class. All that is contained within it is child size. (One of the lasting debts American education acknowledges to Montessori is the small-size furniture which she first developed.) There is an absence of some of the material we are accustomed to see and the inclusion of other materials not

usually seen in nursery classes. There is a sense of order in the way in which the room is laid out. This is not an accidental but an essential feature. There are individual work tables, a rarity in group-oriented American schools. The tables are clustered in small groups but may be rearranged by the children at will. There is a great deal of open floor space, which permits the children to work on the floor. They take their work to mats (roughly the size of bath mats) on the floor and work: squatting, sitting, kneeling and stretching. Ideally, the class opens into a garden or outdoor play area where, weather permitting, the children can continue their activities out of doors. The distinction between work and play is not made in such fashion that one works indoors and plays outdoors however. Children need to learn in all weather, so no effort is made to prevent them from learning in the sunshine.

At first glance, the Montessori prepared environment gives a decentralized impression. Where is the teacher to be found? Anywhere. She has no table or desk as such, but a low chair like that of the children. She works with children individually, or in twos or groups, and is most often found on her knees or haunches working with the children down at their eye level. Since she demonstrates the use of all of the learning activities, the children watch her hands closely in order to copy her actions. The Montessori prepared environment disconcerts adults through its deemphasis on the group. Despite the fact that much evidence exists to support the contention that formation into groups, initiated by the children, is exceedingly rare at the ages of three and four, nonetheless we have been culturally conditioned to expect it. A child working alone in a conventional nursery class often leads the teacher to volunteer a defensive explanation. Quite the contrary in a Montessori class. If the child sees no need to join forces with another, why should the teacher feel a need to explain his action? The impulse to sociability rather than to "togetherness" is the governing one in a Montessori class. "Since sociability in its pure form has no ulterior end, no content and no result outside itself, it is oriented completely about personalities."[3] Reflected in the American Montessori class is the alternating pattern of organization vs. disorganization so

aptly described by Drs. Ilg and Ames.[4] "Careful analysis of behavior trends in the first ten years of life . . . make it apparent that a rather distinctive sequence of behavior stages seems to occur repeatedly as the child matures. Thus the first cycle, and the one we know most about, occurs between two and five years of age, repeats itself from five to ten, and occurs once again between the ages of ten and sixteen . . .

"First of all, we have observed that two years of age, five years and ten years all constitute focal points at which behavior seems to be in good equilibrium, the child having relatively little difficulty within himself or with the world about him. Each of these relatively smooth and untroubled ages is followed by a brief period when behavior appears to be very much broken up, disturbed and troubled, and when the child shows himself to be in marked disequilibrium. Thus the smoothness of 2-year-old behavior characteristically breaks up at two and a half; 5-year-old behavior breaks up at five and a half to six; and ten breaks up at eleven, the 11-year-old child characteristically showing himself to be at definite odds with his environment and with himself.

"Each of these ages is followed, once more, by a period of relative equilibrium at three, six and a half and twelve years respectively, when life's forces seem to be in good balance. The child is happy both within himself and in his environment.

"These are followed by ages when there is a very pronounced inwardizing or drawing in of outer impressions and experiences, to be mulled over, thought about and digested within. These ages are three and a half, seven and thirteen years. At three and a half this inner process often has disturbing side effects of general emotional instability, a variety of fears, poor spatial orientation, hand tremor, whining and high tremulous voice, stuttering and stumbling. Seven and thirteen are more stable ages and better ready to stand the strain of this inwardizing period of growth. The side effects at these latter ages are more apt to be expressed in marked sensitivity and touchiness, excessive withdrawal and moroseness, and a minor and pessimistic attitude toward life in general.

"All three of these ages are followed by periods of extreme expansiveness. Four, eight and fourteen are all times at which

the child's behavior is markedly outgoing in most major respects. He is even in danger of expanding too much. He wanders from home and gets lost at four, he demands to ride his bicycle in the street at eight and may get hit, and he gets all tangled in his multiple and conflicting social plans at fourteen.

"The next three ages (four and a half, nine years and fifteen years) are ones about which we perhaps know the least, but we do know enough to recognize certain similarities about the three periods. In each of them, behavior is less outgoing than at the age which directly preceded. In each it is in less good equilibrium. Child specialists have frequently described each of these three ages by the term "neurotic," though they may each represent perfectly normal stages of growth.

"And then once more, in each instance, we come to ages of stability and of relatively good equilibrium: five, ten and sixteen."

The over-all impression of a Montessori class is one of continual movement coupled with attention. Children, busy at varying tasks, are always involved at sensory and motor levels. This sensory motor involvement has raised a question of the child's dependence on concrete material for understanding. The structured Montessori material is only a stepping stone to abstraction, and it is the general experience of Montessori teachers that children go rapidly from the manipulation of the material in the case of mathematics and language to an ability to do "mental" mathematics and grammar depending on the child's maturation. It is, of course, the task of the teacher to insure the child's continuing progress, through the introduction of progressively more difficult tasks. She must be aware that the fear of new learning because of fear of failure may be a factor in repeated manipulation of material after the child has obviously mastered it and enjoyed it.

The gifts needed in the Montessori teacher include not only a strong back and an intuitive grasp of the child's needs as demonstrated by his ability to communicate through his work. The teacher of the young children—Montessori or otherwise—must be aware of the pitfalls of pride and anger so common among those working with the young. It is extremely easy to feel oneself omniscient when confronted with young children.

Such a feeling often hampers the teacher in her ability to observe the children and to listen to what their work is telling her. Anger, largely in the form of impatience, is another problem for many teachers of the young. The rhythm of the child is a rhythm different from the adult. The child works at a thing until he is satisfied. The teacher has no foolproof way of knowing when this point is reached. The teacher must constantly guard against over-teaching and over-correcting—correcting a child who is unaware that he has made an error, intervening to show a child how to improve a skill he has barely learned. Respecting at all times the child's right to help himself, and to solicit help only when he feels it is needed, requires tremendous patience.

If the teacher appears to be "at one side" of the class rather than in the center, it is because all that the children learn does not come from her. She is not in the center dispensing praise, blame, motivation, encouragement and correction. She is moving about the class, helping where needed, encouraging when asked, praising and blaming where actions warrant it, in a one to one relationship with each child in the early years of his learning. She speaks seldom, but speaks with meaning and authority. The tremendous emphasis on verbal teaching as the principal means of communicating knowledge makes the Montessori teacher (or directress, as Dr. Montessori called her) strangely silent to some American observers. Since many of the difficulties that arise in the use of language between children and adults are due to the child's inability to use words meaningfully, and because the sensory motor foundations for later concept learning are of great importance, the Montessori class does not emphasize learning through talking and listening, but learning through doing and manipulating without interruption. (Obviously a class for older children of six to nine includes both elements, even as it makes provision for group lessons as well as individual work.)

In a lecture given by Montessori, she mentioned that the task of the teacher was "to teach teaching, not correcting." In teaching the children to teach themselves, the Montessori teacher is preparing them for a life of learning, not a single experience of learning.

## *The Practice: An American Montessori Class*

Montessori claimed validly that her approach to the education of the young child was supra-national. The fact that Montessori schools exist in every major European center, in Africa, Asia and America, point to the implementation of this assumption. Yet, the classes in these countries, despite the "classical" Montessori base upon which all are founded, vary greatly from culture to culture and country to country. Any culturally relevant Montessori class must reflect the basic national assumptions upon which education in that country is based. There are many such assumptions which underlie American education, both public and independent. But some assumptions appear more dramatically American than others.

The interest in group activity and the assumption that anything that can be done individually is somehow invested with greater value if done in a group is one such American attitude. Montessori's provision for the individual child in the ungraded class to act as member of the group, learning alone or in concert with others, reflects in the elementary grades the group-oriented attitude of American education. The nomadic tendencies of American families are also reflected in Montessori classes as in all others. The American child is potentially "on the move." No learning institution can count absolutely on the stable child population that characterized the schools attended by our grandparents. The need for expression in large muscle activities and art work on a broad scale is likewise reflective of American culture preoccupations.

Let us imagine a visit to a typical American Montessori class in a school which has been in existence a number of years. The class of three- to six-year-old children, some of whom are in their second and third Montessori years with the same teacher, will be found some forty strong in a very large and light classroom. The classroom might have white walls, incandescent lighting, a light gray floor, and individual tables of gray and white formica, which can be placed, moved about and spotted easily. There are bright-colored paintings on the walls, all the work of the children. Ranged around the room are various sorts of material for work.

In the cloakroom adjacent to the class, one finds the children's names on the pegs for hanging their outdoor clothes, and to each peg is attached a clothespin for attaching cap and mittens. Another is used to clip overshoes together for later identification. Adjoining the cloakroom is a child-sized toilet room, and in the cloakroom is a work sink for painting, cleaning and washing up.

The "exercises of practical life" form part of the Montessori activity. What are these exercises? Washing tables, dusting, waxing, polishing shoes, silver and brass, cutting flowers, changing goldfish water, folding clothes, buttoning, zipping, etc., on frames provided for this purpose—and generally, all the activities which promote a mastery of the child's self and his environment. The equipment used for washing tables (as all other equipment) is very attractive. The child will take a pink plastic apron, which snaps in the front and is therefore manageable, a pink plastic pail, a pink pitcher, pink soap dishes, pink sponge and washing cloth and arrange them in an order already demonstrated to him by the teacher. There is an order in which the washing material is laid, both to expedite the job itself and to offer the child the security of having mastered one way of washing tables "that works." The child will undertake this exercise with extreme care and interest, finding in the working with water the eternal fascination it holds for young children, as well as a structured activity which has a beginning, a middle and an end. At the same time as one young man is washing tables, another might be polishing his shoes, another mopping the floor, another ironing, or engaging in many of the household tasks that are "real" and provide a "reality-bound" school situation.

At the same time as the housekeeping tasks engage some of the children, others are engaged in what Montessori calls the sensorial exercises. These are activities that look like games, designed to provide the children, through sensory motor manipulation, with concepts of weight, volume, dimension, number, etc. Accompanying these activities, vocabulary lessons are presented by the teacher, such as those illustrated by the learning of the names of colors (which the child recognizes but cannot name). For the teaching of vocabulary, Montessori introduced a technique learned by her from Dr. Edouard Seguin called "The Three

Period Lesson." First, the child learns to associate the name of the color with the color; as the teacher shows the child two pairs of color tablets which look like paint chips, she says in touching the yellow one, "Yellow," in touching the blue, "Blue." She then says to the child, "Please give me the yellow. Please give me the blue." At this stage she is asking the child to associate the color with the learned word. The third phase of this exercise, which may or may not follow directly on the heels of the other two, is to ask the child, "Which is this? Which is this?"—anticipating the correct answer of blue or yellow, as the case may be. The child then indicates that he has made the connection between the color and its conventional name.

The many sensory motor activities which form what has been called in the Montessori class "The Indirect Preparation for Academic Learning" occupies many of the other children. Some of the smallest ones might be working alone or with a teacher on the "Sandpaper Letters." These are letters twice the width of a child's finger, which the teacher demonstrates by tracing them herself in the way in which the child will ultimately write them. She then invites the child to follow suit, while repeating the sound of the letter as the child does so—simple breath emissions for the consonants, and first the short vowel sounds for the vowels (as they occur with greater frequency in English). Other children may be composing words and stories with small alphabets; others still are painting and drawing, counting with the red and blue number rods, or composing large numbers with the decimal material and cards with mathematical symbols. The decimal material—on which teachers place value, and which frees the children to compose large quantities and to combine them in the four operations—greatly interests the younger children. Through the manipulation of the decimal material the children are able to add, subtract, multiply and divide with pleasure and interest and success. Where is the teacher or teachers while all this is going on? The teachers are in the classroom as the guardians of that order that must prevail if the children are to be free to learn. In the three-to-six class, the children tend to work with teachers individually, yet the tendency (so deep-seated in America) to group, is also present in some of the older children. If there is a

group, the teacher may be working with it or with one of the children. Throughout the busy hum of the classroom environment, children are working on the floor or at their desks with considerable concentration, asking each other for help when it appears necessary and suffering correction gracefully when it is forthcoming from more accomplished and aggressive colleagues.

When the teacher asks the children for silence, in order to gain their attention, she need ask only once and the class will stop in its work and give the teacher its full attention. The children view the teacher as an authoritative person, there to help them and protect their right to work. Groups of children are allowed to work together. If a child begins to work with another and decides to proceed on his own, he is likewise free to do so. The period in the morning between approximately nine and eleven o'clock is viewed as almost a sacred work-period in Montessori circles. The children are, for the most part, at their learning best—they are working alone to reinforce the lessons learned previously in a group and it is not at all uncommon to see all of the children under the direction of one or two teachers doing different work simultaneously.

To the question "what provision is made for socialization?" one could reply that the very condition of learning in this Montessori environment depends on socialization as an atmospheric element. The teacher who may (and will) intrude, even emphatically, if the good of the whole group requires it, nonetheless never intervenes unless absolutely necessary in the case of differences which arise between the children. An illustration of this might be seen in the following incident. A small boy of three was being pushed off his stool by an older boy each time the older boy came by his table. A girl sitting nearby went over to the child who had been pushed for the third time and was now on the floor and said, "Did you ever consider kicking him?" The pushee said no that he had not. With that, the champion of the underdog said, "Look, it's easy," and gave the offender a smart kick in the shins which sent him hobbling about his business. In such an incident the Montessori teacher would not intervene, but would let the children themselves sort out the difficulty, as they are so capable of doing.

The ground rules which are most apparent in observing a Montessori class are those which deal with the respect for other children and for their work. Any child is free to work with any material he has been shown by the teacher or that he himself has mastered through the observation of another child working with it. Thus, a child who wants to compose large numbers, such as six thousand three hundred fifty one, may have been shown how to do so or has watched others do so and feels competent to try. No child touches another child's work. In a Montessori environment the child who leaves his work, whether he be three or thirteen, leaves in the security of knowing that upon his return everything will be as he left it. Children may work with others who are working on a project only if those working first invite them to do so. As there are not numerous sets of all the material in the Montessori class, the refusal to be allowed to work with a child already doing what one wants to do may result in a long wait. Yet both the refusal and the wait are part of those real conditions which promote awareness of the rights of others. At about mid-morning, a group of children who have finished the first part of their work assume charge of the distribution of juice and crackers to the others. Those children, deeply absorbed, come when they are ready and collect their snack; those who have finished have it together. Never does the Montessori teacher intrude on the learning activities of the child to impose an arbitrary social experience, unless it is absolutely necessary, in her mind. But dismissal at the end of the day is inevitable. Therefore all of the children must be ready to go when their mothers come for them.

If the early skills of learning involve the development of attention through interest in an activity, it is the task of the teacher to respect the growth of interest and to protect the child from constant interruption in his work. When he has finished it to his own satisfaction he will stop. Often a child will repeat an activity, such as counting or composing words or washing tables, long after the teacher sees any reason for him to do so. What looks like meaningless repetition to the adult gives the child pleasure and reinforces his need to repeat until he is satisfied that the task is satisfactorily completed. Montessori explains this thus: "The

first phenomenon that awoke my attention was that of a little girl of about three who was practicing slipping our series of solid cylinders in and out of the block (they go in and out of the holes like the corks of bottles, but they are cylinders of graduated size and each has its own special place). I was surprised to see so small a child repeating an exercise over and over again with the keenest interest. She showed no progress in speed or skill: it was a kind of perpetual motion. My habit of measuring things led me to begin to count the number of times she repeated the exercise. Then I thought I would see how far the strange concentration could withstand disturbance, and I told the teacher to have the other children sing and move about. They did so, but the little girl did not stop her work for an instant. Then I gently picked up the armchair in which she sat, with her in it, and put it on a little table. She had clutched her cylinders to her, and putting them on her knees, continued her task. From the time when I had begun to count, she had repeated the exercise forty-two times. She stopped as though coming out of a dream, and smiled as if she were very happy. Her eyes shone and she looked about her. . . . Here was a first peep into the unexplored depths of the child mind. Here was a very small child, at an age when attention flits from one thing to another and cannot be held down. Yet she had been absorbed in a concentration such that her ego had withdrawn itself from reach of any external stimulus. Then concentration was accompanied by a rhythmic movement of the hands. . . ."[5]

The evident relish with which children repeat activities which to the adult look as though they have been successfully completed characterizes all Montessori classes. This striking attention to activity evidenced by normal young children cannot be explained away. Among those busy children in the buzzing environment are some working with activities involving the children in the first steps to reading, writing, and composition, as well as mathematical concepts. Some children, having mastered a few of the sandpaper letters, will be making small words with a movable alphabet. Others will be working with metal insets, an exercise designed to help the children achieve small-muscle dexterity and the thumb-finger opposition needed for holding a pencil, for

writing with a loose wrist motion and for stroking the paper lightly with the pencil.

The metal insets are simply ten geometric shapes cut out of 5½-inch orange metal squares and colored blue. The way in which the children utilize the insets is initially demonstrated by the teacher. The child takes one metal inset, for example, with its ovoid frame, places it on a small tray together with a piece of paper 5½ inches by 5½. He takes a piece of hardboard of the same dimensions, three differently colored pencils and a little grooved stand for them, and with this material returns to his particular place of work. He carefully arranges the materials before beginning work. He places the three pencils in their holder, places the square of hardboard on the table with the piece of paper over it, and over that he places the frame of the inset. With his sub-dominant hand holding the frame in place over the paper, he traces its outline with one of the pencils. He then sets aside the frame and takes the ovoid, on whose surface is to be found a small knob. With the sub-dominant hand he superimposes the ovoid on the already traced outline and re-traces it, this time with another colored pencil. This tracing is more difficult because he must control the tracing's accuracy and at the same time exert sufficient pressure on the inset to keep it in place. Then he returns the inset to the frame, and with his third pencil lightly strokes diagonally, within the limits established by the twice-traced geometric shape.

The purpose of this exercise is to prepare indirectly for handwriting. It has no more relationship to art than draftsmanship has to freehand architectural rendering. And by breaking down the complex manual skill of writing into its component parts, the Montessori class offers the child the opportunity to acquire skills through the gradual acquisition of small muscle control, skills which we know this culture will demand of him in a few short years. The "explosion into handwriting" that is so characteristic of Montessori classes is hardly surprising when one considers the preparation for it that has taken place over the years preceding it. The child has learned the shapes of the letters, has reproduced them kinesthetically, has acquired the ability to handle a pencil, and has been free to compose words and stories through the

arrangement of a movable alphabet which requires no writing, before he feels the need or desire to write. When the child wants to write he has at hand not only the battery of symbols he needs to express his thoughts, which he has learned to trace in exactly the manner in which he will ultimately wish to write them, but he has the trained hand as well, which will ensure his writing efforts success. "Never let a child risk failure, until he has a reasonable chance of success," Montessori says. The hand that wants to write and can write is the hand truly free to write.

Many American educators know of Montessori only through what they think of as the "toys" she invented. The sensorial materials or apparatus that Dr. Montessori developed cover many aspects of language, number, sensory stimuli, and provide the children with structured perceptual experience. There is a precedent for them in the work of Dr. Edouard Seguin and his "physiological method." Superficially, these materials do resemble some educational toys. But the sensorial materials do not constitute the Montessori environment. One could successfully undertake to organize a class for young children on Montessori principles, without the materials. The materials will not assure any particular result or even guarantee to arouse interest in the child who is not presented them by a "prepared" adult in a situation favorable to his satisfactory use.

Unlike Froebel, Montessori did not believe that "anything can be made of anything." It would be accurate to call the sensorial materials, which appeal to the child's senses, also structured materials, as they are based on certain principles which promote the reduction of confusion in what appears to the child as a "buzzing, blooming confusion," as William James had it. These materials designed to present in sequence notions leading to classification and distinction of objects, and awareness of relationships, provide the child with perceptual possibilities upon which concepts will be built. There is in each piece of apparatus, an isolation of stimulus, so that the child deals with one difficulty at a time. An example of this principle might be found in the red wooden rods, which all look exactly alike. The only difference is that they vary in length from the first which is one decimeter in length to the tenth which is a meter in length. With these rods

the child can compare and distinguish length. If the second rod is taken first (two decimeters in length) he sees that the fourth rod (four decimeters) is twice the length of the second. He also sees that the first and third rods end to end equal the fourth rod. Through working with various sensorial materials, the child "manipulates" length, breadth, color, texture, weight. He also works with form (solid and plane geometric shapes). The next phase of the child's work comes through the acquisition of the vocabulary necessary to express what he has perceived. (This is done through the Seguin three-period lesson described on p. 78.) He learns the word *after* he has an experience of the object.

It is interesting to compare the ways in which Hartmann suggested that children's thinking be improved with the principles of the design and intent of the structured materials developed by Montessori.[6]

The Montessori apparatus or materials provide for the children in the class many and varied "motives of activity." They are inviting to the children by their color, form and design. They are designed to provide interesting perceptual experiences. They contain in their sequence an order related to later learning. Thus the sandpaper tablets provide an experience of "roughness" and "smoothness"; they also prepare the child to stroke the surface lightly to obtain the maximum distinction between roughness and smoothness, when he later strokes the "sandpaper letters," which are, in turn, an indirect preparation for writing and reading.

During the long work-period of the morning, which is uninterrupted by group demands, the children move from job to job. Usually, those activities which involve taking care of the room are the first order of the morning. Montessori speaks of the way in which children will begin with some activities in a minor key and work up to what she calls "il gran lavoro," the great work of the day: that activity which will most completely absorb the child. William Heard Kilpatrick recognized this in his assessment of Montessori education (of which he was also greatly skeptical): ". . . life does not flow in twenty-minute periods. Let the child get genuinely interested and the short period proves all too short. If school life is to repeat and make possible actual life, the tyranny and artificiality of the short period and of overmuch

The extreme care and attention this child gives his work is characteristic of children "absorbed."

Using a farm game, this child is analyzing phrases symbolically (large triangle = noun; smaller triangle = adjective; smallest triangle = article) and is matching animal to phrase.

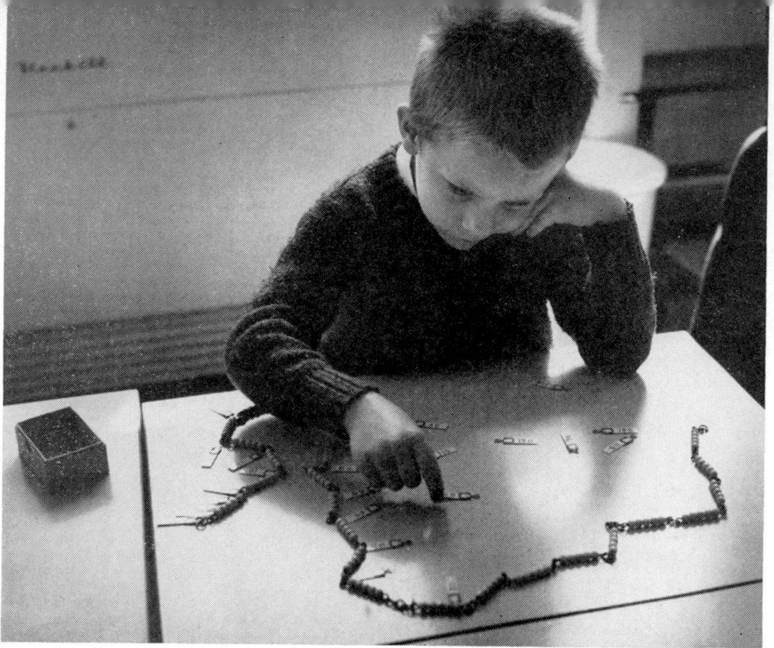

This child is "skip counting" by 5's to 125, as an indirect preparation for raising 5 to the third power.

This boy is doing an exercise in writing "singulars" and "plurals."

direction by the teacher must go. Real thinking and real conduct demand freer rein. . . . The absence of a detailed program [in a Montessori class] and of excessive direction from above afford . . . a fuller opportunity for genuine self-expression."[7]

When children become deeply absorbed in activity that engages them both physically and mentally, their concentration may appear to an adult seeking lighthearted childish responses as humorless and repressed. What such adults frequently lose sight of is the fact that this is not "merely a child" at work, but an emergent man. What he is doing has value not only for the immediate interest it produces in the child and the competence it gives him, but also the child seems to sense the power that such knowledge will give him. A child who is fiercely concentrating is not an unhappy child. Adults judging children too rarely have an opportunity to see concentration in children, and the sense of well-being that accomplishment gives them when they have completed such a task to their own satisfaction.

The visitor to an American Montessori class is struck or possibly upset by the tremendous feeling of order in the class. Among the ground rules of behavior previously alluded to is the notion of the completed task and that of physical order. From the beginning of the school year (when the children come to a virtually empty class) to the concluding day, the children are certain to find everything in the place assigned and are free to take materials from the assigned place, work with them and return them to the assigned place in the condition in which they found them, in order that those who wish to do the same work will have the same opportunity. If a child in the class is working with a map of Africa, and in preparing to return it to its assigned place notices that Tanganyika is missing, he will immediately tell his friends, neighbors and the teacher, in order that a search be instituted. The children automatically check the materials in returning them to the assigned place. This makes possible the use of many varied materials by numerous children without mishap or loss of parts. The importance of order in the Montessori class corresponds both to a need in the child and to an environmental condition which allows individual children greater liberty in initiating choices.

PART III

# The Adult

CHAPTER 5

# The Teacher

IN A culture as rapidly changing as the American one, the image evoked by the word "teacher" may vary widely among generations of the same family. Depending on whether one attended a public or private school, one may see the teacher as the arbiter of on-going social experiences or as the custodian of a coherent past presented to the child with the assurance that adult belief in its immutability is warranted. A third kind of teacher has evolved in the last two generations, one who reflects a new dimension of awareness of child life. "She has come into being as one gifted thinker after another—Froebel, Montessori, Anna Freud—rebelled against the price which modern, urbanized, industrialized Europeans and Americans were paying for their new kind of civilization. From Germany, from Italy, from Vienna, from England and from the United States, there came a demand for some form of education which would fit the little child—a chair and table to fit his body, materials with which he could work out his groping attempts to relate inner and outer world, and teachers who would kneel beside him, who would be the allies of his infancy, rather than the surrogates of the finished world of tradition or the fluid world-in-the-making of the entrepreneur."[1]

But even if the ideal teacher does combine the reverence for tradition with awareness of the immediate goals and a sensitivity to the inner and outer world of childhood, the teacher still risks being out of date in our rapidly changing society. The children of today see the world differently than their ten-year-older brothers and sisters; those siblings born ten years hence will have still another world picture. The task of the American teacher is to

prepare children to face confidently a world not yet seen. Whether or not teaching of children is based on consciously held immutable truths, the mutability of the culture must be recognized and reflected in an educational program for the young.

The problem of teacher effectiveness at any level of teaching must be related to a rapidly shifting culture. A teacher must bear in mind environmental outlooks other than her own, if she is not to become, with increased teaching experience, increasingly outmoded. This danger is perhaps most present to teachers of the young, as the growth of knowledge in child development is continually reversing cherished and long held dicta. The interest currently shown in the process of learning should pose new and justifiable problems for teachers. How much of what young children are taught by adults is learned? Since the child is not using language in the same way as an adult, how effective is speech as a teaching mechanism for the young? Children under five do not have great experience in the pursuit of complex verbal instructions. They are frequently bored by lengthy adult conversations, and simply "tune them out" as any mother well knows. In the highly verbal American culture, teachers frequently talk far too much, thereby diminishing their effectiveness. Must a child be put in contact with content through the words of the teacher?

If nursery teachers are what Margaret Mead implies, child-rearing agents who resemble siblings in primitive cultures, rather than parents (or grandparents), then recruitment of nursery teachers can be seen to pose other problems. These women are often adults closely related to their own childhoods. This teacher might be "a girl from an upper middle class background, who finds herself desperately out of sympathy with the verbal facility and concern for things rather than people that seems to her a predominant characteristic of her world. Very often inarticulate and academically 'slow,' she can become a nursery teacher only if she comes to sufficient terms with her own rebelliousness against adult standards—against, indeed, the whole adult world—so that while she acts as the little child's ally, she does not hold the child back. . . . She is the more successful the less she is acting out some unresolved and overdetermined past, and the

more she has reassimilated and revised her past to fit into the teaching role which she has chosen."[2]

Many parents and teachers discussing currently the role of the teacher have not distinguished clearly enough among the three pedagogical currents mentioned. Educational "progressivists" counseled the teacher to lose the position of external boss and dictator, and take up that of the leader of group activity. This was a rejection of the conventional parental role which teachers had been previously assuming. When pushed to a ludicrous extreme, this new role invested the teacher and the child with approximately the same degree of authority. Parenthetically, this was not what John Dewey had intended. He himself stated, "On the contrary, basing education upon personal experience may mean more multiplied and more intimate contacts between the mature and the immature than ever existed in the traditional school, and consequently more rather than less guidance by others. The problem then is: how these contacts can be established without violating the principle of learning through personal experience."[3]

Montessori, like Mead, implied that the role of the teacher of the young child was not that of a mother substitute. The total identification with the needs of the child, which the best nursery teachers possess, is not possible for a mother, particularly a middle class one, who is unconsciously, even at the time of early childhood, rearing the child to become a "responsible, time bound, goal oriented adult."[4] The teacher of the young child is in the place of the parent, but not in the position of the parent.

Montessori believes that any effective education of the young child must involve the modification of the adult. "The adult considers everything that affects the psyche of the child from the standpoint of its reference to himself, and so misunderstands the child. It is this point of view that leads to the consideration of the child as an *empty being*, which the adult must fill by his own endeavors, as the *inert and incapable being* for whom everything must be done, as a being without an *inner guide*, whom the adult must guide step by step from without. Finally, the adult acts as though he were the child's creator, and considers good and evil in the child's actions from the standpoint of relation to himself.

. . . Any way in which the child departs from the characteristics of the adult is an evil that must be speedily corrected. And in adopting such an attitude, which unconsciously *cancels the child's personality*, the adult feels a conviction of zeal, love and sacrifice."[5] For adult, we can also read Mother.

However, the role of the nursery teacher does bear relation to the mother's role. As long as the teacher is needed by the child, she is for him a mother substitute as well as a mothering adult. However, she assumes the child's point of view, in letting him walk away from her into the life of the group, if only for a short while, not holding him back in a quasi-symbiotic relationship. The importance of the authoritative presence of the adult is everywhere emphasized by Montessori but distinguished by her from an authoritarian role. In reverence to the needs of the child which are believed in though not yet seen, Montessori cautions the adult from over-interference in the work of the child. "A superficial judgment of the Montessori method is too often that it requires little of the teacher, who has to refrain from interference and leave the children to their own activity. . . . It is not that the Montessori teacher is inactive where the usual teacher is active; rather all the activities are due to the active preparation and guidance of the teacher, and her later 'inactivity' is a sign of her success, representing the task successfully accomplished."[6]

Montessori teachers are trained to help the children emerge as they are, and to derive their gratifications as teachers from the provision of possibilities for the children's development rather than from the relationship the child might develop with the teacher. The focus of the school life for the young child is not his relationship to the teacher, but his relationship to himself, to his fellows, and to the environment which he is attempting gradually to master. The Montessori "directress" (as Dr. Montessori called her) establishes through the prepared environment the structure of the day. The morning is devoted to an uninterrupted period of individual activity. It is the teacher's task to protect the child's right to work. Because the child's rhythm is different from that of an adult, there are no arbitrary bells to interrupt him in the midst of what may be the most significant

action of his morning. Montessori maintained that children frequently engage in a few sporadic tasks before they begin what she called "il grand lavoro"—the great work, which is that activity, whether it be at the level of sensorial development, of mastery of self, or of academic learning, which most interests the child or which most corresponds to his particular, unconscious needs at that moment.

In many conventional nursery classes the morning is parcelled out for various activities, and the children, due to the widespread Froebelian influence we find in our schools, are frequently grouped, all doing the same thing at the same time. They also are provided with material with which to stimulate their imagination. That is, they play house, they dress up, play store, etc. In a Montessori class there is a significant absence of so-called play material. This is due not to the absence of recognition that children work and play interchangeably, but due to the fact that Montessori recognized that a reality-bound school situation may prove more beneficial to the child in order to release his creative forces at a time when he is incapable of distinguishing fact from fantasy. In all of this the teacher is present in the class, moving about, working with the children individually or in small groups, ready to help, available for comment, and generally present in an accepting role, though not in an authoritarian one.

She may intervene and does so even decisively, if a child is disorderly or is destructive. Part of the concept of the prepared environment means the preservation of that environment for the good of the whole group. The teacher who allows a child to express himself to the detriment of the whole group is allowing the child an unrealistic indulgence of self in terms of what the group has a right to expect, and also in terms of what the culture into which the child is going will demand of him. Consequently the most effective mechanism for handling recalcitrant children in a Montessori classroom is isolation; that is, not isolation from the group as such, but isolation from independence. The child who is incapable of working independently works near the teacher and must move with her when she moves in order that she keep an eye on him. When *he* feels he is again capable of working independently, he is free to return and set about his

business independently. This need for independence comes from him.

The art of observation must be a highly developed skill in the Montessori teacher. The necessity for observing the children and anticipating their needs becomes of increased importance in a classroom environment where individual work allows a number of children to be engaging in different activities simultaneously under the direction of one teacher. The art of observation is a learned one. In classroom situations where the teacher is the active element and the children the passive, it is not important for the teacher to watch the children, as it is she who determines what will be taught, when it will be taught, how it will be taught, and what gratifications will be forthcoming for the subject matter properly learned. In a Montessori classroom, however, extreme delicacy must be exercised by the teacher to anticipate the needs of the children before they themselves are aware of needs, as well as to reinforce these needs when a child appears to be having difficulty. Therefore, there are rules for the observation of children which are extremely important for the teacher, so that she may have them well in hand.

If the teacher in the class is to be to the children the loving, accepting uncritical adult which they need in order to realize a sense of autonomy and achievement, then it is extremely important that the teacher be aware of the gratifications that working with children can legitimately afford her. Psychic stability is an indispensible condition for working with the young, and where an overly protective maternal attitude is present in a teacher, there is frequently gratification at the wrong level. Teachers of young children have much to learn from clinicians with regard to the importance of observation and non-intervention.

Montessori places great emphasis on the teacher as exemplar in the class. If the children are to acquire the necessary muscular control to open doors, undress and dress themselves, eat neatly and to their own satisfaction, consider the presence of others (though understandably more intent on themselves in their early years), then the teacher must learn to move and act with conscious grace and exaggeration so that her movements can be copied by the

children. The role of watching is an important one in a Montessori class. If the teacher talks, the child watches her mouth. If she moves carefully without speaking, the child watches *her*, and imitates her. The child develops a sympathy for the behavior of the teacher.

"The emotion and attitudes expressed in the word *sympathy* may be at least partly the result of conditioning. Used psychologically, the meaning of the word goes beyond the popular usage denoting agreement, harmony, or being affected by someone else's feelings. Rather it is *identification* with the person. Because the child loves or respects a parent or teacher, the child takes over his patterns of behavior. In the presence of emotional responses the child assumes conditioned attitudes toward other children, adults, school and other features in his environment. Murphy (1937) suggests that these responses may be of major importance in the child's becoming like his parents or peers, and in his taking over the culture of the group."[7] The patterning of the school environment, not an accidental thing in itself, explains some of the suggestibility and imitation in young children.

The reactions of children in any classroom are related to the expectation of the adults who prepared the environment of the class for them. If emphasis is placed by the teacher on freedom to work individually at varied activities the children will obviously gain in independence from this work format, which they did not initiate but which was prepared for them by the teacher, consciously or unconsciously.

## *The Directress*

Montessori refers to the adult working with young children in a learning situation as a directress rather than a teacher. A teacher teaches children, the directress places the children in direct contact with the content of experience. The role of the directress is to prepare the environment, to insure all the children in it an opportunity to find achievement and satisfaction. She establishes norms of behavior by her own behavior and attempts to incarnate those attitudes she wants to promote in the children. Dr. Montessori believed that the directress should truly serve the child:

having prepared the path, she should then step aside and let the child walk. A better word for the Montessori teacher might well be "non-directress." The concept of client-centered therapy has striking analogues in the function of the teacher in a Montessori class.

Lest the directress be thought of as a mechanical robot, standing idle, waiting to be acted upon, it is important to point out that she is a link between the children and the environment, and a *vital* one. It is she who anticipates the children's needs by developing new work, by offering new material when she sees the child has lost interest in what he is doing. Because the children in the Montessori class are often eminently capable of working alone or together without the teacher, she does not thereby become useless. The structure of the class enables her to move from child to child, sometimes working with one, sometimes with a group. There is no diminution of her real authority with the increased autonomy of the children. The fact that the children are capable of independent work frees her to work where she is most needed. She is not held in thrall by the necessity of handling the whole group at the same time.

In the varied diet of the six-to-nine-year-old Montessori class, the directress will offer group or classroom lessons together with the periods of individual work which characterize the class. She will not intervene if the children are working, but will of course if they are doing nothing or are disturbing others. The art of teaching necessarily involves a knowledge of when to intervene and when not to.

What ought to be the gratifications sought in the teaching of the young child? Montessori believed that the love of children must be coupled with true respect for them, if working with them is to free their inner potentialities. Those young women attracted to the teaching of the very young have too often been drawn from those who demonstrated academic ineptitude and hence were considered incapable of "higher" aspirations. Child care has low status value in American culture. The tremendous frustration of well educated mothers who feel "trapped" at home provides eloquent testimony to the fact that they believed that they were educated "for better things." Ideally, the teacher would combine

the objectivity of a clinician with the intuition of an accepting, loving adult. All sensitive teachers allow children the maximum amount of freedom consistent with the internal economy of the group of which they are a part. Such freedom for the young child can be achieved only through a minimum of adult intervention. Montessori constantly cautions against over-teaching and over-direction of the child. By providing many opportunities for the child to act independently and individually, the Montessori teacher insures against the premature absorption of a child into a group which, through her, might reduce the identity of the children's individual selves.

The teacher of the young child needs to bear in mind the world around the corner which the child is entering, even though she does not know the shape of that world. One is forced to conclude that the very important foundations of early learning rest not only on an understanding of the needs of childhood but a relation of these needs to those challenges which the child will later face. "We must devise ways not of cherishing awareness of the self a little longer, which is all the current nursery school really tries to do, . . . but instead ways of making that early awareness a continuing part of the personality into adulthood and old age."[8] What we need is an early education continuous with the whole of the child's development that foreshadows the world of the elementary school and beyond, and forearms him against it.

## *Montessori Teacher Training*

In an approach to learning which unifies theory and practice as intimately as Montessori teaching does, the requirements of the preparation of teachers looms large. From the inception of the Casa dei Bambini in 1907, Montessori realized the grave implications of the preparation of teachers to carry on adequately the great work she had begun. In her San Lorenzo tenement schoolroom which had been offered her as a place to work with children considered unruly, Montessori was to initiate significant teacher training practices, anticipatory of later trends. Her first teachers were simple girls without "teacher training." In fact, Montessori later stated that had they been conventionally trained teachers, they would have found it impossible to follow uncritically her

directions: "I laid no restriction on the mistress, gave her no special duties; I merely taught her how to use the apparatus so that she could present it accurately to the children."[9]

All of the characteristics mentioned as typical of children in Montessori classes were revealed by the first children with whom Montessori worked. Observation convinced her that in favorable circumstances children showed another level of behavior, another dimension of personality. These children came to be referred to as "new children," by virtue of the behavior they manifested to the thousands of observers who came to Rome to learn more of the theory and practice of Dr. Montessori's approach in the years following. Training courses were instituted by Dr. Montessori not only in Rome but in major European capitals. A course was given by Montessori on a visit to California in the year of the exposition, where a model Montessori class was held under the direction of Helen Parkhurst.

The International Training Course designed by Dr. Montessori to give some insight into her methods was usually of six months duration. (There are presently training courses in Europe lasting as long as three years, in teacher-training institutions.) The work of the course was divided into theory—what we would call the philosophical and psychological foundations of the method, and the theory of the teaching material; the practical work with the teaching material, which the student must understand in such a way that the sequence of it becomes habitual in her presentation of it in the class; and observation. It was this last that Montessori emphasized, because it was her contention that it was not what she taught that illuminated the students as much as what the child taught himself. (Details about Montessori teacher training will be found in Appendix B.)

CHAPTER 6

# The Parent

---

## *Montessori–Home Environment*

THERE ARE many more people dealing with young children outside the school than in it. Countless questions rise to the lips of every young mother who deals daily with the perplexities of child nurture. Many parents, interested in achieving some of the gains of the "responsive" or "prepared" environment, want to know how this environment can be achieved in the home. Others do not "believe in" early education (by that I mean organized early education, as no one can deny that a child learns with or without benefit of school, from birth).

The home is an environment different from that of the school, even as the mother is a different order of educator from the teacher. The home, the natural habitat of the family, is in our culture a hierarchical structure with parents firmly at the top. Those in authority presumably keep in mind at all times the needs and the rights of all those within the group, from Father to Baby. The Montessori school is another sort of environment. It is prepared *for the child,* not the family. It is horizontal rather than vertical in structure. The child finds himself among his peers, with an adult intent on his interests, not hers, and the interests of others, which however do not differ as radically as those in a family group.

In two generations, middle class Americans have gone from an extremely rigid form of family life to one increasingly definable as amorphous—one step further from informal. The present extremely loose structure of family life will obviously affect a

mother attempting to structure a home environment. This mother, who "has been reared in a dozen tones of voice, reprimanded, rewarded, cajoled and teased and appeased according to half a hundred systems,"[1] is the product of a fluid and heterogeneous society. Today's mother is as dependent on the reminiscences of her own childhood and the prescriptions of pediatricians as on a consensus of her contemporaries, who have many and varied ways of treating their young.

Though the principles of learning articulated by Montessori may have application in the home, the position occupied by the mother as distinct from the disinterested teacher should be borne in mind. Parents unconsciously orient children toward their own goals. But the goals of early life are within the child and uncommunicable by him to adults. They are internal rather than external goals. Mothers find it difficult to respect the wishes of children in the matter of early learning. Frequently disappointed when a child refuses to show interest in an activity the mother *knows* he is capable of, the mother will nag the child to perform.

Despite the undeniable fact that many young children show tremendous potential for learning, the way in which this potential can be fully realized is only through activity that is meaningful to the child, and autotelic (activity for the child's own ends, not those of his anxious mother). The obverse of the over-anxious mother is the anxious child for whom the mother has too little time, due to the ever present demands being made on her by the family and culture. Beginning with the proposition that the child should be encouraged to "show his needs," the young mother should make provision for him to get in contact with experience, which is the first step of learning for him.

Montessori deplored cribs, calling them cages on wheels, and suggested to parents that they substitute low beds which the children could fall out of with impunity, and to which the children could repair when they were tired. Also allowing a child great possibilities for exploration of the home environment would outlaw the use of the playpen, which is frequently a low-slung substitute for the crib. Mothers say with rightful indignation that it is all very well to let the first baby wander about the house, but that by the time the second child appears it is for his

own protection that he is placed in the playpen to keep him away from the older child's things. (A cartoonist once suggested that in a large family only one playpen was necessary—for the mother to use to protect herself from the onslaughts of her young.)

The way in which children develop mobility from birth through their first year, aptly described by Delacato and Doman,[2] indicates the importance of allowing for creeping and crawling on both hard and carpeted floors when babies are very small. Playpens frequently allow children to stand and walk before they have passed through the phases which ought to precede developmentally. The obvious problems mothers face in preparing a home environment involve protection of the child from objects which can hurt him. Mothers of large families grant their children more independence than many others, simply because it is expedient that the children learn to do as much for themselves by themselves as possible. "Never help a child when he can help himself," Montessori cautions. This caution extends from climbing stairs to pouring milk. If a mother will run the risks of her child's experiences, she must be prepared for mishaps.

Arranging a child's room in an orderly way, with everything to be found in the same place, can both enhance the child's sense of security and make it possible for him to put his hand on anything he wants in the room. Limiting toys and games to a workable number and considering cleaning up as much a part of playing as the actual activity with toys is helpful in building up habits of tidiness. Mothers can show 2½-year-olds how to wash their own hands and faces, by preparing a low table in the bathroom with a pitcher, basin, pail, wash cloth, soap dish, nail brush and towel, so the child will find everything ready for washing and will be able, following a demonstration by his mother, to do this for himself. The pitcher and basin are necessary to make possible pouring activity but eliminate the hazards of attempting to control the temperature of water taps that may run too hot.

With a small mirror, child-height above the table, the child can learn to comb his own hair. All of these activities, if "programmed" in advance in such a way that the repetition of each simple step insures success, will make children at home more capable of caring for themselves, and happier in so doing. All

children love to help their mothers. Allowing even little ones to clean out the bathtub with a damp sponge and a small amount of scouring powder in a dish, or polishing silver or shining shoes, will give children pleasure and helps them achieve skills.

Most young mothers need to be reminded that none of these activities is spontaneous on the part of the child; each must be demonstrated, and reinforced through repetition before the child will find pleasure in doing them. He needs enough practice to acquire each skill to his own satisfaction.

Montessori noted that in almost all activities involving children, the children are expected to go at the adult's pace. With mechanization taking command in the form of strollers, it is now possible for a mother walking to the supermarket to whisk her offspring there in record time. If the mother had the patience and the leisure to let her little one walk, he would derive a great deal more from the trip.

One of the features of the Montessori environment is consistency, which is conspicuously absent in many homes, due to the variety and constancy of demands made upon the mother. If habits of independence are to be built up in the children from an early age, not only must the home be physically set up for this (with low hooks for coats, clothespins to clip snow-boots and mittens together, etc.), but the mother must be willing to devote herself to an unvarying ritual lasting as long as is necessary for the child to internalize the particular activity for himself. Once she has taught the first child to wash his hands, he can then teach the next one and so on, but it is the first lesson that is longest and most in need of regular repetition.

Routine, though not necessarily repugnant to many young housewives, is found less and less in the culture at large, and this makes it difficult for a mother to establish routines for the children. Like the teacher who functions as the exemplar, the mother should be careful in what she does by showing each step to the child clearly enough so that he can repeat it after she has finished. She might also note that in showing children many things, by not speaking, she is freeing them to watch what she does and not watch her mouth.

By encouraging children to do things for themselves, the

mother is making the child the active agent of his own education. The playpen and the television set are but two manifestations of the way in which the child becomes a captive audience. It is in the direct contact with things that the child gets his first percepts. This very important phase of education can be understood and encouraged by mothers from the time the children are very small.

## *The Home as Prepared Environment*

Montessori once related an anecdote about a mother who heard her lecture on the importance of the child's first years. After the lecture, the mother complimented Dr. Montessori and asked her when she might start, and what she might do for her own baby who was only a few weeks old. "Madam, go home at once," said Dr. Montessori, "you haven't a minute to lose." Rarely does one find in an educational theorist the variety of experience and study in Dr. Montessori's background. As a doctor interested in the psychic development of the child as well as in his physical development, she never failed to underscore the importance of the child's first years.

Dr. Montessori has been credited with the invention of child-size furniture. She noticed the impossible demands for adaptation that homes designed for adults made on little ones. She criticized the penchant of parents for making the children sleep too much. Her idea of a low bed, to which he could go when tired, certainly anticipated the trend of "demand" scheduling.

In considering the rhythm of the young child, so different from that of the adult, Montessori underscores the fact that liberty and self-control are the points of arrival for the child, not points of departure. Many parents pride themselves on the immediate obedient responses they get from their young children, failing to see that this can be a very constricting form of conditioning, and one which is not based on the understanding of the parent's words but on a response to the tonality of his voice.

Exploration is the substance of learning in a child's first years. The immediate contact he has with objects and sensations gives him the first information. Opportunities should be given the child wherever possible to play with sand and water, to work

with clay and paint—to get out of the high-chair, playpen, stroller and car seat and get down to where he can put his feet on the ground and see life at his own level. Many mothers have noticed the difference in reactions between children propped on a toidy seat with legs dangling and those who have "potty chairs" their own size. So much of what is provided for young children in the way of furniture is child size but adult level. Children live close to the ground. If American children do not it is because technology has made it possible to crank them up to their mother's level. Surely, it is not unthinkable that the mother do what the Montessorian in the class does—get down to the child's level. By providing the child with a low table, chair or stool, with housekeeping equipment like his mother's, but his own size, by low shelves and a low bed, it would be possible for the child to help himself a great deal more. Mothers accept philosophically the moment when the children learn to climb over the crib side. Would it not be at least as simple to provide a low bed and let the children begin to get in and out with less peril?

An area worth investigating in the area of self-help for the young child is clothes design. It is astounding to find the number of children's clothes that require adult assistance to get in and out of because of buttons in the back or buttons on suspenders threaded through shoulder tabs. In choosing clothes for young children, mothers would do well to look at the clothes from the child's point of view. Is it easy to get in and out of? How would one manage in a hurry? Are the buttons or zipper in front where the child can manage?

The "dressing frames" designed many years ago by Dr. Montessori and currently up-dated to include zippers with jacket closures and dot-snappers for two piece pajamas, are a helpful introduction to the complexity of "doing" oneself up. The tying frame has been thoughtfully provided with left and right laces of different colors so that the child is able to see the anatomy of bow tying. This is otherwise extremely difficult to demonstrate when tying child-size bows with adult fingers.

The area of practical or housekeeping activities is another one rich in possibilities for young children. With the mother bearing in mind the importance of "structuring" a task so that the child

can learn from observing the way in which she does something, and then reminding herself to repeat the task in exactly the same way so that the child can consolidate his knowledge, a mother can teach the child almost any practical skill which is within her competence, from folding diapers to drying silverware to breaking eggs for a cake.

Most adults are quite unconscious of the way in which they do things. Therefore most mothers will be overconfident of their capacity to structure an activity, if they do not think of how to do it in advance, and practice it, so that they will repeat it in the same way. Opening a door is an apparently simple procedure. It does however involve three distinct steps. First, one places one's hand on the knob. Second, one rotates the knob to free the door from the jamb. Third, one draws the door toward one. If any one of these actions is omitted the others will not satisfactorily open the door. The activity pre-structured by the adult, focusing on the sensory-motor skill to be communicated rather than on detailed verbal instructions, constitutes a radically different approach to telling young children how to do things. The training of the Montessori directress, as Dr. Montessori calls her (for she directs and demonstrates rather than teaches), lays tremendous stress on acquiring a structural view of working with children and analyzing what is involved in each sort of action so that upon demonstration in a series of separate though related sequential steps, the child will achieve success in the action.

Hand washing is an activity rarely taught formally to children. Unless the small child has the advantage of a sink down at his own level with the hot water temperature controlled, he has two problems to overcome immediately: one, teetering precariously on a set of steps pulled up to the adult level basin; and two, the present danger of turning scalding water on himself. By providing a low table with hand-washing equipment in the bathroom, the parents can provide an interesting and delightful activity for the child, as well as an eminently practical one. The hand-washing equipment in a Montessori class is color coded so that the plastic apron the child wears, the plastic pitcher and basin, the pail and soap dish as well as the wash cloth and towel are all color related. This is an excellent idea for a home bath-

room. On any low table, covered by a piece of oil cloth or formica, one might place a small basin, a pitcher, and two soap dishes (one containing a hotel size cake of soap, the other a small nail brush). On a rod attached to the table one could place the wash cloth and towel, both of which should be for a two- or three-year-old, about half-size.

In preparing for the handwashing, the pitcher is filled with tepid water by the mother. She then kneels or squats to demonstrate, with the child standing at her right or left, depending on his handedness, which we assume the mother knows. Obviously there are many ways to wash hands. The point behind the structuring of this activity is to show the child a way that if done consistently *always* works and is satisfying to him. She would then do approximately the following:

1. The mother pours the water into the basin, about half-filling it. In so doing, she is careful to stop just at the moment of pouring, after having tipped the pitcher, in order to better control the flow of water.
2. She sets the pitcher down in the place from which she took it.
3. She places her hands in the water, together, with palms down, and then turns them over. She does this twice to insure getting the hands thoroughly wet.
4. She takes the bar of soap from the dish in her dominant hand.
5. With the soap in her hand, she "shakes hands" with the soap, rubbing her palms together with the soap in between.
6. She replaces the soap in the soap dish.
7. She lathers her hands back and front with the soap on her hands.
8. She takes the nail brush from its dish, and starting with the four fingers of the opposite hand she draws the brush across these nails, and then the thumb.
9. She switches the brush to the other hand and does the same with the opposing hand.
10. She rinses the nail brush.
11. She replaces it in its dish.

12. She rinses her hands by repeating twice the gesture for wetting them, making sure the soap is off.

13. She takes a towel and wipes her hands. First one hand, then the other.

14. She replaces the towel.

15. She pulls the pail out from under the table.

16. She pours the soapy water into it.

17. With the wash cloth, she wipes out the bowl and replaces it.

These are approximately the steps involved in hand washing. Many reading this may feel that it is hardly worth the effort to get so involved in order to teach something that can be done for the children by adults or later taught through verbal instructions. The reason for explaining the mechanism of structuring so apparently simple a task as handwashing is to show the way in which the adult must demonstrate with a certain element of exaggeration if the child is to imitate successfully, and to point out the way in which the activity of hand washing becomes an absorbing and interesting experience for a young child when demonstrated in this way. It is also a highly practical skill which at some juncture will *have* to be learned. Once the child has repeated all the steps involved in handwashing as set out, he will literally incarnate them in a satisfactory skill of which he becomes less conscious as his success mounts. He need only pay attention to learn. Once he has learned to his own satisfaction, he is less aware of what was once involved.

Would one call this activity work or play? This would depend upon definitions. Montessori did not agree with Froebel's dictum that one "could make anything out of anything." Certain activities should have a sequence which is apparent to the children and when followed through gives them the indication that the task is complete. The desire to repeat activities is natural to children. It is quite likely that a child having completed the hand washing activity, even though his hands are now clean, would like to start all over again. This is of course encouraged *when* the child evidences an interest. He would then start at the beginning and go through all the steps.

There are any number of home activities which can be structured in this way, by patient mothers.

One might say as did a young mother in a letter to the *Saturday Evening Post*, following the publication of an article on the Montessori Method, "Any mother can use Montessori methods . . . all she has to have are a set of plastic alphabet letters a child can feel; sticks, beads or cards he can count; cardboard jigsaw puzzles with states and countries clearly marked and time to read to him a great deal. When he recognizes the alphabet and a few phonetic sounds, get a primer from the library, and your four-year-old will amaze you by reading as my own did . . ." (Oct. 28, 1961).

What this mother does not realize, and she has a great deal of company, is that the home environment presents special problems for the teaching of the child, though it may not present learning problems for the child. The Montessori apparatus, which has been partially described in this book, resembles well-made educational toys. The apparatus is designed to be used in a certain way (and in some other ways related to that "certain" way) and is to be presented in sequence at the moment that it will interest the child and motivate him to work with it. This moment corresponds to the "periods of sensitivity" described by Dr. Montessori as both important and fleeting. Few five-year-olds will have the patience or the interest to work through the "sand paper letters," as the three-year-olds do.

But the Montessori apparatus constitutes only a small though important part of the Montessori teaching situation. The most important element is the teacher, in terms of preparation; the most important is the child, in terms of growth and development. Both are needed. Without exploring the problem of the mother functioning as a formal teacher and risking the resistance of her child in the process, it is true to say that a mother who is not trained as is a Montessori directress will have great difficulty effectively presenting the material. She does not know the sequence of it; she does not necessarily know the time at which the child will be most apt to be interested in it. Despite the still current adage that "no one understands a child like his mother," the fact remains that as a formal teacher, the mother is not

content to dispose the child to learn, but tends to impose learning on him.

The principle source of difficulty for the mother with the Montessori apparatus in the home is found in the fact that the home is not a prepared environment in the sense in which the school is. The home is designed for quite different ends. The mother can choose only to restructure the home, which is impossible, or to ignore the fact that it is structured differently and proceed as if she were the directress in the class. How then does she behave toward her children the rest of the time when she is not teaching? Mothers are mothers and children want them to remain so. Any amount of incidental learning is often eagerly sought by the child, but once the mother becomes too insistent, there frequently develops complete unwillingness on the child's part to have her teach him. If we are to assume that the child and mother are both willing, despite the unprepared environment, then what problems arise?

If the child in question is the first child and the mother has sufficient leisure to provide a few hours of uninterrupted activity for him, knows the material, suffers no handicap in her relation with the child by presenting it to him, then well and good. If there is more than one child in the family, however, there are immediate problems. Who can build the "pink tower" with the baby cruising nearby? Who can work with the maps when Tanganyika is in imminent danger of disappearing? The ground rules of a Montessori class in the home (unless the trained mother has eliminated temporarily all the other children who are not of the right age, and has devoted herself totally to a class situation) are almost impossible to maintain, without the attendant discipline of a physical environment established in such a way that the children find everything every day as it was left the previous day.

The principal error of Montessori enthusiasts is the failure to recognize that the materials do not teach *automatically*, under any circumstances. The child *must* be in an environment designed to dispose him to work and have at hand a directress who will protect his right to learn. The casual efforts of most mothers are necessarily sporadic. They are casual necessarily, because the

multi-faceted demands of a household and children make it difficult for a mother to set aside the same time every day for working with the children, in the equivalent of the old-fashioned "schoolroom." There is neither time nor place available to most women for this. Not only are rooms multi-purpose, but so are mothers. If one considers the home environment as quite different from the school environment, then it is possible to utilize many of Dr. Montessori's insights in the teaching of a more incidental sort. Key activities can be mastered by the child if structured this way by the mother. Repetition ensures the acquisition of the particular skill.

PART IV

# The Hope

CHAPTER 7

# Education, Six and After

THE DEMANDS of a constantly changing and expanding technology face Americans with the task of learning continually throughout their lives, in order to make sense out of their world. The perceptual information of the early years progressively evolves into conceptual learning, yet the necessity to learn is in no way diminished by the newly felt intellectual power of the slightly older child. The child of six has mastered the first lessons of learning, but he must now acquire vast quantities of information crucial to his culture's demands and his staged development. Montessori believes that to the child of six, the cosmos is not too modest a motive of curiosity. One readily recognizes in children's exposure to television how an interest in Cosmonauts and Astronauts may take shape. In the same manner as the desire to reach the moon evolves, through exposure, so also may the desire to purchase a particular kind of toy by a child viewer evolve if he is exposed to a skillful pitchman.

Yet, there is a difference. The interest in the universe is not only to be explained by current events, but by the capacity of the child to encompass grandiose challenges. The community helpers, the policemen and firemen who continue to people the pages of first readers, are hardly the stuff of heroes. The immediate world of the child of six is not bounded by his neighborhood, despite a long cherished adult belief. Are salmon fishing in Alaska and pineapple picking in Hawaii, studied as human activities, as challenging as the problems of man's re-entry from space and the uses of nuclear energy? As topics, are they a part of the general preoccupation of the culture? "Let us give him

[the child] a vision of the whole universe. The universe is an imposing reality, and an answer to all questions. We shall walk together on this path of life for all things are part of the universe and are connected to each other to form one whole unity. This idea helps the mind of the child to become fixed, to stop wandering in an aimless quest for knowledge. . . . If the idea of the universe is presented to the child in the right way, it will do more for him than just arouse his interest, for it will create in him admiration and wonder, a feeling loftier than interest and more satisfying. . . . the knowledge he acquires is organized and systematic; his intelligence becomes whole and complete because of the vision that has been presented to him."[1]

Montessori rightly assumes that the interest of children in the lower elementary grades is further stimulated because of the learning skills they have mastered before the age of six. "The child of six who has been in a Montessori School has the advantage of not being so ignorant as the child who has missed that experience. He knows how to read and write, has an interest in Mathematics, Science, Geography and History, so that it is easy to introduce him to any amount of further knowledge. The teacher is confronted with an individual who has already acquired the basis of culture, and is anxious to build upon it, to learn and penetrate deeper into any matter of interest. . . . [The teacher] has to prepare a huge amount of information to satisfy the child's mental hunger, and she is not, like the ordinary teacher, limited by a syllabus, prescribing just so much of every subject to be imparted within a set time, and on no account to be exceeded. The needs of the child are clearly more difficult to answer and the teacher can no longer defend herself behind the syllabus and time-table."[2] When Montessori was asked how many seeds should be sown in the mind of a child this age she replied, "As many as possible!"

The age of pre-adolescence, the time in which the child has great psychic stability, having traversed the difficulties of identity in early childhood and not yet confronted by the second crisis of adolescence, is the period, according to Montessori, when the child is susceptible to learning any and all things. This is the age of curiosity, the age of concern with moral judgments, and

an age that needs to work in groups. The child from six to twelve can consolidate the gains of earlier learning by applying his skills to a vast reservoir of factual knowledge.

He also needs imaginative stimulation. Montessori maintains that the child of this age span has an intelligence which "grows under the heat of a flaming imagination." Our aim therefore is not merely to make the child understand, and still less to force him to memorize, but so to touch his imagination as to stimulate him to his inmost core. We do not want complacent pupils but eager ones.[3] Montessori has called those who want to separate the work of the intelligence from that of imagination in children of this age "vivisectionists of the human personality." She believed that the study of the universe in a manner assimilable to a young child combines the stimuli needed to fire both intelligence and imagination.

It is in the early acquisition of the skill subjects, the tools of learning, that Montessori's timetable of learning differs radically from current American practice. When children have learned to read and write before six, the nature of the instruction of the first two elementary grades, at least, will then require revision. What can stimulate the non-reader's imagination sufficiently if it be not a stimulus verbally communicated to him by the teacher? Until a child can read, he is at the mercy of group activity. When he is able to read, he is able to teach himself, and to work at his own pace.

A practical example of the way in which a Montessori ungraded primary class takes advantage of previously learned reading and writing skills is seen in the variety of work available to the children who read, and hence work individually or in groups, getting clues not from the teacher but from structured sequential material, prepared for them by her. Whether they are studying pre-history with the help of a Time Line, on which $\frac{1}{10}$ of an inch represents 100 years, or learning the principal rivers and mountain ranges of Africa; whether they are composing poetry or stories, and illustrating them, dictating spelling words to each other or working on arithmetic, the ability to read and compose frees them from the rigid routine of group recitation and, incidentally, from the repetition of mistakes and wrong

answers. Martin Mayer recently remarked that an extensive visit through United States schools struck him with "one remarkable aspect of learning . . . *the persistence of error*."[4] Although it may appear an oversimplification to say that there are no wrong answers, only wrong questions, the fact remains that teaching which consistently produces and tolerates error is in direct contradiction to the learning process.

Because of the varied ages of the children in a Montessori class, different levels of work on any given subject is possible. There is no "ceiling" on accomplishment at this period. The whole world of learning is open to the children. It is important that they realize at this stage that education and instruction are two quite different things. What is found in a history book is not the whole of history. The text does not encompass the "subject." Referring six-year-olds to a variety of books about pre-history alerts them to the inclusion of different ideas by different authors. The period between six and twelve is one in which new enthusiasms are readily developed. The Montessori teacher needs to know a great deal about a great deal. What she does not know she must know where to find. Like a teacher of the gifted child, she needs to direct children to further work in their chosen areas of interest, as well as insure that they have acquired the expected competence in all the conventional branches of learning. The implications of programmed learning in the Montessori class are especially interesting and pertinent (and will be discussed later), since in the classroom with programmed material the teacher continues to be what she was without it: a person whose job is to help, to put the student in the way of learning.

## *Secondary Education*

As the child approaches adolescence, he returns to a state paralleling that of the learning phase of the three- to six-year-old. He loses assurance and must face again a world of new sights and new sounds, a world powerfully present to him within himself as well as without. Montessori rejected the idea that the adolescent, simply because he was gaining in age, was thereby gaining in strength. She recognized the tremendous burden

This child is tracing the number 8 in sandpaper as an indirect preparation for writing.

This boy is composing words with the movable alphabet, having mastered the sounds and their symbols through the sandpaper letters.

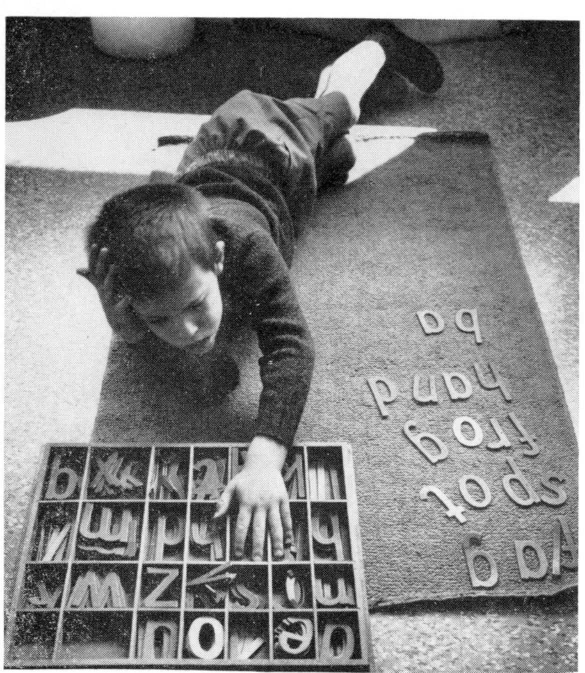

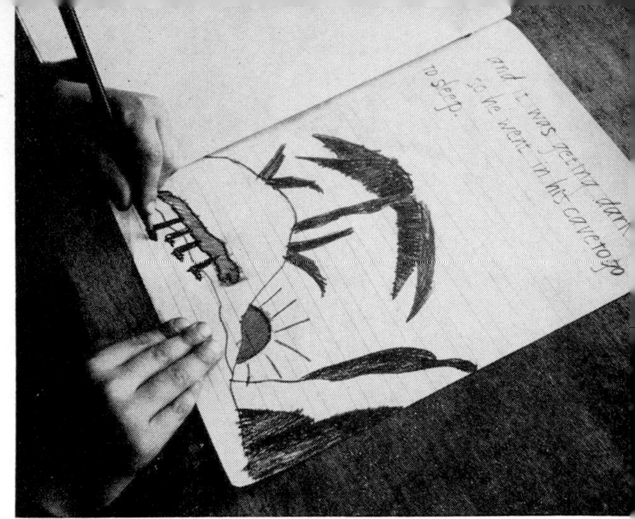

After composing a story, this six-year-old "left hander" embellishes it with illustrations.

A group focuses on a reading lesson. The child in the right foreground works unconcernedly on a metal "inset."

placed on the adolescent by his increased awareness of himself. The adolescent looks inward, preparing to emerge as a socially conscious individual. Montessori believed that the particular sensitivity of the adolescent is his relation to life in society as a social being. American parents would have no quarrel with this insight. "There are doubts and hesitations, violent emotions, discouragement and an unexpected decrease of intellectual capacity. The difficulty of studying with concentration is not due to a lack of willingness, but is really a psychological characteristic of the age. The assimilative and memorizing powers which give young children such an interest in details and material objects seem to change their nature. The chief symptom of adolescence is a state of expectation, a tendency toward creative work and a strengthening of self-confidence. Suddenly the child becomes very sensitive to the rudeness and humiliations which he had previously suffered with patient indifference."[5]

To American ears, Montessori's suggestion that the adolescent be put on the road to the achievement of economic independence may seem trite. Yet many of the problems of "custodial care" which compulsory school-attendance laws force on unwilling teachers illustrate the cogency of this need. Whether or not an adolescent needs to work separately from or in conjunction with his schooling is less important than the fact that he needs to feel the independence that work promotes. "Education should therefore include the two forms of work, manual and intellectual, for the same person, and thus make it understood by practical experience that these two kinds complete each other and are equally essential to a civilized existence."[6] The type of work which Montessori envisions for the adolescent would have the overtones of a secondary vocational interest, and would provide a basis for leisure activity later on in life. Montessori advocated rural and urban centers which provided adolescents with opportunities of work organization and self government. She advocated not a division of labor into learners and workers, but a combination of learning and working skills in the same person, as in contemporary Russian practice.

Montessori's view of education extended from infancy through maturity. "Education should not limit itself to seeking new

methods for an arid transmission of knowledge; its aim must be to give the necessary aid to human development. This world, marvelous in its material power, needs a 'new man.' It is therefore the life of man, and its values, that must be considered. If the 'formation of man' becomes the basis of education, then the co-ordination of all schools from infancy to maturity, from nursery to university, arises as a first necessity: for man is a unity, an individuality which passes through interdependent phases of development. Each preceding phase prepares the one that follows, forms its base, nurtures the energies which urge towards the succeeding period of life."[7]

The number of American critics of higher education who would agree with Dr. Montessori's statement is too great to enumerate. Her contention that universities have become diploma mills will likewise evoke sympathetic assent. Much of the educational reform based on the secondary level of education has failed to concern itself with the foundations of that level of learning, the elementary school. If there is not adequate restructuring of institutions, the reforms in education will be operative only among those hardy competitive students who are learning despite rather than because of any system. The controversy concerning remedial reading stimulated in the Illinois legislature by Dr. Bestor and his colleagues stemmed precisely from their attempt to make of the university a place for adult learning and not an annex to the first grade.

The agonized cries of Robert Maynard Hutchins on equating Cosmetology and Embalming with the Humanities echoes a further intent to make of American universities what universities have historically been. David Riesman counters that "we can no longer look abroad for inspiration for our models of culture and educational advance—nor even react against foreign models which, in so many cases, are busy imitating us."[8] He has also observed that "our colleges and universities however, may be in the situation of the churches today: better attended than ever, bigger and handling more gate receipts, while thoughtful theologians wonder whether religiosity doesn't actually provide an antibody against religion rather than a channel towards it. Education succeeds in emancipating a large proportion of its grad-

uates from the provincial roots, only to tie them the more firmly to the big and more subtly constricting orbits of corporate, academic, suburban and military organizations. With other graduates, higher education lowers its sights in order to avoid despair, and hoping that some culture will rub off on the denizens in four years, often finds that these are only rubbed the wrong way and come out more anti-intellectual than they went in."[9]

Clearly, the confusion of aims in American education has come full circle. For thousands of those exposed to education as to a Schick test, the result is negative. Where are the "unadjusted and unadjustable" men of Bernard Iddings Bell? Many of them have been murdered by the end of the first grade, from gradual doses of "See Spot run, Mother," followed by "See Mother run, Spot."

## *Self Teaching and Montessori*

In any discussion of a learning environment responsive to the needs of the individual child and designed to make individual work possible for him, the need for material with which he can work individually becomes apparent. If we have seriously underestimated the learning capacities of young children, as current research indicates we may have, then those children capable of reading and writing at age six are going to need a different sort of curriculum than that now in favor.

There is a growing recognition of the child's ability to teach himself. This is amply and remarkably demonstrated in his acquisition of his native language, and represents a prodigious achievement taken for granted by those very adults convinced of his ineptitude for learning difficult things. The "unconscious structures of learning" spoken of by Dr. Bruner indicate that the young child builds on the models which he constructs from his absorption of the environment. Montessori wrote sixty years ago that many people think respect for the child and consideration of his physical life means to leave the child without any mental activity. Montessori became interested in the fact that children were capable of learning, prior to any attempt to help them in the learning of anything specific. And present research in self-

teaching stems from an interest in a greater understanding of the psychology of learning. "Just as Dr. Montessori believed that the child will, if given the proper environment, teach himself from birth onwards and from the conscious stage demonstrates how he learns, so Skinner and Crowder and others are discovering that through the use of programmed materials the student can teach himself and at the same time show the scientist how he can best learn. The student is therefore indispensable to those who program subject matter; he helps them determine techniques, sequences and periods in time best suited to his ability to learn."[10] Dr. Montessori's dictum that the environment should reveal the child, not mould him, is a reflection of the teacher's need to be aware of the child's responses.

As has been generally conceded by those working in self-teaching techniques, the child needs the freedom to explore despite the structure represented by the learning experience to be mastered. The reaction of children to discoveries made by themselves is quite different from that same information communicated to them by an adult. The threefold concept in programmed learning of subject matter, student and teacher-programmer reflects the triad of Montessori previously mentioned: the child, the environment with its motives of activity, and the teacher.

In the lower grades where "serious" learning begins, the teacher assumes the role of the parent in imparting information, rather than that of the uncritical adult of the nursery-level who views the work from the child's vantage point. Therefore the subject matter and the teacher tend to be one. The child is acted upon by her, and she is the initiating agent of the learning process. In a Montessori class the child is placed in direct contact with content by the teacher, but what is to be learned does not filter through her personality. In the Montessori triad, self discipline is not an outgrowth of learning, but a very condition of it. What is to be learned, the subject matter itself, produces the discipline. To the degree to which the student becomes the active agent of his own learning, he becomes absorbed in it and informed by the discipline such involvement produces. The method of programmed learning is closer to the Montessori structured material than is the role of the Montessori directress to the creator of programmed

materials. However, the use of the materials in a class, by someone other than their creator, presents the need for the teacher to function as does the Montessori directress, as the *dynamic link* between the child and the material.

In a Montessori class, the children are constantly working individually and independently on materials designed for learning without the teacher. In modern American classrooms, the role of the teacher as Magistra Ludens (at least in the lower grades) would seem to make the notion of programmed learning inapplicable because of its denial of that dependence on the teacher to which the child is being carefully conditioned. Many adults, intent on keeping children "young," wonder what possible benefits early learning offers when children will learn the same things later on, at what may appear to be less cost. The difference can be found in the area of motivation. A child will persist beyond the expectation of an adult at something which interests him. His very ability to persist often indicates his ability to achieve. The desire to achieve is very strong in the youngest of American children, who see older brothers and sisters involved in learning.

In most teaching situations, the motivation must be supplied by the teacher. In a self-teaching situation the motivation is supplied by the learner. Competence and confidence go hand in hand. Dr. Moore is convinced that the strongest learning motivation of the child is the competence drive.[11] Dr. Skinner, in speaking of "completion," is referring to the same thing. So much do men desire competence that they settle for the illusion of it; students tend to give any answer rather than take no action at all. Montessori states that the very classifications and principles in science, history and mathematics hold the same fascination for the child as do classification in language.[12] She insists that "precision attracts the child deeply, this it is that keeps him at work."[13]

There might be here a parallel in the so-called "atomization" of subject matter in automated, programmed teaching methods, a technique allowing the student precision in sequence and precision in "being right." In the learning of the young child at the perceptual level, Piaget compares the separate percepts to frames of a slow motion film which move consecutively (at the pre-

operational level of the child's intelligence) and do not ever speed up sufficiently for him to achieve an over-view of the whole. Sequential learning does however build up ultimate competence by providing steps which, if followed, will lead to the total skill. There is hope, in the child mastering phonemes, that he will eventually master them all as opposed to the "whole word" reader for whom each new word is often treated as wholly unrelated to any other.

Competence is not enough in learning; there must also be curiosity. "The notion of joy in learning has virtually disappeared from learning theory and educational psychology."[14] It seems that in American early education one finds either joy or learning —rarely are they found together. Curiosity is dependent on competence. Dr. Montessori insisted on the need for competence early in life since she was convinced that it insured for young children the opportunity to be curious.

The difficulties in programming learning for children of any age are great, dependent as they are on an understanding of exactly how a child learns. Komoski sums up the requirements for programming: 1) The material must be arranged in topical steps which may be successfully taken by the learner. 2) The learner must be active in his choice. 3) The learner must be re-inforced in his choice (i.e. must know immediately the result of his response, whether right or wrong).[15]

A parallel can be drawn between the requirements of programming and the design of the Montessori apparatus. One lesson to be learned is presented in each piece of Montessori material, each is self-corrective, so that reinforcement is immediate, and each is dependent on the activity of the learner for its use. The cumulative lesson sought from the sequence of atomized subject matter is seen in the Montessori approach to the learning of writing. A series of sequential exercises leading to the so-called "explosion into writing" is undertaken by the child with no conscious awareness of the ultimate skill to be achieved. At the same time, the indirect preparation for this skill through the sequence provides for the child the opportunity to discover the components in a new combination, when actually writing, which was the long range goal all along, though known to the

teacher, not to the child. Montessori saw in the sequential presentation of subject matter a technique of learning suited to the young child, who is incapable of handling general abstract ideas.

Dr. Montessori's view of error was interesting. In self-teaching, mistakes are not as apparently serious as they often seem to be in conventional learning situations. Error is a part of learning, provided it be one's own error: "Correction is irrelevant; each individual should become aware of errors himself, to become interested in his own mistakes."[16]

The role of discipline in self-teaching is worthy of comment. The techniques of self-teaching do away with much of the reward and punishment economy of group learning. "A school system must be called a failure if it cannot induce students to learn except by threatening them for not learning," says Skinner.[17] Montessori long advocated the abandonment of rewards and punishment. She believed the pleasure derived from what was learned was of far greater value to the child than any extrinsic reward.

Any student gaining competence in a given subject may eventually do his own "self-teaching." The learning devices he uses can only prepare for the far greater work of personal exploration. As the student matures and is able to work independently, there is a corresponding shift in the conventional teacher's role. Rather than acting as a supportive agent in his learning, the teacher assumes more of an advisory capacity. The teacher will always be needed to relate the sequences of programmed learning to the logical wholes that the student must master. Skinner points out that the classroom could be at least as automated as the family kitchen, which only provides the tools for creative construction.

The teachers of such students would be freed from much of the drill and routine of teaching and could respond to the needs of individual students more effectively than is possible in a lockstep learning situation. As has been stated, "Any teacher who can be replaced by a machine deserves to be replaced." The teacher who provides the dynamic link between the learner and the knowledge he seeks must be prepared to stimulate the formulation of those problems which can not be raised or solved

by a ready-made program. The programmed sequence stops before creative learning can begin, so the teacher at best is only facilitating one facet of learning through programming. Dr. Montessori warned that the materials did not teach each automatically, nor were they likely to inspire and interest the children without the mediation of the teacher in their presentation.

CHAPTER 8

# The New School

In a recent magazine article describing a Montessori school, the reporter enthusiastically described it thus: "Its old Montessori methods turn out to be a showcase of nearly every 'new' idea that U.S. education has lately discovered."[1] This statement has and will continue to evoke scepticism and irritation among the educators. An examination of the "new" ideas might be helpful to situate old Montessori in the context of new learning notions.

Montessori was the first partisan of the grouping of children in three-year age spans, a conspicuous feature of the "ungraded primary" class of recent date. In the present concept of the ungraded class, the children, according as they are slow, average or bright, are allowed to progress at different rates of speed through the completion of a fixed amount of work necessary for promotion to the next level. As has been previously mentioned, Montessori long decried the overemphasis on syllabus and the teacher's tendency to be satisfied with fulfilling the requirements as laid down therein (and nothing more). So the "open end" curriculum, in which the teacher continues to offer stimulation to the child after he has completed the required amount of work, is implied in Montessori's flexible grouping system.

The notion of the unblocked period of time, in which the children are free to work without interruption was sufficiently arresting to Dr. Kilpatrick to evoke comment in 1914. He admitted the difficulty of respecting this need of the child in the complex programming of a large school, but nevertheless acknowledged its superiority over the sporadic activity of the nursery and kindergarten, which had little regard for the child's need to be unhurried.

The "prepared" environment which Montessori envisaged was one responsive to the needs of the young child, containing possibilities for his satisfaction, achievement and exploration. Among the possibilities were those of the early learning of reading, writing and arithmetic, which Montessori did not deem beyond the capacities of under-sixes when taught in a manner congenial to the level of the child's development. In this assumption she was anticipating current beliefs in the ability of children to learn earlier than has been previously supposed and in the recognition of the need for activity meaningful for the child, which motivates him through his gradually increasing competence.

Montessori's insistence on the directress as an ally of the child rather than as his judge anticipated the trend that has made of teachers of the young a special breed, better adapted to their needs than teachers who impart knowledge with the certainty of parents engaged in an extrinsic goal-oriented existence or grandparents who represent an immutable past and the inference of an equally immutable future. The need of non-intervention of the teacher in the child's attempts to construct himself leads to a de-emphasis on talking and a re-emphasis on showing.

Montessori was aware that the rhythm of the child is different from that of the adult and the time table of early development should be more flexibly viewed than is presently feasible with the school admission policies based on the calendar age of six. Montessori rejected the notion of "pre-school" as opposed to school and saw all learning as continuous, with articulated academic goals. The problems of school placement for American five-to-seven-year-olds underscore the validity of Montessori's arguments.

The need for the education of the young child to be seen in the context of his whole development made Montessori critical of educational procedures which failed to reflect various stages of growth. The awareness of the perceptual level of learning and its reinforcement at an early age to enhance later conceptual learning was but one of the Montessori ideas reflected in her methods.

The idea of *team teaching*, anticipated by Montessori in her discussion of the pre-adolescent, pointed up the need for com-

petency beyond that to be reasonably expected by the ordinary teacher. Through the grouping of children, according to ability and interest within a larger group, it would be possible to alternate large groups of children working independently with smaller groups participating in group lessons and discussion.

The key to the Montessori classroom's flexibility is to be found in the notion of self discipline which informs it. Despite the fond hopes of teachers to evolve a system of teaching which is most respectful of the individual, the lack of education of the child to his individual responsibilities to himself and to the group makes this virtually impossible, and the group becomes one more reflection of the teacher's capacity to inspire obedience and assent through her own personality, rather than through the aggregate of the individual wills of the children.

The importance of the young child, on the threshold of life, mastering the basic disposition of learning if he is to continue to learn long after the formal period of instruction ceases, was as much a reality for Montessori in the nursery as in the university. She understood the roles of motivation, competence and curiosity. She understood the need for the child to be the active agent of his own learning. She understood that the subject matter itself should provide the focus for the child's interest and the necessary discipline.

In short, more than many more modern educators, Montessori saw the child in a broad context of total self realization. She did not speak of teaching the child instead of the subject. She spoke of the child teaching himself, recognizing that what he learned would be related to his personal investment in the learning process.

Montessori believed that the teacher should function as the exemplar of those dispositions she wished to engender in her students. If she were of a dominating cast, she did not belong with the young. If she could not come to grips with her own rebellious feelings about the adult world which she had abandoned for the greater security offered her by young children, she had no place in working with them, as she would impede their progress.

More than many of her contemporaries and successors, Mon-

tessori saw that the nature of conflict between the child and the adult, usually the parent, is to breed an impatience and anxiety on the part of the adult when the child did not correspond to the adult's idea of what should be done when. This annihilation of the child personality was, in Montessori's opinion, a preponderant characteristic of the adult attitude toward the child.

Montessori's remarkable background and her place in a generation that produced Freud, Jung, Adler, Bergson, and Dewey gave her a view of the origins of the child as well as a new vision of his destiny. She saw the child as the Pilgrim of the Absolute, in a world he could shape only through the freedom to grow to the stature of his true self-hood.

Montessori may be credited with adding to the love of the child, so gratifying for adults, respect for his potentialities. She took a serious view of him and that early period of learning which would affect all that subsequent schooling demanded of him. Montessori loved the child, respected him, and believed in him. She was certainly a pioneer in the awakening of the world to the child of today as the man of tomorrow. She fought for continuity in education, seeing that the gains of each developmental period of growth could be consolidated only by continued adult understanding.

Because Montessori wanted the child to achieve for his own sake, to accomplish, she decried competition in the early years of learning. "Never let a child fail, until he has a reasonable chance of success" was her rallying cry. Learning for the right reasons, to please oneself and for the sake of learning, should never be replaced by inferior motives based on reward and punishment. Once the child was competent, he would want to compete, because only then could he show what he knew. He would be less likely to demonstrate his ignorance.

Montessori realized that the work of the young child was the construction of himself. He needed to be a self before he could be absorbed into a group. He could accept or reject the overtures of others only when he possessed a strong sense of his own identity. Montessori believed in liberty for the child for freedom of action, yet within carefully prescribed limits, which made of all his choices good choices, though real ones. If man is to live

as a free man, some awareness of his need for liberty must inform his early education.

Montessori's clinical eye and intuitive grasp provided her with insights which, some two full generations later, seem strangely contemporary. If, as Philip Coombs of the Ford Foundation remarked, it takes about fifty years for an idea to get into the classroom, then a re-evaluation of Montessori is on schedule.

Picture if you will a school of the next decade, a school in which the arbitrary distinctions of pre-school versus "real" school have disappeared, one in which children from age three until age eight are thought of as in the first phase of learning. Such a school would have the physical flexibility that schools designed for team teaching now have, movable walls, etc., to fit them for a variety of purposes. The school of which I speak would have two principal groups around which the daily life is focused: the first group of children from three to six; the second, from approximately five to eight. Within the spacious airy classrooms, with facilities for individual as well as group work, would be a wealth of structured teaching materials and teaching machines, designed for both percept and concept acquisition. In the midst of each group would be a teacher, half hidden because of her intentional activity at the children's level. She would provide the dynamic link between them and all that could be explored, learned and discovered through manipulation of the learning stimuli in the environment.

Ideally, small alcoves off the large classroom, with plenty of open space for floor work, would contain the wherewithal for independent work in art, music listening, reading, scientific experimentation. Special teachers, members of a team, would be in these alcoves at stated times to help children intent on pursuing learning projects. In the first group, the acquisition of the skills of reading, writing and mathematical concepts would characterize the academic portion of the children's learning. In the second class, composition, spelling, grammar, poetry and creative writing, geography, history and math would characterize the work of the class. Remember, these children are under eight. There is still time for them to enjoy what must be learned before it must be learned with or without enjoyment.

The allowance for mobility in both groups might disconcert the observers of the next decade less than those of the present one. The suspicion of mobility dies hard in a culture which equates movement in education with purposelessness. Here movement is purposeful. Every opportunity is given these children to kneel, squat, sit and stand in the course of their work, if the children feel the need of it.

A conspicuous feature of this highly mobile group will be the air of purposeful quiet which pervades the class. There is talking to be sure. Children are working together, dictating spelling words, multiplying large numbers with symbolic material; but the most noticeable source of quiet is the teacher, who speaks sparingly though meaningfully. Given the opportunity to function as the protector of the work environment, armed with the many structured helps that make individual work possible, the teacher is freed from the necessity of talking constantly, even as the children are freed from the burden of group recitation with its attendant errors.

In both age groups, the element of obvious competition is missing. Children who know more than others are helping the slower learners. Some are checking other children's work. The incidental learning of the children forms a real part of the learning situation. The teacher follows a simple rule: she never does for the children what they are capable of doing for themselves. She rarely volunteers help, yet she may intervene with delicacy when she sees a child who is unaware of the nature of his difficulty and is stumped by it.

What will the school experience of these children be, when they leave classes such as these? Will they be subjected to the artificiality of a teacher-inspired curriculum? Or will they be free to continue to work and learn as individuals, lending themselves to a group and capable of withdrawing from the group to work alone if they so desire? These are children who should be resistant to group pressures, who have achieved a sense of self and are not dependent on their peers for their affirmation in being. These are the children who will possess the requisite ability to improvise and create, that is so necessary a part of learning.

What have conventional instructional techniques to do with what has been described? Has the teacher been rendered obsolete by approaches to learning so unabashedly focused for the first time on the child and not the teacher? Not at all. Much of what can be learned in a programmed sequence is information. The exploration and research, the intuition and discovery come later. These can only come about when the teacher is willing to assume a role as humble as that designated as hers by Montessori. Pride and anger, Montessori said, have no place in the teacher. She must decrease that the child may increase. There is no reduction of her need to be in the classroom nor in the acknowledgement of that need by the children once she is there. She functions now in a way that frees her to work with the children at the level of needed stimulus, not to bear mute witness to their obvious accomplishments, which will be echoed in recitation by the whole group.

The structure of the class day in such a school as envisioned would proscribe any unnecessary interruption of work during the entire morning. Three hours of activity will not fatigue these children, who shift from task to task with pleasure, now resting, now redoubling their efforts over a thorny problem. All of the special subjects, the play, the gym, can come after the morning, which is the sacrosanct work period. Ideally, the class for the younger children would open out onto a garden, so that the children could go out of doors to continue their occupations. There should be flowers and vegetables, some play equipment for their large muscles, and a place to sit and commune with nature if that is what the child feels in need of. In nice weather this area, which might be reached by a movable glass wall, can literally be incorporated into the classroom.

With the ground rules of behavior established as previously indicated, the teacher will have many ways in which to work with the children. There will be for her the possibility of providing different activities for almost everyone who wants or needs them. Meanwhile, the business of the requirements, which will be pressing for the members of the second class, must be attended to. On the very real supposition that there are a few in the group who refuse to abide by the rules, there might be established a

corner under the direction of the teacher or an assistant in which the children who are not responsibly independent stay until they feel ready to move out into the group.

This sort of school environment, markedly different from the ultra-traditional one in which the teacher makes all of the decisions and the more permissive one in which the teacher makes most of the decisions while giving the group the illusion of making them, is no idle fancy. These kinds of situations have obtained throughout the world in the best organized of Montessori classes in various countries at various times. Each situation was a reflection of the culture in which it was situated, as would be such an American school as I describe.

In the next decades, the element in the educational triad most likely to assume a new form is not the child who, thwarted or not, will continue to be himself, and less the environment, which superficially may already resemble the physical situation just described. The radical change will be in the teacher. The arbitrary distinction between the job of the teacher at the nursery school level, now involved in giving a child a sense of himself, and the elementary teacher now imparting the rudiments, will shift when these two functions are combined. Children do not change radically at six. Perhaps the school-entering age should be dropped to four to take advantage of early learning; perhaps, as in England, American education should begin to consider the age span three to eight as a more organic pattern of grouping than the present one, which leaves many a five-year-old in the limbo of kindergarten and many an unready six with no option but to repeat a grade which was as little designed for him as he was designed for it. We must do more for our children than we are now doing to meet the challenges of that world, dimly sensed but not yet seen, into which they will be going.

There are fewer constants for our children in our culture than our parents could count upon. But there are some, directly related to the avowed task of education, in either its traditional or contemporary role. The day is past when a man may rest easy on the knowledge he has acquired through formal instruction. We know that our children will need to continue to learn all their lives. They may not, as so many young adults are now doing, live

on the meager intellectual capital amassed during the years of formal schooling. A learning approach which emphasizes the cogency of *learning how to learn,* and the attitude necessary for making this possible, commends itself to our attention. The child who has the disposition, skill and attention necessary for learning will be a freer and more creative learner all his life. He may even be capable in the next generation of reversing the anti-intellectual trend in education, through unprejudiced exposure to subject matter years ahead of the peer group prejudices that he usually absorbs. The next generation may even render extinct the genus "teen ager," and emerge with a continuous growth and learning pattern from infancy to maturity. To make learning palatable is a traditionally educational challenge, to make learning possible earlier than anticipated is a reality. With all there is to know besides knowing oneself, the ideas of Maria Montessori on education appear for our time significantly contemporary.

# Appendix A

---

*Note on the Life of Maria Montessori*

Maria Montessori was born in 1870 at Chiaravalle, in the province of Anconá, Italy. As a child she showed great aptitude in mathematics and decided on a career in engineering, which she later forsook for the study of medicine. Brought up in times of turbulent social stress in Italy, Maria Montessori struck a blow for "a new order" by resisting tremendous criticism and enrolling in the University of Rome Medical School as the first woman in Italy to do so. After Dr. Montessori's graduation as a doctor, in 1896, she did postgraduate work in the Psychiatric Clinic connected with the University. She was appointed directress of the State Orthophrenic School, where she served from 1899-1901. In that year, interested in increasing her knowledge of educational thought, Dr. Montessori returned to the University for further study in Philosophy and Psychology. From 1896-1906 she held the Chair of Hygiene at the Magistro Femminile, Rome (one of two women's colleges in Italy at that time). In 1904 Dr. Montessori became Professor of Anthropology at the University of Rome.

With the foundation of the first Casa dei Bambini in 1906, Montessori's life took a new direction. She directed the work of the Casa until 1911, during which time she also lectured extensively on her approach to education. From that year until her death, Dr. Montessori traveled the earth tirelessly, lecturing, writing, directing research, and establishing in her wake teacher training centers and schools. Her work was of an encyclopedic

nature as were the honors heaped upon her by the governments who counted themselves well served by her efforts. (Dr. Montessori came to America and lectured extensively. She conducted a course in California, and at the San Francisco Exhibition (1915) a model Montessori pavilion was constructed. The work of the Montessori children gained two gold medals.) During the second world war, Dr. Montessori was interned in India as an Italian national. She was permitted to lecture, and during the war years established the Montessori movement in India. Upon her return to Europe, she again took up the work which had been destroyed in Germany and Italy by the war. Dr. Montessori died in Holland in 1952. She was a product of nineteenth century scientific thinking, and an acutely aware social critic, one of the first feminists.

Montessori combined the discipline and training of medicine with tremendous intuitive gifts. Her discovery that the children in the Orthophrenic School, who had been diagnosed as idiots, were capable of reading, writing, and passing the Roman public school examinations, convinced Dr. Montessori that if this were so, then normal children were capable of a great deal more than was customarily expected of them. Montessori realized that if this visual motor involvement could be utilized by the slow learner, then it should be equally valuable technique for working with normal children to stimulate them in the acquisition of perception.

# Appendix B

*Montessori Teacher Training in the U.S.*

The organization of teacher training courses is undertaken by the various national Montessori Societies (e.g., The American Montessori Society, 18 West Putnam Avenue, Greenwich, Connecticut) and reflects national standards of teacher preparation.

In Teacher Training, the necessity of bringing theory and practice closer together has led to the notion of "Foundations" courses, and to an integrated program. There might be a parallel drawn between the present-day liberal arts graduates who are turning to teaching and the unlettered assistants of Montessori's Casa dei Bambini, both groups representing a freedom from those "inert ideas" which would prevent them from allowing children to try learning earlier. The present format of the International Training Course (sponsored by the International Montessori Association and the American Montessori Society) is a fifth-year program for college graduates of an internship type. The elements of theory and practice as laid down by Dr. Montessori are emphasized, as well as the relation between these principles and those underlying American educational practice.

The trainee's day is divided between mornings of observation and practice teaching and afternoons of lectures on Montessori theory and practice, as well as educational and developmental psychology, philosophical and social foundations of American education, and comparative methods. A team of experienced Montessorians, designated by the International Montessori Association, conducts the Montessori portion of the program; qualified university lecturers, the rest. The American Montessori

training takes cognizance of the need for continuing research in teaching methods. The principles underlying the design of the present Montessori apparatus may be expanded into many new sorts of learning materials.

The emphasis on observation is apparent, as seen in the quantitative requirement of approximately 300 hours for the year. The most effective way of learning from children is to watch them. Montessori believed that the child taught much more than any theorist could. The provision for supervised teaching makes it possible for the students to put into practice the theory as they learn it under the direction of a master teacher. The year's work, completed by the compilation of "Apparatus" books (detailed résumés of the use and sequence of the learning materials) made by the students, and oral and written practical and theoretical examinations by external examiners, leads to the International Montessori Diploma which entitles its holder to organize and work in a class of children from 3-8 years. Obviously, one year's training is not enough to assimilate all of the insights necessary for the most effective Montessori teaching. The student's first year of teaching under direction completes the training.

The present demand for Montessori teachers and teachers of teachers reflects tremendous interest throughout America in the ideas of Montessori. The liberal arts background of so many Montessori-trained teachers proves valuable in the direction of classes which require so much dependence on the teacher's resources. Despite the supra-national nature of the child and the common bond shared by children in various cultures, it is a fact acknowledged by the International Montessori Association that the most valuable Montessori training is to be found in the country in which one intends to teach. Consequently, those persons interested in teaching in the United States would be well advised to obtain their training here.

At present, the requirements in various states would necessitate investigation, to assess the validity of the Montessori training as an alternative certification credential.

# DR. MARIA MONTESSORI
## AND THE
# MONTESSORI MOVEMENT:

---

*A General Bibliography of Materials in the English Language, 1909-1961*

*Compiled* by*

GILBERT E. DONAHUE
*Research Librarian*
MONTEITH COLLEGE AND WAYNE STATE UNIVERSITY LIBRARIES
Wayne State University, Detroit 2, Michigan

*To Victoria Ann, Moira Eve, and Christopher Ian*

* The compilation of this bibliography was supported, in part, by the Monteith College Library Research Project, Project #874, Cooperative Research Branch, United States Office of Education.

# INTRODUCTION

Defining the scope of materials relating to the Montessori Movement is not an easy task. The individual works of Dr. Montessori are the central core of this bibliography, of course, but these works and the extensive series of lectures she personally delivered over a period of forty years in Europe, the United States, and Asia sparked intensive reactions throughout the entire educational world. During the past fifty years, accordingly, her movement has gained, and continues to gain, many avid and devoted supporters along with many equally vocal opponents. Given such a situation, an extensive, but scattered literature relating to her movement has been developed in many languages and at various levels of discourse, ranging from the popular to the most technical and scholarly.

The purpose of this bibliography, then, is not only to list the works of Dr. Maria Montessori, but also to present an unbiased documentation of opinion concerning the educational movement which continues to implement her thought and practices throughout the world. The general scope of this work includes, therefore, both supporters and opponents of Dr. Montessori. It also includes scholarly treatises as well as, to speak politely, the not so scholarly materials. In the technical language of bibliography, this work is non-selective and non-evaluative.

The search for this documentation has led through a labyrinth of bibliographical sources and forms to locate the relevant materials. While the primary focus has been the identification of book and journal literature, attention has been also given to newspaper articles and unpublished research studies whenever information on them was available. Whenever possible, book reviews of the items listed in the bibliography have been included. Juvenile literature, fiction and poetry also have been listed when they have dealt directly with Montessorian themes. In terms of publishing agencies, the literature in this bibliography has come from a variety of sources: the mass media magazines, the professional, scholarly journals, commercial book publishers and the university press, as well as the government, both as an initi-

ating agency and publisher of reports. By national origin, the principal sources have come from the United States and Great Britain, but use was also made of Indian, Canadian and Australian literature.

The basic organization of the materials in the bibliography is by historical periods: 1) the pre-World War I period, 1909-1914; 2) the World War I period, 1915-1919; and 3) the individual decades of the 20's, 30's, 40's, 50's and 60's. The rules of entry for the material within each time period are as follows: each item is arranged alphabetically by author, and multiple items by the same author are listed chronologically within each time period. In this listing of works by the same author, book items of the same date are given preference over journal literature. Anonymous items, or entries without known authors, are arranged alphabetically by the first significant word in the *name of the source* and multiple items of this type from the same source are listed chronologically. In government documents and other organizational publications, preference of entry is given to personal authorship, whenever this can be established.

While the search process in the compilation of this work was as complete as time and other resources permitted, this bibliography is only a preliminary step in the documentation needed on the Montessori Movement. Unfortunately, many of the items listed were not available for direct examination during the compilation of this bibliography. There are also known works by Dr. Montessori and other persons which have not been listed because their complete citation could not be verified with locally available information. Any comments, corrections, or additional entries for this bibliography will be gratefully received by the compiler, c/o The American Montessori Society, 18 West Putnam Avenue, Greenwich, Conn.

Bibliography, as has been implied above, is a social process. Not only do the contents of bibliographies reflect some selected social reality, but their compilation would not be possible without the cooperation of many organizations and individuals. Without the prior work of many virtually anonymous persons who produced the bibliographical tools upon which this work is based, it could not have been compiled; nor could it have been compiled without the social institution of the library. The encouragement of the American Montessori Society and the Cleveland Montessori Association was an important factor in the decision to undertake this project. More immediately, I wish to acknowledge the interest and assistance of my colleagues at Monteith College and in the Wayne State University Library, together with the courtesies extended to me by the staffs of the Detroit Public Library and the University of Detroit Library. I am also indebted to Mr. Harry Veeder and Mrs. Eva Gelfman Weiss, of the Monteith College Library Research Project, for their bibliographic assistance during various stages of this work.

Lastly, not in the usual *pro forma* sense, I wish to acknowledge the

contribution of my wife, Sonja, to this work. Her love of our children and her commitment to the necessity of educational reform have been the inspiration of our joint effort to realize the values envisioned by Dr. Maria Montessori. Without that inspiration, this work would have been just that—work. . . .

*References for the Period, 1909-1914*


1. "The Montessori Method," *American Education,* vol. 15 (March, 1912), 302.
2. Anderson, C. A. *Montessori Method of Teaching Hearing Children.* Wash., D.C.: American Association to Promote the Teaching of Speech to the Deaf, 1912. 7p.
3. ———. *Proving the Worth of the Montessori Method.* Washington, D.C.: The Volta Bureau, 1913. 5p.
4. Anderson, J. Scott (Mrs.). "The Montessori Method of Teaching Hearing Children," *Volta Review,* vol. 14 (June, 1912), 154-68.
5. Bailey, Carolyn S. "Don't Touch! Be Still! A House of Children," *Delineator,* vol. 83 (September, 1913), 14.
6. ———. "Freeing of Otello the Terrible," *ibid.,* (October, 1913), 14.
7. ———. "Has Your Youngster Found His Body?" *ibid.,* (November, 1913), 15.
8. ———. "Christ in Bruno; A True Montessori Christmas Story," *ibid.,* (December, 1913), 5.
9. a.———. (Fiction) "Raffaelo's Hunger," *ibid.,* vol. 84 (January, 1914), 8.
10. b.———. "Going Away of Antonio," *ibid.,* (February, 1914), 40.
11. c.———. "Mario's Finger-Eyes," *ibid.,* (March, 1914), 18.
12. d.———. "Andrea's Lily," *ibid.,* (May, 1914), 74.
13. ———. "Our Counciling Mothers; Problems in Applying Montessori Methods," *ibid.,* (June, 1914), 21.
14. Baldwin, W. A. "The Conflicting Pedagogy of Madame Montessori," *Journal of Education,* vol. 77 (February 6, 1913), 147-149.

14-A. Barnes, Earl. "Comparison of Frobelian and Montessori Methods and Principles," *Kindergarten Review,* vol. 23 (April, 1913), 487-490.

15. Bates, Laura McDill. "Montessori Models," *American Annals of the Deaf,* vol. 58 (January, 1913), 16-25.
16. Beaumont, Edith M. "The Montessori System," *South Dakota Educator,* vol. 25 (April, 1912), 12-14.

16-A. Bell, Mrs. Alexander Graham. "What the Montessori Method Means to Me," *Freedom for the Child,* vol. 1(1914), 7-10.

17. Benson, Theresa. "An Experiment in Montessori Work," *Primary Education,* vol. 21(January, 1913), 9-11.

18. Berle, A. A. "Montessori Method and the Home," *Journal of Education,* vol. 77(May 1, 1913), 484-486.

19. Binzel, Alma L. "Early Education: the Kindergarten; the House of Childhood; the 'Exceptional Home,'" *Kindergarten Review,* vol. 24(January, 1914), 271-283.

20. Black, Mae Virginia. "Phases of the Montessori System of Teaching," *Pennsylvania School Journal,* vol. 61(March, 1913), 427-433.

21. Bone, Woutrina. "The Montessori System," North of England Education Conference, 12th Annual Meeting, Bradford, *School Government Chronicle,* vol. 91(January, 1914), 34-37.

22. "Montessori Child," (Poem) *Bookman,* vol. 38(February, 1914), 601.

23. Boone, Richard G. "The Montessori Method," *Sierra Educational News,* vol. 9(February, 1913), 113-121. *Ibid.,* (April, 1913), 270-279.

23-A. "No Naughty Children," *Boston Globe,* December 13, 1913, 5.

23-B. "Dr. Montessori Heard Twice," *ibid.,* December 14, 1913, 50.

24. Boyd, William. "Sense Training in the Montessori System," *Kindergarten Primary Magazine,* vol. 27(June, 1913), 319.

25. ———. *From Locke to Montessori:* A Critical Account of the Montessori Point of View. New York: Henry Holt & Co., 1914. 272p.

Reviewed in:

a. *ALA Booklist* 11:53, October, 1914
b. American *Review of Reviews* 50:252, August, 1914
c. *Athenaeum,* 1:545, April 18, 1914
d. *Boston Evening Transcript,* May 23, 1914, p. 9
e. *Educational Review* 48:427, November, 1914
f. *Nation* 99:320, September 10, 1914
g. *Philosophical Review* 23:693-694, November, 1914
h. *Spectator* 113:464, October 3, 1914
i. *Springfield (Mass.) Republican,* June 11, 1914, p. 5
j. *Survey* 33:339, December 26, 1914

26. Brisby, Drusie P. "The Montessori Method," *Educational Foundations,* vol. 25(February, 1914), 354-361.

27. Bryarly, Katharine Lee. "The Montessori Training Class [in Rome]," *American Annals of the Deaf,* vol. 58(March, 1913), 179-181.

28. Bullock, H. H. "Montessori Method, Self Education," *Primary Plans,* vol. 10(November, 1912), 9-10, 39-40.

29. Burrows, H. "Spontaneous Education: the Montessori Method," *Contemporary Review*, vol. 102(September, 1912), 328-337.

29-A. Bushnell, Ethel. "Montessori and the American Petted Darling," *Kindergarten Review*, vol. 24(1914), 455-458.

29-B. ———. "Homeopathic Treatment in Education: A Study of Specific Values in Montessori," *ibid.*, 515-517.

29-C. ———. "A Comparative Study of Montessori with the Activities of the American Kindergarten," *ibid.*, 546-547.

30. Byoir, Carl. "The Presentation of Montessori Material," National Education Association, *Journal of Proceedings and Addresses*, 50th Annual Meeting, 1912(Ann Arbor, 1912), 613-618.

31. Carmicheal, R. D. "The Montessori Method," *Progressive Teacher*, vol. 19(September, 1913), 11-13.

32. Cobb, C. S. "Montessori Method in Education," London County Council, Conference of Teachers, *Report of Proceedings*. London: P. S. King and Son, 1913, 1-2.

33. Coville, A. P. "Montessori Method: Impressions of a Kindergarten Mother," *Home Progress*, vol. 2(October, 1912), 12-18.

33-A. Cowan, David. "The Montessori System of Education," reprinted from the *Hampshire Chronicle* (Winchester, England: Jacob and Johnson, printer, 1912). 12p.

34. Craig, Clara E. *The Montessori System of Child Culture*. A Report Presented to the State Board of Education. Providence, R.I.: Department of Education, State of Rhode Island, 1913. 16p.

35. Culverwell, Edward P. *Montessori's Principles and Practices*. New York: John Martin's House, 1914. 309p.
Reviewed in:
a. *ALA Booklist* 10:349, May, 1914
b. *Athenaeum*, 2:492, Nov. 1, 1913
c. *Boston Evening Transcript*, January 7, 1914, p. 22

36. "Montessori's Rediscovery of the Ten Fingers," *Current Literature*, vol. 51(October, 1911), 386.

37. "Movement to Revolutionalize Education," *ibid.*, vol. 52 (March, 1912), 311-314.

38. "What America Thinks of Montessori's Educational Crusade," *Current Opinion*, vol. 56(February, 1914), 127-129.

39. "Is the Montessori School Based on a Misconception of the Child Mind?" *ibid.*, (April, 1914), 284-285.

40. "Limitations of the Montessori Method from a Religious Point of View," *ibid.*, 292.

41. Darrach, M. "Pupils Who Never Hear Don't," *Overland Monthly*, n.s. vol. 63(June, 1914), 589-592.

42. "Montessori Certified Teachers; List," *Delineator,* vol. 83 (December, 1913), 51.
43. "Montessori and the American Child," *ibid.,* vol. 84(April, 1914), 76.
44. Dent, L. M. "Are the Montessori Claims Justified?" *Forum,* vol. 51(June, 1914), 883-891.
45. Dillard, Annie. "The Montessori System as Shown in its Application to the City and Country Child," Kentucky Education Association, *Proceedings of the Forty-Third Annual Session* (Louisville, Ky., April 29-May 2, 1914), 158-160, 162-166.
46. Dillingham, H. G. "First Miles," *Home Progress,* vol. 3(July, 1914), 518-522.
47. Drucker, A. P. "Social Value of the Montessori System," *Journal of the American Institute of Criminal Law and Criminology,* vol. 4(January, 1914), 775-778.
48. "Essence of the Montessori Method," *Education,* vol. 34 (January, 1914), 328-329.
49. "American Montessori Courses," *Elementary School Journal,* vol. 15(October, 1914), 61-62.
50. Elsson, J. P. "What Really is the Montessori Method?" *Ladies Home Journal,* vol. 29(November, 1912), 30.
50-A. Fairchild, Marion. "Dr. Montessori's Visit to America," *Freedom for the Child,* vol. 1(1914), 1-3.
51. Findlay, Joseph J. "The Montessori System; Report of an Investigation Recently Conducted at the Fielden School," *Educational Times,* vol. 66(May 1, 1913), 203-207.
52. ———, and K. Steel. *Educative Toys;* Being an Account of Investigations with Montessori and Other Apparatus, Conducted at the Fielden School. London: Blackie and Son, Ltd., 1914. 103 p.
53. Fisher, Dorothy Canfield. *A Montessori Mother.* New York: Henry Holt & Co., 1912. 240p.
Reviewed in:
a. *ALA Booklist* 9:149, December, 1912
b. American *Review of Reviews* 47:765, June 13, 1913
c. *Athenaeum,* 1:243, March 1, 1913
d. *Bookman* 36:672, Feb. 13, 1913
e. *Catholic World* 96:822, March, 1913
f. *Chautauquan* 69:114, December, 1912
g. *Educational Review* 46:410-413, November, 1913
h. *Independent* 74:540, March 6, 1913
i. *Nation* 96:133, February 6, 1913
j. *Springfield (Mass.) Republican,* December 19, 1912, p. 5
54. ———. *The Montessori Manual.* Chicago: W. E. Richardson Co., 1913. 126p.

Reviewed in:
a. *ALA Booklist* 10:267, March, 1914
b. *New York Times* 18:751, December 21, 1913

55. ———. "About the Montessori Method," *Outlook,* vol. 104 (August 30, 1913), 1012-1013.
56. Fisher, Laura. "Montessori System," *School,* vol. 24(December 5, 1912), 123.
57. French, Ruth H. "The Working of the Montessori Method," *Journal of Education,* vol. 78(October 30, 1913), 423-426.
58. ———. "Montessori in Boston," *Journal of Education,* vol. 79(January 1, 1914), 12-13.
59. George, Anne E. "First Montessori School in America," *McClure's Magazine,* vol. 39(June, 1912), 177-187.
60. ———. "Dr. Maria Montessori: An Account of the Achievements and Personality of an Italian Woman Whose Discovery is Revolutionizing Educational Methods," *Good Housekeeping,* vol. 55(July, 1912), 24-29.
61. ———. "A Transplanted Montessori School," *World's Work* (London), vol. 20(August, 1912), 284-294.
62. ———. "Rhythm Work in the Children's House at Washington," *McClure's Magazine,* vol. 41(May, 1913), 182+.
63. ———. "The Montessori Movement in America," Chapter xv, Vol. 1, U.S. Commissioner of Education, *Report,* 1914. Washington, D.C.: Government Printing Office, 1914, 355-362.
64. Gesell, Arnold and Gesell, Beatrice. "The Montessori Kindergarten," *The Normal Child and Primary Education.* Boston: Ginn and Co., 1912, pp. 323-340.
65. Grant, Cecil. *English Education and Dr. Montessori.* London: W. Gardner, Darton & Co., 1913. 105p.
66. Grant, Emma B. "History of Montessori Method and Its Purposes," Illinois State Teachers' Association, *Journal of Proceedings.* 59th Annual Meeting, 1912, 103-107.
67. Graves, Frank P. "Is the Montessori Method a Fad?" *Popular Science Monthly,* vol. 84(June, 1914), 609-614.
68. Gruenberg, S. M. "What is the Montessori Method?" *Scientific American,* vol. 106(June 22, 1912), 564-565.
69. Hailmann, William Nicholas. "A Glimpse of the Montessori Method," *Kindergarten Primary Magazine,* vol. 24(June, 1912), 261-263.
70. ———. "Montessori Method and the Kindergarten," *ibid.,* vol. 25(September, 1912), 6-7.
71. Halsey, Walter N. "A Valuation of the Montessori Experiments," *Journal of Education,* vol. 77(January 16, 1913), 63-64.

72. Hamilton, A. E. "Montessori Obedience," *ibid.*, vol. 79(June 25, 1914), 734-735.

73. Harrison, Elizabeth. *The Montessori Method and the Kindergarten.* U.S. Bureau of Education, *Bulletin*, 1914, no. 28, whole #602. Washington, D.C.: Government Printing Office, 1914. 34p.

74. ———. "Montessori and the Kindergarten," *Kindergarten Primary Magazine*, vol. 27(September, 1914), 27-28.

75. Haskell, F. "Good Word for the Montessori Method," *Journal of Education*, vol. 78(December 18, 1913), 637-638.

76. Heller, H. H. "Appreciation: Maria Montessori," *ibid.*, vol. 79 (January 22, 1914), 96.

77. Holmes, Edmond Gore A. *The Montessori System of Education.* Great Britain, Board of Education Educational Pamphlets, no. 24. London: H. M. Stationery Office, 1912, 27p.

77-A. Holmes, Henry W. "Promising Pointing in the Montessori System," *Kindergarten Review*, vol. 23(April, 1913), 481-486.

78. ———. "Montessori Methods," *Education*, vol. 33(September, 1912), 1-10.

79. Hurd, Anna C. "Montessori and Kindergarten Work as Applied in the Rhode Island School," *American Annals of the Deaf*, vol. 58 (September, 1913), 504-515.

80. Huston, Katharine W. "Montessori Discipline," *Journal of Education*, vol. 79(February 19, 1914), 206.

81. Jacoby, George W. *The Montessori Method from a Physician's Viewpoint.* New York: William Wood and Co., 1913. 25p.

82. Jenkins, Elizabeth. "Impressions of an American Observer in the Montessori Schools," Illinois State Teachers' Association, *Journal of Proceedings*, 59th Annual Meeting, December 26-28, 1912, 109-116.

83. "A Montessori Experiment in Maine," *Journal of Education*, vol. 77(March, 1913), 328.

84. "Montessori's *Pedagogical Anthropology*," *ibid.*, vol. 78(October 23, 1913), 404-405.

85. "Montessori-McClure," *ibid.*, (December 25, 1913), 662-663.

86. Kennedy, Mary Jackson. "The Montessori System," *American Primary Teacher*, vol. 30(June, 1912), 368-369.

87. ———. "Montessori System," *Journal of Education*, vol. 76 (June 27, 1912), 10-11.

88. Kilpatrick, William H. "Montessori and Froebel," *Kindergarten Review*, vol. 23(April, 1913), 491-496.

89. ———. "The Montessori Method," International Kindergarten Union, *Proceedings* of the 20th Annual Meeting, April 29-May 2, 1913, Washington, D.C. (Cleveland, Ohio,

1913), 122-127; abstract in U.S. Bureau of Education, *Bulletin,* 1914, No. 6, Whole Number 577 (Washington, D.C.: Government Printing Office, 1914), 118-120.

90. ———. "The Montessori System in the Light of the Best American Educational Theory," North Carolina Teachers' Assembly, *Proceedings* of the Thirteenth Annual Session (Raleigh, N.C., November, 1913), 68-71.

91. ———. *The Montessori System Examined.* Boston: Houghton, Mifflin, 1914. 71p.

92. "What Can We Learn from the Montessori System?" *Kindergarten Review,* vol. 23(December, 1912), 266-270.

93. Law, Mary E. "Montessori Method and the Kindergarten," *Kindergarten Primary Magazine,* vol. 25(June, 1913), 273.

94. ———. "Montessori Method, the Kindergarten and the Gary School," *ibid.,* vol. 26(April, 1914), 222-223.

95. Lidbetter, Evelyn. "Teaching of Writing and Reading—The Value of Muscular Memory," London County Council, Conference of Teachers, *Report of Proceedings,* London: P. S. King and Son, 1913, 5-6.

96. "Montessori Schools in Italy," *Literary Digest,* vol. 47(October 11, 1913), 637-638.

97. "Most Interesting Woman of Europe," *ibid.,* (December 20, 1913), 1226-1227.

98. "When Helen Keller Met Montessori," *ibid.,* vol. 48(January 17, 1914), 134.

99. Logan, Anna E. "Montessori and Froebel," *Kindergarten Review,* vol. 23(May, 1913), 553-561.

100. ———. "Ideals of Scientific Pedagogy and the Montessori Experiment," Wisconsin Teachers' Association, *Proceedings* of the 60th Annual Session, November 8-10, 1912 (Madison, 1913), 175-180.

101. Long, J. Schuyler. "The Montessori Method: A Comparison," *American Annals of the Deaf,* vol. 58(March, 1913), 117-125.

102. "Information about the Montessori Method," *McClure's Magazine,* vol. 37 (October, 1911), 702-704.

103. "Montessori Bibliography: Books and Articles Published up to April, 1913," *ibid.,* vol. 41(July, 1913), 170+.

104. McMunigle, Mary G. "Why Columbia University Rejects the Montessori Method," *Pittsburgh School Bulletin,* vol. 6 (October), 1437-1440; *ibid.* (November, 1912), 1461-1465.

105. MacMunn, Norman. *A Path to Freedom in the School.* London: G. Bell and Sons, 1914. 162p.

106. Margulies, A. Reno. "Montessori Method and the Deaf Child," *Volta Review,* vol. 14(April-May, 1912), 48-49 and 74-85.

107. ———. "Montessori Method Applicable to the Deaf," *ibid.*, (June, 1912), 146-147.

108. ———. "Dr. Montessori and Her Method," *ibid.*, vol. 15 (October, 1913), 334-338; also in *American Annals of the Deaf*, vol. 58(September, 1913), 496-502.

109. May, Maude G. "A New Method of Infant Education," *Journal of Education* (London), vol. 31(September, 1909), 645-647.

110. Merrill, Jenny B. "New Method in Kindergarten Education," *Kindergarten Primary Magazine*, vol. 22-23(December, 1909-March, 1910), 106-107, 142-144, 211-212, 297-298.

111. ———. "New Method in Infant Education," *ibid.*, vol. 24 (December, 1911), 96-98.

112. ———. "Neglected Corner in Montessori Method," *ibid.*, vol. 25(January, 1913), 125.

113. ———. "Appreciation: Montessori," *ibid.*, vol. 26(January, 1914), 146.

114. Montessori, Maria. *The Montessori Method;* Scientific Pedagogy as Applied to Child Education in "The Children's Houses." Translated from the Italian by Anne E. George. New York: Frederick A. Stokes Co., 1912. 377p.
Reviewed in:
a. *ALA Booklist* 8:408, June 1912
b. American *Review of Reviews* 45:766, June 12, 1912
c. *Athenaeum*, 1:645, June 8, 1912
d. *Catholic World* 99:253, May, 1914
e. *Chautauquan* 68:116, September, 1912
f. *Dial* 52:392-4, May 16, 1912—M. V. O'Shea
g. *Educational Review* 43:529-33, May 12, 1912–E. Y. Stevens
h. *Independent* 73:263, August 1, 1912
i. *Journal of Experimental Pedagogy*, March, 1913, 48+
j. *Nation* 94:563-5, June 6, 1912
k. *New York Times* 17:242, April 12, 1912
l. *School Arts Magazine* 12:66, Sept., 1912–H. T. Bailey
m. *Spectator* 109:245, August 17, 1912
n. *Survey* 28:421, June 8, 1912
o. *Times Educational Supplement*(London), June 4, 1912, 69

115. ———. "Disciplining Children," *McClure's Magazine*, vol. 39(May, 1912), 95-102.

116. ———. *Pedagogical Anthropology*. Translated from the Italian by Frederic Tobin Cooper. New York: Frederick A. Stokes Co., 1913. 508p.
Reviewed in:
a. *America* 10:130-2, November 15, 1913

b. *ALA Booklist* 10:21, September, 1913
c. American *Review of Reviews* 48:380, September, 1913
d. *Anthenaeum,* 2:313, September 27, 1913
e. *Athenaeum,* 2:422, October 18, 1913
f. *Boston Evening Transcript,* August 6, 1913, 18
g. *Catholic World* 99:253, May, 1914
h. *Independent* 75:748, September 25, 1913
i. *New York Times* 18:425, August 10, 1913
j. *North American Review* 198:733, November, 1913
k. *Outlook* 104:962, August 23, 1913
l. *Springfield (Mass.) Republican,* September 25, 1913, 5
m. *Time Educational Supplement* (London), October, 1913

117. ———. "Plan for an International Institute," *McClure's Magazine,* vol. 40(March, 1913), 221+.

118. ———. *Dr. Maria Montessori's Own Handbook.* New York: Frederick A. Stokes & Co., 1914. 121p.
Reviewed in:
a. *ALA Booklist* 11:11, September, 1914
b. American *Review of Reviews* 50:252, August, 1914
c. *Athenaeum,* 1:545, April 18, 1914
d. *Boston Evening Transcript,* June 17, 1914, 22
e. *Independent* 78:454, June 8, 1914
f. *Nature* 93:659, August 27, 1914
g. *Saturday Review* 117:441, April 4, 1914
h. *Spectator* 113:464, October 3, 1914
i. *Survey* 33:338, December 26, 1914

119. Moore, Annie E. "Impression of Montessori Schools in Rome," Southern Educational Association, *Journal of Proceedings and Addresses,* 23rd Annual Meeting, November 28-30, 1912 (Nashville, Tenn., 1913), 160-166.

120. Moorehead, F. B. "Shocked into Smartness," *Technical World,* vol. 19(April, 1913), 218-221.

121. Morgan, S. A. *The Montessori Method: An Exposition and Criticism.* Ontario Department of Education, *Bulletin,* No. 1, 1912. Toronto: L. K. Cameron, 1913. 72p.

122. Myers, Katrina. "Seguin's Principles of Education as Related to the Montessori Method," *Journal of Education,* vol. 77 (May 15, 1913), 538-541.

123. Naumburg, Margaret. "Maria Montessori: Friend of Children," *Outlook,* vol. 105(December 13, 1913), 796-799.

124. "Woman as Child Trainer; Maria Montessori's Houses of Childhood in Italy," *New York Evening Post,* January 22, 1912.

125. *New York Times,* 1913
"American students enrolled in Rome," March 16, section

IV, p. 5, column 1
"(Montessori method) will be shown by motion picture films," July 13, III, 2:7
"Children becoming egomaniacs," letter by Dr. H. C. R. Norriss, July 24, 6:7
"Letter by 'Jane Burr,'" August 1, 6:6
"Mme Montessori tells of spread of her method, letter," August 10, II, 10:6
"Dr. Maria Montessori coming to America to study educational methods and to deliver lectures, Nov. 20, 10:8; leaves Rome, Nov. 21, 3:2; arrives in New York, plans to establish a laboratory school in Rome, opinions on the education of children, Dec. 4, 9:1; editorial, Dec. 4, 8:4; entertained in Washington by Mr. and Mrs. Alexander Graham Bell, Dec. 7, IV, 17:6; special article on her method of education and its reflection in her personality, Dec. 7, X, 12:1; will lecture in New York again, to meet Helen Keller and Thomas A. Edison, Dec. 8, 11:5; Dr. John Dewey presides at lecture, Dec. 9, 8:2; guest at luncheon given by Mr. and Mrs. P. Stuyvesant Pillot, lectures announced, meets Helen Keller, Dec. 11, 2:8; lectures in Brooklyn Academy of Music, plans to visit Harvard University, Dec. 12, 6:2; methods compared with kindergarten system, letter, Dec. 12, 10:6; last lecture in New York, Dec. 16, 3:7; exhausted by tour, to rest at Battle Creek, Dec. 21, II, 1:7; reception given in her honor by Women's Cosmopolitan Club; sails for Liverpool, comment on America, Dec. 24, 4:3.

126. *New York Times,* 1914
"Maria Montessori gives reception to American delegates at meeting of International Council of Women, May 17, 1914, III, 2:7.
"Maria Montessori to personally supervise school at Panama Exposition," August 3, 1914, 8:7.

127. Newell, Bertha Payne. "Aspects of the First Three Gifts and Some Montessori Materials," *Kindergarten Review,* vol. 23 (October, 1912), 73-79.

128. "The Montessori School," *Northwest Journal of Education,* vol. 23(April, 1912), 353-354.

129. O'Connor, M. J. "Madame Montessori," *America,* vol. 10 (December 27, 1913), 270-272.

130. O'Grady, Alice. "American Kindergartens and Montessori Schools," *Educational Bi-Monthly,* vol. 8(April, 1914), 298-306.

131. O'Shea, Michael Vincent. "The Montessori Method of Teaching," *Dial,* vol. 52(May 16, 1912), 392-394.

132. ———. "The Newest Educational Enthusiasm," *Popular Educator,* vol. 30(February, 1913), 311-313.

133. "Dr. Montessori and Her Teachings," *Outlook,* vol. 105 (December 27, 1913), 864-865.

134. Palmer, Luella A. "Montessori and Froebelian Materials and Methods," *Elementary School Teacher,* vol. 13(October, 1912), 68-79; also in *Kindergarten Review,* vol. 24(November, 1913), 129-140.

135. Peterson, Joseph. "A New Emphasis on Activity in Education, Experiments Which Bear Upon the Age in Which to Start Children to School," *Utah Educational Review,* vol. 5 (March, 1912), 8.

136. Pollock, Horatio M. "Notes on the Development of the Montessori System," *American Education,* vol. 17(January, 1914), 268-271.

137. Reeder, R. R. "Montessori Method of Educating Children," *Survey,* vol. 27(January 20, 1912), 1595-1597.

138. Roland, Allen. "Montessori Method and Missionary Methods," *International Review of Missions,* April, 1913.

139. Salter, Emma G. "Montessori Method: Some Recent Criticisms," *World's Work* (London), vol. 22(July, 1913), 158-161.

140. "Woman pioneer in education," *Scientific American,* vol. 106 (May 25, 1912), 470.

141. Scudder, Myron T. "The Montessori Method in Relation to the Rural Schools," *School Journal,* vol. 80(February, 1913), 135-136.

142. ———. "The Montessori System," New York State Association of District Superintendents, *Proceedings* of the First and Second Meetings, 1912-1913 and 1913-1914, 144-148.

143. Shaw, Elizabeth Ross. "The Scientific Spirit in Education; Its Effects Upon the Kindergarten in Relation to the Distinctive Characteristics of the Montessori Method," National Education Association, *Journal of Proceedings and Addresses,* 51st Annual Meeting, 1913 (Ann Arbor, Michigan, 1913), 439-445; also in *School Journal,* vol. 80(October, 1913), 372-374 and in the *Atlantic Educational Journal,* vol. 9(December, 1913), 125-129.

144. ———. "Kindergarten and the Montessori Method," *Kindergarten Primary Mazagine,* vol. 26(December, 1913), 96-97.

145. Simpson, M. M. *Report on the Montessori Methods of Education.* Australia. New South Wales, Department of Public Instruction, 1914. 47p.

146. Smith, Anna Tolman. *The Montessori System of Education.* United States Bureau of Education, *Bulletin,* 1912, no. 17;

Whole no. 489. Washington, D.C.: Government Printing Office, 1912. 30p.

147. Smith, H. Bompas. "The Montessori Conference (Report of Conference at East Runton, England)," *Educational Times* (London), vol. 67(September 1, 1914), 418-419.

148. Smith, Sadie. "The Montessori System and the Deficients," *Ohio Educational Monthly,* vol. 62(August, 1913), 431-434.

149. Smith, Theodate L. "Dr. Maria Montessori and Her Houses of Childhood," *Pedagogical Seminary,* vol. 18(December, 1911), 533-542.

150. ———. *The Montessori System in Theory and Practice.* New York: Harper and Bros., 1912. 78p.
Reviewed in:
a. *Independent* 73:798, October 3, 1912
b. *Outlook* 102:321, October 12, 1912

151. Stevens, Ellen Yale. "Montessori and Froebel—A Comparison," *Elementary School Teacher,* vol. 12(February, 1912), 253-258.

152. ———. "The Montessori Method and Primary Education," *Primary Education,* vol. 20(June, 1912), 313-316.

153. ———. "Montessori Method and the American Kindergarten," *McClure's Magazine,* vol. 40(November, 1912), 77-82.

154. ———. "The Montessori Method and the Modern Kindergarten," *World's Work* (London), vol. 21(December, 1912), 105-109.

155. ———. *A Guide to the Montessori Method.* New York: Frederick A. Stokes & Co., 1913. 240p.
Reviewed in:
a. *ALA Booklist* 9:446, June, 1913
b. American *Review of Reviews* 47:765, June, 1913
c. *Educational Review* 46:396, November, 1913
d. *Boston Evening Transcript,* April 3, 1913, 25
e. *New York Times* 18:253, April 27, 1913

156. ———. "The Montessori Movement in America," *McClure's Magazine,* vol. 40(February, 1913), 222-224.

157. ———. "The Montessori Movement—A McClure Department," *ibid.,* vol. 41(July, 1913), 170-174; *ibid.,* (August, 1913), 201-203.

158. Stewart, J. A. "Madame Maria Montessori," *Journal of Education,* vol. 75(June 20, 1912), 702.

159. ———. "Teaching Tots to Read and Write," *ibid.,* vol. 80 (July 9, 1914), 46-47.

160. Townsend, Janet S. "Montessori Training Class for Teachers in Rome," *McClure's Magazine,* vol. 41(June, 1913), 184-194.

161. Tozier, Josephine. "An Educatoral Wonder-Worker: Maria Montessori's Methods," *McClure's Magazine,* vol. 37(May, 1911), 3-19; also in *Fortnightly Review,* vol. 90(August, 1911), 309-327.

162. ———. "Montessori Schools in Rome," *McClure's Magazine,* vol. 38(December, 1911), 122-137; also in *World's Work* (London), vol. 19(February, 1912), 250-265.

163. ———. "Montessori Apparatus," *McClure's Magazine,* vol. 38(January, 1912), 289-302; also in the *World's Work* (London), March, 1912.

164. ———. "If Mme. Montessori Taught Music, This Engaging New Method which is Phenomenally Successful Would Probably Be Her Way of Doing It," *Delineator,* vol. 84 (February, 1914), 16-17, 61.

165. Tuttle, Madge. "A Comparison of the Montessori and Froebelian Systems," *Primary Plans,* vol. 11(June, 1913), 9, 41.

166. U.S. Bureau of Education. Library Division. *List of References on Maria Montessori and Her Methods.* Washington, D.C., 1913. 4p. 1914. 6p.

167. "Montessori Method in Specially Designed School; 'Northampton Charts' will also be a Feature of Instruction at Torresdate House," *Volta Review,* vol. 14(December, 1912), 553.

168. Vorse, Mary Heaton. "New Freedom for Little Children," *Women's Home Companion,* vol. 40(October, 1913), 9; *ibid.,* (November, 1913), 18.

169. ———. "How Children See with Their Hands," *ibid.,* vol. 41(February, 1914), 11-12.

170. ———. "Importance of Play," *ibid.,* (March, 1914), 23; *ibid.,* (April, 1914), 13.

171. Voss, Marian. "The Montessori Method," *Utah Educational Review,* (January-February, 1913), 25-27.

172. Walker, Jane. "The Montessori Method of Education," *Educational Review,* vol. 46(October, 1913), 300-307.

173. Ward, Florence Elizabeth. "Impressions of the Montessori System," National Education Association, *Journal of Proceedings and Addresses,* 50th Annual Meeting, 1912, 609-613; also in *Kindergarten Review,* vol. 23(November 1912), 139-143.

174. ———. *The Montessori Method and the American School.* New York: Macmillan & Co., 1913. 243p.
Reviewed in:
a. *ALA Booklist* 10:366; May, 1914
b. *Boston Evening Transcript,* February 21, 1914, 8
c. *Chautauquan* 72:493, February 21, 1914

d. *Educational Review* 47:421, April, 1914
e. *Nature* 93:659, August 27, 1914
f. *Spectator* 113:464, October 3, 1914
g. *Survey* 33:339, December 26, 1914

175. ———. "Place of Art and Handwork in the Montessori System," Western Drawing and Manual Training Association, *Proceedings* of Meeting held at Des Moines, Iowa, May 7-10, 1913, 89-96.

176. ———. "School Health Ideas of Dr. Montessori," *Kindergarten Primary Magazine*, vol. 26(November, 1913), 66-67.

177. Warren, Howard C. "The House of Childhood; A New Primary System," *Journal of Educational Psychology*, vol. 3 (March, 1912), 121-132.

178. Wheelock, Lucy. "Comparison of Montessori and Froebel," Vermont State Teachers' Association, *Report* of the 64th Annual Convention, October 22-23, 1913 (Brattleboro, 1913), 77-85.

179. White, Jessie. *Montessori Schools as Seen in the Early Summer of 1913.* London: H. Mifford, 1914. 185p.

180. Wild, Laura H. "Montessori System and the American Schools for the Deaf," *Journal of Education*, vol. 76(August 22, 1912).

181. Williams, L. A. "Estimate of the Montessori System of Child Training," *New York Teachers Monographs*, vol. 14(June, 1912), 25-32.

182. Winship, A. E. "Montessori Methods," *American Primary Teacher*, vol. 35(April, 1912), 285-286.

183. ———. "Montessori Methods," *Journal of Education*, vol. 75(April 11, 1912), 399-400.

184. Witmer, Lightner. "A Caution on Montessori," *ibid.*, vol. 76 (July 4, 1912), 39.

185. ———. "The Montessori Method," *Psychological Clinic*, vol. 8(March 15, 1914), 1-5.

186. Wood, Walter de Burley. *Children's Play and Its Place in Education*, with An Appendix on the Montessori Method. New York: Duffield, 1913. (2nd edition: 1915)

187. Zaner, C. P. "The Montessori Method as Applied to Writing," *Colorado School Journal*, vol. 28(June, 1913), 21-25.

*References for the Period, 1915–1919*

188. "Dr. Montessori in England," *Anglo-Italian Review*, (November, 1919), 135-140.

189. Bailey, Carolyn S. *Montessori Children.* New York: Henry Holt & Co., 1915. 188p.
Reviewed in:
a. *Bookman* 41:213 April, 1915
b. *Boston Evening Transcript* May 10, 1915, 24

c. *Independent* 81:428 March 22, 1915
d. *Nation* 100:361 April 1, 1915
e. *New York Times* 20:266 July 25, 1915

190. Barnard, Grace Everett. "Montessori Conference [at the NEA 1915 Meeting]," *The Kindergarten and First Grade*, vol. 1 (February, 1916), 87-88.

191. Bell, Alexander Graham. "Auto-education continued in the primary school," *Freedom for the Child*, vol. 2(January, 1916), 8-15.

192. Bertolini, Pietro. "The Case for Madame Montessori," *World's Work* (London), (May 1915), 561-573; *ibid.*, (June, 1915), 86-91; *ibid.*, (July, 1915), 185-190.

193. Blakely, Paul L. "Learning to 'Don't,'" *America*, vol. 14 (March 25, 1916), 573-574.

194. Boggs, L. Pearl. "The Eternally Feminine in the Montessori System," *The Kindergarten and First Grade*, vol. 2(May, 1917), 195-196.

195. Claremont, Claude A. "The Freedom of the Child in the Montessori School," *Child-Study*, vol. 9(November-December, 1916), 99-104.

195-A. ———. "The Montessori Apparatus," *Child*, vol. 9(July, 1919), 436-439.

195-B. ———. *Has Dr. Montessori Made a True Contribution to Science?* A paper read privately, December 15, 1917 (Hampstead, England, A. R. Jackson, printer, 1917), 18p.

195-C. ———. *A Review of Montessori Literature*. London: J. M. Dent & Sons, Ltd., 1919. 32p.

196. Claus, H. T., "Outdoing Montessori Here," *Boston Evening Transcript*, January 20, 1917.

197. Craig, Clara E. *The Beginnings of Reading and Writing in the Rhode Island Normal School*. Providence: Rhode Island Normal School, 1919. 32p.

198. Davidson, Percy E. "The Prospect for the Scientific Study of Kindergarten Education [with critical attention to the methodology of Dr. Montessori]," *Kindergarten and First Grade*, vol. 2(May, 1917), 189-194.

199. Dillard, Annie. "Montessori in a public school first grade," *Freedom for the Child*, vol. 2(October, 1915), 10-16.

200. Drummond, Margaret. *The Dawn of Mind;* An Introduction to Child Psychology. London: E. Arnold, 1918. 179p.

201. ———. "The Nursery School: An Educational Problem," *Contemporary Review*, vol. 115(April, 1919), 451-460.

202. ———. "Mme. Montessori; letter," *Spectator*, vol. 123 (November 15, 1919), 653-654.

203. Ellis, Evelyn. "Comparison of Results of the Kindergarten and Montessori Methods," *Kindergarten Review*, vol. 26 (December, 1915), 209-214.

204. Frabbito, Paul Francis. "A Critical Evaluation of Madame Montessori's Pedagogy," Unpublished Master's thesis, New York University, 1917. 81p.

205. Hailmann, William Nicholas. "Is Montessori the Educational Columbus?" *Sunset:* the Pacific Monthly, vol. 34(June, 1915), 1110-1115.

205-A. Hardy, Mattie C. "The Derivation of the Montessori Didactic Apparatus," *Elementary School Journal,* vol. 18(December, 1917), 294-300.

206. Hill, Patty S. "*Advanced Montessori Method,*" [Review] *Educational Review,* vol. 56(December, 1918), 432-438.

207. Holmes, Edmond G. A. "Drudgery and Education: A Defense of Montessori Ideals," *Hibbert Journal,* vol. 15(April, 1917), 419-433.

208. Hurd, Anna C. "The Montessori Method Applied to Deaf Children," *Volta Review,* vol. 17(June, 1915), 239-242.

209. Hutchinson, Lily. "Montessori in the Classroom," *Child* (London), vol. 7(September, 1917), 624-630.

210. Kimmins, Charles William. "A Montessori Experiment [at Sway, Hampshire]," *Child-Study,* (May, 1915), 69-72 .

211. ———. "The Liberty of the Child in Education," *Problems of Reconstruction,* Lectures and Addresses Delivered at the Summer Meeting at the Hampstead Garden Suburb, August, 1917. London: T. Fisher Unwin, Ltd., 1918. 315p.

212. "Baby Prodigees," *Kindergarten Primary Magazine,* vol. 27 (June, 1915), 310.

213. Locke, B. "Montessori Method and the Kindergarten," *ibid.,* vol. 28(October, 1915), 67-68.

214. MacLear, Martha. *The Kindergarten and the Montessori Method; a Synthesis.* Library of Educational Methods. Boston: R. G. Badger, 1915. 114p.

215. Merz, Charles. "Montessori for Presidents," *New Republic,* vol. 8(August 26, 1916), 89-91.

216. Montessori, Maria. "My System of Education," National Education Association, *Journal of Proceedings and Addresses,* vol. 53 (1915), 64-73; also in *Educator-Journal,* vol. 16 (October, 1915), 63-71. (Reprinted as pamphlet by the National Montessori Promotion Fund, 1915.)

217. ———. "Organization of Intellectual Work in School," National Education Association, *op. cit.,* 717-722. (Reprinted as pamphlet by the National Montessori Promotion Fund, 1915.)

218. ———. "Education In Relation to the Imagination of the Little Child," National Educational Association, *op. cit.,* 661-667; also in *Kindergarten Primary Magazine,* vol. 29 (November, 1916), 84-87.

219. ———. "The Mother and Child," National Education Association, *op. cit.*, 1121-1130. (Reprinted as pamphlet by the National Montessori Promotion Fund.)

219-A. ———. "The Children of the World, with Special Reference to the American Child," Wisconsin Teachers' Association, *Proceedings* of the 64th Annual Session, November 2-4, 1916 (Madison, 1917), 299-304.

220. ———. *The Advanced Montessori Method.* Vol. 1: *Spontaneous Activity in Education,* translated from the Italian by Florence Simmonds. 355p. Vol. 2: *The Montessori Elementary Material,* translated from the Italian by Arthur Livingston. 464p. New York: Frederick A. Stokes & Co., 1917.
Reviewed in:
a. *Boston Evening Transcript,* October 17, 1917, 8
b. *Bookman,* April 1918, 28-30, by John Adams
c. *Educational Review* 56:432-438, December, 1918, by P. S. Hill

220-A. National Montessori Promotion Fund. *Directory of Montessori Classes and Montessori Teachers in the United States.* Revised to May 10, 1916. New York: The Fund, 1916. 24p.

221. "Children's House—Closing Exercises," *New York Times,* June 3, 1915, 12:8.

222. "Dr. Maria Montessori—gives summer course at Exposition in San Francisco," *ibid.,* July 22, 1915, 18:1.

223. "Montessori Class—Miss M. Naumburg resigns because class received no supplies or heat," *ibid.,* February 5, 1916, 20:6.

224. Palmer, Luella A. "Montessori Suggestions for Kindergartners," *Kindergarten Review,* vol. 25(February, 1915), 349-353.

225. P.N.E.U. Mother. "Montessori and Other Matters," *Parents Review,* (April, 1916), 284-287.

226. Rasmussen, Vilhelm. *Child Psychology.* London, 1913.

227. Rawnsley, Willingham. "The Montessori Method," *Parents Review,* (December, 1915).

228. Rusk, Robert R. "Montessori," Chapter XII, *The Doctrines of the Great Educators.* London: Macmillan & Co., 1918. pp. 262-288. (2nd edition, 1954, pp. 258-283.)

229. Ryan, W. Carson, Jr. "The Montessori Demonstration School," *Educational Exhibits at the Panama-Pacific International Exposition, 1915.* United States Bureau of Education, *Bulletin,* 1916, No. 1. Washington, D.C. Government Printing Office, 1916. pp. 98-99.

230. "International Montessori Training Course," *School and Society,* vol. 2(July 10, 1915), 59-60.

231. "As to Montessori Mothers," *Scribner's Magazine*, vol. 60 (October, 1916), 513-514.
232. Smith, H. Bompas. "Conference on New Ideals in Education," *Educational Times* (London), vol. 68(September 1, 1915), 334-336.
233. "Montessori Cult's Eclipse," *Sunset:* The Pacific Monthly, vol. 35(October, 1915), 657-658.
234. "Report of Lectures by Maria Montessori," *Times Educational Supplement* (London), September 4—December, 1919.
235. "With Dr. Montessori at Barcelona," *ibid.,* May 1, 1919, p. 208.
236. "The Montessori Method at Work—Tolstoy and Montessori," *ibid.,* August 7, 1919, 397.
237. Watson, Foster. "The Significance of Dr. Montessori's Work," *Athenaeum,* September 12, 1919, 872-874.
238. Webb, C. "Madame Montessori and Mr. Holmes as Educational Reformers," *Hibbert Journal,* vol. 14(April, 1916), 578-591.
239. Wells, Rose. "The Montessori Spirit and the Teaching of French," *Modern Language Teaching* (July, 1917), 113-114.
240. White, Jessie. "Progress of the Montessori Method in England," *School Guardian,* vol. 43(October 19, 1918), 277-279. (London)
241. ———. "Misconceptions of the Montessori Method," *ibid.,* vol. 44(December 21, 1918), 29-31.
241-A. "Maria Montessori," *Who's Who.* London: Black, 1915-1952.
241-B. Williams-Ellis, A. "Mme. Maria Montessori," *Spectator,* vol. 123(November 1, 1919), 572-573.

*References for the Period, 1920–1929*

242. Adler, Alfred. "The Dangers of Isolation," The *Call of Education,* vol. 1(1924), 128-134.
243. Anderson, M. "Montessori Method," *New Era,* vol. 10(July, 1929), 191-192.
243-A. Batchelor, C. S. "The Montessori Method I: Its Progress and Influence on the Teacher," *The Sower,* no. 86 (January, 1928), 262-265.
243-B. ———. "The Montessori Method II: The School and the Child," *ibid.,* no. 87(April, 1928), 286-289.
244. Blackburn, Mary. *Montessori Experiments in a Large Infants School.* New York: L. P. Dutton and Co., 1921. 372p. Reviewed in:
a. *Boston Evening Transcript,* August 10, 1921, 6
b. *Literary Review* (N.Y. *Evening Post*), July 16, 1921, 10

245. Borland, Jean K. "Mental Development–Montessori and Other Methods," *Journal of the Royal Sanitary Institute,* (March, 1926), 459-464.

246. Boyd, William, "Montessori System," *Journal of Education and School World* (London), vol. 55(March, 1923), 155+.

247. ———. "The Montessori System," *Education Movements and Methods,* ed. by John Adams, New York: D. C. Heath and Co., 1924, pp. 49-62.

248. The *Call of Education* (Amsterdam, published by H. J. Paris and by Van Holkema en Warendorf; Dr. Maria Montessori, chief editor), vol. 1, 1924; volume 2, 1925. Ceased publication, 1925.

249. "The Montessori Movement in Holland," *ibid.,* vol. 1(1924), 157-161.

250. "The Montessori Home School, Rondebosch, South Africa," *ibid.,* 255-258.

251. "The Montessori Movement in Ireland," *ibid.,* vol. 2(1925), 65.

252. "Cardboard Model of an Old Amsterdam House Made by Girl 9¼ Years of Age," *ibid.,* 299-230.

253. "To the Readers" [request for manuscripts giving concrete example of Montessori learning experiences, etc.], *ibid.,* 231-235.

254. Campondonico de Crespo, Mrs. Elida L. " 'Casa dei Bambini' in Panama," *ibid.,* 70.

255. "Montessori Progress," *Child,* (July, 1926), 298-300.

256. Clarement, Claude A. "Why is the Montessori Method A Science?" The *Call of Education,* vol. 1(1924), 36-41.

257. ———. *Intelligence and Mental Growth.* London: Kegan Paul, 1927. 138p.

257-A. ———. "The Montessori Movement in England," *New Era,* vol. 9(1928), 75-76.

258. Cornish, D. H. "Bilingualism and Sensitive Periods: from a Phonetician's Point of View," The *Call of Education,* vol. 2 (1925), 176-181.

258-A. Craig, Clara E. *Teaching Reading and Writing in the Henry Barnard School.* Rhode Island College of Education *Bulletin,* no. 21, June, 1924. Providence, R.I., 1924.

259. Crichton-Browne, Sir James. "Introductory Address: Montessori Conference, Wembley Exhibition, May 9, 1924," *ibid.,* vol. 1(1924), 162-166.

260. Droogleever Fortuyn, Ae. B. "Sensitive Periods," *ibid.,* 104-112.

261. Drummond, Margaret. *Five Years Old or Thereabouts.* Some Chapters on the Psychology and Training of Little Children.

New York: Longmans, Green and Co., London: E. Arnold, 1920. 180p.

262. ———. "[Address to Montessori meeting]," *Times Educational Supplement* (London), February 17, 1921, 71.

263. ———. *The Psychology and Teaching of Number*. Yonkers-on-Hudson, N.Y.: World Book Co., 1922. 125p.

264. ———. *Some Contributions to Child Psychology*. New York: Longmans, Green, and Co.; London: E. Arnold, 1923. 151p.

265. ———. "Numbers for Infants," *New Era*, vol. 7(1926), 153-157.

266. Fynne, Robert John. *Montessori and Her Inspirers*. London: Longmans, Green and Co., 1924. 347p.

267. Glückselig, Elfriede. "Children of the First Public Montessori Elementary Class in Germany, Jena," *The Call of Education*, vol. 2(1925), 293-303.

268. Godefroy, J. C. L. "Perspectives [provided by Montessori Method]," *ibid.*, vol. 1(1924), 24-31.

269. Gould, G. "Theories and Fairies," *Saturday Review*, vol. 147 (May 4, 1929), 604-605.

270. Grunwald, Clara. "The Montessori Movement in Germany," The *Call of Education*, vol. 1(1924), 247-254.

271. Halbert, Anna Evelyna. "Problems of Self-Activity in Modern Educational Theory with Special Reference to Rousseau, Harris, Dewey, and Montessori." Unpublished Ph.D. dissertation, New York University, 1925. 185p.

272. Hitchings, Barbara. "Bowling Green Nursery School [New York City]," National Society for the Study of Education, *Preschool and Parental Education*, 28th Yearbook. Bloomington, Illinois: Public School Publishing Co., 1929, pp. 140-147.

273. Holmes, E. G. A. "Drudgery and Education," *Freedom and Growth*, and Other Essays. New York: L. P. Dutton and Co., 1923. pp. 96-116.

274. Hutchinson, Lily. "A Review of the Montessori Movement in England," The *Call of Education*, vol. 1(1924), 68-73.

275. Katz, David. "On the Psychology of the Human Hand," The *Call of Education*, vol. 2(1925), 110-115.

276. Kinel, L. "Montessori System, As Applied in the Mary Crane Nursery of Chicago," *Visual Education*, vol. 5(July, 1924), 196-197.

277. Levy, D. M. and Bartelme, P. "Measurement of Achievement in a Montessori School and the Intelligence Quotient," *Pedagogical Seminary*, vol. 34(March, 1927), 77-89.

278. Maccheroni, Anna. "The Old Idea of Discipline and the Mon-

tessorian: A Comparison," The *Call of Education,* vol. 2 (1925), 138-143.

279. McCormick, P. J. "Montessori and Religious Instruction," *Thought,* vol. 2(June, 1927), 56-71.

280. Miller, H. Crichton. "The Montessori Method," *Child,* (January, 1921), 103-106.

281. Montessori, Maria. "The Call," The *Call of Education,* vol. 1 (1924), 8-12.

281-A. ———. "Study of Very Little Children," *ibid.,* 48-54.

282. ———. "Questions and Answers Relating to the Development of the Social Life in the Montessori School," *ibid.,* 62-65.

283. ———. "Child Character," *ibid.,* 95-103.

284. ———. "Questions and Answers: Why Should Not the Children Be Left Free to Make What Use They Like of the Material?" *ibid.,* 150-152.

285. ———. "On Discipline—Reflections and Advice," *ibid.,* 183-196.

286. ———. "Analysis," *ibid.,* vol. 2(1925), 92-102.

287. ———. "The New Mistress," *ibid.,* 124-129.

288. ———. "Montessori Training Course at London: Final Lecture," *ibid.,* 323-324.

289. ———. *The Montessori Didactic Apparatus.* New York: House of Childhood, 1926. 70p.

290. ———. [Reports on Lectures in England]. *Times Educational Supplement* (London), May 14-July 23, 1927, pp. 224, 236, 247, 260, 271, 282, 296, 309, 322, 337, 343.

291. ———. *Child in the Church;* Essays on the Religious Education of Children and the Training of Character, edited by E. M. Standing. St. Louis: B. Herder Book Co., 1929. 191p.
Reviewed in:
a. *America* 42:607, March 29, 1930
b. *Blackfriars* 10:1466-7, November, 1929
c. *Catholic World* 130:628, February, 1930
d. *Fortnightly Review* 37:23, January, 1930
e. *Irish Eccl. Rec.* 5 ser. 35:222-23, February, 1930

292. ———. "Blazing New Trails in Education," *Parents' Monthly,* vol. 4(April, 1929), 18-20.

293. Montessori Father. "Some Observations of a Father on the Development of His Daughter," The *Call of Education,* vol. 1(1924), 221-223.

294. Nasgaard, S. "Montessori Movement in Denmark," *New Era,* vol. 10(January, 1929), 61.

295. Neguenzoff, Chr. "The Montessori Movement in Bulgaria," The *Call of Education,* vol. 2(1925), 68-69.

296. "Montessori Child Education Foundation Training School, New York City, Baccalaureate Sermon, by Dean Robbins," *New York Times,* June 6, 1927, p. 12, column 3. "Commencement Exercises," *ibid.,* June 8, 1927, 18:2.

297. "Montessori–Editorial on Article on Her Aims and Achievements in *Children* (magazine)," *ibid.,* March 24, 1929, III, 4:5.

298. Ochs, Elsa. "The Children's Home in Berlin-Wilmersdorf," The *Call of Education,* vol. 1(1924), 143-149.

299. Philippi, C. "The School Adapted to the Needs of Child Development," *New Era,* vol. 6(1925), 132-133.

300. Radice, Shiela. *New Children; Talks with Dr. Maria Montessori.* New York: Frederick A. Stokes and Co., 1920. 168p. Reviewed in:
  a. *Weekly Review* 3:480, November 17, 1920
  b. *Spectator* 124:619, May 8, 1920
  c. *Survey* 45:136, October 23, 1920

301. Revesz, Geza. "Introductory Note" [on the purposes of the journal, The *Call of Education,* and the Montessori Method], The *Call of Education,* vol. 1(1924), 31-33.

302. ————. "Questions and Answers: Why Should Children Begin Attendance at the Montessori School at 3-4 Years of Age," *ibid.,* 211-215.

303. ————. "*Progressive Education* [review of a new journal]," *ibid.,* vol. 2(1925), 71-73.

304. ————. "Order and Formation of Series," *ibid.,* 267-282.

305. St. John, A. "Montessori and Social Progress," *Sociological Review,* vol. 19(July, 1927), 197-207.

306. "British Montessori Centers," *School and Society,* vol. 13 (February 5, 1921), 166-167.

307. Shreve, Edith. "A Modification of the Counting Frame," The *Call of Education,* vol. 2(1925), 144-145.

307-A. Standing, Edward Mortimer. "The Montessori Method on a Large Scale," *The Sower,* no. 82(January, 1927), 147-148.

308. ————. "The Montessori Method and Catholicism," *Catholic Mind,* vol. 27(July 22, 1929), 261-270.

309. Stern, William. "The Bearing of the Child's Games on Its Nature," The *Call of Education,* vol. 1(1924), 201-205.

310. Thompson, S. R. "Intellectual Machinery and Education," The *Call of Education,* vol. 1(1924), 113-116; "postscript," by J. C. L. Godefroy, 116-119.

311. "Dr. Montessori's English Visit," *Times Educational Supplement* (London), January 1, 1920, 1-2.

312. "Dr. Montessori in Holland," *ibid.,* February 12, 1920, 84.

313. "The Montessori Method," *ibid.,* November 11, 1920, 595.

314. "Dr. Montessori's First Lecture: Theory and Reality," *ibid.*, April 7, 1921, 159; "Editorial," *ibid.*, April 28, 1921, 195.
315. "Training for Brotherhood," *ibid.*, May 6, 1921, 203, 204.
316. "The Montessori Society," *ibid.*, December 17, 1921.
317. "A Neapolitan Nursery School," *ibid.*, July 8, 1922, 319.
318. "Teaching of Reading in a Montessori School," *ibid.*, Sept., 1926, 30, *ibid.*, October, 1926, 459.
319. "Reading and Writing," *ibid.*, June 8, 1929, 264; "Some Practical Experiences," *ibid.*, October 22, 1929, 468.
320. Tromp, C. W. "Observations on the Development of the Intelligence in a Montessori School," The *Call of Education*, vol. 2(1925), 38-46.
321. Van Dorp, E. F. "On Lessons," *ibid.*, 206-212.
322. Weill, Blanche. "The Montessori Method and Sub-Normal Children," *ibid.*, 283-292.
323. White, Jessie. "Mrs. Curwen's Review of the *Advanced Montessori Method*," *Parents Review*, (August, 1921), 566-572.
324. ———. "Relations between the Dalton Plan and the Montessori Method," *Times Educational Supplement* (London), November 25, 1922.
325. Wilkinson, Major Sir Nevile. "Titania's Palace," The *Call of Education*, vol. 1(1924), 76-84.

*References for the Period, 1930-1939*

325-A. Bird, Grace E. "A Successful Experiment in Child Education," [The Henry Barnard School, Rhode Island College of Education, Providence] *Elementary School Journal*, vol. 30 (March, 1930), 539-546.
326. Claremont, Claude A. "Education of the Movements," *Towards a New Education*, edited by Wm. Boyd. London and New York: A. A. Knopf, 1930, 145-149.
327. ———. "Montessori Science and Idealism," *ibid.*, 358-364.
328. ———. *The Chemistry of Thought;* Introducing a New Basis for the Descriptive Analysis of Constructive Thought and Creative Imagination. London: G. Allen and Urwin, Ltd., 1935. 259p.
329. ———. *A Child's Paradise*. London: Studio House, 1938.
330. ———. *Spanning Space*. London: Sir I. Pitman and Sons, Ltd., 1939. 124p.
331. "Montessori Method and the Subnatural Mind," Conference of Educational Associations (London), *Report* of the 18th Annual Conference, 1930, 23-27.
332. "Recent Developments in the Montessori Method," *ibid.*, *Report* of the 19th Annual Conference, 1931, 98-105.

333. Drummond, Margaret. *The Gateways of Learning;* An Educational Psychology having Special Reference to the First Years of School Life. London: University of London Press, 1931. 190p.

334. ———. "Montessori Method as a Basis of Modern Education," Conference of Educational Associations, *Report* of the 23rd Annual Conference, 1935, 21-25.

335. "Madame Montessori and American Imitators," *Elementary School Journal,* vol. 30 (April, 1930), 570-571.

336. Glückselig, Elfriede. "Writing in a Montessori School," *Towards a New Education,* edited by Wm. Boyd. London and New York: A. A. Knopf, 1930, 144-145.

337. Joosten-Chotzen, R. "Advanced Montessori Material from 6-12 Years," *ibid.,* 150-51.

338. "Montessori in Vienna; Interview," *Living Age,* vol. 340 (July, 1931), 510.

339. Lochhead, Jewell. "The Montessori System," *The Education of Young People in England.* Teachers College Contributions to Education, No. 521. New York: Bureau of Publications, Teachers College, Columbia University, 1932. pp. 33-40.

340. Maccheroni, A. M. "Mathematics and the Montessori Method," *New Era,* vol. 15 (January, 1934), 8-11.

341. Meyer, A. E. "Montessori Method," *Modern European Educators and Their Work.* New York: Prentice-Hall, Inc., 1934. pp. 19-33.

342. Montessori, Maria. "The Adult and the Child" and "The Teacher's Task," *Towards a New Education:* A Record and Synthesis of the Discussions on the New Psychology and the Curriculum at the Fifth World Conference of the New Education Fellowship held at Elsinore, Denmark, in August, 1929, edited for the N.E.F. by William Boyd. London and New York: Alfred A. Knopf, 1930, 106-112.

343. ———. "The Child's Environment," *ibid.,* 138-141.

344. ———. "Geometry," *ibid.,* 151-155.

345. ———. "Psychological Principles in Education," *ibid.,* 354-358.

346. ———. "Adult and Child in Modern Education," *The Sower,* no. 101 (December, 1931), 101-108.

347. ———. "Ideals and Facts in Education," *Saturday Review,* vol. 152 (December 5, 1931), 711-712.

348. ———. "Environment for the Child," *ibid.,* (December 19, 1931), 783-784.

349. ———. "Education of Defective Children," *ibid.,* vol. 153 (January 2, 1932), 7.

350. ———. "New Method in Education," *ibid.*, (January 16, 1932), 64.

351. ———. *Mass Explained to Children.* London: Sheed and Ward, 1932. 116p.
Reviewed in:
a. *America* 49:572, September 16, 1933
b. *Catholic World* 140:251, November, 1934
c. *Commonweal* 18:413, August 25, 1933

352. ———. *Peace and Education.* Geneva: International Bureau of Education, 1932. 22p.

353. ———. "Social Questions of the Child," Conference of Educational Associations (London), *Report* of the 20th Annual Conference, 1932, 298-304.

354. ———. "Disarmament in Education," *New Era,* vol. 13 (September, 1932), 257-259; also in *American Childhood,* vol. 18(January, 1933), 14.

354-A. ———. "Spiritual Regeneration of Man," Conference of Educational Associations, *Report* of the 22nd Annual Conference, 1934, 171-176.

355. ———. *Mass Explained to Boys and Girls;* Adapted for Use in American Schools by Ellamay Horan. Chicago: W. H. Sadlier, 1934, 144p.
Reviewed in:
a. *America* 51:595, September 29, 1934
b. *Extension* 29:53, October, 1934
c. *Homiletic and Pastoral Review* 34:557, February, 1934
d. *Orate Fratres* 9:47, December, 1934

356. ———. *The Reform of Education During and After Adolescence.* Amsterdam: Association Montessori Internationale, 1939.

357. ———. *The Secret of Childhood,* translated and edited by Barbara Barclay Carter. London: Longmans, Green and Co., 1936. 278p.
Reviewed in:
a. *Clergy Review* 12:415-16, November, 1936
b. *Downside Review* 55:284, April, 1937
c. *G. K.'s Weekly* 23:404, September 3, 1936
d. *Month* 169:182-3, February, 1937
e. *Tablet* (London) 168:245, August 22, 1936

358. ———. "Child's Place in Society," Conference of Educational Associations, *Report* of the 24th Annual Meeting, 1936, 41-44.

359. ———. "Functions of the University, *ibid., Report* of the 27th Annual Meeting, 1939, 377-385.

360. ———. *The Erdkinder and the Functions of the University.* London: Montessori Society of England, n.d. 32p.

361. ——— and Child, Phoebe. "Teaching General Science to Small Children," *New Era*, vol. 20(July, 1939), 200-203.

362. Mookerjee, K. "Dr. Maria Montessori and Child-Centric Education," *Calcutta Review*, (June, 1937), 319-326.

363. "Teacherless Plan," *New York Times*, March 15, 1931, Section III, page 7, column 4.

364. "Int. on Educating Children, Portrait," *ibid.*, May 7, 1933, IV, 8:2.

365. "International Montessori Association Plans for Congress," *ibid.*, July 25, 1936, X, 11:5.

366. "Dr. Maria Montessori to give course in Holland," *ibid.*, August 28, 1938, II, 5:4.

367. "Comment on Dr. Montessori's *Secret of Childhood*," *ibid.*, August 20, 1939, II, 5:2.

367-A. O'Hern, Edward Philip. "The Montessori Method: Its Value for Teaching Religion and Morals in the Catholic School." Unpublished Master's thesis, Catholic University of America, 1932. 76p.

368. O'Neil, John F. "Clara E. Craig's Adaptations of the Montessori Methods at the Rhode Island College of Education." Unpublished Master's thesis, Catholic University of America, 1937. 39p.

369. Rotten, E. "Rights of the Child," *New Era*, vol. 19(January, 1938), 25-26.

370. Roubiczek, Lili. "Montessori Material for the Development of Mental Functions," *Towards a New Education*, edited by Wm. Boyd. London and New York: A. A. Knopf, 1930, 141-144.

371. Rusk, Robert R. "Montessori," *A History of Infant Education*. London: University of London Press, 1933, 69-89.

371-A. Sister Mary. "Appreciation of Dr. Maria Montessori's *The Child in the Church*," *Journal of Religious Instruction*, vol. 3(October, 1932), 108-117.

372. Sister of Notre Dame. *Scottish Montessori School.* The Primary Department of Notre Dame High School, Dowanhill, Glasgow. St. Louis, Mo.: B. Herder Book Co., 1932. 128p.

373. Standing, Edward Mortimer. "Montessori Method in Relation to Moral Training and Catholic Dogma," *The Sower*, no. 98(March, 1931), 23-31; also in *Catholic Educational Review*, vol. 29(September, 1931), 412-424.

374. ———. "Montessori Practice and Thomist Principles," *Blackfriars*, vol. 17(March, 1936), 204-212.

375. ———. "Proof of the Pudding; An Enquiry into the Results of Montessori Method," *The Sower*, no. 119(June, 1936), 73-77.

376. ———. "Sensitive Periods in Child Development and Their Importance in Education," *ibid.*, no. 122(March, 1937), 9-18.
377. ———. "Place of Reason in Education: Some Recent Developments," *ibid.*, no. 124(September, 1937), 137-144.
378. ———. "Normality and Deviation (in children and the Montessori school)," *ibid.*, no. 130(March, 1939).
379. "Catalunya and the Montessori Method; Communication from M. Montessori," *Tablet* (London), vol. 160(October 29, 1932), 569.
380. "Child's Place in Society," *ibid.*, vol. 168(September 5, 1936), 321-322.
381. "Religious Education; Summary," *ibid.*, vol. 174(August 19, 1939), 251.
382. "Montessori in Copenhagen," *Time*, vol. 30(August 10, 1937), 41.
383. "Childhood Secrets," *ibid.*, vol. 34(July 31, 1939), 30.
384. "Montessori Thirty Years After," *Times Educational Supplement* (London), No. 1110(August 8, 1936), 293.
385. Tromp, C. W. "The Montessori Movement in Holland," *Towards a New Education*, edited by Wm. Boyd. London and New York: A. A. Knopf, 1930, 149-150.
386. Usill, Harley. "The Montessori Method," *The Yearbook of Education, 1933*. London: Evans Brothers, Ltd., 1933, 168-171.
387. Van der Leeuw, J. J. "Unique Character of the Montessori Method," Conference of Educational Associations, *Report* of the 21st Annual Conference, 1933, 303-307.


*References for the Period, 1940-1949*


388. Chisholm, M. "Woman Who Made School Fun," *School*, vol. 35(February, 1947), 351-356.
389. Claremont, Claude A. "The Activity School: How It Differs from Montessori," *Times Educational Supplement* (London), No. 1778(May 27, 1949), 350.
390. ———. "The Purposefulness of Montessori," *ibid.*, No. 1779 (June 3, 1949), 369.
391. Crowley, Rose Marie. "A Comparative Study of Three Established Methods of Educating Children in the Kindergarten and Primary Grades." Unpublished Master's thesis, St. John's University, 1943. 62p.

391-A. "Maria Montessori," *Current Biography, 1940*. New York: H. W. Wilson Co., 1940, pp. 591-592.

392. Drummond Margaret. "Basic Education: The Montessori Method," *Hibbert Journal*, (October, 1946), 70-73.

393. ———. *Learning Arithmetic by the Montessori Method.* London: George C. Harron and Co., 1947. 64p.

394. Fitzburgh, Harriet L. and P. K. Fitzburgh. "Maria Montessori," *Concise Biographical Dictionary of Famous Men and Women.* New York: Grosset, 1949, pp. 480-481.

395. Hoehm, Matthew, (ed.). "Marie Montessori," *Catholic Authors.* St. Mary's Abbey, 1948, 544.

396. Hovre, F. de. "Masters of Contemporary Catholic Education," *Catholic School Journal,* vol. 40(January, 1940), 12.

397. Hoyo, Pearl. "Comparative Study of the Views of Maria Montessori and Susan E. Blow on the Training of Children." Unpublished Master's thesis, Catholic University of America, 1944. 70p.

398. Kucia, Sister May Marcella. "A Study of the Psychological Principles Embodied in the Montessori System." Unpublished Master's thesis, Sisters' College, Cleveland, Ohio, 1946.

399. Maccheroni, Anna. *True Romance: Dr. Maria Montessori as I Knew Her.* Edinburgh: Darien Press, 1947. 110p.

399-A. McPolin, F. "Montessori System of Auto-Education," *Irish Ecclesiastical Record,* series 5, vol. 63 (February, 1944), 87-99.

400. Montessori, Maria. *Education for a New World.* Asundale Montessori Training Centre, Adyar, Madras, Publication Series, No. 1. Kalakshetra, Madras 20, India, 1946. 89p.

401. ———. *The Child.* [Reprinted from *The Theosophist,* December, 1941] 2nd ed. Adyar, Madras 20, India: The Theosophical Publishing House, 1948, 26p.

402. ———. *Child Training;* [Twelve Talks Broadcast from the Madras Station of All India Radio, June 1-12, 1948.] Government of India, Publications Division, Ministry of Information and Broadcasting, 1948. 36p.

403. ———. *The Discovery of the Child,* [3rd edition, *The Montessori Method],* Adyar, Madras, India: The Theosophical Publishing House, 1948. 336p.

404. ———. *Reconstruction in Education.* [Reprinted from *The Theosophist,* February, 1942] 2nd edition. Adyar, Madras, India: The Theosophical Publishing House, 1948. 13p.

405. ———. *To Educate the Human Potential.* Adyar, Madras, India: Kalakshetra Publications, 1948. 124p.

406. ———. *What You Should Know About Your Child.* Colombo: Bennet and Co., 1948.

407. ———. *The Absorbent Mind,* Adyar, Madras, India: The Theosophical Publishing House, 1949. 421p. [2nd rev. ed., translated from the Italian by C. A. Claremont, Adyar,

Madras, India: The Theosophical Publishing House, 1959; 297p.] Reviewed in *Jubilee* 7:44 November, 1959 by H. Kelly.

408. Montessori, Mario M. "Freedom and Its Meaning," *American Teacher,* vol. 33(March, 1949), 14-16.

409. Muyzenberg-Willemse, Van Den. "Development of the Montessori Movement in the Netherlands," *New Era,* vol. 27 (April, 1946), 106.

410. "Dr. Maria Montessori Interned in India; Movement for Her Release Started," *New York Times,* July 2, 1940, II, 5:2.

411. "Methods Used by Child Education Foundation [Montessori Group]," *ibid.,* September 21, 1941, II, 5:7.

412. "Maria Montessori: portrait; Return from Exile Noted," *ibid.,* June 8, 1947, VI, 8.

413. Plank, Emma N. "Montessori's Contribution to the Development of the Concept of Number." Unpublished Master's thesis, Mills College, Oakland 13, Calif., 1947.

414. Richardson, Mary Faison. "The Relationship of the Montessori Method of Pre-School Education to Current Nursery School Theory and Practice in America." Unpublished Master's thesis, Vassar College, 1940. 68, 37p.

415. Rongione, L. A. "Montessori Method and St. Augustine," *Catholic Educational Review,* vol. 42(February, 1944), 99-104.

416. "First Progressive," *Time,* vol. 50(October 20, 1947), 56.

*References for the Period, 1950-1959*

417. Burke, O. "Whitby School," *Jubilee,* vol. 6(February, 1959), 21-27.

418. Cassidy, J. F. "Dr. Maria Montessori," *Ava Maria,* vol. 76 (October 25, 1952), 519-521.

419. "Maria Montessori: An Italian Educational Reformer," *Catholic Educational Review,* vol. 50(June, 1952), 416.

420. "Plea to Educators to Understand Children," *ibid.,* (September, 1952), 491.

421. Claremont, Claude A. "Montessori Appeal," *The Times Educational Supplement* (London), No. 1939(June 27, 1952), 560.

422. ———. "Unrecognized Colleges: Progress Stifled," *ibid.,* No. 2155 (September 7, 1956), 1093.

423. ———. "Montessori in Britain: Fiftieth Anniversary of Dr. Montessori's First School," *New Era,* vol. 38(June, 1957), 122-125.

424. "On Bubbles and Such," *ibid.,* vol. 40(March, 1959), 55; *ibid.,* (June, 1959), 145, 147.

425. Cole, Luella. "Montessori and Her Schools," Chapter XX, *A History of Education: Socrates to Montessori.* New York: Rinehart and Co., 1950. pp. 563-589.

426. Costa-Minneci di Villareal, Joyce. "Methods and Materials of the Montessori System: An Interpretation." Unpublished Master's thesis, The American University, 1957. 72p.

427. ———. "The Montessori Elementary Curriculum Content and the Corresponding American Curriculum: A Cross-Cultural Study." Unpublished Ph.D. dissertation, The American University, 1958.

428. Ellison, Louise. "A Study of Maria Montessori's Theory of Discipline through an Examination of Her Principles and Practices and an Experiment with Pre-School Children." Unpublished Master's thesis, Tufts University, 1957. 378p.

429. Fox, John Thomas. "Remedial Reading: An Adaptation of the Montessori Method." Unpublished Master's thesis, Illinois State Normal University, 1951. 31p.

430. Horwirtz, Caroline and H. H. Horwirtz. *Treasury of the World's Great Heroines.* New York: Hart and Co., 1951, 164-170.

431. Lubienska, H. "The Child, His Body, and His Soul," *Jubilee,* vol. 5(June, 1957), 37-39.

432. McDonald, Donald. "Student Freedom, Yes; Anarchy, No," The *Catholic Messenger,* vol. 77(March 5, 1959), 10.

433. Montessori, Maria. "Nursery Schools and Cultural Environment," *Journal of Education* (London), vol. 82(December, 1950), 655-657; also in *Catholic School Journal,* vol. 50 (October, 1952), 52A.

434. ———. "As the Twig is Bent," *Rotarian,* vol. 82(January, 1953), 11.

435. ———. *The Formation of Man,* translated by A. M. Joosten. Adyar, Madras, India: The Theosophical Publishing House, 1955, 135p.

436. Montessori Obituaries:

a. *Americana Annual,* 1953, 456-457.
b. *American School Building Journal,* 124:66, June, 1952
c. *British Medical Journal,* 4767:1085, May 17, 1952
d. *Current Biography,* 13:36, June, 1952
e. *Current Biography Yearbook,* 1952, 1953, 434
f. *Illustrated London News,* 220:854, May 17, 1952
g. *Isis,* 43:367, 1952
h. *Journal of Education* (London), 84:286, 288
i. *Nature* 169:992-993, June 14, 1952
j. *New York Times,* May 7, 1952, 27
k. *Publishers' Weekly,* 161:2211, May 31, 1952
l. *School and Society,* 75:318, May 17, 1952

m. *Spectator,* 188:599, May 9, 1952
n. *Tablet* (London), 199:405, May 17, 1952
o. *Times Educational Supplement* (London), No. 1932: 385, 388, May 9, 1952; No. 1934:447, May 23, 1952; No. 1935:473, May 30, 1952
p. *Wilson Library Bulletin,* 27:22, September, 1952

437. Montessori, Mario M. *Doctor Montessori and Her Work.* London: W. Knott and Son, Ltd.
438. ———. "The First Six Years: Character Founded," *Times Educational Supplement,* No. 2017(December 25, 1953), 1081.
439. ——— and Claremont, Claude A. "Montessori and the Deeper Freedom," *Yearbook of Education* (London), 1957. Evans Brothers Ltd., 1957, 414-426.
440. A Montessorian. "This Doctor Became an Educationist," *New Era,* vol. 32(June, 1951), 120-130.
441. ———. "The Children's Garden and the Children's House," *ibid.,* vol. 33(March, 1952), 50-54.
442. ———. "The Child-Adult Relationship and Educational Research," *ibid.,* (June, 1952), 134-138.
443. Moore-Rinvolucri, M. J. "Maria Montessori: A Revaluation," *Irish Eccl. Record,* vol. 80(October, 1953), 217-224.
444. "Profile: Maria Montessori," *The Observer* (London), May 13, 1951, 2.
445. Plank, Emma N. "Observations on Attitudes of Young Children toward Mathematics," *Mathematics Teacher,* vol. 43 (October, 1950), 252-263.
446. Rambusch, Nancy McCormick. "Learning Made Easy," *Jubilee,* vol. 1(September, 1953), 46-53.
447. ———. "The Sense of Silence," *Jubilee,* vol. 3(January, 1956), 44-45.
448. ———. "Children's Toys," *ibid.,* vol. 4(May, 1956), 54-55.
449. ———. "Freedom, Order and the Child," *ibid.,* vol. 5 (April, 1958), 37-40.
450. "Life's Work on Behalf of Children," *The Sower,* vol. 184 (July, 1952), 58-59.
451. Standing, Edward Mortimer. "Note on the Historical Development of the Montessori Movement," *Blackfriars,* vol. 37 (November, 1956), 467-473.
452. ———. *Maria Montessori, Her Life and Work.* Fresno, Calif.: Academy Library Guild, 1959. 354p. (English edition: Hollis & Carter, 1957.)
Reviewed in:
a. *America* 102:200, November 14, 1959
b. *ALA Booklist* 56:216, December 1, 1959
c. *Blackfriars* 39:239, May 1958

d. *Commonweal* 72:43, April 8, 1960
e. *Catholic Educational Review* 57:572, November, 1959
f. *Magnificat* 104:40, November, 1959
g. *Marriage* 41:54, December, 1959
h. *Critic* 18:25, December, 1959
i. *New Era* 39:100, April, 1958, by C. A. Claremont

453. Strong, Jay. *Of Courage and Valor;* Heroic Stories of Famous Men and Women, "Maria Montessori," 293-299. New York: Hart, 1955.

454. "La Dottoressa," *Time,* vol. 59 (May 19, 1952), 70-72.

455. "Montessori Gathering; Pioneer Honored," *Times Educational Supplement,* No. 1825 (April 21, 1950), 304.

456. "Montessori Congress: Sense of Intellectual Adventure," *ibid.,* No. 1881 (May 18, 1951), 394.

457. "Dr. Montessori," *ibid.,* 395.

458. "The Montessori Attitude: Freedom under Authority," *ibid.,* No. 1882 (May 25, 1951), 415.

459. "Montessori in Holland," *ibid.,* No. 1934 (May 23, 1952), 447.

460. "Montessori in India," *ibid.,* No. 1952 (September 26, 1952), 784.

461. "Glance at Montessori," *ibid.,* No. 1999 (August 21, 1953), 734; reply: C. A. Claremont, "Montessori Apparatus: Precision Needed," *ibid.,* No. 2000 (August 28, 1953), 750.

462. "Approach Play by Signor Montessori: Advanced Work," *ibid.,* No. 2131 (March 23, 1956), 377.

463. "History for Juniors: Keeping In Time," *ibid.,* No. 2161 (October 19, 1956), 1251.

464. "Montessori in Britain," *ibid.,* No. 2178 (February 15, 1957), 206; *ibid.,* No. 2180 (March 1, 1957), 274.

465. "New Ideas," *ibid.,* No. 2228 (January 31, 1958), 155.

466. "Mathematics Made Visible," *ibid.,* No. 2235 (March 21, 1958), 459.

467. "Montessori Now," *ibid.,* No. 2239 (April 18, 1958), 607.

468. UNESCO. *World Survey of Education.* Vol. II: *Primary Education.* Paris, 1958. 1387p.
Index entry for Montessori:
Bolivia, p. 159; Brazil, 167; Ceylon, 223; Chile, 234; Ecuador, 328; El Salvador, 347, 350; France, 384; Fr. Cameroon, 418; Germany, Fed. Rep., 457; Guatemala, 491; India, 538; Iran, 562; It. Somaliland, 621, 622; Italy, 610; Japan, 634; Luxembourg, 687, 690; Nepal, 735; Netherlands, 742, 747; Nicaragua, 796; Panama, 823; Paraguay, 830; Portugal Surinam, 764.

469. Wallbank, P. "Montessori Now," *Times Educ. Sup.* No. 2184 (Mar. 29, 1957), 415.

*References for the Period, 1960-1961*

470. Claremont, Claude A. "On Coping with Gravitation," *New Era*, vol. 41(January, 1960), 15-16.

470-A. Daltry, C. T. "Why Should Mathematics Seem Difficult, and What Can We Do About It?" [Paper presented at the 12th International Montessori Congress, Bad Godesberg, Germany, August 22-27, 1960] *International Review of Education*, vol. 7(1961), 187-194.

471. Flynn, Mary C. "Headmistress [Nancy McCormick Rambusch]: Personality Sketches," *Today*, vol. 17(November, 1961), 3-5.

472. Montessori, Mario M. "Maria Montessori's Contribution to the Cultivation of the Mathematical Mind," [Paper presented at the 12th Int'l Montessori Congress, Bad Godesberg, Germany, August 22-27, 1960] *International Review of Education* vol. 7(1961), 134-141.

472-A. Morris, Joe Alex. "Can Our Children Learn Faster," *The Saturday Evening Post*, vol. 234(September 23, 1961), 17-25.

473. [Whitby] First Permanent Building Dedicated; School will be Headquarters for American Montessori Association," *New York Times*, May 7, 1961, Section IV, p. 13, column 4.

474. Pribonic, Catherine. "Montessori Re-Examined." Unpublished Master's thesis, Department of Education, Cornell University, 1961.

475. Rambusch, Nancy M. "Montessori Reappraised," *Jubilee*, vol. 7(April, 1960), 42+.

476. ———. "Montessori Approach to Learning," National Catholic Education Association, *Bulletin*, vol. 58(August, 1961), 320-322.

477. Sister M. Alban, S.C. "The Montessori Method—Applied," *Catholic School Journal*, vol. 61(December, 1961), 23-26.

478. Standing, E. M. "Seeds of Evil in the Child's Soul," *Downside Review*, vol. 78(Winter, 1960), 52-53.

479. "Joy of Learning, Whitby School," *Time*, vol. 77(May 12, 1961), 63.

480. "Montessori and Maths: Doctrine and the Individual," *Times Educational Supplement*, No. 2363(September 2, 1960), 259.

481. Wagenschein, Martin. "The Teaching of Mathematics—A Tragedy," [Paper presented at the 12th International Montessori Congress, Bad Godesberg, Germany, August 22-27, 1960] *International Review of Education*, vol. 7(1961), 155-162.

# Notes

## INTRODUCTION

1. Marc Oraison, *Love or Constraint* (New York: P. J. Kenedy, 1959), p. 15.
2. Margaret Mead, *Growing Up In New Guinea* (New York: New American Library, 1953), p. 164.
3. Robert Lindner, *Must You Conform?* (New York: Rinehart & Co., 1956), p. 167.
4. Lawrence A. Cremin, *The Transformation of the School:* Progressivism in American Education, 1876-1957 (New York: Alfred A. Knopf, 1961), p. 242.
5. Paul Woodring, *A Fourth of a Nation* (New York: McGraw, Hill, 1957), *passim.*
6. R. M. Hutchins, "Our Basic Problems and Our Educational Program," *McCall's Magazine*, vol. 87 (May, 1960), p. 200.
7. Sheila Radice, *The New Children* (London: Hodder & Stoughton, 1920), p. 49.
8. J. S. Bruner, *The Process of Education* (Cambridge: Harvard University Press, 1960), p. 33.
9. Clifton Fadiman, Introduction to *The Case for Basic Education,* ed. by J. D. Koerner (Boston: Little, Brown & Co., 1959), p. 10.

## CHAPTER 1

1. Fadiman, *op. cit.*, p. 5.
2. Edouard Seguin, *Idiocy and its Treatment by the Physiological Method* (New York, 1866).
3. Maria Montessori, *The Discovery of the Child* (Adyar, Kalakshetra Publications, 1948), p. 371.
4. Radice, *op. cit.*, p. 122-123.

## CHAPTER 2

1. Gardner Murphy, *Human Potentialities* (New York: Basic Books, 1958), p. 164.
2. G. K. Chesterton, *Orthodoxy* (New York: Dodd, Mead & Co., 1946), p. 108.
3. Maria Montessori, *The Absorbent Mind* (3rd ed., Adyar, Theosophical Publishing House, 1961), p. 117.

4. Alfred North Whitehead, *The Aims of Education* (New York: New American Library, 1949), p. 27-28.
5. Montessori, *The Absorbent Mind,* p. 21.
6. *Ibid.,* p. 139-141.
7. Jerome S. Bruner, *The Process of Education* (Cambridge: Harvard University Press, 1960), p. 8.
8. Montessori, *The Absorbent Mind,* p. 118.
9. *Ibid.,* p. 22.
10. *Ibid.,* p. 139 ff.
11. Lyman Bryson, *The Next America* (New York: Harper, 1953).
12. William H. Kilpatrick, *The Montessori System Examined* (Boston: Houghton Mifflin Co., 1914), p. 14.
13. Jean Piaget, *The Language and Thought of the Child* (New York: Harcourt, Brace & Co., 1926), p. 57.
14. David Russell, *Children's Thinking* (Boston: Ginn & Co., 1956), p. 215-216.
15. E. M. Standing, *Maria Montessori:* her life and work (Fresno: Academy Library Guild, 1957), p. 100.
16. *Ibid.,* p. 115.
17. Maria Montessori, *The Advanced Montessori Method* (London, 1918), vol. 2, pp. 304-306.
18. Sir Herbert Read, *Education Through Art* (New York: Pantheon, 1945), p. 113-114.
19. *Ibid.,* p. 113.
20. *Ibid.,* p. 14.

## CHAPTER 3

1. Maria Montessori, *The Formation of Man* (Adyar, Theosophical Publishing House, 1955), p. 96.
2. Erik Erikson, *The Healthy Personality* (New York: Norton, 1960), p. 53.
3. Ruth Benedict, "Continuities and Discontinuities in Cultural Conditioning," *Psychiatry,* vol. 1 (February, 1938), p. 162-163.
4. These are a series of four oblong blocks, into which cylinders are placed, ten cylinders in each block varying in dimension from thickest to thinnest, from shortest to tallest in varying degrees. All of the cylinders are grasped by a small knob which necessitates the use by the child of the three fingers which he will ultimately use in holding a pencil.
5. Jean Piaget, *The Psychology of Intelligence* (Patterson: Littlefield, Adams & Co., 1960), p. 53.
6. *Ibid.,* p. 5-6.
7. Maria Montessori, *Education for a New World* (Adyar: Kalakshetra, 1946), pp. 61-63.

8. Erikson, *op. cit.*, p. 32.
9. *Ibid.*, p. 34.
10. From the Preface by E. Claperede to Jean Piaget, *The Language and Thought of the Child* (New York: Meridian Books, 1957), p. 14.
11. David Riesman, *Individualism Reconsidered* (Glencoe: The Free Press, 1954), p. 105.
12. John Dewey, *Experience and Education* (New York, 1946), pp. 41-42.
13. David Riesman, *Constraint and Variety in American Education* (New York: Doubleday Anchor Books, 1958), p. 143.
14. *Ibid., loc. cit.*
15. John Dewey, *How Much Freedom in New Schools Today*, p. 220.

## CHAPTER 4

1. Carl Delacato, *Prevention and Treatment of Reading Problems* (Philadelphia: Charles Thomas, 1959), *passim.*
2. Maria Montessori, *The Secret of Childhood* (Calcutta: Orient Longmans, 1961), p. 207.
3. Georg Simmel, "The Sociology of Sociability," in Talcott Parsons *et al* (eds), *Theories of Society:* Foundations of Modern Sociological Theory (New York: The Free Press of Glencoe, Inc., 1961), vol. 1, p. 158.
4. Frances L. Ilg and Louise Bates Ames, The Gesell Institute's *Child Behavior* (New York: Dell Publishing Co., 1955), pp. 20-22.
5. Montessori, *The Secret of Childhood*, pp. 133-134.
6. G. Hartmann, *Educational Psychology* (New York: Ronald, 1941), Chapter Nine, "Improving Thinking and Reasoning," p. 283 ff. Many of Hartmann's propositions could be used to describe Montessori's materials:
    1. The reduction of abstract relations to direct perception;
    2. The constant search for similarities and differences among experiences;
    3. The exercise of the ability to classify and categorize a large and heterogeneous body of material;
    4. The development of facility in employing word, number and other symbols;
    5. The use of models and "schematic pictures" for the sake of a better anchorage to the reasoning sequence;
    6. The apprehension of the way in which things are organized in a certain configuration as a prerequisite to the understanding of details.
7. Kilpatrick, *op. cit.*, p. 19.

### CHAPTER 5

1. Margaret Mead, *The School in American Culture* (Cambridge: Harvard University Press, pp. 26-27.
2. *Ibid.*, p. 30.
3. John Dewey, *Experience in Education,* pp. 8-9, 84.
4. Mead, *The School in American Culture,* p. 20.
5. Montessori, *The Secret of Childhood,* p. 12.
6. Montessori, *Education for a New World,* p. 109.
7. Russell, *op. cit.*, p. 180.
8. Montessori, *The Secret of Childhood,* p. 132.
9. Mead, *The School in American Culture,* p. 40.

### CHAPTER 6

1. Mead, *The School in American Culture,* p. 22.
2. Delacato and Doman, *Mobility Scale,* Philadelphia, Rehabilitation Center.

### CHAPTER 7

1. Montessori, *To Educate the Human Potential,* pp. 10-11.
2. *Ibid.*, pp. 9-10.
3. *Ibid.*, p. 19.
4. Martin Mayer, *The Schools* (New York: Harper Bros., 1961), p. 82.
5. Maria Montessori, *The "Erdkinder"* (London: The International Montessori Society, n.d.), p. 8.
6. *Ibid.*, p. 9.
7. *Ibid.*, pp. 24-25.
8. Riesman, *op. cit.*, p. 32.
9. *Ibid.*, pp. 64-65.
10. Jean Scheidenhelm, *New Ideas in Teaching Technologies and the Montessori Method,* 1961, unpublished paper.
11. Omar K. Moore, *Time* (November 7, 1960), pp. 91-92.
12. Montessori, *The Formation of Man,* p. 53.
13. Montessori, *The Absorbent Mind,* p. 179.
14. Mayer, *op. cit.*, p. 83.
15. P. Kenneth Komoski, "Teaching Machines," *Instructor,* March 1961, p. 32.
16. Montessori, *The Absorbent Mind,* p. 247.
17. B. F. Skinner, "Teaching Machines," *Science,* vol. 128, no. 3330, October 24, 1958, p. 976. He adds, "What [John Dewey] threw out, he should have thrown out. Unfortunately, he had little to put in its place."

### CHAPTER 8

1. *Time,* May 12, 1961, p. 64.

# Index